A Grammar of Khowar

GRAMMARS OF WORLD AND MINORITY LANGUAGES

Series Editors
Lily Kahn and Riitta-Liisa Valijärvi

This series consists of accessible yet thorough open-access grammars of world and minority languages. The volumes are intended for a broad audience, including the scholarly community, students and the general public. The series is devoted to less commonly taught, regional, minority and endangered languages. Each volume includes a historical and sociolinguistic introduction to the language followed by sections on phonology, orthography, morphology, syntax, and lexis, as well as additional material, such as text samples. The series aims to promote and support the study, teaching and, in some cases, revitalisation of languages worldwide.

Lily Kahn is Professor of Hebrew and Jewish Languages, UCL.

Riitta-Liisa Valijärvi is Associate Professor of Finnish and Minority Languages, UCL and *Docent* (Associate Professor) of Finno-Ugric Languages at Uppsala University, Sweden.

OTHER TITLES IN THE SERIES

A Grammar of Akajeru
Raoul Zamponi and Bernard Comrie
https://doi.org/10.14324/111.9781800080935

A Grammar of Elfdalian
Yair Sapir and Olof Lundgren
https://doi.org/10.14324/111.9781787355392

A Grammar of Paraguayan Guarani
Bruno Estigarribia
https://doi.org/10.14324/111.9781787352872

A Grammar of Khowar

Descriptive and comparative analysis

Elena Bashir

UCLPRESS

First published in 2025 by
UCL Press
University College London
Gower Street
London WC1E 6BT

Available to download free: www.uclpress.co.uk

A CIP catalogue record for this book is available from The British Library.

ISBN: 978-1-80008-815-3 (Hbk)
ISBN: 978-1-80008-816-0 (Pbk)
ISBN: 978-1-80008-817-7 (PDF)
ISBN: 978-1-80008-821-4 (epub)
DOI: https://doi.org/10.14324/111.9781800088177

بارابار ای میزانہ درُستی زبان ادمو
اسپہ کھووار ڇھیتراره خوُر ای نِشّان ادمو

barabár i mizána drustí zabán adémo
ispá khowár ċhetrára xur i niṣán adémo

"All the languages of humanity are equal in importance
In Chitral our Khowar is yet another gift of humanity.

زٖبان کھُلی ادمو ہر ای تنار گَمبوُری
گُرزینو مثلِ ڇھیترار مثالِ کھووار

zabań khulí adémo har i tanár gambúri
gurzéno mísl-e-ċhetrár misál-e-khowár

All the languages of humanity – each one is a unique flower.
Chitral is one garden of many; Khowar is one flower of many."

Inayatullah Faizi

This work is dedicated to the people of Chitral—in particular the many individuals who have shared their knowledge of the culture and language of Chitral and their hospitality with me—in our shared hope that this language will continue to be appreciated and used in all aspects of Chitrali life. I hope that it will stimulate interest among the younger generations and encourage them to pursue studies and research on Khowar.

For their continued friendship and hospitality over the years, I am forever grateful to the following persons and their families: Haider Ali Shah in Chitral Town, Inayatullah Faizi in Laspur, the late Maula Nigah Nigah in Zondrangram, Muhammad Arap Khan in Sorech, the late Naji Khan Naji in Shotkhar, the late Rahmat Akbar Khan Rahmat in Chapali, Sher Wali Khan Aseer in Bang and Charun, and the late Taj Muhammad Figar in Zargarandeh.

Contents

Publisher's note on the digital formats of the book

Screen reader software does not currently support accurate audio rendition of Khowar text.

List of maps and figures

Maps

Figures

List of tables

Using the grammar

List of abbreviations

Abbreviations for grammatical terms and forms used in the morphological analysis of example sentences are:

1	first person
2	second person
3	third person
ABL	ablative
ADJ	adjective
ADV	adverb(ial)
ADV.P	adverbial participle
AG	agent noun
AUG	augment (OIA preterital marker)
C	consonant
CAJ	cajolative particle
CAUS	causative
CAUS.DES	causative desiderative
CLF	classifier
CLO	closeness
COMP	complementiser
D	direct
DAT	dative
DES	desiderative
DIST	distal
EXCL	exclusive
FUT	future
HAB	habitual
HORT	hortative
I	indirect
IOM	identified object marking
IPFV	imperfective
INF	infinitive
INS	instrumental case
INS.N	instrumental noun

IRR	irrealis
LOC1	locative 1
LOC2	locative 2
LOC3	locative 3
LOC4	locative 4
MIR	mirative
N	noun
NEC	necessitative
NEC2	second necessitative morpheme
NMLZ	nominaliser
NP	noun phrase
NS	non-specific
OBL	oblique
PFV	perfective
PL	plural
POT	potential
PRF	perfect
PROH	prohibitive
PROX	proximal
PRS	present
PRS/FUT	present/future
PST	past
PTCP	participle
QUOT	quotative
REAL	realis
REDUP	reduplication
REFL	reflexive
REL	relative
REM	remote
RES	resultative
S	specific
SBJV	subjunctive
SG	singular
TAG	tag question
TOP	topic marker
UNCERT	uncertainty
V	vowel
VC	causative verb
VI	intransitive verb
VOC	vocative
VT	transitive verb

Other symbols and abbreviations

.	indicates a syllable boundary, as for example in *lo.łík*
*	indicates an ungrammatical or unacceptable form
<	indicates a form descended historically from an earlier one
>	indicates a form which develops into a later one
←	indicates a form derived synchronically from a base form
→	indicates a base form from which another form is derived
~	indicates an alternate form
:	vocative, or expressive vowel lengthening (non-phonemic)
Ar.	Arabic
Bur.	Burushaski
Eng.	English
id.	idiomatic usage
lit.	literally
OIA	Old Indo-Aryan
p.c.	personal communication
Prs.	Persian
RV	Rig Veda
[S]	sentence
TAM	tense-aspect-mood
Tnnnn	where n represents a numeral from 0–9, entry number in Turner (1962–6)
Ur.	Urdu
Wkh.	Wakhi
Yd.	Yidgah

Glossing conventions

These abbreviations, and the glossing conventions used, follow the Leipzig glossing rules (https://www.eva.mpg.de/lingua/resources/glossing-rules.php) as far as possible. In accordance with these best practices, one-to-many correspondences in either the object language (Khowar) or the metalanguage (English) are handled as follows. When one word in one language corresponds to a multi-word expression in the other, the parts of the multi-word expression are separated by periods, as in the following examples. In (i), the two elements of the Khowar conjunct verb correspond to the infinitive of an English verb; in (ii) one Khowar word corresponds to a four-word English phrase; and in (iii) a complex verb form *botí asúr* consists of a perfective participle plus the present tense of 'be' (animate), which together make up a present perfect tense-aspect form. In some cases, such forms may be mentioned by the resultant tense-aspect name, and the elements of the complex verb will be demarcated with a period as in (iii). Usually, however, each constituent part will be labelled separately, as in (iv).

(i) *lu.dik*
'to speak'

(ii) *ṣuçkooγ*
'clay.dissolved.in.water'

(iii) *botí.as-úr*
tie.PRS.PRF
'is.tied'

(iv) *bot-í as-úr*
tie.PFV.PTCP be(ANIM)-PRS.3SG
'is tied'

Since there is no sex-based grammatical gender in Khowar, third-person singular subjects of verbs in example sentences will be glossed with 's/he' or 'it'. 'She' or 'he' will only appear in glosses or translations where required by the cultural or textual context. However, since in English 'she' refers only to female persons, but 'he' can refer to either a male or female person, in ordinary English-language text in the book, a generic, non-specific human will usually be referred to as 'he'. Non-human animates and inanimates will be referred to as 'it'.

The reader may notice that a particular word is spelled differently in different examples. When this occurs, it is intentional and reflects my attempt to represent the variation I have encountered in my research.

Presentation of example sentences

Example sentences are presented in the traditional three-line format: (i) Khowar sentence in roman representation, with morpheme boundaries marked with a hyphen; (ii) morphological analysis, each morphological element vertically aligned with its roman representation, in which grammatical category labels are in SMALL CAPS; and (iii) English gloss/translation. (iv) If the example is from a source other than the author's own materials, the source is given in parentheses following the English gloss. When a person's initials are given in parentheses here, it means that the sentence was given to me by that person during my field research and appears in my notes exactly as such.

The English translations of example sentences will include English punctuation—mainly full stops and commas. However, I have avoided putting this punctuation in the Khowar examples, since most of them were presented to me orally and I don't want to imply that Khowar speakers would choose to punctuate Khowar in the same way that English is punctuated.

(i) *uγ ma ṭhur-á-ve*
(ii) water I.OBL sip-CAUS-IMP.2SG
(iii) 'Give me a sip of water.' (iv) (DSAL, Bashir et al. 2022 [2005])

Roman representation

Khowar words and example sentences are presented in a roman transcription using characters familiar to most people. It is important to note that these representations are transcriptions, which represent the sounds, not transliterations, which represent the spelling of words in the object language (Khowar). For a list of these characters, see Table 2.3.

Acknowledgements and list of contributors

The work represented in this book would not have been possible without the help and contributions of many persons in Chitral. I would like to thank the following people for the many hours they spent with me discussing various points of Khowar grammar. In my early days studying Khowar in 1986, Inayatullah Faizi, at that time Lecturer at the Government Degree College, Chitral, gave me my first introduction to Khowar and to people who shared my interest in the language, mainly members of the Anjuman-e-Taraqqi Khowar, Chitral. I am grateful to him for these introductions and for the time he spent with me.

After completing my dissertation on the Kalasha language, I began my focused research on Khowar, working first with Rahmat Karim Baig, at that time Lecturer in the Government Degree College, Chitral. At a gathering following a meeting of the Anjuman-e-Taraqqi Khowar, I also met the following persons, who have remained of central importance in the preparation of this work: Maula Nigah Nigah, Mukarram Shah, Rahmat Akbar Khan Rahmat, Sher Wali Khan Aseer, Taj Muhammad Figar, and Yousaf Shahzad.

Abbreviations for the names of individual persons cited as the source of a specific example or piece of information and their home regions are listed here.

		Home Village
AK	Adina Khan	Chapali, Tehsil Mastuj
AKM	Amir Khan Mir	Chumurkun, Tehsil Chitral
AR	Abdur Rauf	Parwak, Tehsil Mastuj
ARC	Amin-ur-Rehman Chughtai	Drosh, Tehsil Drosh
GMKH	Gul Murad Khan Hasrat	Parkusap, Tehsil Mastuj
GNK	Gul Nawaz Khaki	Singur, Tehsil Chitral
IF	Inayatullah Faizi	Laspur, Tehsil Mastuj
IFM	Mother of Inayatullah Faizi	Laspur, Tehsil Mastuj
IWA	Ismail Wali Akhgar	Mastuj, Tehsil Mastuj
MA	Mir Ahmed	Rayin, Torkhow
MAK	Muhammad Arap Khan	Sorech, Tehsil Torkhow
MH	Mumtaz Hussain	Charun Owir, Tehsil Mastuj

MK	Mustafa Kamal	Uzhnu, Tehsil Torkhow
MNN	Maula Nigah Nigah	Zondrangram, Tehsil Mulkhow
MS	Mukarram Shah	Warijun, Tehsil Mulkhow
MYS	Muhammad Yousaf Shahzad	Laspur, Tehsil Mastuj
NKN	Naji Khan Naji	Shotkhar, Tehsil Torkhow
RAKR	Rahmat Akbar Khan Rahmat	Chapali, Tehsil Mastuj
RKB	Rahmat Karim Baig	Zondrangram, Tehsil Mulkhow
SWKA	Sher Wali Khan Aseer	Bang, Yarkhun, Tehsil Mastuj
TMF	Taj Muhammad Figar	Chitral Town, Tehsil Chitral
TMFD	Daughter of Taj Muhammad Figar	Chitral Town, Tehsil Chitral
TMFW	Wife of Taj Muhammad Figar	Chitral Town, Tehsil Chitral
WSiC	Woman storyteller	Chapali, Tehsil Mastuj
ZHD	Zahoor ul Haq Danish	Zondrangram, Tehsil Mulkhow
ZMZ	Zakir Muhammad Zakhmi	Booni, Tehsil Mastuj

Those examples which I recorded during the course of my fieldwork without noting a specific speaker are indicated by (EB field notes).

Storytellers who told traditional tales for me in various villages have made important contributions to this work. They include Zarkoti Khan in Village Bang in Yarkhun; Ruzgar Khan in Sorech, Torkhow; the wife of Syed Nasir Shah of Parwak, Tehsil Mastuj; Nur Muhammad Shah of Village Uthul, Tehsil Mulkhow; Rahmat Ghani and his mother in Village Kari, Tehsil Chitral; Safitullah in Parwak, Tehsil Mastuj; Khan Mahmat, Village Shotxar in Torkhow; a woman storyteller in Chapali, Tehsil Mastuj; and the wife of Syed Nasir Shah in Parwak, Tehsil Mastuj. These oral texts mostly involve the adventures of a protagonist (usually a man, but sometimes a woman) in conflict with a human or supernatural adversary.

More recently, Mumtaz Hussain of Charun Owir has contributed a *šiloóγ* 'folk tale' in written form; this appears as the Appendix to this book.

1
Introduction

1.1 Scope and purpose of this grammar

This is a descriptive reference grammar based on fieldwork conducted by the author in Chitral during the period 1986–2010, mainly with senior persons who speak the conservative varieties of the language spoken in Upper Chitral. Conversations with these people (mostly men) were carried out in their home villages, in Urdu, the link language of Pakistan. During these conversations they offered sentences to illustrate the meanings of specific words or explain cultural phenomena, only occasionally to illustrate grammatical constructions. I include almost exclusively spontaneously produced materials, not sentences elicited by presenting an Urdu sentence and asking 'How do you say this in Khowar?', since this method usually results in unnatural sentences.

My work attempts to capture a 'snapshot' of the language at a point in time when it was undergoing rapid change, before many of its characteristic features are eroded or lost. It is not intended as a pedagogical grammar; nor does it attempt to develop any specific linguistic theory. Rather, it employs the approach and terminology set out in Dixon's *Basic Linguistic Theory* (Dixon 2009), a method which prioritises fieldwork and empirical language data.

The intended audiences for this book are: first, Khowar speakers curious to see how one linguist describes their language, and other people in Pakistan who want to learn more about the languages spoken in their country; second, linguists of all kinds whose research could benefit from the data and analysis of this under-described language in this book; and finally, anyone else interested in learning about languages new to them.[1] I have tried to avoid overly technical or theoretical terms in order to keep the language such that any educated non-specialist can understand and benefit from the book.

1.2 The Khowar language

1.2.1 Location, speakers

Khowar (ISO 639-3: khw) is spoken primarily in Upper and Lower Chitral Districts in the Khyber Pakhtunkhwa Province of Pakistan, where it is the lingua franca of those districts. Upper and Lower Chitral (bifurcated into two districts in 2018) consist of the main river valley of the Chitral/Kunar River and several major side valleys including Lotkuh, Mulkhow, Torkhow, and Laspur. In 1947, after the Partition of India and Pakistan, Chitral declared its intention to accede to Pakistan but remained a princely state under the Kator dynasty until 1969, when it finally merged with Pakistan. Under the princely state, the official language of Chitral was Persian, and the archives of pre-Pakistan times are all in Persian.

Khowar is referred to by various other names, both in the colonial literature and by other ethnic communities in the region. Colonial names include Chitrali, Arniya, and Qashqari. Qashqari ~ Kashkari are terms used by Pashtuns ~ Pakhtuns ~ Pathans and adopted by the British; Patuamon is the Kalasha name for Khowar; and Gokwar is a term for Khowar in Torwali.

The spelling of the name of this language remains a topic of some discussion. For a time both 'Kohwar' and 'Khowar' were used; in fact, most of the articles of Sher Nawaz Naseem and older papers by Inayatullah Faizi use 'Kohwar'. Recently, however, 'Khowar' has become the accepted standard spelling.[2]

The population of Chitral is concentrated in the arable river valleys. My best estimate of the number of first-language Khowar speakers is around 400,000.[3] Within Chitral, the language of Upper Chitral is the most conservative and is considered the original variety of Khowar. Additionally, Khowar is spoken in the Ushu and Mataltal valleys of upper Swat (Akhunzada 2013), and in the Gupis-Yasin and Ghizer Districts of Gilgit-Baltistan, where minor dialectal variations are found. Recently

[1] I am grateful to two anonymous reviewers, whose comments and suggestions have done much to improve this work. Needless to say, any shortcomings or errors remain solely my responsibility.

[2] It is possible that the earlier spelling, Kohwar, reflects an earlier perception of the historical origin of the language.

[3] Based on a 2003 estimate of approximately 300,000.

many Khowar speakers have also migrated to the major urban centres of Peshawar, Rawalpindi, and Karachi, where their speech is subject to influences from the local and dominant languages of those cities.

1.2.2 Genetic affiliation

Khowar is one of those languages traditionally referred to by the geographical cover term 'Dardic' but better termed 'Far Northwestern Indo-Aryan' languages.[4] Its closest linguistic relative is Kalasha, which is spoken mainly in three side valleys on the right bank of the Chitral River south of Chitral Town—Birir, Bumburet, and Rumbur. Khowar and Kalasha have many inherited similarities, but also many differences. For recent discussion of these, see Bashir (2022).

1.2.3 Neighbouring languages and areal affiliations

At present, the core Khowar-speaking area is contiguous with those of Palula and Dameli on the south and Kalam Kohistani (Garwi), and Dir Kohistani on the south/southeast; Kalasha, Kām Kátaviri, Yidgah, and Ishkashmi on the west; Wakhi on the north; and Hunza Burushaski and Shina on the east. Yasin Burushaski is spoken in the Yasin valley, a small linguistic enclave separated from Hunza Burushaski (Map 1.1).[5] At present, Khowar is dominant over the other indigenous languages spoken in Chitral, but this was not so in the past, when interactions before the time of the modern nation states involved all of these languages in situations of symmetrical multilingualism, in which no language enjoyed a privileged position over another. As a result of these multiple interactions over centuries, several identifiable small linguistic areas (sprachbunds)[6] have developed in the Hindukush–Karakoram region. For discussion of this aspect of Khowar's history,

[4] The term 'Far-Northwestern Indo-Aryan languages' has been proposed by Richard Strand (2022) and is beginning to gain currency, with increasing recognition that there is no single stammbaum node to which all these languages can be traced. Morgenstierne (1961: 139) states that "there is not a single common feature distinguishing Dardic, as a whole, from the rest of the IA languages". I think it is a better term for these languages than the problematic and potentially misleading 'Dardic', which some people understand to mean descent from a single stammbaum node, and some understand to include Wakhi and Burushaski as well. 'Dardic' should be understood only as a geographical cover term.

[5] I am grateful to Dale Mertes, Media Application Specialist at the University of Chicago, for his work in creating Maps 1.1 and 1.2.

[6] A classic definition of linguistic area (sprachbund) is "an area which includes languages belonging to more than one family but showing traits in common which are found not to belong to the other members of (at least) one of the families" (Emeneau 1956: 16, fn. 28).

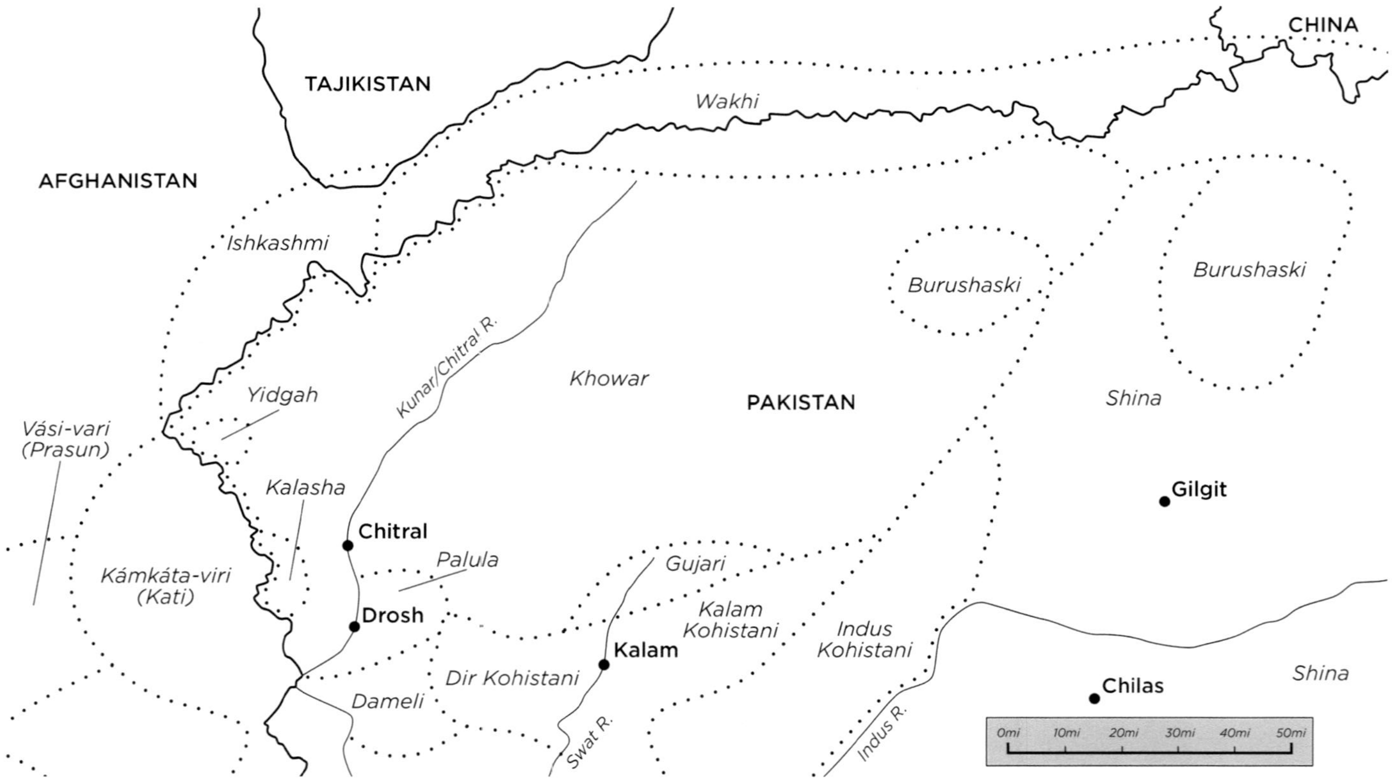

Map 1.1 Khowar and neighbouring languages. Created by Dale Mertes, Media Application Specialist at the University of Chicago.

see Bashir (1988a, 1996a, 2022), Liljegren and Svärd (2017), and Liljegren (2021). In addition to these kinds of interactions, superstratal languages—Persian, Turkic, Urdu, and now English—have much influenced the development of Khowar.

1.2.4 Dialectal variation

The first reference to the question of dialectal variation within the Khowar-speaking area was in Morgenstierne (1947: 5): "There are no well-defined dialects, perhaps partly because the peasants are frequently being transferred from one part of the state to another by the big landowners." This opinion was repeated in Decker (1992). However, subsequent work has begun to yield a more granular picture. Faizi (2021 [1985]) distinguishes six linguistic zones: (1) Chitral and Drosh; (2) Torkhow and Mulkhow; (3) Biyar; (4) Lotkuh, Karimabad, and Arkari; (5) Laspur; and (6) Ghizar, Yasin, Warashgum, and Ishkoman in Gilgit-Baltistan (Map 1.2). Akhunzada (2013) discusses the Khowar spoken in the Ushu and Mataltan Valleys of upper Swat and notes that the Khowar spoken there does not differ much lexically from the Khowar of the main Chitral Valley, but the pronunciation and intonation of the language there is quite different, similar to that of Gawri (Kalam Kohistani) and the Khowar spoken in Arandu. A small pocket of Khowar speech in Village Vrang in then-Soviet Wakhan, called Kivi by Paxalina (1987), was recognised by Buddruss (1989) as almost identical with the Khowar of Chitral.

As a new generation of Khowar native speakers begin to research their own language, more such detailed studies of the Khowar of specific areas can be hoped for.[7]

1.2.5 Typological overview

Khowar is an agglutinative language, in which each morpheme carries specific meaning(s) and most are readily identifiable and separable. Important morphological features of Khowar are its replacement of an inherited mainly sex-based grammatical gender by an animacy-based gender system, retention of a Nominative–Accusative (NOM–ACC) alignment system, and the importance of grammaticised evidentiality

[7] Although this work focuses mainly on the Khowar of Faizi's zones 2 and 3, there are occasional references to forms characteristic of other areas. I have attempted to capture regional differences as best I can.

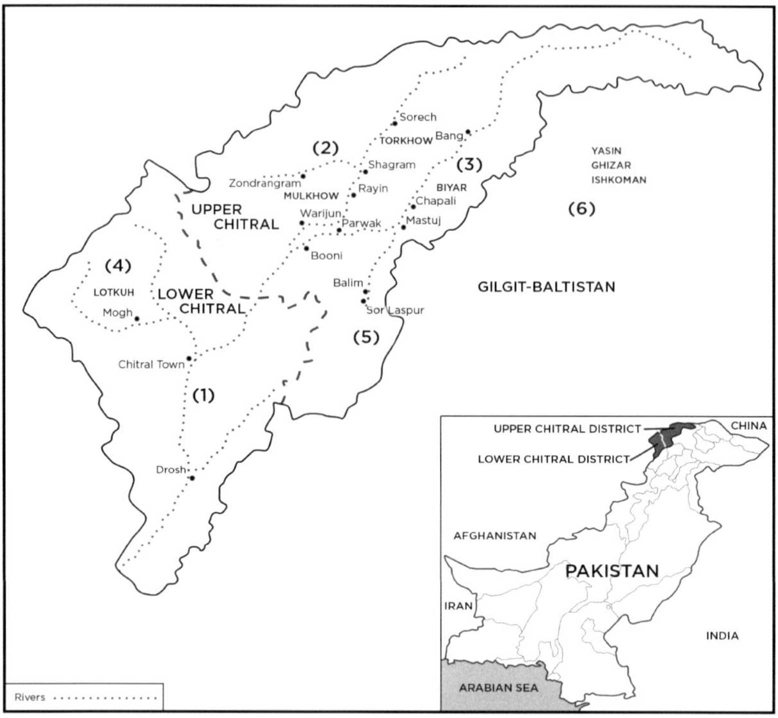

Map 1.2 Khowar dialect regions according to Faizi (2021 [1985]). Created by Dale Mertes, Media Application Specialist at the University of Chicago.

and mirativity distinctions. The distinction between verbal and nominal (non-verbal) predicates is central; certain types of predicates, namely identity and class inclusion, are consistently expressed with nominal sentences. With regard to lexicalisation of the elements of complex motion events—PATH, MANNER, and MOTION—Khowar is a language which usually combines MOTION and PATH in the verb and expresses MANNER adverbially in what is called a satellite.[8] For example, the sentence meaning 'She ran to me quickly' would be expressed in Khowar as 'She came to me running quickly' (see Section 8.7.1 for more discussion and examples).

Khowar has basic Subject Object Verb (SOV) word order, with Adjective Noun (ADJ N), Genitive Noun (GEN N), and Noun Phrase Postposition (NP POSTP) orders, but employs much flexibility in conveying information and discourse structure. Since person and number

[8] Early presentation of this idea is to be found in Talmy (1975, 1985), and more recently in Levin et al. (2010).

information of the sentence subject is encoded in the verb, full pronouns seldom appear as subjects, and Khowar is one of those languages often referred to as 'pro drop'. In general, new information is in pre-verbal focus position, making it a Type XXIII language (Greenberg 1966; Kim 1988), and old information is in sentence-initial or topic position.

The basic or most salient meaning of a particular word can be identified as one of the traditional parts of speech (noun, verb, adjective, adverb), but part-of-speech interpretation is flexible. For example, most adjectives can function freely as nouns; some nouns function as adverbs or adjectives, for example, *dahrt* ~ *daht* ~ *daxt*, a noun meaning 'pus', is frequently used adjectivally to mean 'dirty', 'nasty' (of water, eatables, persons). Adjectives can function adverbially; for example, *čan*, an adjective meaning 'naked', 'bare (body, room)', 'simple', 'plain', 'lonely', also functions adverbially, meaning 'only', as in: *čan í thuék* 'only one rifle'. The basic adverb *ṣoy* 'near', 'close', as in *ta dur ṣoy šerað* 'Is your house nearby?', can also be used as a noun 'nearness', 'near place', as in *hasé ṣóya gíti di no pašír* 'S/he can't see even from close up.' Khowar has a large number of basic adjectives.

Khowar is in the process of evolving from a left-branching language to include some right-branching elements (Bashir 1988a). With regard to head and dependent marking (Nichols 1986), Khowar is predominantly a dependent-marking language, with only the clause carrying markings of person and number on its head, the verb. Reference tracking is accomplished through use of locative expressions, deictic pronouns, and importantly by the choice between a switch reference mechanism employing the oblique infinitive and the perfective participle (see Section 10.10).

Important phonological characteristics of Khowar are the retention of three Old Indo-Aryan (OIA) sibilants and the presence of three affricates—dental-alveolar, palatal, and retroflex—the partial occurrence of lexical tone, and the almost complete disappearance of OIA voiced aspirate plosives (see Section 2.1).

Central to the conceptualisation and expression of meaning in Khowar are: (1) the interaction of its three-term deictic system with the array of locative case endings and spatial terms referencing the parameters of verticality and horizontality, (2) the interaction of evidentiality with tense-aspect-mood forms, and (3) the distinction between temporally bounded and recurrent actions or permanent states.

1.3 The Khowar lexicon

The Khowar lexicon represents accretion of words from multiple sources—Iranian, Turkic, Burushaski, and neighbouring NWIA languages—at various times, building over time on its OIA (Sanskrit) base (Bashir 2023a). Just as words have been continually added to the language, they are also falling into disuse, becoming obsolete and eventually extinct (Faizi 2021 [1982]).

1.3.1 The Old Indo-Aryan base

Old Indo-Aryan is usually called Sanskrit, although many varieties of it existed, including the Vedic language preserved in the Vedas, and other unrecorded local varieties.[9] Some OIA-origin words have changed considerably over time, like *yeč* 'eye', a reflex of Vedic *ákṣi* 'eye' (T43), or *andrén-* 'inside' < *ántara* 'interior', 'near', Rig Veda (RV) 'neighbouring' (T357). Others, like *ašrú* 'tear (produced by weeping)', are almost identical to their OIA ancestor *áśru* 'tear', RV (T919). Morgenstierne (1957) contains discussion of these forms and a list of several hundred OIA-origin words.

1.3.2 Burushaski substratal element

It is thought by several scholars of the Hindukush–Karakoram area, including the area where Khowar and other languages of northwest Pakistan are spoken, that Burushaski was once spoken over a considerably larger area than it is today. See Morgenstierne (1935: xxiff.; 1947: 92ff), Lorimer (1937: 67), Fussman (1972), Tikkanen (1988), and Zoller (2005: 16), among others, for discussion of this topic. Lists of Khowar words of Burushaski origin, for example *iskí* 'heel' (cf. Hunza Burushaski *iski* 'sole', 'surface' (Lorimer 1938: 48)), *naváhʦ* 'inconvenient', 'uncomfortable' (cf. Burushaski *apárʦ* 'the wrong way' [*a* + *varʦ*]); Burushaski words of Khowar or other IA origin, like *bʌŋgut* 'fortification', 'breastwork' (Lorimer 1962: 46; Berger 1974: 132); and mixed words, like Khowar *lóšṭing* 'clod of earth' (< T11157 *lɔṣṭá* 'lump of earth' + Burushaski plural suffix *-ing*), are presented in Bashir (2022). In addition to lexicon, Bashir (2022) and Chapter 4 in this book describe certain morphological and semantic influences of Burushaski in Khowar, for example the marking of pluractionality (Section 4.1.2.2).

[9] See Emeneau (1966) on the dialects of OIA.

1.3.3 Iranian influences

Words originating in various Iranian languages at different time depths are numerous. Morgenstierne (1936) classifies Iranian-origin loanwords in Khowar into four groups: (1) from Modern Persian, (2) from some Middle Iranian language(s), (3) from Pamir languages, and (4) from undefinable or unknown Iranian sources. Examples of each of these groups include the following.

(1) *phost* ‘skin’ and *bathán* ‘native country’ from Modern Persian. Both of these words show the secondary aspiration that frequently develops in Khowar, usually when a monosyllabic word begins with a voiceless plosive, or when voiceless plosives immediately precede stressed syllables.

(2) Most likely from Middle Iranian languages are *harén* ‘mirror’, *čáxur* ‘spinning-wheel’ (cf. Sogdian *čaxr* ‘wheel’), *niméž* ‘prayer’, and *-γon* ‘like’, ‘resembling’ (cf. Sogdian *γon* ‘manner’, ‘kind’).[10]

(3) From languages spoken in the Pamir area,[11] mainly Wakhi (Wkh.) and Yidgah (Yd.), come the following Khowar words: *γéik* ‘to spin’ < Yd. *γīum*; *vrazní* ‘pillow’ < Yd. *virzane* < **varznai* < **barznika-* ‘pillow’; *šunǰ* ‘needle’, cf. Yd. *šinǰo, šunǰo*. From Wakhi there are *doγúr* ‘fingernail’; *rigíṣ* ~ *regíṣ* ‘beard’ < Wkh. *regiṣ̌*, *rəγ̌īš*; *roxní* ‘embers’ < Wkh. *rəxni(g)* ‘fire’; *γerík* ‘to turn (into)’ < Wkh. *γ̌īr-* ‘to turn round’.[12]

(4) Some words whose origin is not precisely identifiable are among the most frequently appearing words in the language; some of these are *menú* ‘guest’, *pálum* ‘fine’, ‘small’, *ṣa* ‘black’, *ṣapík* ‘bread’, ‘a meal’, *verkhú* ‘lamb’, *ḍaq* ‘boy’ and *γoṭ* ‘feeble-minded’, ‘dumb (unable to speak)’. The words *ḍaq* and *γoṭ* are particularly interesting in that they include both IA retroflexes and the non-IA sounds /q/ and /γ/ (Morgenstierne 1936: 43).

Iranian languages have also had important influence on Khowar phonology. Iranian languages lost aspiration soon after their separation from Old Indo-Iranian. Contrastive aspiration has persisted in some Iranian languages, but not in Modern Persian. Khowar, in contrast

[10] Antje Wendtland has graciously supplied the following additional etymological information: Old Iranian **gauna-ka* ‘of the kind’, Sogdian *γwn ʾk*, and Manichean *γwny(y)*.

[11] ‘Pamir languages’ is now considered a geographical cover term, like ‘Dardic’, rather than a genetic grouping.

[12] For further discussion of Khowar–Wakhi interactions, see Bashir (2001).

with Kalasha, for example, has lost aspiration on voiced consonants; it retains contrastive aspiration, however, on some words.[13] Strand (2022: 447–8) argues that, as a result of influence from Iranian languages, anterior phonation[14] has increased in prominence in those Indo-Aryan languages that lie in the Iranian–Indic contact zone.

Further, he argues that one result of the new prominence of anterior phonation in these languages is weakened or lost posterior phonation and loss of whispery-voiced consonants (voiced aspirates), especially in Khowar.[15]

Morphological influences from Iranian languages include the plural ending *-an* (originally only for animates), and loss of inherited sex-based grammatical gender. The complementiser *ki* is an increasingly frequently used element from Persian.

1.3.4 Turkic elements

The founder of the Rais dynasty of rulers of Chitral, Shah Nadir, was originally from eastern Turkistan, today known as the Xinjiang Uyghur Autonomous Region, China (Baig 2004: 2). Along with the Rais rulers came some Turkic terms for concepts related to governance. A few of these are: *asaqál* ~ *aqsaqál*, literally 'white-bearded elder', the title of the minister for food (Baig 2004: 40); *méhtar* literally 'leader', title of the ruler of Chitral, is immediately from Turkic but ultimately from Persian (Baig 2004: 100). While *mírza* 'secretary' (Baig 2004: 39) probably immediately came from Turkic sources it is ultimately of Persian origin. *ataléγ*, of Uzbek origin, meant 'elder', 'father', or 'head of the family'; in Chitral he was a state official of the highest rank. This was one of the earliest administrative posts created by the Mehtars (Baig 2004: 52). The *yasavul* was superintendent of the royal kitchens, overseeing arrangements for guests and courtiers (Baig 2004: 40). This is one of the words ending in *-avul* which denote the bearers of official and administrative duties in Turkish and Turco-Mongol states (Bosworth 2001: 302). A title of great antiquity is *tarxán* 'military commander in Turkic armies' (Aydin 2009: 111).[16] Also, *xan*, a title used mainly for a subordinate ruler, and its feminine counterpart *xánum*, as well as *beg* 'Turkic title for a chieftain' and its feminine counterpart *bégum* 'lady (honorific)', must have come

[13] See Section 2.1.1.2 for further discussion of aspiration.

[14] See Section 2.2.2.2 for further discussion of phonation types.

[15] It seems to me that this also accounts for the perceptible, but non-phonemic, differences in stress and pitch contours of some monosyllabic words.

[16] It seems possible that this is the source of the village name Tarxanándeh 'village of the Tarxans'.

into Khowar and other South Asian languages from Turkic (Aydin 2009: 106). A few other words denoting culturally salient concepts are an honorific term for 'wife', and the name of a type of falcon. The Arabic plural *ʕayāl* 'family members' came to mean 'wife' in many Turkic languages (Erdal 2004: 272, fn 460).[17] This seems to be the likely source of Khowar *aẓyál* 'wife (honorific)'. Khowar *taiyún* 'a beautiful, white hawk/falcon' (Naji 2008: 132) comes into Khowar apparently unchanged in meaning from Turkic (Bosworth 2001: 311).

A few words pertaining to quotidian life also appear to be of Turkic origin. Khowar *arqá* 'back (body part)' (cf. Turkish *arka* 'back'), *yaẓéik*, which now means 'to crawl on the skin and cause itching' or 'to go on a tour (as of a government officer)' seems to originate in Turkic *gezmek* 'to walk', 'visit', 'tour', 'wander in'. Turkic *kulučka* 'brood of chicks' looks like a likely source of Khowar *kułúči* 'young chicken, up to the time it leaves its mother'. Similarly, Turkic *turp* 'radish' might be the source of Khowar *trup* ~ *tʰrup* 'radish', 'salt'. But note that Khowar *trup* 'salt' is also traced to an OIA source (T5934) *tr̥prá* 'pungent', a meaning which could give rise to both 'salt' and 'radish'. A fermented milk product widespread in Central Asia is *qurút*, found in Khowar with the same meaning. In Turkic languages, *čeček* 'flower' is the term for smallpox.[18] A trace of this conceptualisation of 'smallpox' is in the use of Khowar *isprú* 'blossoms' to mean smallpox. Another set of terms of probable Turkic origin is words for horse coat colours (see Section 1.3.6).

In addition to individual lexical items, Turkic seems to be the source of some grammatical elements. The morpheme *-élik* ~ *-éli* > Kalasha *-éli*, which conveys the deontic modal meaning of necessity, seems likely to be of Turkic origin. Menges (1968: 139) gives the first-person imperative *-ały*, to which *-m* for first-person singular or *-q* for first-person plural are added. Also, as a rigidly left-branching language, Turkic has reinforced Khowar's inherited left-branching tendencies.

Khowar adjectives show a variety of morphological patterns indicating intensification. At least some of them can be compared with Turkic patterns. For example, in Khowar *oç* 'blue/green' and *taq oç* 'bright blue/green'; *ʣehč* 'yellow' and *taq ʣehč* 'bright yellow'; and *savz* 'green (mid ranges like leaf-green)', and *taq savz* 'dark green'. Khowar *taq* in this adverbial function can be compared with the Chagatay adjective *toq* 'full' (Bodrogligeti 2001: 100).[19] Some Chagatay words showing

[17] In the same way as in modern Urdu the English 'family' is often used to mean 'wife (and children)'.
[18] The word *čéčak* has travelled into Urdu in the meaning of 'smallpox', but not of 'flower'.
[19] These Khowar forms are due to the late Maula Nigah Nigah, a well-known poet and litterateur of Village Zondrangram, Tehsil Mulkhow.

similar semantics are *bom-boz* 'very light blue', *qap-qara* 'entirely black', *qip-qirmizi* 'entirely red', *qip-qizil* 'very red', *sap-saríg* 'very yellow', and *sar-sabz* 'fresh green' (Bodrogligeti 2001: 97–8).

1.3.5 Recent borrowings from Urdu and English

English loanwords began to enter the language during the colonial era. An early English loanword was *bayskóp* (< bioscope) 'movie', 'cinema', which is no longer in use; *braṭ* 'bread', which is still in use, also may be an early English loan. Recent borrowings are too numerous to list, and with rapid social and technological change, the rate of borrowing from English continues to accelerate. Some of these recent loanwords have begun to appear in recent lexicographical works; for example, *ṭal maṭól* 'intentional delay' from Urdu (Naji 2008: 153); and *ákṭiv* 'active, alert' from English (Chitrali 2019: 35). Faizi (2021 [1982]) noted this development over 40 years ago, listing new vocabulary items in Khowar from both Urdu and English and expressing his hope that Khowar words will not be unnecessarily abandoned: "What is needed ... is to make concrete efforts to preserve the words dying out with the passage of time, so that the language may be able to get new blood, without losing the base and veins to be used for its absorption."

1.3.6 Colour terms

Colour terms afford an interesting example of this historical accretion. The basic terms for 'red' *kruy* (T3585), 'white' *išpéru* (T12774), 'black' *krížna* (T3451), and 'green', 'blue' ('grue') *oc̣h* (T24) are of OIA origin. A secondary layer, of Iranian origin, includes 'yellow' *ʣehč* (Morgenstierne 1936: 671), 'black' *ṣa* (Morgenstierne 1936: 669), 'white' *safíd*, as in *safidék* 'white variety of spikeless wheat', and 'green (mid shade)' *savz* (Bashir 2023b). A third group consists of specific terms for colours of horses, most of which are of Turkic origin.[20] These are *ǰiráng* 'reddish', 'yellowish-brown' (Abdramanova 2017); *qizíl* 'reddish', a colour produced by a mixture of red and white hairs (< Turkic); *surxún* 'white', 'a white horse' (Abdramanova 2017); *thulfár* an imaginary fast horse (< Turkic *tulpár*, 'a mythological winged horse'); *turúy* 'brown' (Bashir 2023b); *samánd* 'yellowish-white' (Bashir 2023b); *qašqá* '(adj.) white-faced (of horse)', (n.) 'horse with a white blaze on its forehead' (considered inauspicious if star-shaped). The

[20] For more on Turkic words for horse colours (in Sanskrit), see Berger (1967–8).

Turkic words, *kaška/kaškalï* (Yorulmaz & Baran 2022: 10–11), which are the apparent source of these terms have initial /k/ instead of Khowar /q/. Other horse colour terms, whose origins are unclear to me, are *kumáy* 'black' and *khabút* 'bluish grey', produced by mixture of white and black hairs, which gives a shade like light/sky blue.

1.4 Sociolinguistic environment

Khowar is spoken as the home language in (almost) all Chitrali households where Khowar is the first language. It is the language used in the bazaars and in government and private-sector offices except when Urdu has to be used when non-speakers of Khowar are present. It is the dominant language and lingua franca for all of Upper Chitral except for the Wakhi-speaking area in Baroghil, and for most of Lower Chitral except for the southernmost parts, where Pashto is now fairly frequently spoken, and in Madaghlasht, where a variety of Persian is spoken. In Lower Chitral, it is spoken along with or replacing other mother tongues in the Kalasha- and Palula-speaking regions (Munnings 1990b: §1.7.7). It is also spoken by many male Dameli speakers (Perder 2013: 8).

The literacy rate in Chitral is quite high, approximately 63 per cent overall (https://www.dcuc.gov.pk/about.php), and people's enthusiasm for education, for both boys and girls, is strong. Most of the educated population read (and speak when necessary) Urdu in addition to Khowar, and the number of English-knowing persons is also increasing.

Most Khowar speakers feel strong language loyalty, and activities by writers and language activists, at first through the Anjuman-e Taraqqi Khowar. Founded in 1965 by Shahzada Hussam ul-Mulk, the Anjuman is the first organisation dedicated to the preservation and promotion of the Khowar language.[21] Now, encouraged by recent government recognition that Khowar should be taught in primary schools, language loyalty is being reinforced and much work has been done towards developing a curriculum for Khowar instruction in primary schools. In 2009, a new education policy stated that Urdu, English, and a regional language should be included in the curriculum. Then, in 2011, it was decided by the Khyber Pakhtunkhwa government to include five indigenous languages, one of which is Khowar, as compulsory subjects

[21] For more information on the Anjuman-e Taraqqi Khowar, see https://www.mahraka.com/anjuman_taraqi_khowar/index.html, an article primarily in Urdu, but including many valuable historical photographs.

in the area in which they are spoken (Akhunzada 2021),[22] and Khowar is now beginning to be taught as a subject in primary schools in Chitral. The Mother Tongue Institute for Education and Research (MIER) has participated in the production of a series of textbooks for primary school children.

1.5 Research on Khowar

1.5.1 Early work

Early works on Khowar are mentioned here in chronological order. O'Brien (1895) is a grammar and vocabulary of Khowar which includes some nominal and verbal paradigms and a good collection of example sentences, mostly relevant to military contexts, with translations. Grierson (1919) contains a 16-page section on Khowar, which is valuable as one of the few sources about earlier forms of the language. D.L.R. Lorimer's collection of Khowar texts and his Khowar vocabulary (7,000 entries), were left to the School of Oriental and African Studies, London, but because they are difficult to access, they have not received the attention and use they deserve. The writings of Morgenstierne (1936, 1947, 1955, 1957) are the most important linguistic work of this period. Morgenstierne and Shah (1959) is a collection of some Khowar songs. Endresen and Kristiansen (1981), a summary of Khowar research up to 1981, contains a discussion of the earliest exploratory works on Khowar and describes Morgenstierne's research experiences in specific and colourful detail. It gives a list of Morgenstierne's unpublished manuscript materials, which he originally bequeathed to the Indo-Iranian Institute at the University of Oslo and that are now preserved in the Norwegian National Library, as well as mentioning Lorimer's unpublished notes. Additionally, it includes a short Khowar prose text, with glossary, and a discussion of Khowar phonology. Following in Morgenstierne's tradition was Georg Buddruss, whose 1982 discussion of Khowar as written in the Perso-Arabic script remains as relevant in 2025 as it was in 1982. Additionally, he published an article (Buddruss 1989) on a variety of Khowar locally called Kivi which was spoken in Village Vrang of then-Soviet Wakhan.

[22] Liljegren and Akhunzada (2017) is a comprehensive article on the sociolinguistic position of many of the languages of northern Pakistan, including Khowar.

1.5.2 Recent studies

Recent work on Khowar falls mainly into four categories: (1) sociolinguistic studies, (2) lexicography, (3) descriptive, comparative, and typological/areal studies, and (4) literary works and discussions of literature.

1.5.2.1 Sociolinguistic studies

An early sociolinguistic study of Khowar is an unpublished paper by Munnings (1990b). In this paper, Munnings concludes that:

> Khowar has lost something of the prominence it once enjoyed in Chitral. In the past, it met most, if not all, of the linguistic needs of the Kho. In the last fifty years, however, its role in government and administration has been severely curtailed, its traditional dominance in the commercial life of the district has been challenged and it has been given no place in the modern institutions of formal education. (§1.8)

The first published sociolinguistic study that I know of is Decker (1992), which reports on literacy and education percentages, multilingualism, and language vitality. Decker's conclusions are less pessimistic than Munnings's, and he concluded that Khowar language use is active. My own perceptions of these matters are also perhaps not as pessimistic as those of Munnings. I see Khowar regularly spoken in homes, with no attempt to introduce Urdu into this realm. It is also used in offices, both government and private-sector, when non-speakers of Khowar do not need to participate in the conversation.

Recently a younger generation of Khowar-speaking researchers have begun to write about changing language use by Khowar speakers. Islam Bibi et al. (2019) is a study of the linguistic habits of female students at the Intermediate level in Lower Chitral. Lower Chitral was chosen to explore this topic as it is more exposed through educational institutions and electronic media to the effects of English than other parts of Chitral. This study finds that among these young women the use of English has become somewhat of a status symbol and that traditional Khowar expressions are being abandoned. This is perhaps an extreme case, but it indicates the vast changes taking place in the language. Farid Ahmad Raza writes on the changing trends in naming persons (Raza n.d.), noting that traditional Khowar names are falling into disuse. A recent paper, Anbreen et al. (2020) discusses the linguistic practices of 20 Khowar-speaking Facebook users living in Rawalpindi and Islamabad. The authors find that English is the language of choice, followed by Urdu, and then Khowar. Given that the subjects of this study all resided in major urban centres, this result is not surprising. However, since the use of various social media is expanding in Chitral itself, it is probably indicative of the direction of change there too. Khan et al. (2021) discusses the adaptation of English words into Khowar.

1.5.2.2 Lexicography

Lexicography is an area in which considerable work has been done. An early Khowar–English dictionary, albeit by a non-linguist and suffering from under-differentiated representation of consonant sounds, is Sloan (2006 [1981]). Many Khowar speakers are intensely interested in their language and keep lists of words in private notebooks. A recently published Khowar–Urdu dictionary written and compiled by a native speaker is Naji (2008). A Khowar–English–Urdu dictionary has been published by Rehmat Aziz Chitrali (2019). Another, as yet unpublished, source is the work of the late Gul Nawaz Khaki on a Khowar–Urdu dictionary, which, according to the Mahraka website (http://mahraka.com), is expected to contain about 35,000 entries. The Khowar–English dictionary prepared as a pilot project under the aegis of the Digital Dictionaries of South Asia Project at the University of Chicago, which includes example sentences and audio files, can be found at https://dsal.uchicago.edu/dictionaries/khowar/ (Bashir et al. 2022 [2005]). Bashir (2023b) is a collection of words and cultural observations gathered during her fieldwork from 1986 to approximately 2010.

1.5.2.3 Descriptive, comparative, and typological/areal studies

Some recent studies focus on phonological, typological, and historical questions. They include the work of Bashir and more recently Liljegren. Bashir (1996a) looks at the areal position of Khowar, and an unpublished paper examined Burushaski–Khowar relationships (Bashir 1997). Bashir (2000b) treats the representation of spatial relationships in Khowar; Bashir (2001) discusses Khowar–Wakhi contact relationships; and Bashir (2007) discusses recent phonological, morphological, and syntactic contact effects. Most recently, Bashir (2022) discusses similarities and differences between Khowar and Kalasha. Liljegren (2014) and (2019) are areal-typological studies of Khowar and its immediate neighbours. Liljegren et al. (2021) is a database relevant to Hindukush areal typology. Liljegren and Khan (2017) is a study of Khowar phonetics and phonology.

1.5.2.4 Literature

Khowar is rich in poetry, which is widely enjoyed and appreciated by the public, and mushairas 'poetry recitations' are frequently held in various towns and villages by local branches of the Anjuman-e-Taraqqi Khowar. Recently some people, notably Farid Ahmad Raza, have urged the parallel development of prose literature. A few prose publications have begun to appear. Hussain (2016) is a collection of 14 Chitrali folktales, mainly animal tales with a concluding moral, presented for children; Raza and Danish (2019) is a collection of folktales with both Khowar texts and English translations available; and Raza (2024) is a collection of his short stories. Khan (2016) is a collection of Khowar proverbs.

There is a large body of published work on Khowar literature, in both Khowar and Urdu. The publications of the Anjuman-e-Taraqqi Khowar and the early journal *Jamhur-e-Islam*, published by the Press Information Department in Peshawar, contain many articles on Khowar literature. A series of valuable articles by Sher Nawaz Naseem, six published in 1987 and one appearing in 1988 in *The Frontier Post*, Peshawar, discuss the lives and achievements of some prominent Khowar literary figures: (Naseem 1987a) discusses Rehmat Akbar Khan Rehmat; (Naseem 1987b) is about Baba Ayub, ghazal producer; (Naseem 1987c) is on Gul Nawaz Khaki; (Naseem 1987d) focuses on Mirza Firdous Firdousi; (Naseem 1987e) is on Ustad Amir Gul Amir; Naseem (1987f) is on Amin-ur-Rehman Chughtai; and (Naseem 1988) discusses the contributions of Shahzada Hisam ul-Mulk. These articles are now available on http://mahraka.com. Akhgar (2008) is an authoritative and accessible English-language treatment of modern Khowar poetry. Two more recent studies are Shafket Ali (2020) and Shah and Wali (2021).Very recently, a few women have begun to write in Khowar.

Recently, Khowar materials have begun to appear online. A collection of articles on Khowar literature in Urdu, as well as English translations of some Khowar poetry and traditional tales, is found at https://www.mahraka.com/literature.html, a website started and maintained by Mumtaz Hussain. Another website, https://khowari.com/ was established in the early 2020s by Fakhr-e-Alam. Additionally, numerous videos of Khowar singers and poetry recitations appear on sites like YouTube and social media sites.

2

Phonology

This chapter discusses the sound system of Khowar. It first presents inventories of consonant and vowel phonemes, then discusses their contrastive features and combinatorial possibilities, and syllable structure.[1] Sound symbolism and the Khowar writing system are treated in Sections 2.5 and 2.6, respectively.

2.1 Consonants

The Khowar consonant sounds as represented in this book are shown in Table 2.1. In this table, and in citations of historical forms, aspirated consonants are indicated with superscripted *h*, for example <t^h> for aspirated /t/; however, for simplicity and ease of reading, in Khowar words and example sentences in the main text, aspirated consonants are written without superscripting aspirated *h*; thus <*th*> for aspirated /t/. This does not cause ambiguity with consonant /h/, because consonant /h/ is always preceded by a vowel. Sounds whose status is unclear are enclosed in parentheses. International Phonetic Alphabet (IPA) symbols for these sounds are found in Table 2.13 below.

[1] For detailed discussion of the articulatory phonetics underlying the Khowar sound system, see Strand (2012, 2022).

Table 2.1 Consonant phonemes

Closure type	Place of articulation						
	Labial	Dental-alveolar	Post-alveolar (palatal)	Post-alveolar (retroflex)	Velar	Post-velar	Glottal
Plosive voiceless	p p^h	t t^h		ṭ ṭ^h	k k^h	q (q^h)	
voiced	b	d		ḍ	g		
Affricate voiceless		ʦ ʦ^h	č č^h	c̣ c̣^{h}			
voiced		(ʣ)	ǰ	j̣			
Fricative voiceless	f	s	š	ṣ	x		h
voiced		z	ž	ẓ	γ		
Flap		r					
Approximant	ʋ		y				
Lateral approximant		ł	l				
Nasal	m	n					

Khowar, along with several other Far-Northwestern Indo-Aryan (IA) languages, Burushaski, and Iranian Wakhi, notably has three voiceless fricatives (sibilants) and three voiceless affricates—dental-alveolar, palatal, and retroflex—all with both unaspirated and aspirated phonemes.[2] This is a rare situation globally; Liljegren (2017: 118) finds that the presence of palatal, dental, and retroflex affricates is much more frequent in the Hindukush area than worldwide. Based on his sample of 31 IA languages, he finds this feature in 20 Hindukush languages, 65 per cent of his sample, whereas the global distribution shows this feature in 10 languages, which represent only 2 per cent of that sample.

In Khowar, /q/, /x/, /γ/, and /f/, which are often restricted in other IA languages to Perso-Arabic loans, occur frequently in native words, for example, *ḍaq* 'boy', *qaf* 'claw', *af* 'down(ward)', *doγúr* 'fingernails', *xal* 'taste', *γał* 'game like hockey or polo'. In fact, there is a specific word, *łaváṭi*, for persons who cannot pronounce /k/ and produce /q/ instead.[3] The voiced velar fricative /γ/ occurs very frequently in Khowar. In addition to appearing in words where it is original, it develops in at least two other situations. First, ع, a voiced pharyngeal approximant in words

[2] Retroflex affricates are original in Burushaski, so their appearance in Khowar is part of a local micro-areal pattern (Tikkanen 2008). Liljegren (2021) further investigates these phenomena.

[3] Information courtesy of Maula Nigah Nigah. This is the opposite of the situation in the IA languages of the Indo-Gangetic plain, where most people cannot pronounce /q/ and produce /k/ instead. A historical example of this is the word *oq* 'vomit' which is a reflex of OIA **okk* 'vomit' (T2538).

of Arabic or Persian origin, becomes غ, a voiced velar fricative in Khowar, for example in the frequently used adjective *láγal* 'very nice', 'beautiful' < Prs. لعل [laˤl] 'ruby', 'species of wild rose', 'red wine'. Also, when a vowel-final word (often an oblique pronoun) is followed by a vowel-initial suffix, a hiatus-filling /γ/ appears, as in the forms *hato-γó*, third-person proximal singular oblique pronoun', *i-γó-γon* 'like one another', or *verkhu-γíši* 'lambskin'. It has also been observed that some vowel-initial words are occasionally pronounced with an epenthethic syllable-initial consonant, for example, *arám* 'ease', sometimes produced as *γarám* (see example 9.128 below).[4]

Although /ɫ/ has been called 'retroflex' by some writers, and the Khowar writing system represents it with ڑ, the character used for Urdu retroflex /ṛ/, which does not occur in Khowar, /ɫ/ is a velarised dental-alveolar (not retroflex) lateral, which is found also in Kalasha and Palula. The post-alveolar lateral /l/, on the other hand, is slightly palatalised.

The status and appropriate treatment of the dental-alveolar affricate /ʣ/continues to be discussed. This sound occurs frequently in the speech of some areas of Upper Chitral.[5] For example, in addition to being the dominant pronunciation of native Khowar words like *ʣa* 'wet, moist', 'moist dish', it often appears instead of /z/ in Urdu words including /z/. For instance, *zaxmī* 'wounded' is often heard as *ʣaxmí.* This sound is represented by a unique letter, ځ, in Naji's *Khowar–Urdu Lughat* (2008) and in Chitrali's *Khowar–Urdu–English Dictionary* (2019).[6] Although minimal pairs for /ʣ/ and /z/ may not be found, for those advocating and using a separate character for /ʣ/ the question is about maintaining and accurately representing the characteristic pronunciation of important local varieties, rather than phonemic status over all varieties. For this reason, it is also used in the University of Chicago's *A digital Khowar–English dictionary with audio* (Bashir et al. 2022 [2005]),

[4] This may also explain the form of *yeč* 'eye', about which Morgenstierne (1972: 91) wondered, "*γech* < *akṣi* – with unexplained prefix *γ*".

[5] There is dialectal variation between affricate and fricative pronunciations: /ʣ/ and /ts/ are pronounced in Terich, while /z/ and /s/ tend to be heard in Mastuj, for example *tsónʣur* 'awl' in Zondrangram, but *sónzur* in Mastuj (MNN).

[6] The *Khowar Qaida* by Samsam ul-Mulk (n.d.) does not include a character for this sound. Nor does one appear in the 1921 *Hurūf-e tahjī-e zabān-e Khowār* by Shahzada Nasir ul-Mulk, as made accessible in German by Buddruss in his 1982 article. Munnings (1990a) argues for the phonemic status of /ʣ/, contrasting *ʣah* 'curry, wet dish' with *za* 'wet'. These, however, are two alternate pronunciations of the word whose basic meaning is 'wet', 'moist'. Liljegren and Khan (2017: 5) have this to say about this: "The contrast between the voiced fricatives /z/, /ʐ/, /ʑ/ and their affricate counterparts /d͡z/, /d͡ʐ/, /d͡ʑ/ is marginal, partly allophonic, and far from uniform throughout the speaker community."

which is based on the speech of Terich in Tehsil Mulkhow; in Bashir (2023b); and in this book.[7]

The labial approximant /ʋ/ has two noticeably different allophones, depending on the surrounding consonant and vowel sounds. Preceding front vowels and /r/, it is more like a voiced labio-dental fricative, similar to the English /v/, as in *ʋrázun* 'wing', *sangaʋí* 'otter', *ʋez* 'gunpowder', 'medicine'; while preceding back vowels it is closer to a bilabial approximant, like English /w/, as in *aʋá* 'I', *naʋáhʦ* 'uncomfortable', 'dangerous', *ʦoʋú* 'orphan'.

2.1.1 Contrastive features

The following consonantal features are contrastive in Khowar: voice (voiceless versus voiced), aspiration (unaspirated versus aspirated), and place of articulation. Khowar has contrastive dental-alveolar versus post-alveolar (retroflex) plosives; dental-alveolar versus post-alveolar (palatal) versus retroflex fricatives and affricates; velarised dental-alveolar versus palatal laterals; and velar versus post-velar plosives. Illustrative examples for these contrasts are given in Tables 2.2–2.8 and Sections 2.1.1.1–2.1.1.3.

2.1.1.1 Voice

Plosives, affricates, and fricatives contrast in voicing, as illustrated in Table 2.2. Though some of these examples are not true minimal pairs, the contrast holds.

[7] In Wakhi, spoken adjacent to Khowar in the north, /ʣ/ occurs with the same alternation with /z/ as is found in Khowar. It is represented with the symbol ʒ (Latin-based system) or ز with two vertical dots above (Ahmed Jami Sakhi system), in the consonant charts in Beg et al. (2022: 133, 134). Satoko (2005) represents it with d͜z. The long and close local and cross-border interaction of Khowar speakers in the northern parts of Chitral with Wakhi speakers probably explains the more frequent occurrence of this sound in Upper Chitral (see Bashir 2001). According to Steblin-Kamensky (1999: 35), /ʣ/ is not very frequent in Wakhan. With regard to Hunza Burushaski, Berger (1998 Vol. I: 21) finds /ʣ/ in syllable onset only in the word *zizí* 'mother of kings', pronounced *ʣizí*, and often syllable-finally in loanwords from Urdu, like *čīz* 'thing', which is heard as *číʣ*. The similarity in distribution, occurring as a variant of /z/, in Khowar, Wakhi, and Burushaski, suggests a micro-areal development.

Table 2.2 Voiceless and voiced contrastive pairs

Place of articulation and closure type	Voiceless	Voiced
bilabial plosive	/p/ *pec̣* 'hot'	/b/ *beč* 'aunt'
dental-alveolar plosive	/t/ *ta* 'you (OBL)', 'your'	/d/ *dá* 'here! (take it)'
post-alveolar (retroflex) plosive	/ṭ/ *ṭaq* 'thoughtlessness', 'haste'	/ḍ/ *ḍaq* 'boy'
velar plosive	/k/ *kan* 'tree'	/g/ *gan* 'wind'
palatal affricate	/č/ *čúmur* 'iron'	/ǰ/ *ǰamár* 'son-in-law'
post-alveolar (retroflex) affricate	/c̣/ *c̣ang* 'embracing', 'encountering'	/ǰ̣/ *ǰ̣enǰ̣ér* 'chain'
dental-alveolar fricative	/s/ *sor* 'head'	/z/ *zor* 'force', 'strength'
post-alveolar (palatal) fricative	/š/ *šun* 'lips'	/ž/ *žúnu* 'alive'
post-alveolar (retroflex) fricative	/ṣ/ *ṣok* 'path made in snow by repeated walking'	/ẓ/ *ẓaq* 'thick', 'viscous'
velar fricative	/x/ *xam* 'flat/level' (land)	/ɣ/ *ɣam* 'sorrow, grief'

2.1.1.2 Aspiration

Voiceless plosives and affricates contrast in aspiration. Illustrative pairs for consonants showing contrasting aspiration are listed in Table 2.3. Some of these are not true minimal pairs, but they do illustrate the contrast.

Table 2.3 Unaspirated and aspirated plosives and affricates

	Unaspirated	Aspirated
Bilabial plosive	/p/ *par* 'wooden vessel for flour or grain' (Naji 2008: 97)	/pʰ/ *pʰar* 'over there'
Dental-alveolar plosive	/t/ *trin* 'yogurt', 'curd'	/tʰ/ *tʰrínguɫ* 'three-pronged pitchfork'
Dental-alveolar affricate	/ʦ/ *ʦat* 'enough', 'sufficient'	/ʦʰ/ *ʦʰar* 'food offered in charity after someone's death to ensure his being blessed'
Post-alveolar (retroflex) plosive	/ṭ/ *ṭong* 'variety of pear'	/ṭʰ/ *ṭʰongí* 'small axe'
Post-alveolar (retroflex) affricate	/c̣/ *c̣ang* 'embrace'	/c̣ʰ/ *c̣ʰan* 'leaf'
Post-alveolar (palatal) affricate	/č/ *činí* 'china cup'	/čʰ/ *čʰiník* 'to break (vt)'
Velar plosive	/k/ *kar* 'ear'	/kʰ/ *kʰar* 'vegetable garden'
Post-velar plosive	/q/ *qaq* 'dry', 'desiccated'	/qʰ/ *qʰoteék* 'to breathe heavily or sniffle (while talking)'

Aspiration in some words is inherited from Old Indo-Aryan (OIA), as in *kʰar* 'vegetable garden' (< OIA *kʰātá* 'dug up' T3862), *čʰiník* 'to cut' (< OIA *čʰinátti*, pl. *čʰindánti* 'cuts off', 'splits' Rig Veda (RV) [√cʰid] T5046), *pʰal* 'ploughshare' (< OIA *pʰā́la* 'ploughshare' T9072). In some, it has developed from OIA /kṣ/, as in *ç̣ʰir* 'milk' (< OIA *kṣīrá* 'milk', 'thickened milk' T3696). In Khowar, OIA aspirated voiced plosives have almost completely lost their aspiration, traces of which remain in the low tone on some words, like *doón* 'ghee' (< **dʰadan* < OIA *dadʰan* 'coagulated milk') (Morgenstierne 1932: 46; 1972: 89).

In numerous words, however, spontaneous, non-historical aspiration develops. With some words, both unaspirated and aspirated variants are heard, for example, *kamáł* and *khamáł* 'skull'. Non-contrastive, non-inherited phonetic aspiration appears frequently in the onset of or preceding stressed syllables. For example, for the agent noun of *maṣkík* 'to ask for' both *maṣkák* and *maṣkhák* 'beggar' are attested (with the aspirated variant more likely to occur in Lower Chitral), as are *ṭaṭóri* 'millet bread' and its variant pronunciation *ṭaṭhóri*. Persian *post* 'skin', 'hide' becomes *phost* in Khowar, with the same meaning. The oblique form of the English loanword *koṭ* 'coat', which has the stressed *ó* oblique ending, becomes *koṭhó*.[8] It even appears in unstressed contexts, for example *khabáb* 'kabab', borrowed from Urdu *kabāb* and *kharegár* 'expert', 'skillful person' < Urdu *kāregār*, or *phurgám* 'plan' < Eng. 'programme'.

There are (still) some words for which only the aspirated or the unaspirated pronunciation is accepted, for example *khol* 'threshing floor' (aspirated) and *kan* 'tree' (unaspirated), but for many, both aspirated and unaspirated pronunciations are equally acceptable. Given the ubiquity of this non-historical, non-contrastive aspiration, it seems that the strength of the aspiration contrast in Khowar is weakening. This is probably at least partially a result of the extensive influence on Khowar of Iranian languages, which have lost all aspiration. Written evidence for this weakening is the fact that quite a few words occur, and are attested in dictionaries, in both aspirated and unaspirated forms; examples are

[8] Some scholars analyse this phenomenon as involving neutralisation of an inherent aspiration in word-final position, an analysis which would give the underlying form of 'camel' as uṭʰ, the aspiration of which surfaces in the oblique form *uṭʰó* (Endresen & Kristiansen 1981: 240). Liljegren and Khan (2017: 5) also adopt this analysis, giving /krɔʈʰ/ [kroʈ] 'tree trunk.DIR' versus /krɔʈʰɔ/ [krɔˈʈʰɔ] 'tree trunk.OBL'. However, Strand (2012) considers that aspirated consonants do not occur in final position, but final consonant /h/ does, as in *kuh* 'wide valley', *ayh* 'up'. Yet another possibility is that this [h] in *koṭ-hó*, for example, arises because of the strong preference for consonant-initial syllables, and could thus be considered syllable-initial consonantal /h/ rather than aspiration.

kušún ~ *khušún* 'smoke', 'household' (DSAL), and *kišti* ~ *khišti* 'boat', 'begging bowl' (Naji 2008: 377). For some people, *trup* means both 'salt' and 'radish'; others have aspirated *thrup* for 'radish' and *trup* for 'salt'.

The various pronunciations attested for 'scarecrow'—*pathránʦk* (Chitrali 2019: 438), *pathránsk* (EB field notes), *pathránzk* (Sloan 2006 [1981]: 120; Naji 2008: 101), *patránsk* (O'Brien 1895: 103)—reflect several characteristics of Khowar phonology. First, the instability/variability of aspiration (*phatránsk* versus *pathránsk*); second, the tendency for an intrusive (non-phonemic) dental-alveolar plosive [t] to appear before a dental-alveolar fricative (especially after /n/) (*pathránʦk*);[9] and third, underlyingly voiced segments surfacing as devoiced before a voiceless plosive (*pathránsk* versus *pathránzk*).

Aspirated /q^h/ is heard in a fair number of Khowar words, for example *ẓiqhéik* 'to squeak' and *çiqhéik* 'to squeak intermittently', *ṭoqhéik* 'to cluck (hen after laying an egg)'; *çoqhík* 'to coo', 'to flatter', *vaqhík* 'to bark'. In all of the above words, however, /q/ is a root-final consonant and the aspiration appears before the stressed vowel of the infinitive suffix. The only word I have encountered with /q^h/ not in the onset of a stressed syllable or immediately preceding a stressed vowel is *qhoteék* 'to breathe heavily or sniffle (while talking)'. Two hypotheses suggest themselves. First, an alternate pronunciation of this word is *qohteék*, which suggests that for this word /q^h/ may arise from the transposition of the glottal fricative /h/ and resulting aspiration, as described for Balochi in Birahimani (2021). Given this, and in the absence of more detailed evidence about the occurrence and distribution of /q^h/, it is also possible that Khowar's /q^h/ results from the secondary (non-historical) aspiration described above.[10]

It is widely accepted that Khowar has no voiced aspirates (Strand 2012; Liljegren & Khan 2017); indeed, voiced consonants are hardly ever aspirated. Morgenstierne, however, (1932: 49–50) found traces of

[9] Munnings (1990a: 26) calls affricates arising in this way 'pseudo-affricates' and contrasts them with true affricates.

[10] Masica (1991: 108), based on data available at the time, said, "For example, an aspirated *q^h is a perfectly possible phoneme, one existing in various Caucasian and Amerindian languages, but it is not found in NIA [New Indo-Aryan]." /q^h/ is also found in Hunza and Nager Burushaski, including in initial position and not only in stressed syllables (Berger 1998: 13, 20–21), but neither Berger (1974) nor Tiffou (2014) mentions /q^h/ in Yasin Burushaski. Lorimer (1962) also lists no words beginning with <q^h>. On the other hand, the title of Skyhawk (2022) is "The Jamáal Qháan story of Alíi Gouhar of Ḍomošáal (Hunza)", suggesting that /x/ of Urdu, for example, is regularly pronounced as /q^h/. The Burushaski–Urdu dictionary compiled by the Burushaski Research Academy in Karachi (2006) regularly uses the letter خ to represent /q^h/, not /x/ as it does in Urdu or Khowar. /q^h/ is also found in Domaki, presumably under the influence of Burushaski.

aspiration with voiced plosives in some varieties of the language. I have also found a few apparent counterexamples to the accepted generalisation; from my own fieldwork there are *udhulík* 'to spread (rumour)', *dher* 'rock pile', *dhaák* 'a runner' (agent noun of *deék* 'to run'), *bhum* 'earth', 'ground', each of which I have heard from one speaker only.[11] It seems, thus, that some traces of the residual aspiration noted by Morgenstierne have survived until the end of the twentieth century. Naji (2008: 31) gives *udhudhu* 'the sound of thunder'; given the *ururú* 'roaring sound' attested elsewhere in my field notes, it seems that this may be another rare surviving variant.

2.1.1.3 Place of articulation

Tables 2.4–2.8 show contrastive examples of consonant sounds produced at various points of articulation.

Table 2.4 Dental-alveolar and post-alveolar (retroflex) plosives

Dental-alveolar		Post-alveolar (retroflex)	
Phoneme	Example	Phoneme	Example
/t/	*tir* 'arrow'	/ṭ/	*ṭír* 'in deep sleep', 'unconscious'
/tʰ/	*tʰas* 'water container with spout'	/ṭʰ/	*ṭʰašṭ* 'flat, round vessel'; 'basin'
/d/	*dal* 'split grains or legumes'	/ḍ/	*ḍal* 'group'

Table 2.5 Dental-alveolar, palatal, and post-alveolar (retroflex) affricates

Dental-alveolar		Post-alveolar (palatal)		Post-alveolar (retroflex)	
Phoneme	Examples	Phoneme	Examples	Phoneme	Examples
/ʦ/	*ʦáraq bik* 'to indulge in excesses', 'to exceed limits' *ʦeq* 'small'	/č/	*čaršambéh* 'Wednesday' /č/ *čaq* 'ready'	/c̣/	*c̣iq* 'part of water mill'
/ʦʰ/	*ʦʰangéik* 'to shake down (grain in a sack)'	/čʰ/	*čʰiník* 'to cut/ break (vt)'	/c̣ʰ/	*c̣ʰuník* 'to tread/step on'

[11] These few instances were heard from senior persons living in conservative dialect areas.

Table 2.5 (continued)

Dental-alveolar		Post-alveolar (palatal)		Post-alveolar (retroflex)	
Phoneme	Examples	Phoneme	Examples	Phoneme	Examples
/ʥ/	*dahlénʥ* 'large open room, space at entrance of a house which serves as an insulating chamber' *ʥox* 'thorn'	/ǰ/	*khanǰ* 'wall' *ǰer* 'line', 'queue'	/j̣/	*lénj̣u* 'tree bark' *j̣enj̣ér* 'chain'

Table 2.6 Dental-alveolar, palatal, and post-alveolar (retroflex) fricatives

Dental-alveolar		Post-alveolar (palatal)		Post-alveolar (retroflex)	
Phoneme	Examples	Phoneme	Examples	Phoneme	Examples
/s/	*sor* 'head'	/š/	*šor* 'a hundred'	/ṣ/	*ṣor* '(very) salty'
/z/	*zar* 'gold' *zoík* 'to agree to' *zor* 'force', 'strength'	/ž/	*žareék* ~ *žaréik* 'to absorb' *žoík* 'to have sexual intercourse with' *žun* 'person', 'individual' *múži* 'in the middle'	/ẓ/	*ẓoγ* 'thin', 'weak' (humans, animals) *ẓar* 'poison' *ẓaq* 'thick', 'viscous' *múẓi* 'small skein of yarn'

Table 2.7 Velarised dental-alveolar and palatal laterals

Velarised dental-alveolar		Palatal	
Phoneme	Example	Phoneme	Example
/ł/	*doł* 'loudly, strongly'	/l/	*doól* 'drum'

Table 2.8 Velar and post-velar plosives

Velar		Post-velar	
Phoneme	Examples	Phoneme	Examples
/k/	*kušún* 'smoke', 'household' *kam* 'little', 'few'	/q/	*quš* 'living quarters' *qamqám* 'metal trap for rats and other animals'

2.2 Vowels

Khowar has a simple, five-vowel system, shown in Table 2.9.[12]

Table 2.9 Vowels

	Front	Central	Back
High	i		u
Mid	e		o
Low		a	

These vowels are all contrastive. The following words demonstrate the contrast between /a/, /o/, /u/, and /i/ in stressed syllables.

išlák 'unfermented', 'unleavened'
išlók 'piece', 'shaving', 'chip (wood)'
išlúk 'dried up (animal no longer giving milk, or a spring or canal in which water is no longer flowing)'
išlík 'smooth'

The following unstressed verb roots show the contrast between all five vowels.

ra- 'bark'
ru- 'grow long'
re- 'speak'
ro- 'dye'
ri- 'leak'

/e/ and /i/ contrast in forms like the imperative singular ending *-é*, as in *koré* 'do!' and the ending of the perfective participle, *-í* ~ *-i*, as in *korí* 'having done'. This contrast also appears in pairs like *thuík* 'to spit' versus *thuék* 'rifle'.[13]

/e/ and /a/ contrast: *baṣ* 'share'; 'modal particle' and *beṣ* 'extra, excessive'; *kan* 'tree' and *ken* 'turn', 'number (as in a queue)', 'rock shelter'

[12] See Liljegren and Khan (2017) for a recent analysis of the Khowar vowel system. Among their interesting results is: "The distinguishing features are front /i ɛ/ versus back /u ɔ ɑ/; open /ɛ ɑ ɔ/ versus close /i u/; and unrounded /i ɛ ɑ/ versus rounded /u ɔ/. Our conclusion is therefore that the main distinguishing feature between /ɑ/ and /ɔ/ is roundedness rather than tongue position." (2017: 6)

[13] Some words show dialectal variation between /e/ and /i/ between Upper and Lower Chitral, as with *néki* 'is not' and *regíṣ* 'beard' (Zondrangram) but *níki* and *rigíṣ* (Lower Chitral).

/e/ and /o/ contrast: *bel* 'small, squarish scoop for ashes and coals', *bol* 'armed force'[14]

/e/ and /u/ contrast: *axér* 'end', *ṣaxúr* 'ray (of the sun)'

However, in unstressed syllables, /u/ and /o/, and /i/ and /e/ are sometimes very close, as in *mux* ~ *mox* 'face', and *dexdéx* ~ *dixdíx* 'just about to'. In his Khowar–Urdu dictionary, Naji often gives two spellings for words pronounced with unstressed /e/ [ɛ] ~ [i]: one with the diacritic ◌ِ for short /i/ and another with the full vowel symbol ی representing /e/; for example, بیشٹو بِشٹو *bɛṣú* ~ *biṣú* 'species of bush used for fuel' (Naji 2008: 95, 80).

2.2.1 Suprasegmental features

Vowels can contrast phonemically in stress and tone (pitch contour), but not in length or nasality.

2.2.1.1 Stress

Stress, as used in this work, means the prominence of one syllable relative to others. This syllable prominence is produced by a speaker exerting more energy while producing the stressed syllable than with others.[15] It is perceived by a listener as greater loudness, and sometimes higher pitch and greater duration (length).[16] In Khowar, word stress is lexically determined; that is, in each word a specific syllable is stressed. Stress has several functions in Khowar. First, it is lexically contrastive, indicating a meaning difference in several pairs of basic underived words; see examples in Table 2.10. Stress plays a morphological role in several contexts, for example in deriving nouns from adjectives, as in *iskúrdi* 'short' → *iskurdí* 'shortness'.

[14] Some infinitives show dialectal variation /e/ ~ /o/ between Torkhow and other areas in Chitral, for example *bałóik* 'to overcome by force' in Torkhow versus *bałéik* ~ *baleék* ~ *baléyk* in other areas.

[15] With some speakers, the difference between the intensity of a stressed syllable and that of an unstressed syllable is greater than with others.

[16] Three degrees of phonetic length are heard: short (*don* 'tooth'); medium (*to:nǰ* 'destroyed', 'lost'); and long (*doón* 'ghee').

Table 2.10 Minimal pairs involving contrastive stress

Stress on first syllable	Stress on final syllable
káłi 'dish of strips of dough boiled in onion broth'	*kałí* 'plough part: two wooden sticks suspended from the yoke on the sides of the bull's head'
táru 'fast (runner)'	*tarú* 'batter' (Liljegren & Khan 2017: 6)
béłu 'basket', 'weight measure (about 20 kg)'	*bełú* 'flute', 'blowpipe'
tóri 'above', 'upper'	*torí* 'having reached'
gáłi 'car', 'vehicle'	*gałí* 'watch', 'clock', 'timepiece'

Stressable syllables are those which can, given the necessary positional or syntactic context, bear stress. Monosyllabic nouns like *dur* 'house', are considered to be inherently stressable, that is, stressed in certain contexts; thus *dúr-i* 'house-LOC2' but *dur-ó* 'house-OBL'. Disyllabic nouns are stressed either on their final syllable: *apák* 'mouth', *arqá* 'back'; or on their initial (in this case penultimate) syllable: *áłi* 'duck', *náqul* 'proverb', *υrázun* 'wing'. Trisyllabic nouns can be stressed either on the penultimate syllable, as in *išnári* 'thing', *iskúrdi* 'short', or on the final syllable, for example, *adiná* 'Friday', *panǰaráṣ* 'full moon', *iskurdí* 'shortness'. Adjectives can be monosyllabic, like *peç̣* 'hot'; disyllabic with initial stress, as in *múṭu* 'dull'; disyllabic with final stress, for example, *laház* 'ill'; or trisyllabic, as in *učóγun* 'liquid', with stress on the penultimate syllable. Trisyllabic adjectives are mostly native Khowar words like *łoυaáki* 'round (cylindrical)', *išpéru* 'white', *dudéri* 'distant', and *iskúrdi* 'short'.[17] Enclitic elements like *di* 'also' are unstressed (unless emphasised for discourse reasons).

Morphological processes, either derivational, as in *iskúrdi* 'short' → *iskurdí* 'shortness' (see also Chapter 3), or inflectional, as in *ç̣hétur* 'field.DIR' → *ç̣hetr-ó* 'field-OBL', *ç̣hétr-o* 'field-LOC4', result in stress shift and morphophonological changes. The oblique singular case suffix /o/ is a stressable syllable, sometimes taking primary word stress and sometimes not.[18]

With most monosyllabic nouns, oblique /o/ takes stress and the stem vowel is unstressed, as with *dust* 'friend.DIR' → *dust-ó* 'friend-OBL', *šam* 'evening.DIR' → *šam-ó* 'evening-OBL'. However, there are two classes of monosyllabic nouns in whose oblique forms the stress remains on the

[17] From most of these adjectives abstract nouns can be derived by addition of the stressed nominalising suffix *-í*, which replaces the unstressed final /i/ of the adjectival form.

[18] For discussion of similar morphophonemic changes in Gilgit Shina, see Radloff (1999a).

stem. The first is those nouns which have a stem vowel with low tone and its accompanying length; examples are: *leén* 'hollyhock.DIR', *lén-o* 'hollyhock-OBL'; *laál* 'affectionate term of address for elder brother.DIR, *lál-o* 'elder brother.OBL'; *žuúr* 'daughter.DIR', *žúr-o* 'daughter-OBL'; *braár* 'brother.DIR', *brár-o* 'brother-OBL', *boók* 'wife.DIR', *bók-o* 'wife-OBL'. I analyse this behaviour as a consequence of low tone inducing a lengthening of the vowel, with the second mora of these elongated vowels bearing stress. In Strand's (2022) analysis, words with low tone and elongated vowels have accented posterior phonation. This is similar to the pattern observed with polysyllabic words, in which oblique *-o* immediately following a stressed vowel is not stressed. A second class of monosyllabic nouns includes those whose stress in the oblique form is on the stem but which do not have low tone. These include *nan* 'mother.DIR', *nán-o* 'mother-OBL'; *tat* 'father.DIR', *tát-o* 'father-OBL'; *beč* 'aunt.DIR', *béč-o* 'aunt-OBL'; *mik* 'uncle.DIR', *mík-o* 'uncle-OBL', and *lu* 'word', 'utterance.DIR, *lu-o* (word-OBL)'.[19]

The reason for retention of stress on the stem of these words needs explanation. One hypothesis is that, since most of the observed monosyllabic words in this class are kinship terms, this may be an analogical development modelled on *braár* 'brother' (< *bhrā́tr̥* RV, T9661) and *žuúr* 'daughter' (< *duhitŕ̥* T6481), both of which are reflexes of OIA words containing /h/, of which their low tone is a trace.

The case of *žav* 'son.DIR', *žav-ó* 'son.OBL', and *vav* 'grandmother.DIR', *vav-ó* 'grandmother.OBL' is different. Though they are also basic kinship terms, they behave differently, perhaps because they are not reflexes of OIA words with /h/. Or, more likely, the stem-final *v* of these words induces a syllable break in the oblique form, yielding a structure like *va.vó*, with a favoured consonant-initial second syllable, as happens with *łov* 'fox', whose oblique is *ło.v-ó* 'fox-OBL'.[20]

However, *lu*.DIR 'word', 'speech', retains stress on the stem vowel in its oblique form *lú-o* (word-OBL), as in *ma lú-o mo det* 'Don't tell about me.'[21] Given that other nouns of apparently identical structure, like *šu* 'porcupine', 'bolt of cloth' and *ṣu* 'layer of easily split rock', have stress on their oblique forms, as in *šu-ó mo maré* 'Don't kill the porcupine' and *avá ṣu-ó nezítam* 'I split off a layer of rock',[22] the question of why *lu* 'word' behaves differently remains a puzzle to me.[23]

[19] The words *nan* 'mother', *tat* 'father', and *beč* 'aunt' can be compared to Wakhi *nan* 'mother', *tat* 'father', and *beč* 'uncle', and with words in other Pamir languages.
[20] See Section 2.2.2.1 Diphthongs.
[21] From an oral text from Village Sorech.
[22] These two examples are from Zahoor ul Haq Danish.
[23] It is possible that these behaviours may be explained by employing Strand's (2022) analysis of posterior and anterior phonation.

Low-rising tone with an elongated vowel is also seen on the final syllable of some disyllabic nouns, for example *vezeén* 'evening.DIR'. In such words, the final vowel retains stress but preceding the oblique ending loses its low tone and induced length, as in *vezén-o-te* 'evening-OBL-DAT', *baçhoół* 'calf.DIR', *baçhół-o* 'calf-OBL'. This happens with the normally stressed oblique plural ending *-án* as well; for example, *maáṣ* 'husks.DIR', *máṣ-an* 'husks-OBL.PL', *ivaák* 'root.DIR', *ivák-an* 'root-OBL.PL', not **ivak-án*. Some disyllabic pairs of words contrast only in pitch contour, with its consequent vowel elongation; for example, *sarék* 'the narrow end of an egg', with stressed non-lengthened vowel, and *sareék* 'to seem, appear', with low tone and lengthened /e/.

A disyllabic word with final stress but not having low tone retains its stress unchanged before the oblique singular and oblique plural endings. With such nouns, the oblique *-o* or *-an* is unstressed, as with *šapír* 'wolf.DIR', *šapír-o* 'wolf-OBL'; *reṣú* 'bull.DIR' *reṣú-o* 'bull-OBL'; *kuṭhúk* 'fruit pit.DIR', *kuṭhúk-an* 'fruit pit-OBL.PL', *kahák* 'hen.DIR', *kahák-an* 'hen-OBL.PL'. Since the infinitive ending *-ík* is always stressed, the *-o* of an oblique infinitive is always unstressed.

If a disyllabic word has initial stress and unstressed /u/ in the final syllable as in *léšu* 'cow.DIR', the unstressed /u/ is elided before the oblique suffix, yielding *leš-ó* 'cow-OBL'. If elision of unstressed /u/ results in an unacceptable syllable-final consonant cluster, as with *čúmur* 'iron.DIR' → **čúmr-*, or *gósun* 'trash.DIR' → **gosn*, adding the oblique ending yields an unproblematic final CV syllable, *čum.r-ó* 'iron-OBL' or *gos.n-án* 'trash-OBL.PL', and the oblique ending is stressed in the pattern observed with most disyllabic words with final stress.[24] Final unstressed /i/ behaves similarly, except that instead of being elided, the final unstressed /i/ is weakened to a /y/ glide and stress is on the oblique, as in *kéłi* 'sheep.DIR', *keły-ó* 'sheep-OBL' and *áłi* 'duck.DIR', *ały-ó* 'duck-OBL'.

If the final syllable of a disyllabic noun ends in a stressed /é/ or /ó/, that vowel merges with oblique /o/, resulting in lengthening it; for example, *griṣpó* 'summer.DIR', *griṣpo-oó* 'summer-OBL'.[25]

Trisyllabic nouns with stress on the penultimate syllable and unstressed vowels in the final syllable behave like disyllabic nouns with final unstressed vowels, stress remaining on the penultimate syllable. With final unstressed /u/, the /u/ is elided, as in *ružáyu*.DIR 'daughter.in.law',

[24] This behaviour is discussed by Munnings (1990a: 23), who analyses it as 'u-insertion' into an underlying form *čumr*, preventing a non-occurring final consonant cluster /mr/. However, it can also be analysed as analogous to the widely discussed 'schwa deletion' in other Indo-Aryan languages. For example, Urdu *aurat* 'woman.DIR.SG' becomes *aurt-ẽ* 'women.DIR.PL'.

[25] Some speakers have *griṣp* as the direct form and *griṣpó* as the oblique.

rużáy-o 'daughter.in.law-OBL', *kumóru* 'girl.DIR', *kumór-o* 'girl-OBL'. With final unstressed /i/, the vowel becomes a consonantal glide /y/ preceding the oblique marker /o/ as with disyllabic nouns: *kiphíni* 'spoon.DIR', *kiphín.y-o* 'spoon-OBL', *gambúri* 'flower.DIR', *gambúr.y-o* 'flower-OBL'.

Trisyllabic nouns with final stressed /í/ or /ú/ behave like disyllabic nouns with a stressed final syllable; the stressed final vowel is not elided or weakened and retains its stress, as in *božoní* 'boundary.DIR', *božoní-o* 'boundary-OBL'; *lablabú* 'beet.DIR', *lablabú-o* 'beet-OBL'. With stressed final /é/, for example in *pia.yé* 'PIA.DIR', /e/ merges with oblique *-o* and lengthens it, as in *pia.y-oó* 'PIA-OBL'.[26]

With compound words, the primary stress of the first element becomes secondary (marked when necessary with the symbol < ˙ > above the secondarily stressed syllable), for example *bašȧr.dóyu* 'member of a funeral procession', in which the stress of the final syllable of the first element of the compound has become secondary. If a stressed derivational or inflectional suffix attaches to a polysyllabic word, the primary stress shifts to the position appropriate for it in the final word form. For example, singular *novés* 'nephew', 'grandchild' becomes plural *novės-gíni* when the stress-bearing plural suffix *-gíni* is attached. Short participial relative clauses like *kȯṭanǰíru* '(person) [who is wearing a coat]' behave as a single word, with primary stress on its penultimate syllable. The expression [*dȯnžúrdu*] *reéni*, literally 'a dog [that has eaten ghee]', is idiomatically used of a person ashamed of himself for having done something wrong. In this case, the long, low-toned vowel of *doón* 'ghee' loses its length and second-mora stress.

Sentence stress is to be distinguished from lexical stress. In sentences or multi-word utterances, stress can shift to indicate various kinds of emphasis or focus, as shown in the difference between example (2.1), with normal, non-emphatic intonation, and (2.2) with emphatic, insistent stress shifted to the present/future specific marker. I have indicated this type of stress when it occurs. For example, (2.2) might be uttered if a speaker had already said s/he didn't have time, but the interlocutor kept pressing him/her to come.

(2.1) *ma γoš no bóy-an. avá gík-o no*
my time NEG become.3SG.PRS/FUT-S I come.INF-OBL NEG
bo-m
be.able-1sg.PRS/FUT.NS
'I won't have time; I won't be able to come.'

[26] PIA = Pakistan International Airlines. This example is from Chitral Town.

(2.2) *yoš no boy-**án**. gík-o no bom-án*
'(I've told you already) I **don't** have time; and I can't come.'

The final syllable in a sentence, usually the verb ending, is often phonetically lengthened and its tone somewhat lowered, signalling the end of an utterance. Such sentence stress or phonetic effect is not marked in the examples in this book.

2.2.1.2 Tone

Lexical tone is a distinctive pitch contour associated with a word.[27] If tone is contrastive in a language, yielding differences in meaning, the language is called a tone language. In Khowar, a low-rising pitch, accompanied by extended duration (length) contrasts with high-falling pitch in a small number of pairs. This is found mostly with monosyllabic words; however, some disyllabic words too contrast only in pitch contour, with consequent vowel elongation; for example *sarék* 'the narrow end of an egg', with stressed non-lengthened vowel, and *sareék* 'to seem/appear', with low tone and lengthened /e/; and *išpén* 'portion given by someone from his own share to someone of equal or lower status' and *išpeén* 'species of bush'.

Table 2.11 displays some contrastive pairs. In this book, vowels with low-rising tone are indicated with a doubled vowel symbol with an acute accent on the second copy, as <aá>.[28]

Table 2.11 Lengthened vowel and low-rising pitch contrasted with high-falling pitch

High-falling pitch	Low-rising pitch, elongated vowel
bas 'overnight stay' (Kho.), 'bus' (< Eng.), 'enough' (< Ur.)	*baás* 'flame'
don 'tooth'	*doón* 'ghee'
len 'knot'	*leén* 'hollyhock'
goł 'throat'	*goół* 'gully', 'dry streambed'

[27] The majority of the Indo-Aryan languages in the greater Hindukush region make tonal distinctions of various types. See Baart (1997, 1999, 2003, 2004) and Radloff (1999b).

[28] This notation was originally developed by Berger (1960) for Burushaski, and subsequently adopted by Buddruss (1996) and Radloff (1999b) for Gilgit Shina, and Schmidt and Kohistani (2008) for Kohistani Shina. It represents the analysis that when stress falls on the second mora of a phonemically long vowel, it produces a low tone. I use this notation here to indicate the elongation of the vowels in syllables with low tone, since the analysis of the elongated vowels in such syllables seems to explain the retention of stress on the root of such words in Khowar when the oblique ending /o/ is suffixed. The use of this notation makes no claim, however, that pitch and tone play the same role in Khowar as they do in Shina or Burushaski.

Table 2.11 (continued)

High-falling pitch	Low-rising pitch, elongated vowel
bol 'army, armed force'	*boól* 'appearance of the Pleiades and the moon together'
dí 'now', *di* 'also' (enclitic)	*dií* 'yes'
ḷang 'hard', 'stiff'	*ḷaáng* 'hearth'
dron 'bow (used with arrows)'	*droón* 'wormwood'
sarék 'the narrow end of an egg'	*sareék* 'to seem, appear'
išpén 'portion given by someone from his own share to someone of equal or lower status'	*išpeén* 'species of bush'

Given the limited number of minimal pairs in which tone is contrastive, it seems appropriate to say that tone plays a relatively minor role in Khowar, and it can be considered only partially a tone language.

However, quite a few other words also have elongated vowels accompanied by a low-rising pitch (cf. Strand's accented posterior phonation), although they may not contrast in minimal pairs. Some words of this type are *goóm* 'wheat', *koółl* 'bone', *čhaáγ* 'shade', *çhiír* 'milk' (Mulkhow pronunciation), *doól* 'drum', *doóγ* 'milk and milk products', *droó* 'body hair', *giír* 'an intensive particle used with concept of darkness', *guúẓ* 'describes a person or animal which prowls around with head down (looking for something)', *heén* 'wooden lever, used for prying up stones', *hiím* 'snow' (Mulkhow pronunciation), *šiloóγ* 'story', 'traditional tale', *usneék* 'to swim', *vezeén* 'evening', *ḍaḍoóri* 'round wooden block from which round serving vessels were fashioned'. To the best of my knowledge, these are all OIA-origin Khowar words, which is consistent with Strand's analysis attributing the increase of anterior phonation in languages of the contact zone between Iranian and Indo-Aryan languages to the influence of Iranian languages.[29]

2.2.1.3 Length

Vowel length is not contrastive (phonemic) in Khowar, but phonetic length does arise as a consequence of stress.[30] This means that three

[29] Strand (2022: 449–50) explains the pitch contour of words such as these as a consequence of anterior versus posterior phonation as follows: "Accented phonation is produced with either tight anterior voicing or posterior voicing, concomitant with the oral articulation of a vowel. Accented anterior voicing raises the pitch of the vowel, while posterior voicing lowers the vowel's pitch."

[30] The position of length in Khowar is similar to that found for Wakhi. Grjunberg and Steblin-Kamensky (1976: 542–5) present experimental evidence that synchronic vowel length is not phonemic but correlates with positional and intonational factors. They suggest that there co-exist

degrees of phonetic length are perceptible—short (*don* 'tooth'), medium (*to:nǰ* 'destroyed, lost'),[31] and long (*doón* 'ghee'). This can be seen in the word *barabá:r* 'equal, fine, good', in which the /a/ of the final, stressed syllable is phonetically slightly longer than the /a/ of the first and second syllables.[32]

The apparently long vowels heard in words like *hayaá* (*hayá-a*) 'this-LOC1' 'here' and *hardií* (*hardí-i*) 'heart-LOC2' 'in the heart' result when a vocalic suffix attaches to a word ending in the same vowel. Affective lengthening appears in conversation and in stories to emphasise the duration of an action or state or for emphasis as in ***bi:l**khúl* 'com**plete**ly!' (first syllable of *bilkhúl* which is elongated, and second syllable of 'completely' emphatically stressed). Elongated vowels also appear as a vocative marker when addressing someone; for example *é na:n* 'o Mother'.

2.2.1.4 Nasalisation

Nasalisation of vowels is almost never heard in Khowar. For example, when an Urdu word with a nasalised vowel, like Urdu *yahā̃* 'here', is used in Khowar, it is often pronounced as *yahán*, with a full nasal consonant /n/. The only words in which I have heard clear nasalised vowels are the expressive particle *ẽẽ* ~ *hẽẽ* 'Aha! So (I see)!' and the word *ōṣ̌ṭ* 'eight' (with some speakers). So the question of phonemic contrast does not arise. Weak phonetic nasalisation is induced on a vowel preceding a nasal consonant, especially a nasal-velar consonant sequence preceding a stressed vowel as in /an.gár/, [ãgár] 'fire'.

Examining nasalisation in neighbouring and/or related languages is worth a detailed digression. The contrast with Kalasha is striking. Kalasha has phonemically contrastive nasalised counterparts for its five basic vowels, a, e, i, o, u. For example, *bag* 'garden' versus *bãg (dyek)* 'to poke' (Kochetov et al. 2020). Kalasha has had close contact with Nuristani languages, about which Strand (2007–11) says, "Nasalised vowels appear in all dialects except Western Kât´avari. Nasalisation derives

two separate phonological systems, one for native Wakhi words including old borrowings and one for (more recent) borrowings (Bashir 2009: 827). This is similar to the conclusion that one might reach from Strand's analysis of anterior and posterior phonation in far-northwestern Indo-Aryan languages, especially Khowar; that is, that with the influx of Iranian words into Khowar, previously existing (IA) posterior phonation is increasingly yielding to (Iranian-influenced) anterior phonation.

[31] In Strand's analysis, this word has anterior phonation. Liljegren and Khan (2017: 8) find that vowels are often pronounced with longer duration if followed by a voiced consonant.

[32] Some dialectal difference in the pronunciation of vowels is reported by Maula Nigah Nigah, such that there is a tendency to have longer vowels in Lower Chitral than in Upper Chitral, for example, *jam* 'good' in Upper Chitral but *ja:m* in Lower Chitral. This observation seems consistent with Strand's (2022) analysis, in which anterior phonation is increasing relative to posterior phonation in areas more influenced by Persian or Urdu (Lower Chitral).

from a reduction of ancient *n." Buddruss and Degener (2017: 61) also note nasalisation in some Prasun (Vâsí-vari) words but find that it is not phonologically distinctive. It seems likely that nasalisation in Kalasha may be a shared phonological feature induced by contact with some Nuristani languages.

In some other IA languages neighbouring Khowar, nasalisation is not so prominent. In Dameli, according to Perder (2013: 27), nasalised vowels occur—mostly long, as in *žũũ* 'louse', but also short, for example *ãš* 'token'; but he does not discuss the question of whether or not nasalisation is contrastive. Regarding Palula, Liljegren (2016: 61) says that "nasalisation seems to be a marginal suprasegmental feature of a limited number of lexemes. Apart from those, nasalisation is a non-contrastive phonetic property of vowels occurring adjacent to a nasal consonant." In Kalkoti, nasalisation is found but its phonemic status is uncertain (Liljegren 2013: 138).

However, in Kalam Kohistani (Gawri), contrastive nasalised vowel phonemes are found (Baart 1997: 31, 37). In Torwali, spoken adjacent to Gawri, nasalised vowels are common, and nasalisation is phonemic (Lunsford 2001: 32). Farther to the west, in Pashai, Morgenstierne (1973a: 148) noted only that for some dialects of northwest Pashai, "before a sibilant /n/ is realised as nasalisation of the preceding vowel". Discussing the northeast group of dialects, he says: "Nasalised vowels are probably to be interpreted as combinations of vowel + nasal [consonant]" (p. 208). He does not mention any contrastive function of nasalisation. Lehr (2014) also does not mention nasalisation in her work on the Pashai of Darra-i Nur. More recently, she notes (p.c.) that she has heard (phonetic) nasalisation in vowels preceding retroflex [ṇ] and velarized [ŋg], for example with *ãṇa* 'egg', *ãŋguṛek* 'finger', *ãŋgar* 'fire', but sees no contrastive nasalisation. Strand (2005, 2012) mentions nasalisation as a 'coproduced component' associated with the nasal consonants but makes no mention of phonemic nasalisation. Nasalisation is also not mentioned for Tirahi (Morgenstierne 1934).

Given the variation in salience of vowel nasalisation in neighbouring languages, to what can we attribute the almost complete absence of nasalisation in Khowar? I have previously (Bashir 1988a) commented on the likely influence of Burushaski on Khowar. In Hunza Burushaski, nasalised vowels occur only in expressive (probably onomatopoetic) words like *thíãũ ét-* 'sneeze', *ṣṹũ ét-* 'smell', *hẽ* 'come on!', while in Nager Burushaski they appear in these expressive words and rarely in some place names (Berger 1998 Vol. 1: 16. For Yasin Burushaski, neither Berger (1974) nor Tiffou (2014) mentions nasalised vowels.

The situation in historical and contemporary neighbouring Iranian languages also seems highly relevant. There is no mention of vowel nasalisation for Parachi, which may have been in contact with *pre-Khowar (Kieffer 2009). New Persian, which has heavily influenced Khowar, does not have contrastive nasalised vowels. Aside from Persian, the Iranian language which has had the longest and closest contact with Khowar is Wakhi, which appears to have no vowel nasalisation (Bashir 2009). Mock (1998) makes no mention of vowel nasalisation, either in his own field observations or in the work of any other scholar.

2.2.2 Vowel sequences

Sequences of two vowels can be of two types—diphthongs and disyllabic sequences. Diphthongs are complex vowel sounds in which the articulators move from the position of an initial vowel sound to the position of a second one, producing not a full second vowel but a semivowel or consonantal off-glide. Diphthongs function as single vowels in a single syllable. Disyllabic vowel sequences, on the other hand, participate in two syllables. An important question for Khowar is whether an apparent diphthong, for example /ai/, or /au/, is better analysed as a diphthong, a vowel–semivowel sequence, VV or as a vowel–consonant glide sequence, VC.[33]

2.2.2.1 Diphthongs—VC sequences

For Khowar, the solution to this question adopted in this book is that most apparent (or historic) diphthongs are synchronically better analysed as either single vowels or VC sequences. Illustrative cases are the third person singular past ending and the third-person singular present/future ending. Adopting the VC solution gives *-ay* instead of *-ai*, for example *širáy,* the mirative of *š*- 'be (INAN)', *biráy* the mirative of *b*- 'become', and *ruphítay* 's/he, it got up', past direct of *ruph*- 'get up'. Present/future forms like *boy* 'it is/will be' instead of *boi,* and *koy* 's/he, it does/will do' instead of *koi* result. Several Khowar writers seem to prefer the VC analysis, as suggested by their spelling choices in romanised spellings.[34]

[33] The analysis and classification of diphthongs is fraught with complications, and perhaps no single statement applies equally well to an entire speech community. Catford (1977: 215–17) is an authoritative presentation of these issues.

[34] An argument for the VC analysis of putative diphthongs is the behaviour of monosyllabic words like *ƚov* 'fox' in the oblique, where the oblique form *ƚo.vó* behaves as having a consonant-initial final syllable. (See Section 2.2.1.1 Stress.) A strong conclusion was reached by the late Carla Radloff for Gilgit Shina several years ago—that it entirely lacks diphthongs (Radloff 1999b: 52; 2003 passim).

Transitive/causative stems end in stressed *é* (< *ái*), like *khul.é-* 'finish off'. With an infinitive like *khulé-ik*, with a V́V sequence, the question is whether the normally stressed *í* of a basic infinitive ending survives as a weakened, unstressed *i*, whether it has further weakened to a consonantal off-glide, or whether it is now a simple vowel, *é*. That is, whether to treat sequences with now unstressed /i/ in causative infinitives as containing a VC sequence, *éy*, represented as *khuléyk*, for instance, or *khulék* with a single vowel, instead of *khuléik* with a V́V sequence. Some writers have adopted the VC solution for representing such infinitives with roman characters, while others prefer the single-vowel or the V́V *-éi-* analysis.[35]

In this book, forms containing such sequences will appear as VV sequences in tables of paradigms in order to maintain continuity in the literature, but as VC sequences in the main text and in example sentences, in an attempt to better represent the perceived and actually pronounced sounds of the words today.

2.2.2.2 Disyllabic sequences

Disyllabic vowel sequences can have an initial or a final stressed vowel, VV́ or V́V.

2.2.2.2.1 VV́ sequences

VV́ sequences are more frequent than V́V sequences and arise in several situations. Some VV́ sequences occur in nouns, for example, *ta.ít* 'charm' 'amulet', *ši.áq* 'mud (for building)', *ṣa.úk* 'slipknot', 'stitch (in knitting)', *bo.ík* 'bird'. With these and other VV́ sequences, some speakers insert an epithentic [y] or [ʋ] to break up the CV.VC sequence and create a more favoured CV.CV(C) sequence, for example, *thu.ék* ~ *thu.ʋék* 'rifle', *bo.ík* ~ *bo.yík* 'bird'.

Several such situations arise when vowel-initial suffixes attach to vowel-final stems of basic verbs. Since the infinitive ending *-ík* of basic verbs is always stressed, the infinitive of vowel-final roots necessarily includes a VV́ sequence, as in *do.ík* 'to milk (an animal)', *čho.ík* 'to be frostbitten', *no.ík* 'to be visible', *búhtu.ík* 'to fear'.

The perfective participle ending, *-í* ~ *-i*, when suffixed to a vowel-final stem, presents another such situation. With the verb *khulé-* 'finish off', whose causative stem ends in the stressed front vowel /é/, the question is whether the /i/ of the perfective participle ending is shortened and loses its stress but remains vocalic, or whether it is further

[35] Rehmat Aziz Chitrali, for one, uses the spellings *-eyk* for the infinitives of transitive verbs in his dictionary (Chitrali 2019).

reduced to /y/, producing a V́C sequence *éy*. The perfective participle could be represented as *khulé-i* 'having finished off' to preserve the *i* of the perfective participle ending, or *khulé-y* to represent the present pronunciation more closely. In this book, in order to not lose morphological information, I spell all perfective participles with final *-i*, giving *khulé-i*.

With verbs whose roots end in unstressed *-i*, the stem-final /i/ merges with the /i/ of the perfective participial ending, yielding forms with a lengthened vowel like *thií* 'having remained still/stopped', as in *thií nišé* 'sit still!'. But with a stem ending in an unstressed /u/ as in *búhtu-* 'fear', the /í/ of the participial ending retains its stress and the consonantal /ʋ/ does not appear before the *-i* of the participial ending, yielding *buhtuí* 'having feared'.

The same changes apply with the past direct morpheme, *-í(s)(t)-*, of *-i*-final roots, giving *thiítay* 'came to rest/stopped moving'. This is seen clearly with other verbs with vowel-final roots like *zo-* 'agree to', *ro-* 'dye', *su-* 'sew', *łu-* 'howl', 'bray', *buhtu-* 'fear'. Such words yield VV́ sequences in PST.D forms like *o.í* in *ro.ítay* 's/he dyed (something)', *u.í* in *su.ítay* 's/he sewed', *buhtu,ítay* 's/he, it became frightened'.

The thematic vowels in present/future paradigms are stressed, giving forms like *pašír* 's/he, it sees/will see', *góni* 'they come, will come'. With vowel-final roots like *ri-* 'leak', *buhtu-* 'fear', or causative stems like *rié-* 'cause to leak', PRS/FUT forms like *ri-úran* 'it is leaking (water)', *buhtu-íran* 's/he is afraid' *ri-éran* 'it is leaking (bucket)' result. All of these have VV́ sequences.

Some nominalising suffixes with an initial stressed vowel result in VV́ sequences. For example, the nominalising suffix *-í*, seen for instance in *muka-í* 'shotgun' ← *muká* 'shot (used in a gun)'. This suffix produces several words which participate in VC and VV́ contrasting pairs. The contrast between the VC sequence *uy* and the disyllabic VV́ sequence *u.í* can be seen in the following pairs: *ç̣huy* 'hungry', *ç̣hu.í* 'hunger'; and *čhuy* 'dark', *čhu.í* 'darkness', 'night'. Another such suffix is *-úṭi*; following /a/, in *andra.úṭi* 'strap on a load or backpack such that hands are left free' and *ža.úṭi* 'shoot that grows from the roots of a mature tree', it retains stress on *ú* and resists reduction to consonant ʋ. The instrumental noun-forming suffix *-íni,* as in *so-íni* 'instrument for sweeping or brushing together', also produces VV́ sequences. On the other hand, *-íki* following /a/, as in *xonza.íki* ~ *xonʣa.íki* 'female of a species of large, long-haired ratlike animal with a long tail' sometimes loses its stress and is pronounced as *xonzáyki*.

2.2.2.2.2 V́V sequences

V́V sequences occur less frequently. They arise when a noun ending in a stressed vowel takes an unstressed vocalic case ending, as in *phyu* 'shoulder blade.DIR', *phyú-a loɫík* 'shoulder blade.LOC1 look' (to look at an animal's shoulder blade as a form of divination). V́V sequences also arise at the morpheme boundary between a vowel-final prefix with an originally stressed vowel like *bé-* 'without' or *ná-* 'not' and a vowel-initial word, for example *ė.i* in *bė.izzatí* 'disgrace' and *ȧ.u* in *nȧ.umét* 'hopeless'. In such cases the originally primary stress on the prefix becomes secondary, with the resulting word conforming to the usual word-stress patterns.[36]

2.3 Allophonic effects

Both consonants and vowels exert allophonic effects on adjacent segments. For example, following velarised /ɫ/, /e/ and /i/ are somewhat backed, for example, *ɫex* 'dull curved blade used for scooping dough onto the breadboard' sometimes sounds like [ɫɨx]. On the other hand, /l/, which is slightly palatalised, can front and raise a following vowel, for example, *lašṭ* 'plain (land)' sounds like [læšṭ]. In some words, /í/ induces strong palatalisation on a preceding consonant, as in *gív* ~ *g^yív* 'a gathering of women at night to clean and prepare wool for spinning'.

2.4 Phonotactics

2.4.1 Consonant clusters

A consonant cluster is two or more adjacent consonant sounds pronounced together with no vocalic sound or morpheme boundary intervening. Initial, medial, and final clusters occur in Khowar; however, medial clusters are not being considered here, since they often arise across syllable or morpheme boundaries, for example, the *lt* in *pol.tá* 'wick', or the *kt* in *ṭék-tu* 'top-LOC3' 'up on the top', or in a reduplicated form like *kl* in *lak.laká* 'a joke'. Some word-medial clusters are found in Persian/Urdu loans, for example *fl* in *γaflát* 'negligence'.[37]

[36] It is worth noting that both of these words involve Perso-Arabic origin elements.

[37] There is a tendency in children's speech to change a medial /ṭr/ cluster to initial /br/, creating a more frequent initial /br/ cluster instead of medial /ṭr/, for example the English word 'battery' is heard as *briḍí* in children's speech, which becomes *biṭrí* in adults' speech (MNN).

2.4.1.1 Initial clusters

The second consonant in native Khowar word-initial two-element syllable onset clusters may be /l/, /ɫ/, /k/, /p/, /r/, /d/, /y/, or /ʋ/. In my data, initial /ḍr/, /ṭr/, /sk/, /sl/, and /pl/ appear only in words borrowed from English. Words with such non-native clusters are often modified by inserting an epenthetic vowel. For English 'plaster', the *pl* cluster is 'repaired' by inserting epenthetic *a*, giving *palastér*. Instead of /klip/ 'hair clip', *kilíp* occurs, and for 'slipper' we have *silipér*. The /sk/ cluster is sometimes repaired, and sometimes not. For example, instead of /skul/ 'school', *sikúl* or *iskúl* is sometimes heard. However, /skoṭ/ 'Scout' is unchanged, as is *sken* 'scan'

Syllable-initial clusters I have found in Khowar are sorted by their second consonant in Table 2.12. *k* occurs as second consonant only in English borrowings.

2.4.1.2 Final clusters

I have found the following two-consonant syllable-final clusters, sorted here by their second consonant, arranged in Khowar alphabetical order.[38]

/p/ as second consonant

/rp/ *phorp* 'corral for cattle'
/hp/ *phohp* 'corral for cattle'
/sp/ *aɫósp* 'wakefulness, consciousness'
/šp/ *xošp* 'dream'
/ṣp/ *poṣp* 'wool'

/t/ as second consonant

/ft/ *ǰuft* 'pair, even number'
/ht/ *geht* 'dust'
/rt/ *tʰuhrt* 'ford (river)'[39]
/st/ *qast* 'true'
/št/ *rošt* 'light'
/xt/ *saxt* 'very, extremely'

[38] Endresen and Kristiansen (1981: 239) listed 33 syllable-final clusters. They apparently found word-final cluster /kt/ in unpublished data from Morgenstierne. Unfortunately, I do not have access to those data; the clusters listed here are those which I have found in my own materials. There may well be others which I have not encountered.

[39] In original /hrt/ clusters, the /r/ is frequently devoiced, becoming /h/, which often then becomes /x/, giving developments like *tʰuhrt* > *tʰuht* > *tʰuxt* 'ford (river)', *bohrt* > *boht* > *boxt* 'rock', and *duwáhrt* > *duwáht* > *duwáxt* 'door'. The h > x change is particularly noted in Lower Chitral.

Table 2.12 Syllable-initial consonant clusters

First consonant	Second consonant						
	l	ł	k	p	r	y	ʊ
b	*blayík* 'to wither'	*błaʦ* 'round', 'thick'			*braár* 'brother'	*byółi* 'Byori' (village name)'	
d					*drayáṇj* 'famine'	*dyak* 'giver', 'beater'	
ḍ					*ḍrayvér* 'driver' [< Eng.]	*ḍyeh ḍyeh* 'call to summon chickens'	
ʣ					*ʣrap* 'close together' (~ *ʦrap* ~ *zrap*)		
f		*fłaq* 'suddenly'			*frax* 'loose', 'wide (clothes)'		
g		*głox* 'place in a tree from which limbs branch out'			*grah* 'snapping turtle'	*gye* 'come!'	
ɣ		*ɣłaʦhéik* 'to knead, squeeze'			*ɣraṭ* 'healthy, with a strong, well-fleshed body'		
k		*kłok* 'broody (of a hen when she is ready to hatch eggs)'			*kramík* 'to thresh with animals'	*kya* 'some', 'any'	
m					*mraː̣* 'mulberry (tree or fruit)'	*myaná* 'wallet, small purse for money'	
n						*nyof* 'nine'	

Table 2.12 (continued)

First consonant	Second consonant						
	l	ł	k	p	r	y	ʋ
p	*plakh* 'spark plug' (< Eng.)	*pɫik* 'all', 'finished (off)'		*praš* 'side, ribs'	*pyadél* 'on foot'		
pʰ	*pʰláš* 'soft'	*pʰɫis* 'naked'			*pʰreṣú* 'tress', 'lock of hair'	*pʰyu* 'shoulder blade'	
q		*qɫef* 'hook'			*qreq* 'belch'		
s	*slip korík* 'to slip (vehicle)' (< Eng.)		*skoṭ* 'Scout' [< Eng.] *sken* 'scan' [< Eng.]	*spanduúr* 'species of small beans'	*srung* 'horn (of animal)'	*syahčéšum* 'species of black-eyed hawk'	*svab* 'act of religious merit'
š					*šron* 'upper part of thigh (human or animal)'		
ṣ						*ṣyal* 'jackal'	
t				*tprušéy*(?) 'call to send away sheep'	*troq* 'bitter'		
tʰ					*tʰraṣk* 'scraping sound of foot on ground'		
ʦ					*ʦrap* 'firmly'		
ṭ					*ṭrekṭér* 'tractor' (< Eng.)	*ṭyof* 'species of small hawk'	

ʋ				*ʋrázun* 'wing (of bird)'	
x	*xłik* 'hiccough, gasp'			*xrizoxráš* 'magic formula to unfreeze something'	*xyal* 'thought, opinion'
z				*zroṭhík* 'to untie (knot)'	*zyan* 'loss'
ž				*žriγ* 'shriek'	

/ṭ/ as second consonant

/šṭ/ *õšṭ* 'eight'

/ǰ/ as second consonant

/nǰ/ *ponǰ* 'five'
/rǰ/ *sayúrǰ* 'falcon'

/j̣/ as second consonant

/nj̣/ *dragánj̣* 'famine'

/č/ as second consonant

/hč/ *ʣehč* 'yellow'
/rč/ *ʣehrč* 'yellow'
/xč/ *ṣaxč* 'hut'

/x/ as second consonant

/łx/ *tałx* 'enthusiastic'

/ʦ/ as second consonant

/rʦ/ *ohrʦ* 'bear'
/hʦ/ *ohʦ* 'bear'

/ʣ/ as second consonant

/nʣ/ *vrenʣ* 'sharp pain in chest'[40]
ṭinʣ 'a vertical jump'

/d/ as second consonant

/nd/ *band* 'closed'
/žd/ *qužd* 'a shout'
/rd/ *bord-* 'grow (intransitive)'

[40] Mulkhow variety; this appears as *vrenz* in the speech of those people who do not have /ʣ/ in their lect.

/ḍ/ as second consonant

/nḍ/ *lenḍ* 'knot'[41]

/r/ as second consonant

/γr/ *γayr* 'without'

/z/ as second consonant

/γz/ *mayz* 'brain'
/nz/ *υrenz* 'sharp pain in chest'
/rz/ *υarz* 'head', 'beginning point'
/υz/ *laυz* 'word'

/q/ as second consonant

/šq/ *išq* 'passion'
/υq/ *šaυq* 'interest, enthusiasm'

/k/ as second consonant

/čk/ *hinčk* 'place where river flows through a narrow gorge'
/çk/ *ṣuçk* 'clay used for coating slates for writing'
/łk/ *hołk* 'scar'
/nk/ *thonk* 'thin (of flat things, like paper or cloth)'
/sk/ *frosk* 'straight'
/šk/ *mišk* 'small flower similar to a morning glory'
/ṣk/ *naṣk* 'beak'
/tk/ *sotk* 'bud', 'red gemstone'

/g/ as second consonant

/ng/ *ṭong* 'pear'
/rg/ *buzúrg* 'elder', 'holy man'

Repair of impermissible clusters also occurs in syllable coda position. For example, we hear *silíf* for English 'self', 'self-starter (of vehicle)'.

I have found a few three-consonant final clusters; one of them begins with /n/: /nʣk/ ~ /nzk/ ~ /nsk/, as in *pathránsk* 'scarecrow', or

[41] This is an alternate pronunciation of *len* 'knot' in Strand (2012) and Chitrali (2019: 338).

ṭinsk 'species of small bird'; and several of them begin with /hr/: /hrʦ/ in *ohrʦ* 'bear', /hrt/ in *gehrt* 'dust', /hrč/ in *ʣehrč* 'yellow'. The final clusters /hrt/ and /hrʦ/ are still heard in some words, like *bohrt* 'stone', *ohrʦ* 'bear', especially in Upper Chitral; now, however, /hr/ is often simplified to /h/, giving *ohʦ*, *geht*, and *ʣehč* ~ *zehč*.

2.4.2 Syllable structure

I have found the following syllable patterns:

V	*i*	'one'
VC	*af*	'down', 'downward'
VCC	*ȭšṭ*	'eight'
VCCC	*ohrʦ*	'bear'
CV	*ǰu*	'two'
CVC	*bom*	'I will be'
CVCC	*phost*	'skin', 'hide'
CVCCC	*ṭinsk* ~ *ṭinʣk* ~ *ṭinzk*	'species of small bird'
CCV	*droó*	'single hair'
CCVC	*błok*	'bud'
CCVCC	*grinǰ*	'rice'
CCVCCC	*pa.thransk*	'scarecrow'

Consonant-initial syllables are preferred. This can be seen, for example, in the effect of the LOC-1 ending on the Persian-origin word *umr* 'age', 'life'. In the direct form, it is sometimes heard as *úm.bar* with an epenthetic [b], but in the LOC-1 form it is regularly *úm.ra*, where no epenthetic consonant is needed to produce a consonant-initial syllable.

Any single consonant can occur in syllable onset.

2.5 Sound symbolism

Some iconic sound symbolic effects are found in Khowar.[42] I use 'iconic' according to Peirce's original meaning, that is, of a sign (signifier) having a resemblance between its form and its meaning (signified) (see Peirce 2012). In verbs denoting specific kinds of sounds, voicing can be contrastive, the voiced version indicating a more continuous or stronger version of what is the same or a similar sound, for example, *ẓiqhék* 'to

[42] I am grateful to Maula Nigah Nigah for the information in this section on sound symbolism.

squeak' versus *çiqhék* 'to squeak intermittently'. With the pair *thraṣkék* 'to rustle (like dry leaves)' versus *draṣkék* 'to make a scraping, scuffing sound (as of shoes on the ground)', + voice indicates a more forceful version of same type of action. In verbs denoting kinds of sounds, back vowels are associated with lower pitch of the sounds being compared. For example, *muγék* 'to moan (as while asleep)', *maγék* 'to mew, meow (lamb, kid, cat)', and *miγék* 'to talk in a high-pitched voice', 'to whimper'.

Reduplication of vowels, elongation, is used iconically to intensify meaning, as with *laš* 'slowly' → *laáš* 'very slowly and carefully'. Reduplication of consonants, resulting in phonetic gemination, emphasises the repetitive and extended nature of an action, as in example (2.3). Reduplication of an entire morpheme can signify repetition of an action, for example *brax* 'sound of clattering' and *braxbráx* 'repeated/intermittent sound of clattering'; to denote actions which are inherently repetitive, for example *khangnakháng bik* 'to stagger'; or in onomatopoetic words like *khúṣukhúṣu korík* 'to whisper'.

(2.3) *kandúri zamán b-aγ-áy* *kandúri vaxt b-aγ-áy*
so much time go-PST.D-3SG so much time go-PST.D-3SG

kandúri anús b-aγ-áy *kos-ítt-ay* *kos-ítt-ay …*
so.many days go-PST.D-3SG walk-PST.D-3SG walk-PST.D-3SG

'He travelled for so long, for so much time, for so many days—he walked and walked …' (oral text, Village Bang)

2.6 Written Khowar

2.6.1 Khowar's Perso-Arabic writing system

The original Arabic alphabet had 28 consonant characters, 3 of which were also used to represent the long vowels /ā/, /ī/, and /ū/. Short vowels were represented with the diacritics ◌َ <ă>, ◌ِ <ĭ>, and ◌ُ <ŭ>. As the Arabic script was adapted for writing numerous other languages—including Persian, Pashto, Sindhi, Kashmiri, Urdu, and many Central Asian languages—the original 28 Arabic characters were modified to create letters needed to represent sounds present in these other languages but not in Arabic.

In 1921, Prince Nasir ul-Mulk, the Mehtar of Chitral at that time, published a suggested alphabet for Khowar, which incorporated modified Perso-Arabic characters to represent Khowar consonant sounds not represented in either the Persian or Urdu alphabets (ul-Mulk 1921). Later, Prince Samsam ul-Mulk wrote a short grammar of Khowar (ul-Mulk 1966), a phrase book, and a Khowar *qaida* 'primer' (ul-Mulk n.d.), which included the characters څ، ݮ، ݯ، ݰ، ݱ needed for the Khowar consonants /ʦ/, /j̣/, /c̣/, /ṣ/, and /ẓ/, respectively, but not ځ for /ʣ/. These five characters, plus ځ to represent /ʣ/, have been accepted and remain in use for the consonant sounds. The Arabic letter ع 'ayn' appears in a few Arabic-origin words used in Khowar. This letter, however, is not associated with a specific sound in Khowar. The Arabic letters ط ، ظ ، ص ، ض appear in some words which have entered Khowar from Arabic, Persian, or Urdu, but not in native Khowar words.

Practices and problems of Khowar orthography were discussed in detail over 40 years ago by Buddruss, who identified the issues which still persist in 2025 (Buddruss 1982: 22). He said, among many other things, "While the spelling common today of the consonants is well regulated and, on the whole, can be regarded as phonemically based, the designation of the vowels is inconsistent and ambiguous with an (unconscious) tendency to follow phonetic rather than phonemic principles." Although people both inside and outside Chitral have been discussing these problems for many years, for the most part, the situation today (2025) remains the same as Buddruss described it in 1982.

The main problems are still with the representation of vowel sounds. In general, these problems arise because the Khowar writing system is originally based on Arabic, in which vowel length was important, and then on the orthography as modified for Persian and Urdu. Khowar differs from Urdu in the phonological status of four features—stress, length, nasalisation, and tone. In Khowar, stress is contrastive, whereas in Urdu it is not. Nasalisation is contrastive in Urdu, but in Khowar it is mostly non-existent. There are no tonal distinctions in Urdu, whereas Khowar has a distinctive low-rising tone, which makes a difference in meaning in some pairs of words, for example *doón* 'ghee' versus *don* 'tooth', *dií* 'yes' versus *di* 'also', and *baás* 'flame' versus *bas* 'day'.

Most of the problems arise from the fact that length is contrastive in Urdu, whereas in Khowar it is not. This means that the problem of when to use the letters ا، و، ی، ے, which are used in Urdu only for long vowels, and when to use the diacritics ◌َ (used in Urdu for /ă/ [ə]), ◌ِ (used in Urdu for ĭ), and ◌ُ (used in Urdu for ŭ) in Khowar, which has no phonemically long vowels, is severe and persistent. ا and آ are used in Urdu for /ā/; و is used in Urdu both consonantally for /ʋ/ and for the vowel sounds /o/ and /ū/), and ی is used in Urdu consonantally for /y/ and initially and finally for /ī/ or medially for /ē/. In Urdu, length is the determining factor in vowel prominence, but in Khowar it is stress.

Educated people in Chitral have been taught with Urdu as the medium of instruction and have learned to interpret the Perso-Arabic letters as they function in Urdu. Therefore if, in Khowar, the full vowel letters ا, ی, and و were to be used consistently for all vowels, or even to indicate stress, there would be an interference effect from Urdu orthographic practice causing Khowar speakers to perceive this as inappropriate, since in Khowar stressed vowels are prominent but not long. A further complicating factor is that stress sometimes induces a degree of phonetic lengthening, which in some cases can be perceived as reason to use the full vowel symbols.

So far, no system has been devised or agreed upon to indicate tone in Perso-Arabic spellings, and quite possibly most Khowar writers consider that it is not necessary.

For these reasons, I have not attempted in this book to represent Khowar words and sentences in Perso-Arabic script. Although Khowar is now widely written, spelling conventions are not yet standardised, particularly for the vowels, and much variation is found. It is hoped that as more and more people write in Khowar, a consensus about forms to be considered as standard will emerge.

2.6.2 Representation of Khowar in this book

Table 2.13 presents the Perso-Arabic Khowar letters, their phonetic descriptions, their IPA symbols,[43] and the transcription system used in this book. Consonants are listed in their Khowar alphabetical order.

Table 2.13 Khowar letters, IPA symbols, and the transcription system used in this book

Consonants			
Phonetic description	Khowar letter	IPA symbol	Transcription used in this book
voiced bilabial plosive	ب	b	b
voiceless bilabial plosive	پ	p	p
aspirated voiceless bilabial plosive	پھ	p^h	ph
voiceless dental-alveolar plosive	ط، ت	t	t
aspirated voiceless dental-alveolar plosive	تھ	t^h	th
voiceless post-alveolar (retroflex) plosive	ٹ	ʈ	ṭ

[43] As given in: https://www.internationalphoneticassociation.org/content/full-ipa-chart.

Table 2.13 (continued)

Consonants			
Phonetic description	Khowar letter	IPA symbol	Transcription used in this book
aspirated voiceless post-alveolar (retroflex) plosive	ٹھ	ʈʰ	ṭh
voiced palatal affricate	ج	ɟ	ǰ
voiced post-alveolar (retroflex) affricate	ݮ	d͡ʐ	j̣
voiceless palatal affricate	چ	t͡ɕ	č
aspirated voiceless palatal affricate	چھ	t͡ɕʰ	čh
voiceless post-alveolar (retroflex) affricate	ݯ	t͡ʂ	ç̣
aspirated voiceless post-alveolar (retroflex) affricate	ݯھ	t͡ʂʰ	ç̣h
voiceless glottal fricative	ہ، ح	h	h
aspiration	ھ	ʰ (with voiceless consonants)	h
		ʱ (with voiced consonants)	ɦ
voiceless velar fricative	خ	x	x
voiced dental-alveolar plosive	د	d	d
voiced post-alveolar (retroflex) plosive	ڈ	ɖ	ḍ
voiceless dental-alveolar fricative	څ	t͡s	ʦ
aspirated voiceless dental-alveolar fricative	څھ	t͡sʰ	ʦʰ
voiced dental-alveolar fricative	ځ	d͡z	ʣ
dental-alveolar flap	ر	ɾ	r
velarised dental-alveolar lateral	ڑ	ɫ	ɫ
voiced dental-alveolar fricative	ز، ذ، ظ، ض	z	z
voiced palatal fricative	ژ	ʝ	ž
voiced post-alveolar/ (retroflex) fricative	ݱ	ʐ	ẓ
voiceless dental-alveolar fricative	س، ث، ص	s	s
voiceless palatal fricative	ش	ç	š
voiceless post-alveolar (retroflex) fricative	ݰ	ʂ	ṣ
voiced pharyngeal approximant in Arabic; no specific sound in Khowar	ع	ʕ	varies, depending on pronunciation of specific word

Table 2.13 (continued)

Consonants			
Phonetic description	Khowar letter	IPA symbol	Transcription used in this book
voiced velar fricative	غ	ɣ	γ
voiceless labio-dental fricative	ف	f	f
voiceless uvular plosive	ق	q	q
aspirated voiceless uvular plosive	قھ	q^h	qh
voiceless velar plosive	ک	k	k
aspirated voiceless velar plosive	کھ	k^h	kh
voiced velar plosive	گ	g	g
post-alveolar lateral	ل	l	l
bilabial nasal	م	m	m
dental-alveolar nasal	ن	n	n
bilabial approximant	و	ʋ	ʋ
palatal approximant	ی، ے	j	y

Vowels			
Phonetic description	Khowar letter	IPA symbol	Transcription used in this book
central low vowel	◌َ ا	ɑ	a
mid front vowel	ے ی	e	e
high front vowel	◌ِ ی	i	i
lower-mid back vowel	و	ɔ	o
high back vowel	◌ُ وُ	u	u

The transcription system used in this book uses standard roman characters with a few modifications, mentioned here. Palatal post-alveolar sounds are indicated with a haček (caron) above the letter; thus <č> represents the voiceless palatal affricate چ, and <ǰ> represents its voiced counterpart ج. A dot under a consonant letter <̣> represents post-alveolar (retroflex) articulation. Greek gamma <γ> is used to represent the voiced velar fricative to avoid potential confusion caused by a representation like <gh>, which is sometimes used for this sound. The character <ʋ> is used instead of roman <w> or <v>, since neither of those accurately represents the sound of /ʋ/, which usually represents a bilabial approximant but often, depending on its phonetic environment, is closer to a voiced labio-dental fricative. Two Khowar letters are used for /h/, three for /s/, and four for /z/, because when words of Arabic or Persian origin, including Urdu words, are used in Khowar they usually retain the spelling they have in Arabic or Persian. The consensus of Khowar writers is that the historical Arabic or Persian spellings should be retained for words originating in those languages. I have not, however, either in this work or in Bashir (2023b), retained آ, aleph madd, for ā (long a) in Urdu words to represent word-initial 'long a'. For example, Urdu آم /ām/ 'mango' is spelled ام in Khowar, since in length is clearly not contrastive in Khowar, and this word is actually pronounced /am/.

Stress in the roman representations of Khowar words is indicated by an acute accent over the vowel in a stressed syllable. Thus, in *púši* 'cat', the /ú/ is stressed. Most monosyllabic words are shown here as stressable but unstressed, although there are phonetically distinguishable degrees of stress. When stress is phonemic for a monosyllabic word, it is marked.

3
Word formation

Khowar has a rich derivational morphology, generating nouns and adjectives by affixation, verbs by affixal derivation and by conjunct verb formation, and various meanings by reduplicative processes.[1] Compounding also yields numerous words.

3.1 Prefixal elements

Most affixes are suffixal, but there are a few prefixal elements, all of which have negative meanings. With the exception of native *no-* 'un-' 'not', like *nopočíru* 'uncooked', 'unripe' and *nonoyoóku* 'invisible', these are of Persian origin, some directly from Persian and some via Urdu. In older borrowings, Persian *be-* 'without' has become Khowar *ve-*, as in *ve-žánu* 'lifeless', 'very weak', *ve-xál* 'tasteless'. More recent borrowings, through Urdu, have *be-*, for example *be-gúnah* 'without sin', 'innocent'. Numerous words include the negative element *na-*, acquired from Persian at varying time depths. Some are older words, like *naxávn* 'without support, as an animal which has not been properly looked after' (Naji 2008: 458), *nažór* 'indigestion' (Naji 2008: 458), and *nałám* 'disobedient' (Naji 2008: 458). Many are newer borrowings, ultimately from Persian, but immediately through Urdu and having meanings almost identical to their Urdu senses, like *naráz* 'angry', 'displeased', *naqábil* 'unfit', 'unworthy', or *naláyq* 'incompetent', 'ne'er-do-well'. A few recent borrowings from

[1] Since nouns, pronouns, and verbs are the only lexical categories that undergo inflection, inflection of these categories will be discussed separately in the chapters on nominal morphology and verbs (Chapters 4 and 6), respectively.

Urdu also include the element *γayr-* 'without', 'not' as a prefix, for example *γayrházir* 'not present', 'absent (in educational or employment context)' < Urdu *γærhāzir*.[2]

3.2 Noun-forming suffixes

The stressed suffix *-í* added to an adjective regularly derives nouns, like *vor* 'fragrant' → *vorí* 'fragrance'; *ċhuy* 'hungry' → *ċhuí* 'hunger'. Many of these are abstract, for example, *ṣieéli* 'beautiful' → *ṣielí* 'beauty'. A noun + *-í* also forms a noun denoting a person having a habitual relationship with that noun, for example *boóng* 'marijuana' + *-í* → *bongí* 'marijuana user' and *afyún* 'opium' + *-í* → *afyuní* 'opium user'.

Several noun-forming suffixes are applicable to most verbs, while others have more restricted domains. An instrumental noun-making suffix *-íni* or *-éni* with derived transitives/causatives is suffixed to the root of most verbs, forming a noun of instrument for V-ing, like a machine or other device, for example *zap nigíni* 'clothes washing instrument', which can then be used adjectivally as in *zap nigíni mašín* 'clothes washing machine'. A few more examples are presented in Table 3.1.

Table 3.1 Instrumental nouns formed with *-íni / -éni*

Verb	Gloss	Instrumental noun	Gloss
maž-	'sweep'	*mažíni*	'broom'
su-	'sew', 'stitch'	*kauš.suíni*	'awl with hook, used for stitching shoes'
axl-	'comb'	*axlíni*	'comb'
ɫunɫ-	'clean or card wool'	*ɫunɫíni*	'instrument for carding'
avr-	'ride on'	*avríni*	'long stick used to support a load carried on one's back when coming downhill'
beɫ-	'wrap', 'swaddle (baby)'	*beɫíni*	'woven strip used to bind baby's diaper or swaddling cloth'
gan usné-	'lift the lever and bolt used to regulate speed of the water wheel/turbine in a water mill'	*gan usnéni*	'wooden rod used to regulate the height of the upper millstone'

[2] *γayr*, which appears to have been borrowed at multiple times, usually functions as a Layer 3 case-marking element (postposition) 'without' (see Masica 1991: 230–48). It follows the ablative case of nouns as follows, NP-ABL *laṭén-ar γayr* 'without a lantern', and the oblique + ablative of pronouns, as with *ma-sar γayr* 'without me'.

The noun *kiphíni* 'oval shaped wooden spoon with handle on the long side' is an interesting case. This word is also sometimes heard as *pikhíni*. If this is the original pronunciation, changed by metathesis to *kiphíni*, it would have originally meant 'instrument for drinking' (*piík* 'to drink' + *-íni*). The basic noun *ligíni* 'tongue' seems to be a formation of this type, probably from the Wakhi verb *lix-* 'lick' (Bashir 2001: 10) or possibly from the Khowar verb *li-* 'lick'. This suffix can also form nouns of place, like *nišíni* 'place to sit' from *niš-* 'sit' (ul-Mulk 1966: 15). Some nouns can also take *-íni*; for example, from *goṣ* 'dough' comes *goṣíni* 'flat wooden stick for turning bread on cooking iron'.

Instrument nouns from nouns or verbs with infinitives in *-é(i)k* are formed with *-éni*. Several of these refer to vessels used for some specific purpose. Some examples are *braγnéni*, 'an open cylindrical vessel for keeping dough and fermenting it for the next bread-cooking session' is derived from *braáγ* 'fermentation starter', 'yeast'; *truphéni* 'salt box' (Strand 2011); *kaphéni* 'wooden plate, used for presenting bread'; and *mušṭíki.pačéni* 'vessel for baking *mušṭíki*' a type of bread, cooked by burying in ashes'. Others refer to objects used for specific purposes, like *khol.daphéni* 'a wooden mallet used for packing earth of a threshing floor, made of heavy wood like apple or beech', from *khol* 'threshing floor' and *daphé-* 'pound', 'pack'; and *nimežéni* 'prayer mat', literally 'place for saying prayers'. Occurrence of a word like *fuṭu.néni* 'camera', a children's word meaning literally 'device for taking pictures', indicates that this instrumental noun formation is still productive.

The nominalising suffix *-ánu* can convey two types of meaning:

(1) Added to a verb root it forms nouns meaning 'a place where V-ing occurs' or 'a place where something specific is found or kept'. Some examples are *γernánu* 'place where there are eddies, whirlpools' ← *γerdík* 'to revolve'; *nišmánu* 'a place which is easy to reach but difficult to come back from' ← *níšum bik* 'to get stuck on a difficult mountain path'; *xałȧvánu* 'mouse hole', 'place where a mouse can reach easily' ← *xałáv* 'mouse'; *tuhtánu* 'place in river where water is shallow and it can be forded' ← *tuht* 'ford in river'; *usnánu* 'swimming place, where current is not fast and it is safe to swim' ← *usneék* 'to swim'; *daránu* 'woodpile' ← *dar* 'wood'; *yozánu* 'stock of ice kept underground for summer' ← *yoz* 'ice'; *driyánu* 'landslide', 'a place where a scree slope collapses' ← *driíž* 'scree slope'; *ambaránu* 'state stores of food, grain and provisions' ← *ambár* 'stock of food' (Baig 2004: 40). According to Baig, this suffix is no longer productive in this sense.

(2) Suffixed to some place names, it forms a noun referring to a person from that place, for example *dros* + *ánu* → *drosánu* 'person from Drosh'; *birіránu* 'person from Biríг'; *bumburetánu*, 'person from Bumburet'; *byoɫyánu* 'person from Byori'; *ǰinǰiretánu* 'person from Jinjiret'; *asuretánu* 'person from Ashret'; *rumburánu* 'person from Rumbur'.[3]

Several other suffixes also form nouns referring to persons from specific places.[4] Some of these are:

-u	suffixed to a place name with *ú* as the nucleus of its final syllable indicates a person from that place, *žuγúr* + *-u* → *žuγúru* 'person from Zhughur'; *ʦ~singúr* + *-u* → *ʦ~singúru* 'person from Singur'.
-éγ	*denín* + *-éγ* → *deninéγ* 'person from Denin'; *parpiš* + *éγ* → 'person from Parpish'.
-ék	*khot* + *-ék* → *khoték* 'person from Khot', *úžnu* + *ék* → *užnék* 'person from Uzhnu', *c̦hetrár* + *-ék* → *c̦hetrarék* 'person from the town of Chitral (said by a person not from Chitral Town)'.
-éku	*šoγór* + *-éku* → *šoγoréku* 'person from Shoghor'; *drošp* + *-éku* → *drošpéku* 'person from Village Droshp'; *sin* + *-éku* → *sinéku* 'person from Village Sin'.
-grémi	used with place names ending in *-grám*, indicates a person from that village, *ṣágram* + *-émi* → *ṣagrémi* 'person from Shagram'; *zondrángram* + *-émi* → *zondrangrémi* 'person from Zondrangram'.
-í	*arándu* + *-í* → *aranduí* 'person from Arandu'.
-íči	*ṣágrom* + *-íči* → *ṣagromíči* 'person from Shagrom'; *γordá* + *-íči* → *γordaíči* 'person from Ghorda'; *sonóγur* + *-íči* → *sonogríči* 'person from Sonoghur'.
-ík	*brep* + *-ík* → *brepík* 'person from Brep'; *ɫáspur* + *-ík* → *ɫaspřík* 'person from Laspur'.
-íki	*gaht* + *-íki* → 'person from Gaht'.

Several variant suffixes, *-íri*, *-íši*, *-éɫi*, *-íli* when added to a noun denoting an animal, indicate either the meat or skin of that animal.[5] Some derivations of this type are: *tic̦* + *-íri* → *tic̦híri* 'skin of adult male goat',

[3] These terms all refer to places in Lower Chitral, south of Chitral Town. Except for Drosh and Ashret, these are all places where Kalasha is (still) spoken or was spoken until fairly recently.
[4] Information about these place-name suffixes is from Maula Nigah Nigah.
[5] I am grateful to Maula Nigah Nigah for information about these words.

basír + *-íri* → *basiríri* 'skin of adult female goat', and *istoŕ* + *-íri* → *istoríri* 'skin of horse'. Formations with *-íši* include *bran* + *-íši* → *braníši* 'skin of ram', *čhaní* + *-íši* → *čhaniγíši* 'kidskin',[6] *verkhú* + *-íši* → *verkhuγíši* 'lambskin', *gáraṭ* + *-íši* → *gàraṭíši* 'skin of dead (not properly slaughtered) animal'. The suffix *-éłi* is found in *keréłi* 'sheepskin' → *kéłi* + *éłi*.[7] Another variant appears to be *-íli*, as in *avṣekíli* 'sloughed off snakeskin', as in *avṣekíli peʦhík* 'to slough off skin (of a snake)'. These suffixes appear to be only partially productive now.

-γeér is a bound morpheme meaning 'a field from which X has been harvested' or 'field in which X is to be planted', for example *gomγeér* 'field from which wheat has been cut'. This is a productive noun-forming process. Words so formed appear not to be used adjectivally.[8]

-γár is a bound morpheme meaning 'material or supplies for making or doing something', as in *čalayγár* 'cloth for making clothing'. When added to a noun denoting a specific type of garment(s), it refers to cloth specifically intended for use in making that garment, for example *phakołγár* 'cloth for making a *phakół*, the traditional Chitrali men's cap', *žaráp* + *γár* → *žarapγár* 'wool for making socks'. This suffix is not, however, restricted to items of clothing; for instance, *ʦhar* + *-γár* yields *ʦharγár* 'meat reserved for preparing *ʦhar*, a meal given in charity after a person's death', and *žeriγár* 'provisions for a *žéri*, a celebratory feast'.

The suffix *-kóṭi* suffix carries several adjectival and nominal senses: 'like something', as in *šerkóṭi* 'brave', lit. 'like a lion'; 'affected or afflicted by something', *honkóṭi* 'flood-affected', *gilkóṭi* 'smeared with mud of animal manure'; having a diminutive sense, 'a little one' for instance *naγzikóṭi* 'dirty little one' (spoken affectionately to a baby); *durkóṭi* 'small house' (ul-Mulk 1966: 15) 'young of, or a small one (animal)', *šarakóṭi* 'small/young male markhor'. Another diminutive-forming element is *-γúłak*, as in *ǰuwanγúłak* 'a small young man' (ul-Mulk 1966: 15).[9]

Words denoting the young of animals for which there are not unique words can be formed with the suffixal element *-žéri* 'offspring of', for example *pùšižéri* 'kitten', *lovžéri* 'fox kit', *kaγžéri* 'offspring of a crow'.

Suffixed to a noun, *-dóyu* denotes a person or persons involved in an institutionalised group activity. For example, a *yardóyu* is a (member of a) cooperative work party of villagers helping to complete a big job and *bardóyu* ← *bar* 'load' + *-dóyu* means 'load carrier', 'party of

[6] Note the hiatus-filling *γ* between *í*-final *čhaní* and *-ú-* final *verkhú* and *-íši*.
[7] Note the avoidance of two *ł* sounds in succession.
[8] **gomγeér ç̣hétur* was not accepted by MNN.
[9] This suffix is cognate with Kalasha *kúạk* 'child', 'little one' (Trail & Cooper 1999: 175), as in *istrížagúạk* 'girl' (p. 132).

persons who carry baggage (and dowry) of a bride to the house of the groom'. A *ʦhołumdóyu* is a person who tags along behind someone else unwantedly, a 'fifth wheel'; *dar* 'wood' + *-dóyu* → *dardóyu* 'person(s) who carry wood'; *gividóyu*, '(member of) a group of women gathered at night working together in cleaning, carding, and spinning wool'; *sosirí* + *-dóyu* → *sosirdóyu* 'person(s) who takes his or her turn to graze goats'; *uγ* + *-dóyu* → *uγdóyu* 'person(s) who go(es) to bring water'.[10]

-garí, suffixed to a noun yields a noun meaning 'habit of behaving like the referent of that noun', for instance *rėnigarí* 'quarrelsome nature' (lit. 'doglike habits') ← *reéni* 'dog', *ḍaqigarí* ← *ḍaq* 'boy' 'childish behaviour', or *roygarí* 'proper behaviour for a person', 'humanity'.

-árum, when added to a verb root, forms a collective noun denoting 'things to V', where V is a verb referring to basic quotidian actions. Frequently used instances of this formation are *piyárum* 'things to drink', *žibárum* 'things to eat', *γeyárum* 'things to use/utensils', *anǰárum* 'things to wear', *ispanárum* 'things with which to fill in an abutment or terrace wall'. This suffix is not currently productive, viz. **rárum* '*things to read' (Baig 1997: 219).

The nominalising suffix *-áli*, added to a verb root, forms nouns denoting payment for performing an institutionalised activity like: *šu koráli* 'payment for weaving woollen cloth'; *baṣ angáli* 'gift or money given to a person who brings *baṣ* to a house where a daughter or sister lives'; *roçháli* 'payment for grazing animals'; *kramáli* 'payment for threshing'; *brenáli* 'payment for shearing sheep'; *kuṣáli* 'payment for slaughtering an animal' (3.1); *bar bareáli* 'porterage'. *daráli* was a wage paid in exchange for fostering a child in the time of the Mehtars (Baig 2004: 32). This suffix is still grammatically productive but requires a very specific context (Baig 1997: 213).

(3.1) *avá qasáb-o-te kuṣ-áli phrét-am*
I butcher-OBL-DAT slaughter-fee give.PST.D-1SG
'I gave the butcher his fee for slaughtering (an animal).' (MNN)

-íl is a suffix denoting a place where a specific kind of plant grows; for example, *phapakíl* 'place where *phapaáki, a* species of wild bush, *Tamarix dioica,* grows'; *ʣoxíl* 'place where thorns grow'; *droníl* 'place where *droón* grows'; *čikaríl* 'place where the *čikár* willow grows'.[11]

[10] These words incorporating the suffix *-dóyu* are from Maula Nigah Nigah, who states that this suffix is no longer productive. In this specific context, the phrase 'his or her' is used intentionally, since the task of tending goats was done by both girls and boys.

[11] I am grateful to Inayatullah Faizi, who has supplied this term; it appears that *-ík* is an alternate form of this suffix, as in *droník* 'place where *droón* 'wormwood' grows (RKB).

Some words ending in the nominalising suffix *-u* refer to things that are too large, or excessive. They include: *davắlu* 'a very ugly hairstyle of an old, mad, or sick person'; *ṣavắlu* 'a too-large room, extra big room'; *ravázu* 'a too-tall (ugly-looking) person'; *thaváẑu* 'a sex-driven male goat'; *naváṣu* 'an animal or tree too big in shape'.[12]

3.3 Adjective-forming elements

The morpheme *-véni* means 'having or owning X', as in *durvéni* 'having/owning a house'. This is a productive element. It can be suffixed to nouns and some past participles to form adjectives, for example *ažirvéni* 'having children', but not to all adjectives. For instance, **thulvéni* 'having fatness' was not accepted. Like other adjectives, these words frequently function as nouns. Thus, *durvéni* often means 'a person who owns a house'.

A suffix *-eéγ*, added to the names of seasons, yields words referring to different varieties of crops, for example, *griṣpeéγ paloóγ* 'summer (ripening) apples', *šareéγ paloóγ* 'fall (ripening) apples', *bosundeéγ goóm* 'spring (planted) wheat'.[13]

A bound element *-γári* 'afflicted/taken away by (an animate agent or a natural force like wind)' appears in a context like that in (3.2).

(3.2) *ǰam kumóru gor-γári h-oy*
good girl witch-afflicted become.PST.D-3SG
'A good girl was afflicted by a witch.' (MNN)

A similar meaning is conveyed by *-žúni* 'afflicted by', 'suffering from' (inanimate circumstances, typically diseases and misfortunes), which appears with either native Khowar words (3.3) or loanwords, like *γam-žúni* 'sad' 'grief-stricken'.

(3.3) *hasé andáv-žúni b-íti as-úr*
s/he fever-afflicted become-PFV.PTCP be(ANIM)-PRS.3SG
'S/he is suffering from a fever.' (MNN)

A limited number of adjectives describing position are formed with the suffix *-ónar*, for example, *riphónar* 'in a standing position' (← *riph-* 'get up', 'stand up') and *nišónar* 'in a sitting position' (← *niš-* 'sit').[14]

12 Inayatullah Faizi is the source of these words (email 3 February 2014).
13 An excrescent [d] frequently follows the homorganic nasal [n].
14 These words are from Rahmat Karim Baig.

Suffixed to an adjective, *-roó* (T10803) adds the sense of '-ish', 'rather', as with *phukroó* 'rather small', 'smallish'; or a comparative sense '-er', as in *ʦiroó* 'younger' or *loṭhoroó* 'elder' (for example, of brothers). A similar meaning is added by *-γóni* '-ish' or 'like' (cf. the postposition *γon* 'like'). This element takes the main stress of the word formed when it is attached. It can be added to an adjective, for example *išpėruγóni* 'whitish', or a noun like *braryóni* 'like a brother', or *γoṭγóni* 'like a dumb (non-speaking) person'.

The element *-óku*, suffixed to a verb root, contributes the sense of causing the action of V to happen. Some examples are *ušuphóku* 'slippery' (← *ušup-* 'slip'); *pošóku* 'causing to be seen' (← *poš-* 'see'); *noyóku* 'causing to appear' (← *noy-* 'appear'); *hardišanóku* 'worrisome', 'worried' (← *hardí* 'heart' + *šan-* ~ *šen-* 'worry').

The suffix *-óṣ* suffixed to nouns forms nouns or adjectives denoting a person with a habit of doing something specific, for example *xašṭár lióṣ* 'a person who licks dirty dishes' (Naji 2008: 422). There are also *ṭiroóṣ* 'little shitter' and *miyoóṣ* 'little wetter' (both terms affectionately used for a baby) (Bashir 2023b).

3.4 Reduplicative processes

A simple and useful definition of reduplication is "the systematic repetition of phonological material within a word for semantic or grammatical purposes" (Rubino 2005: 12). Reduplication takes many forms in Khowar: full reduplication, in some cases where the base morpheme is no longer used and in other cases where it is; full reduplication with a vowel change in the reduplicated (first) element; partial reduplication of various types; and echo reduplication with *m-* in the reduplicated element. In all these derived forms, the main word stress falls on the penultimate syllable. I also consider vowel lengthening and consonant lengthening (gemination) as types of reduplication (see Rubino 2005). Several different kinds of meaning are generated; these are discussed in Section 10.10.

3.4.1 Full reduplication

3.4.1.1 Full reduplication with unchanged base form

This form of full reduplication is the repetition of an entire word, preceding the base form. Some words which show full reduplication of a base form are found synchronically only in their reduplicated form, which suggests that they belong to an old stratum of the lexicon. These include:

γavγáv 'verbal fight' (**γav*)
čurčúr 'broken into tiny pieces' (**čur*)
ẓavẓáv 'again and again' (**ẓáv*) (MNN)
qetiqéti 'tickling', 'itching' (**qeti*) (MNN, ZHD)
t͡sent͡sén 'broken into tiny pieces' (**t͡sen*)
t͡sirt͡sír 'tight', 'firm' (**t͡sir*) illustrated in example (3.4)

(3.4)

qalám-i	*çok-í*	*t͡sirt͡sír*	*b-íti*
pen-LOC2	adhere-PFV.PTCP	tight	become-PFV.PTCP

hal.h-óy
remained.PST.D-3SG

'S/he held onto the pen tightly (for example, if someone tried to take it from her/him).' (MNN)

Others, however, repeat a base form which is still in use. Examples are:

zruxzrúx 'quietly (of weeping)' (ZMZ, in Bashir 2023b) ← *zrux* 'relieved (of some distress)' (ZHD)
ǰamǰám 'good' (plural) (← *ǰam* 'good')
kamkám 'little by little' (← *kam* '(too) little') (3.6)
kyávat kyávat 'from time to time' (← kyávat 'sometime', 'ever' (lit. 'sometime sometime')
ẓarẓár 'very quickly' (← *ẓar* 'quickly') (3.5)

(3.5)

ẓarẓár	*kós-i*	*gye*	*ispá*	*ta*	*ves-í*
quickly	walk-PFV.PTCP	come.IMP.2SG	we	you	await-PFV.PTCP

malál	*hó-t-am*
late	become-PST.D-1PL

'Walk quickly; we are late because of waiting for you.' (Ali n.d.)

(3.6)

dukandár	*tan*	*išnári-an*	*kamkám.korí*	*bezem-í*
shopkeeper	REFL	thing-OBL.PL	gradually	sell-PFV.PTCP

khul-é-t-ay
finished-CAUS-PST.D-3SG

'The shopkeeper gradually finished selling his goods.' (Ali n.d.)

3.4.1.2 Full reduplication with vowel change in reduplicated (preceding) element

Examples of this formation include:

łipłáp 'moment', 'instant' (← *łap* 'a flash') (MNN)
thrịṣkuthráṣku 'sound of rustling, scraping (paper, shoes on ground)' (← *thraṣk* 'a scraping sound')
ṭungṭáng ~ *ṭumṭáng* 'very dark', 'dust cloud'

3.4.1.3 Full reduplication with m-initial reduplicated element

In this pattern the base form is followed by a reduplicated form with initial *m-*.[15] This pattern is widespread among the languages of northern Pakistan, Persian, Turkish, some Caucasian languages, and even Russian; it is often discussed in the literature as 'echo reduplication'. A few representative examples are:

kačmáč 'silk thread and accompanying things'
čeyméy 'tea and accompanying things'

3.4.1.4 Full reduplication with infixed -na-

Base form + *na* + base form.REDUP + *-i* . In this structure, *na* + the reduplicated base word + *-i* follows the base word. This structure including *-i* yields adjectives and/or nouns, and without *-i*, adverbs. The meanings generated all involve some kind of repeated movement. Some examples are:

leknaléki adj. 'of a person having an artificial affectation, especially one who walks with an artificial gait'; n. 'affectation', 'habit of walking with an artificial gait' (MNN)
toqnatóqi 'all muddy' (← *toq* 'mud')
ṭoqnaṭóqi 'confused', 'upset'; 'state of looking around in surprise' (SWKA) (← *ṭóqi* 'making fun of someone')
yošnayóši 'searching for walnuts left over after owner has collected the main harvest'
thalnatháli 'quivering, as of a thick liquid like mercury' (MNN)

[15] Semantically similar forms in languages of the Indo-Gangetic plain use [š] (Panjabi), or [ʋ] (Urdu, Hindi).

phirnaphíri 'stroking affectionately, as a mother with a child' (← *phiri* 'stroking') (MNN)
γernaγér 'turning again and again', 'zigzag' (← *γer-* 'turn') (DSAL)

Sometimes a modified or different element follows *-na-*, yielding variants having the same or similar meaning, for example *phatnapúli dik* 'to stumble and fall', ~ *phalnaphúl bik* (GNK), and ~ *palnaphúli dik* 'to stumble (persons)' 'to stagger (persons)' (MNN).[16]

3.4.1.5 Full reduplication with infixed -a-

A base noun + *-a* + base form.REDUP + *-i* forms adjectives describing a place where the base noun is prevalent or frequent.

prašapráši 'sloping' (← *praš* 'side') (Strand 2011)
ḍokaḍóki 'hilly' (← *ḍok* 'elevated, high; mound' (Ali n.d.)
daγadáγi 'stained all over' (← *daγ* 'stain', 'spot') (Ali n.d.)

Some words following this pattern but without the final *-i* appear to be adverbs formed on verb roots. For example:

ličalíč 'hanging, swinging' (← *lič-* 'move horizontally') (RAKR)
łaqałáq 'hanging, swinging' (RAKR) (Naji 2008: 267)

3.4.1.6 Full reduplication + -áki

The pattern: base word + fully reduplicated base word + *-áki* forms some words referring to aspects of behaviour:

c̣hum-c̣hum-áki 'extremely happy' (← *c̣hum* 'delicate (of a smile)') (MNN)
ṭix-ṭix-áki 'cheerful', 'gay', 'laughing' (← *ṭix* 'cheerful and happy (of women)') (ARC)

3.4.1.7 Full reduplication with infixed -bi- ~ -pi-

Another pattern involving complete reduplication is formed from: base word + *-bi-* ~ *-pi-* + base word.REDUP + nominal ending *-u*. It is seen in words like *υorbiυóru* 'dried and ground coriander seeds' (← *υoór* 'fragrant'). A variant of this formation with devoiced *p* ← *b* is also found, as in *γonpiγónu* 'different kinds of' (Ali ms).

[16] This significant variation suggests an old word/formation.

3.4.2 Partial reduplication

Two types of partial reduplication are found. The first is partial reduplication with no vowel change in the copied element. In this type a CV reduplicated syllable precedes the base CVC form. This pattern yields plural meanings of adjectives or nouns. Examples are:

> *thuthúl* 'thick (plural)' (← *thul* 'fat', 'thick')
> *phuphúk* 'small (plural)' (← *phuk* 'small')
> *ʦeʦéq* 'small (plural)', also 'children' (← *ʦeq* 'small')

A second type has partial reduplication with a vowel change in the reduplicated syllable:

> *lilóṭ* 'big (plural)' (← *loṭ* 'big')
> *žižáv* 'sons' (← *žáv* 'son')

3.4.3 Vowel lengthening

Vowel lengthening appears in partially reduplicated forms of some adjectives, where the vowel in the reduplicated CV element preceding the base form is the same as the base vowel, but expressively lengthened with a low pitch contour, as in *loólóṭ* 'very, extremely large' (← *loṭ* 'big').

Vowel lengthening can also accompany stress orally in a verb form to indicate strong emphasis, as in *anǰumá:n* 'I **am** putting it on! (I already told you.)' It also conveys temporally extended action, as in (3.7).

(3.7) *sithár-i* *pr-ay* *pr-a:ay*
sitar-LOC2 strike.PST.D-3SG strike.PST.D.REDUP-3SG

pr-a:ay *orár-i* *dré-t-ay* *to-ó*
strike.PST.D-REDUP.3SG sleep-LOC2 put-PST.D-3SG REM.SG-OBL

'She kept on playing and playing the sitar and put him to sleep.'
(oral text, Village Bang)

3.4.4 Consonant lengthening

Consonant lengthening (gemination) is frequently heard in oral narratives, for example the geminated /t/ in (3.8), where it conveys extended repetition of an action.

(3.8) *kos-ítt-ay* *kos-ítt-ay*
walk-PST.D-3SG walk-PST.D.REDUP-3SG
'He walked and walked …' (many oral texts)

3.5 Compounding

Compounding refers to the combining of two or more free morphemes into a longer word with more complex meaning. This process is very productive, forming adjectives or nouns. A few of these productive types are mentioned here. Nouns denoting edible items, when combined with the element *-oóy* (← *uúy* 'water'), yield words meaning a soup-like or watery dish, like *aluoóy* 'potato soup/curry with much liquid', *čamboroóy* 'dried apricots cooked in water', *kaviroóy* 'watery curry containing *kavír* 'capers''. Used in compounds where the first noun is a place name, *-oóy* indicates a stream originating in that place, for example *roṣgoloóy*, 'the stream which originates in Roshgol'. The compound noun *ganusnéni* 'a piece of wood which controls the speed of a water mill' combines *gan* 'a lever and bolt used to regulate the speed of the turbine in a water mill' with the instrumental noun *usnéni* 'thing which lifts up'.

The noun *hardí* 'heart' occurs in numerous compounds, for example *hardiçakónu* 'interesting' (lit. 'that which sticks to the heart'); *hardiphát* 'homesick' (lit. 'heart-broken'), 'lonely'; *loṭhardí* 'having a big heart', 'generous'; *hardišanoóku* 'anxious', 'worried', 'worrisome'; *kamhardí* 'having little courage'; *phukhardí* 'cowardly'.

A compounding element *kal* (T3084) meaning 'time (for a routine activity)' yields nouns such as *hasyákal* 'breakfast time'; *botákal* 'time for the late-evening meal'; *kiṣbotákal* 'ploughing time'; *lešuaverákal* 'time for cows to come home and be put in their stalls' (SWKA); *lešudoyákal* 'cow-milking time' (SWKA).

The noun *máłi* 'home/abode of an animal' combines with numerous elements, some of which have developed idiomatic meanings: *bubukmáłi* 'hoopoe's nest'; *çhirmáłi* 'a house where milk is always present'; *gormáłi* 'witch's home' (id. sense 'a house where women talk too much'); *łoumáłi* 'fox's den'; *maçhimáłi* 'beehive'; *pùšimáłi* 'cat's den/home' (id. sense 'a very small room').

Pairs of closely associated words like *nan* 'mother' and *tat* 'father' or *moóš* 'husband' and *boók* 'wife' give dvandva compounds like *nantát* 'parents' and *mošboók* 'married couple'.

yečhen-tukhúnu 'sharp-eyed', adjective or noun, consists of the locative plural case of *yeč* 'eye' + the adjective *tukhúnu* 'sharp'.

γaridúri ← *γarí* 'summer pastures' + *dur* 'house' means 'house in the summer pastures'.

A compound word consisting of a noun or adjective plus a past participle can function as a short participial relative clause (adjectival), for example *koṭanǰíru* '(a person) wearing a coat' (← *koṭ* 'coat' + *anǰíru*, past participle of *anǰík* 'to wear').

Compounds can be equivalent to complex phrases, for example *yorotmuxnokorák* 'sunflower'. Morphological analysis of this word is shown in (3.9).

(3.9) *yor-o-t-mux-no-kor-ák*
sun-OBL-DAT-face-NEG-do-AG
'that which does not turn its face toward the sun' (sunflower)

3.6 Verb formation

3.6.1 Causative derivation

A basic derivational process for verb formation is to suffix the causative marker *-é* ~ *-eé* ~ *-éy* (< *ái*) to a noun or an adjective; thus, from *kam* 'less', 'little' comes *kamé-* ~ *kaméy-* 'decrease', 'reduce'. From the noun *šuruúγ* 'a beginning' is formed *šuruγé-* 'start/begin (a task or process)'.[17] From *bas* 'period of a day, including night' or 'night stay' comes *basé-* 'invite/give permission to spend the night', 'put hens in their coop for the night'. Some verbs of this type denote the production of a characteristic sound by an animal, like *maγeé-* ~ *maγé-* 'bleat (lamb, kid)', 'meow (cat)'. Another meaning denoted is 'produce a visual effect', as with *łap* 'a flash' → *łapheé* ~ *łaphó-* (Torkhow) or *łuphé-* ~ *łupheé-* 'twinkle', 'shine' 'glisten' (like the sun); or *bakhé-* ~ *bakheé-* 'shine', 'glimmer' and reduplicated *baqbaqé-* 'radiate light', 'shine brightly'.[18] Yet another meaning is 'produce a sensation in a conscious being', as with the adjective *qayí* 'heavy', from which comes *qayé-* 'be/feel heavy', or from *angáh* 'aware', 'awake' comes *angahé-* 'warn', 'awaken'.[19] This process operates on both

[17] *šuruúγ* 'beginning' is also used in conjunct verb formation (Section 3.6.2).

[18] Note the variation between /q/ and /kh/.

[19] This process reminds one of the 'denominative verbs' in Sanskrit discussed by Burrow (1973 [1955]: 361), about which he says, "Denominative verbs are those that are formed on the basis of a noun stem. Ultimately, as already observed, all verbal stems are not to be distinguished from the corresponding noun stems, but they have acquired independence. The denominative proper is a formation by which verbal stems continue to be made from the nouns existing in the language. The suffix employed in making denominatives is accented *-yá-*".

OIA- and Iranian-origin words, but so far I have not found it used with English borrowings.

3.6.2 Conjunct verb formation

Another important process for verb formation consists of a nominal or adjectival form plus most frequently *b-* 'be(come)', yielding intransitives, or *kor-* 'do', forming transitives. Verbs so generated are traditionally called 'conjunct verbs' and more recently 'complex predicates' in the South Asianist linguistics literature.[20] In Khowar we find conjunct verbs incorporating elements from OIA, Persian, and even Burushaski (see Bashir 2023b). With elements from OIA we find *avǰí b-* 'be persuaded' 'be misled', *avǰí kor-* 'mislead someone', and *čhin b-* 'be broken', *čhin kor-* 'break (transitive)'. From Khowar adjectives, examples are *abathá b-* 'get lost' 'be mistaken', *abathá kor-* 'mislead someone', 'cause someone to go astray', and *broól b-* 'become numb', *broól kor-* 'numb (as by an injection)'.

The Burushaski noun *bits* 'front facing of *šuqá*' (Lorimer 1938: 84), 'armpit', 'side', 'gusset' (Lorimer 1962: 56), with the meaning 'breast', 'chest' in Khowar, appears in *bits kor-* 'carry on the front of the shoulder (usually a child)'. Persian/Arabic elements in conjunct verbs are numerous, for example, *arzí kor-* 'institute a legal case'; *gehrt kor-* 'stir up dust' with the idiomatic sense 'run away'; *iqrár kor-* 'acknowledge', 'admit', 'confess'; *mum kor-* 'soften', 'melt (like wax)'; *šuruúγ* 'beginning', 'start' → *šuruúγ b-* 'to begin' (intransitive), *šuruúγ kor-* 'start, begin (something)' (transitive).

It seems that this construction has proliferated fairly recently in Khowar's development. Conjunct verbs existed but were not common in OIA. Gambhir (1993: 81) says, "In general, the use of complex verbs is quite limited in the Vedic and classical Sanskrit periods. It, however, appears that there are relatively more examples of complex verbs in the genres of commentaries and story narration than in others." Writing about the conjunct verb construction, Lorimer finds that it is "not a marked feature in Kho. or Wkh. Wkh. forms compounds with the verb 'to make', but in Kho. even these are not very common" (Lorimer 1937: 96). This process had initially gained momentum with the close contact of

[20] In the Iranianist literature, these formations are called 'compound verbs'.

Khowar and Persian[21] and is now increasingly being driven by the large number of borrowings from Urdu and English. From recently borrowed words we have *kal kor-* 'call on phone' (< Eng.); *badél kor-* 'change (clothes)' (< Ur.); and from the Urdu adjective *pūrā* 'full', 'complete' comes *purá kor-* 'to complete'. This raises the interesting question of the relative proportion of simple versus conjunct verbs in Khowar. Investigation of this question and comparison of the current proportion in Khowar with those in other neighbouring or related languages could yield interesting historical insights. (For further discussion of conjunct verbs, see Section 6.9.1.)

[21] Windfuhr (1979: 113) says about these constructions in Persian, "The continuous development in Persian from a formerly inflectional to an increasingly synthetic language has brought with it the expansion of compound verbs, virtually the only source of verbal innovation for many centuries." There are many types of conjunct verbs in Persian (see Lambton 1957: 85–95), as compared to the relatively few types in Khowar. See also Windfuhr (2009) for discussion of conjunct verbs (aka compound verbs) in numerous Iranian languages.

4 Nominal morphology

4.1 Nouns

Nouns bear the grammatical categories animacy, number, and case. They are morphologically marked for case and sometimes number, but not for animacy. In addition to simple lexical nouns, certain deverbal forms—infinitive, instrumental noun, agent noun, and a causative/desiderative form in *-áru*—are inanimate nouns.

4.1.1 Animacy

The three-gender—masculine, feminine, neuter—OIA system, which was largely sex-based but with phonological and other semantic criteria also operative, has been replaced in Khowar by an animacy-based noun classification (gender) system.[1] Nouns are not morphologically marked for animacy and are classified as animate or inanimate solely on semantic grounds. The grammatical effect of animacy is observed in the verb system in those finite forms which include the existential or locative 'be' verbs *as-* 'be(animate)' or *š̌-* 'be(inanimate)'.

The boundary between animate and inanimate classes varies from language to language. For instance, in some languages, entities with higher (potential) agentivity, like natural forces or machines, can sometimes be classified as animate, and lower animates, like insects or microorganisms, can sometimes be grouped with inanimates. Neither of these effects is

[1] This has also happened in Kalasha. Morgenstierne (1947: 7) connects the fact that "the inflection of the ancient bases in *-a* has prevailed upon all other stems" with the loss of the OIA category of gender.

observable in Khowar. Indeed, in Khowar, amoebae, bacteria, and even viruses are treated as animate, as seen in examples (4.1)–(4.5).

(4.1) *hayá múži čayna-á i noγ vayrás nis-í*
this in China-LOC1 one new virus emerge-PFV.PTCP
as-úr
be(ANIM)-PRS.3SG
'These days a new virus has emerged in China.' (ZHD)

(4.2) *hayá úγ-o ṭip bekṭíriya / ǰarasím as-úni*
this water-LOC4 many bacteria / germs be(ANIM)-PRS.3PL
'There are many bacteria/germs in this water.' (ZHD)

(4.3) *hayá uγ-ó mo pi-yé hay-uú*
this water-OBL PROH drink-IMP.2SG this-LOC4
amibá / ǰarasím as-úni
amoeba / germs be(ANIM)-PRS.3PL
'Don't drink this water; there are amoebas/germs in it.' (ZHD)

Khowar differentiates between viruses affecting living beings and those affecting computers, based on whether these forms reside and replicate in living organisms or in electronic devices. Electronic computer viruses are thus treated as inanimate. A Khowar speaker would, for example, say the sentence in (4.4).

(4.4) *ma kampyúṭar-o vayrás š-éni*
my computer-LOC4 virus be(INAN)-PRS.3PL
'There are viruses in my computer.' (ZHD)

(4.5) *ta yuesbí-o ṭip vayrás šir-áni,*
your USB-LOC4 lots.of virus be(INAN)-PST.I.3PL
avá sken a-r-ét-am
I scan AUG-do-PST.D-1SG
'There turn out to be lots of viruses in your USB; I scanned (it).' (ZHD)

With regard to the question of whether artificial intelligence programs that are made to imitate humans, given human-sounding names, and speak with human(like) voices ('Alexa', 'Cortana', 'Hey Google', and others), are treated as animate or inanimate, Zahoor ul-Haq Danish states that all artificial intelligence programs and technologies are treated as inanimate in Khowar.[2] Following similar logic, nouns referring to institutions, which are inherently comprised of humans (4.6), (4.8), or abstract nouns referring to groups of people, like 'leadership' in (4.7), are treated as animate. Such nouns are singular, even though the constitutive elements are plural, as in (4.6), (4.7), and (4.8).[3]

(4.6) *kámpani ahmád-o nez-í veṣé-i*
company Ahmad-OBL eject-PFV.PTCP send-PFV.PTCP
as-úr
be(ANIM)-PRS.3SG
'The company has dismissed Ahmad.' (ZHD)

(4.7) *parṭí-o purá qiyadát çhetrár-tu as-úr*
party-OBL entire leadership Chitral-LOC3 be(ANIM)-PRS.3SG
'The leadership of the party is all in Chitral.' (ZHD)

(4.8) *yunivársiṭi hayá faysal-ó kor-í as-úr*
university this decision-OBL do-PFV.PTCP be(ANIM)-PRS.3SG
ki sitámbar-i khuláv b-oy
that September-LOC2 open become-3SG.PRS/FUT.NS
'The University has decided that it will open in September.' (ZHD)

All plants are treated as inanimate, perhaps because they do not visibly move of their own accord.

4.1.2 Number

4.1.2.1 Plural marking

Direct case plural is usually marked only for animates; the plural marker is *-án* (< Persian), for example, *buzúrg* 'elder', *buzurgán* 'elders'. Even for animates, in conservative dialects plurality is not usually marked in the direct case; example (4.9) shows a typical case where an animate subject is not marked for plurality but plurality is clearly marked on the verb. Inanimates do not usually have a distinct direct case plural, as seen in (4.10).

[2] Email 10 February 2020.
[3] Zahoor ul-Haq Danish, p.c., 6 June 2020.

(4.9) *ḍaq poṣ saré-ni-an*
boy manure haul-3PL.PRS/FUT-S
'The boys are hauling manure.' (DSAL)

(4.10) *zom bo dudéri š-éni*
mountain very far be(INAN)-PRS.3PL
'The mountains are very far away.' (MNN in Bashir 2023b)

However, inanimates denoting mass substances like meat or ice can appear with plural endings when referring to countable portions of such things, as in (4.11).

(4.11) *rék-o thé čey-án af ser-ít-ay*
say.INF-OBL then tea-OBL.PL down carry-PST.D-3SG
šoxór-an al-áy af ser-ít-ay
sugar-OBL.PL bring.PST.D-3SG down carry-PST.D-3SG
'When he_a said (this), he_b carried the (boxes of) tea down; he_b brought (sacks of) sugar (and) carried them down.' (oral text, Village Kari)

The tendency to mark plurality on direct case nouns is increasing. In ul-Mulk (1966: 30–1) none of the direct case plural forms, either animate or inanimate, show direct plural *-án*. Sentences like (4.12), (4.13), and (4.14) are now, however, common.[4]

(4.12) *kimėri-án žo-ó γotsí-ni-an*
woman-PL.DIR grain-OBL clean-3PL.PRS/FUT-S
'The women are cleaning (the) grain.' (RKB)

(4.13) *baça-án haṣ ki vazir-án-an sar γayr kórum*
king-DIR.PL such that minister-PL-OBL.PL ABL without work
no koráv-tani
NEG do.IPFV.PTCP-HAB.D.3PL
'Kings (were) such that they didn't do any work without (their) ministers.' (oral text, Village Uthul)

[4] Whether or not overt plural marking on direct case subjects is associated with definiteness or specificity remains a topic for further research. In (4.12) it appears to be so, but in (4.13) and (4.14) not.

(4.14) *ǰaméli-o xafá kor-ík-o arváh-an diš*
ǰaméli-OBL annoyed do-INF-OBL spirits-PL.DIR annoyed
b-óni
become-3PL.PRS/FUT.NS
'When one offends a *jameli*,[5] the ancestral spirits are annoyed.' (DSAL)

Oblique plural is always marked for both animates, *vazir-án-an* in (4.13), and inanimates, *ȧykun-án* in (4.15). If an animate plural takes a postposition, this can result in plurality being doubly marked, as is *vazir-án-an* in (4.13). Double marking of plurality also occurs with reduplicated plurals like *lilóṭ-an* 'elder.PL-OBL.PL', that is, 'elders-OBL.PL' or Arabic broken plurals used in Khowar, like *arváh-an* 'spirit.PL-OBL.PL' (< Ar. *ruh*, 'spirit', *arváh*.PL 'spirits') in (4.14).

(4.15) *kahák ȧykun-án γurdé-r-an*
hen egg-OBL.PL move.around-3SG.PRS/FUT-S
'The hen is moving her eggs around.' (DSAL)

Kinship terms have special plural forms ending in *-gíni*: *nangíni* 'mothers', *vavgíni* 'grandmothers', *bapgíni* 'grandfathers', 'ancestors', *tatgíni* 'fathers', *žurgíni* 'daughters', *brežȧygíni* 'sisters-in-law', *novėsgíni* 'grandchildren' or 'nieces and nephews', *mikgíni* 'uncles', *bečgíni* 'aunts', *ispsȧrgíni* 'sisters', *kaygíni* '(elder) sisters', *brargíni* 'brothers', *mošgíni* 'husbands', *bokgíni* 'wives'. The oblique of these plural kinship terms is marked with *-án*, as with *brar-gini-án* 'brother-PL-OBL.PL', again resulting in double-marked plurality.

Reduplicative processes also function to form plurals, with a CV partial reduplication of the base word prefixed to it, for example *ži-žáv* 'sons' (← *žav*).[6] When an adjective is pluralised in this way, it can function either nominally or adjectivally, as in *li-lóṭ* 'elders' or 'elder.PL', *phu-phúk* 'small-PL', *ʦe-ʦéq* 'little ones', usually meaning 'children'.

An irregular plural in *-rán* is seen in *boigrán* 'birds' (← *boík* 'bird'). Morgenstierne (1947: 15) noted a direct case plural in *-bák* for *ṣádar* 'servant' and *lanḍi* 'unfaithful wife'.[7]

[5] A *ǰaméli* is the offspring or descendant of a female relative (out of the line of patrilineal descent).
[6] The plural suffix *-gíni* is now sometimes heard with 'son', especially in Lower Chitral.
[7] These forms probably consist of a noun + the agent noun of *b-* 'be, become' used in a plural context.

4.1.2.2 Mass versus count distinction and pluractionality

The mass versus count distinction in nouns is reflected in the quantitative interrogative adjectives *kamaá* 'how many', which is appropriate only with count nouns, and *kandúri* 'how much', 'how many', which can (now) modify either count or mass nouns.

A verbal phenomenon which resembles the use of plural forms with countable portions of mass nouns is the use of plural marking on the verb to indicate multiple actions rather than agreement with a plural subject. This is known as pluractionality (Newman 2012). It is observed in Khowar and Yasin Burushaski (Tiffou & Patry 1995), and possibly in Kalasha. Example (4.16) is frequently heard in Chitral. The plural marking occurs because 'electricity', while in the abstract not a countable thing, is conceptualised as something like 'lights', that is, manifestations of electricity occurring in multiple (individuated, countable) locations.

(4.16) *bišlí* *baγ-áni*
electricity go.PST.D-3PL
'The electricity has gone off.' (Chitral Town)

Pluractionality draws on the same semantics as does plural marking on mass nouns. Khowar consistently uses plural marking for mass nouns occurring in multiple (countable) portions: *pušúr-an*, meat-PL 'pieces of meat', *yoz-án*, ice-PL 'pieces of ice', *čey-án* tea-PL 'packets of tea', as in (4.11) above, where the conversion of mass substances, like tea leaves and sugar, into countable units is indicated by the use of plural marking. When a mass substance is found in multiple or extended locations as in (4.17), the oblique plural *ṣá-an* 'soots' indicates the occurrence of soot at more than one place, on both eyelids. This occurrence of something in extended or multiple locations also influences the choice of locative case ending (Section 10.3.2).

(4.17) *tav-ó* *ṣá-an* *γéč-i* *ki* *c̣haré-iru*
griddle-OBL soot-OBL.PL eye-LOC2 when sprinkle-PST.I
mox-ó *ḍox-ár* *ayh* *man-í* *as-úr*
face-OBL mound-ABL upwards rub-PFV.PTCP be(ANIM)-PRS.3SG
'When it sprinkled soot from the cooking iron on its eyelids, it has rubbed it from its cheeks up (to its forehead).' (oral text, Village Bang)

4.1.3 Case

All nouns have four case forms, direct (DIR), oblique (OBL), ablative (ABL), and vocative (VOC).[8] With most monosyllabic nouns, the oblique ending *-o* is stressed, as in *bil* 'lid.DIR' *bil-ó* 'lid-OBL'. Monosyllabic nouns which retain stress on the base in their oblique form are discussed in Section 2.2.1.1. Although Morgenstierne (1947: 11) stated that the ablative case *-ar* is used only with inanimates and this statement has been repeated up to now, this is not entirely the case. See Section 4.1.3.4 for examples of occurrences of the ablative with animates. An instrumental (INS) and four locative (LOC) cases (see Section 4.1.3.5) occur with inanimates. Vocative (VOC) forms are normally used only with humans; however, if an animal or inanimate is personified, as in poetry, it can appear with a vocative ending. A unique vocative ending, *-áa*, is used when addressing God, *xodáy-áa* 'O, God' (see example (5.5) below). A vocative particle, *é:*, usually precedes the noun referring to the person addressed. In addition, the stem vowel of that noun is often lengthened, for example *é: na:n* 'o, mother'.

Table 4.1 shows the singular and plural case endings for animate and inanimate nouns. All case endings attach to the direct form of the noun.

Table 4.1 Case endings

Case	Singular		Plural	
	Animate	Inanimate	Animate	Inanimate
Direct	Ø, or *-án*	Ø	*-án*, *-gíni*, reduplication	Ø, (*-án*)
Oblique	*-o* (stressable)	*-o* (stressable)	*-an* (stressable)	*-an* (stressable)
Locative 1		*-a* (unstressed)		*-en* (stressable)
Locative 2		*-i* (unstressed)		*-en* (stressable)
Locative 3		*-tu* (unstressed)		*-en* (stressable)
Locative 4		*-o* (unstressed)		*-en* (stressable)
Instrumental		*-en* (stressable)		*-en* (stressable)
Ablative	*-ar* ~ *-ári*	*-ar* (stressable)	*-ar* ~ *-ári*	*-ar* ~ *-ári*
Vocative	*-é* *-aá* (for God)		*-án* (used with VOC particle *é:* 'hey, o' …)	

[8] Masica (1991: 231) discusses indication of case and case-like relationships in terms of 'layers'. He says: "There are at least three layers of forms with case-like functions (here I, II, III) in most NIA languages, typically made up of inherited synthetic, new agglutinative, and quasi-analytic elements."

Other case and local relationships for animates are (semi-)postpositional (Layer II). The ablative postpositions *-sar*, and *-γar*, which are formed on the ablative case ending *-ar*, both follow the oblique case, but they cannot stand as free morphemes. They are used with both inanimates and animates. Dative relationships for both animates and inanimates are also postpositional; the dative postposition *=t* ~ *=te* ~ *=ten* ~ *=tene* follows the oblique case and attaches like a clitic. Instrumental and ablative-based plurals are formed with *sóra* 'with' and *-sar* 'than' and other ablative senses, following the oblique plural.

4.1.3.1 Direct case

The direct case, the unmodified base form of a noun or pronoun, is used for all sentence subjects and indefinite or non-specific direct objects.

4.1.3.2 Oblique case

The oblique case occurs in several functions; it:

- marks specific or definite direct objects (4.18)
- precedes most postpositions (4.19)
- expresses genitive relations like possession, both alienable (4.18) (4.20) and inalienable (6.17) below
- expresses a temporal locative relation (4.21)
- functions as a switch reference marker with the oblique infinitive (4.22)

(4.18) *toó* *dazbo-ó* *gaán-t-am* *axlíni-o*
REM.SG.OBL prayer.beads-OBL take-PST.D-1SG comb-OBL

gaán-t-am
take-PST.D-1SG

'I took his prayer beads, I took his comb.' (oral text, Village Bang)

(4.19) *madiyán istór* *loṭhoró* *žav-ó-te* *žavúk*
female horse elder son-OBL-DAT to.be.returned.after.foaling

pr-ay
give.PST.D-3SG

'He gave the mare to his elder son to be returned after foaling.' (oral text, Village Bang)

(4.20) *hayá haté bȧrzangí-o davlát—tá-te phré-t-am*
prox.sg rem.sg giant-obl treasure you.obl-dat give-pst.d-1sg
'This is that giant's treasure—I give it to you.' (oral text, Village Bang)

(4.21) *baríki pon-én čhuy-ó kos-ín no*
narrow path-loc.pl night-obl walk-pot.ptcp neg
boy
become.3sg.prs/fut.ns
'One can't walk on narrow paths at night.' (DSAL)

(4.22) *žižáv-an-te boók no al-áy no*
sons-obl.pl-dat wife neg bring.pst.d-3sg neg
ang-ík-o háse phíski ré-t-ay.ki
bring-inf.obl rem.sg youngest say.pst.d-3sg
é: brȧrgíni-á:n
o brothers-voc.pl
'(The king) didn't bring wives for (his) sons. When he didn't bring (wives), the youngest one said, "Hey, brothers…"' (oral text, Village Bang)

In (4.22), the subject of the first clause is the king. This clause is linked to the next one by the oblique infinitive *angíko*, which signals that the subject of the next clause will be different: the youngest son.

4.1.3.3 Instrumental case

The basic use of the instrumental case (ins) is to mark an object used for some action, like the blowpipe in (4.23). It also often means 'by way of', as in (4.24). The instrumental is also used with a noun or pronoun denoting the cause or reason for something, as in (4.25).

(4.23) *bełú-en angár-o phu-é*
blowpipe-ins fire-obl blow-imp.2sg
'Blow the fire with the blowpipe.' (DSAL)

(4.24) *pisá diší-o pon-én bí-mi-an-aá,*
you.pl badness-obl road-ins go-2pl.prs/fut-s-q
ǰamí-o pon-én b-ími-an
goodness-obl road-ins go-2pl.prs/fut-s
'Are you going by way of the road of evil (or) by the road of goodness?' (oral text, Village Bang)

(4.25) *ma namutí-en tu ǰit h-av*
my barefootedness-INS you victorious become.PST.D-2SG
'You won because of (by exploiting) my barefootedness.' (MNN)

If the cause/reason is referred to by a pronoun like 'that' or 'this', as in *he-γén díti* 'because of that/this', the pronominal form *he-γén* includes a hiatus-filling epenthetic /γ/, as in (4.26).

(4.26) *avá raγéšṭi por-í as-t-am heγén.díti*
I early lie.down-PFV.PTCP be(ANIM)-PST.D-1SG therefore
ẓot riph-ít-am
early get.up-PST.D-1SG
'I went to bed early; that is why I got up early.' (SWKA in Bashir 2023b)

When the cause/reason for something is a predication including a subject and a verb, 'because of [S]', as in (4.27) and (4.28), the instrumental case suffix is attached to the infinitive expressing the action/event/state of [S].

(4.27) *or-áru behč-ík-en ma kapál ҫham-úr-an*
sleep-CAUS.DES remain-INF-INS my head pain-3SG.PRS/FUT-S
'Because I didn't get enough sleep, my head is hurting.' (MNN)

(4.28) *avá sabáq no r-ék-en urdú huṣ*
I lessons not study-INF-INS Urdu understanding
no kó-m-an
not do-1SG.PRS/FUT-S
'Because I didn't study, I don't understand Urdu.' (MNN in Bashir 2023b)

With nouns naming days of the week, *-én* expresses temporal location, as in (4.29).

(4.29) *hasé uxtí adin-én šadí kor-ák bir-áy*
he next Friday-INS marriage do-AG.N become.MIR-3SG
'(I have learned that) he is going to get married next Friday.' (DSAL)

The original sense of *sór-a* (head-LOC1) is 'on top of' 'after one another', as in *iyó sóra* 'one after the other'. Used as a postposition, it is also used to express instrumental meaning, 'with', as in (4.30).

(4.30) *ṭał-ó sóra qulf-ó hur-é*
key-OBL with lock-OBL open-IMP.SG
'Unlock/open the lock with the key.' (MNN)

For further discussion and examples, see Section 8.6.3.

4.1.3.4 Ablative case

The ablative case ending (ABL) *-ar* ~ *-ári* ~ *-γar* ~ *-γári* is used mostly with inanimate nouns and spatial terms, like *muž-ár* 'from in(side)', *paxtí-ar* 'of/from the rice', *kur-ár* 'from where?'. However, see examples (4.31) and (4.32) for attestations with animate nouns, in (4.31) with a concrete and in (4.32) an abstract sense. The simple ablative case ending *-ar* attaches to the direct form of nouns and to infinitives, past participles, adverbs, and causative/desiderative nouns.

(4.31) *istór-ar af xom-ít-ay*
horse-ABL down descend-PST.D-3SG
'He got down from the horse.' (oral text, Village Bang)

(4.32) *avrát-ar gan-í kulán-a pat no*
woman-ABL take-PFV.PTCP man-LOC1 up.to NEG
behč-é-r-an
remain-CAUS-3SG.PRS/FUT-S
'It/he isn't sparing (anyone), from women to men.' (oral text, Village Sorech)

A hiatus-filling [γ] appears between a vowel-final pronoun and *-ar* ~ *-ári*. After the demonstrative bases of distal *he* 'that', and remote *(ha)te* 'that', *-γar* and *-γári* appear: *he-γár* 'from/of that', *(ha)te-γár* 'from/of that' (4.33). The ablative form *-γári* appears in (4.33) and (4.34). This form appears to consist of ABL *-ar* plus LOC2 *-i*, and to occur when an element of physical motion or the (abstract) passing of time is involved. See (4.38) below for another example of this.

(4.33) *činár-o múł-a g-íti te-γár-i*
chinar-OBL base-LOC1 come-PFV.PTCP REM.SG-ABL-LOC2
rahí a-ré-ni
departure AUG-do.PST.D-3PL
'They came to the foot of a chinar tree and (then) departed from there.' (oral text, Village Bang)

(4.34) *ṣáyoz çak-ék-o thariqá çhetrár-a*
glacier attach-INF-OBL method Chitral-LOC1

bo qadim-ár-i behč-í
very ancient.times-ABL-LOC2 remain-PFV.PTCP

girú kórum
come.PST.PTCP practice

'The technique of making artificial glaciers is a practice which has survived and come down to us from a long time ago.' (MNN in Bashir 2008)

In contrast, the ablative form in (4.35), *te-γár múłi* 'beneath that one', denotes a static location. In (4.35) and (4.36) the ablative expresses spatial comparison.

(4.35) *te-γár múłi bȧk(a)s-ó bil-ó ayh a-ré-r*
REM.SG-ABL below box-OBL lid-OBL up AUG-do.PST.D-3SG

ki ʦhap ašrafí
when full.of gold.coins

'When he lifted the lid of the box below that one, (he saw that) it was full of gold coins.' (oral text, Village Sorech)

(4.36) *hayá ṣa dov rét-ay hamo-γár tóri*
this black demon say.PST.D-3SG this.OBL-ABL above

dov níki
demon is.not

'"This is the black demon," he said, "There is no (other) demon above this one."' (oral text, Village Sorech)

Non-finite verbal forms like the infinitive (4.37), past participle (4.38) and (4.39), and the causative/desiderative nominal in *-áru* (4.40) can also take the ablative case ending. The ablative conveys various senses including physical separation (4.41); source (4.42); temporal sequence with the postpositions *áči* 'after' (4.37), (4.38) and *prúšṭi* 'before' (8.60), (8.61) below, material (4.43); or absence, with the postposition *γayr* 'without' (4.44).

(4.37) *buc̣huṣ-ík-ar áči gambúry-o bi savz*
bloom-INF-ABL after flower-OBL seed made
b-óni
become-3PL.PRS/FUT.NS
'After blooming, a flower's seeds are formed.' (DSAL)

(4.38) *avá asúm ma bir-dú-ar áči ma*
I be(ANIM).PRS.1SG my die-PST.PTCP-ABL after my
xazaná-i b-oγúr
treasury-LOC2 go-IMP.PL
'I am (alive now); after my death go into my treasury.' (oral text, Village Sorech)

(4.39) *khošt-é-r-ar poy-ári kandúri zamaná*
hidden-CAUS-PST.PTCP-ABL after-ABL so.much time
phar baγáy
away go.PST.D.3SG
'After hiding (the body), a long time passed.' (oral text, Village Parwak)

(4.40) *or-ár-ar ruph-ík-o no b-ét-am*
sleep-CAUS.DES-ABL get.up-INF-OBL NEG be.able-PST.D-1SG
'I wasn't able to wake up.' (lit. 'get up from sleep' (DSAL)

(4.41) *dudéri-ar xesmát b-íti h-ay*
distance-ABL tired become-PFV.PTCP come.PST.D-3SG
'S/he came from far away, tired out.' (DSAL)

(4.42) *ẓ̌oγ keły-ó kutér-ar kya šang*
thin sheep-OBL knife-ABL what fear
Proverb. 'A thin sheep has no fear of the knife.' (Sense: 'A desperate person has nothing to lose.') (DSAL)

(4.43) *poṣp-ár šu savz b-oy*
wool-ABL handloom.cloth made become-3SG.PRS/FUT.NS
'From wool handloom cloth is made.' (DSAL)

(4.44) *močí* *roxní-ar* *γayr* *kórum* *kor-ík-o* *no*
blacksmith charcoal-ABL without work do-INF-OBL NEG

b-oy
be.able-3SG.PRS/FUT.NS

'A blacksmith can't work without charcoal.' (DSAL)

The postposition *-sar*, usually 'than', is a development of the ablative case, and is used with either animates or inanimates. It is a bound morpheme, only following the oblique form of a noun or pronoun. All pronouns take *-sar* with their oblique forms: *má-sar* 'from me', 'than me', *tá-sar* 'than you(SG)', *ispá-sar* 'than us', *pisá-sar* 'than you(PL)', *hamó-sar* 'from/than him, her, this', *horó-sar* 'than him, her, that, it', and *hatoó-sar* 'than him, her, that, it', *hamítan-sar* 'than these', *hétan-sar* 'than them, those', *hatétan-sar* 'than them, those'. For some examples of the various senses of *-sar* see Section 8.6.2.

4.1.3.5 Locative cases

The distribution of the four locative cases is based on the parameters of verticality and horizontality. LOC2, *-i*, encodes horizontal motion or location/extent. LOC3, *-tu*, expresses location or motion upward, or location with respect to vertically oriented objects. LOC4, *-o*, encodes motion or location downward. LOC1, *-a* is not specified for verticality or horizontality. Examples of the uses of these cases follow.

4.1.3.5.1 Locative 1

The locative 1 (LOC1) case marker *-a*. expresses pointlike locations as opposed to those having linear extent; it also does not express direction or motion. With three-dimensional pointlike locations, the most frequent gloss is 'at', for instance *sikúl-a* 'at school', or, with two-dimensional locations 'on', as in *istán-a* 'on the roof'. Being unmarked for verticality or horizontality, LOC1 *-a* is the most general of the locative endings and is subject to much semantic and grammatical generalisation, to the extent that it acts like a second oblique, preceding the postposition *pat* 'up to', 'until', as in (4.46). Constructed with a finite form of *d-* 'give', 'strike', the infinitive + *-a* gives an inceptive meaning 'begin to', as in *boṣík-a pray* 'It began to rain', also (4.45).

(4.45) *tseq* *keł-ík-a* *pr-ay*
child cry-INF-LOC1 beat/give.PST.D-3SG
'The child began to cry.'

(4.46) *chuy-ó* *rošt* *d-ík-a* *pat* *ištrox-ít-am*
night-OBL light strike-INF-LOC1 until sneeze-PST.D-1SG
'Last night I sneezed until dawn (all night).' (DSAL)

4.1.3.5.2 Locative 2

The locative 2 (LOC2) case marker is *-i*. With three-dimensional bounded entities at approximately the same height as the deictic centre, and possessing an element of horizontal extent, *-i* can be glossed as 'in', for example *sikúl-i* 'in (the) school'. Example (4.47) illustrates this aspect of the meaning of LOC2. To see the difference between LOC1 and LOC2, compare examples (4.48) and (4.49), which provide a semantic minimal pair.

(4.47) *c̣hétr-i* *ǰoṣ* *š-éni*
field-LOC2 weed be(INAN)-PRS.3PL
'There are (lots of) weeds in the field (significant horizontal extent).'

(4.48) *khánǰ-i* *niveš-í* *o-š-óy*
wall-LOC2 write-PFV.PTCP AUG-be-PST.D.3SG
'The wall was written on.' (over a large horizontal extent, implying that a long text or many things were written) (Bashir 2000b: 21)

(4.49) *khánǰ-a* *niveš-í* *o-š-óy*
wall-LOC1 write-PFV.PTCP AUG-be-PST.D.3SG
'It was written on the wall.' (smaller, pointlike location) (Bashir 2000b: 20)

4.1.3.5.3 Locative 3

The locative 3 (LOC3) ending is *-tu*. LOC3 involves upward location or direction, or close contact with vertically oriented objects, for example *kán-tu* 'up in(to) the tree'. Examples (4.50) and (4.51) involve upward motion (4.50) or (static) direction (4.51).

(4.50) *avá buní-tu* *b-ím-an*
I Booni-LOC3 go-1SG.PRS/FUT-S
'I am going up to Booni.' (if travel up valley is required, for example from Chitral Town)

(4.51) *nan* *dúr-tu* *as-úr*
mother house-LOC3 be(ANIM)-PRS.3SG
'Mother is (up) in the house.'

4.1.3.5.4 Locative 4

The locative 4 (LOC4) case marker is *-o*. LOC4 encodes downward location or motion, as in (4.52), (4.53), and (4.54).

(4.52) *loṭ boht čókul g-íti khánǰ-o pr-ay*
big rock downward come-PFV.PTCP wall-LOC4 hit.PST.D-3SG
'A big rock came down and hit the wall.'

(4.53) *avá ċhetrár-o b-ím-an*
I Chitral-LOC4 go-1SG.PRS/FUT-S
'I am going down to Chitral.' (from a location higher upriver than Chitral, for example Booni) (MNN)

(4.54) *čéy-o trup kam wa*
tea-LOC4 salt less EMPH
'There is too little salt in the tea.' (location) (Bashir 2000b).

In (4.54) locative4 occurs because the tea is in a cup, a vertically oriented container.

4.1.3.5.5 Locative plural

A locative plural ending, in my data appearing only with inanimates, is *-en*. With most monosyllabic nouns, *-én* is stressed (4.55). With polysyllabic nouns stressed on the final or antepenultimate syllable, it is unstressed (4.56), (4.57).

(4.55) *som γeč̌h-én kánu*
both eye-LOC.PL blind
'blind in both eyes' (MNN)

(4.56) *dukán-en bašár kor-é*
shop-LOC.PL question do-IMP.SG
'Ask in the shops.' (MNN)

(4.57) *sarhád-en šalí no b-oy*
mountainous.regions-LOC.PL rice NEG become-3SG.PRS/FUT.NS
'Rice doesn't grow in mountainous regions.' (DSAL)

4.1.3.5.6 Vocative

Vocative (VOC) statements are those that address someone/something. Vocative meaning is expressed in two ways: (1) with the vocative case ending *é* (SG) (4.58) or *án* (PL) (4.59), and (2) with vowel lengthening plus the vocative particles *é:* (4.59) and (4.61), or (*h*)*ét*, preceding the addressee. *hét* has a derogatory sense and is used in addressing disrespected or despised persons/creatures (often encountered in oral folk narratives), as in (4.60). Both the particle *é:* and vowel lengthening appear in (4.59) and (4.61).

(4.58) *ẹaáɣłí-é: ẹaáɣ mo kor-é avá biabán-a*
rook-VOC.SG cry PROH do-IMP.SG I wilderness-LOC1
as-úm
be(ANIM)-PRS.1SG
'O rook, don't sing; I am (wandering) in the wilderness.' (Stanza from Baba Sayyar) (DSAL)

(4.59) *é: et-á::n*[9], *brargíni-á:n, es no*
hey you.guys-VOC.PL brothers.VOC.PL this NEG
gan-ími-an-aá osoíni no gan-ími-an-aá
take-2PL.PRS/FUT-S-Q handkerchief NEG take-2PL.PRS/FUT-S-Q
'Hey you guys, brothers, don't you want to buy it? Aren't you going to buy a handkerchief?' (oral text, Village Kari)

(4.60) *hé:t rét-ay.ki ta pušúr ma-t losnúk no*
hey.you say.PST.D-3SG your flesh me-DAT morsel NEG
b-es-ír ta ley ma-t ṭhur no
become-SBJV-3SG your blood me-DAT sip NEG
b-es-ír
become-SBJV-3SG
'"Hey you", she (a witch) said, "Your flesh wouldn't be even a morsel for me, your blood not even a sip."' (oral text, Village Bang)

(4.61) *é: ma bulbú:l*
VOC my nightingale
'O, my nightingale' (endearment)

[9] See Table 5.2 for the demonstrative bases. The extreme vowel lengthening represented in this example is expressive.

4.2 Pronouns

Since person and number information of the subject is encoded on finite verb forms, independent pronouns referring to the subject of a sentence occur infrequently in natural discourse. In some linguistics literature this property is called 'pro drop'. Full pronouns usually occur when there is a specific reason to emphasise the (identity of the) subject or agent. For this reason, in sentences supplied in isolation, without additional context, personal or demonstrative pronouns occur more frequently than in natural conversation or continuous text or narrative. Hence their frequent appearance in the examples in this book and in dictionaries like Bashir (2023b). Khowar does not have pronominal suffixes, suffixal/enclitic elements expressing possessive and other case relationships; significantly, these are found in Kalasha and some other languages of the Greater Hindukush area (Di Carlo 2011).

4.2.1 Personal pronouns

The personal pronouns are displayed in Table 4.2. Only the first- and second-person singular pronouns have distinct direct and oblique forms. The second-person plural is not, as is commonly done in Urdu for example, used to convey respect or politeness. Direct forms of the personal pronouns occur infrequently as subject in natural, connected discourse; oblique forms, however, are obligatory in other argument positions. For third-person entities, the demonstrative pronouns are used. These are treated in Chapter 5.

Table 4.2 Personal pronouns

Person	Sg.	Pl.
1. DIR	*avá* 'I'	*ispá* 'we'
OBL	*ma* 'me', 'my'	*ispá* 'us', 'our'
2. DIR	*tu* 'you'	*pisá* ~ *sa* 'you'
OBL	*ta* 'you', 'your'	*pisá* ~ *sa* 'you', 'your'

Postpositions indicating other case relations (dative, locative, ablative, instrumental) follow the OBL, as in *má-t(e)(n)(e)* I(OBL)-DAT 'to me', *má-sar* 'from/than me'. In these alternate forms the basic dative postposition, *-t*, is often followed (for euphonic or idiolectal reasons) by *-e*, *-en*, or *-ene*.

4.2.2 Interrogative and indefinite pronouns

The interrogative and indefinite pronouns are closely related, mostly homophonous. A difference in intonation distinguishes interrogative *kyaγ* 'what?' from indefinite *kyaáγ* 'something'. Indefinite *kyaáγ* has a low pitch, induced by stress on the second mora of an elongated /a/, or, in Strand's analysis by posterior phonation. Table 4.3 shows the main interrogative and indefinite pronominal forms and their adjectival forms and meanings.

Table 4.3 Interrogative and indefinite pronouns

Pronominal			Adjectival	
Interrogative		Indefinite	Interrogative	Indefinite
DIR OBL	*ka* 'who?' *kos* 'whom?'	*kaá* 'someone' *kos* 'someone'	*kos* 'whose', 'whom'	*kos di* 'whosever', 'whomever'
DIR OBL	*kyá* 'what?' *khyo* 'what?'	*kya* 'some'; 'any' in negative contexts	*kya* 'what'	*kya* 'a', 'some'
DIR OBL	*kyaγ* 'what?' *khyo* 'what?'	*kyaáγ* 'something'; 'some'; 'anything (with NEG)' *khyo* 'something'	*kya* 'what'	*kya* 'a', 'some', 'any' *kyá.di* 'any'
DIR OBL	*kí* 'which one?' *kí* 'which one?'	*kivál(u~i) di* 'whichever one' *kiválo di* 'whichever one'	*kí* 'which? (out of a specific set)' *khyo* 'what?'	*kya* 'a', 'some', 'any' *kyá.di* 'any'

Examples (4.62) and (4.63) illustrate the use of *kyaáγ* indefinite.

(4.62) *žanvár-an múži kyaáγ phuk kyaáγ loṭ*
animal-OBL.PL among some small some big
'Among animals, some are small, some large.' (DSAL)

(4.63) *paysá š-áv-a kyaáγ gan-ín*
money be(INAN)-IPFV.PTCP-LOC1 something take-POT.PTCP
b-óy
be.able-3SG.PRS/FUT.NS
'When there is money, something can be bought.' (MNN)

Example (4.65) shows interrogative *kyaγ* 'what?' in a context which shows clearly that the set of possible referents is not delimited. Either *kyaγ* (4.64) or *khyo* (4.65) can function as direct object. Oblique *khyo* suggests that the speaker has a potentially specific direct object in mind, while *kyaγ* suggests a non-specific indefinite object.

(4.64) *kyaγ ž-utí asús bo qreq*
what eat-PFV.PTCP be(ANIM)-PRS.2SG much belch
k-ós-an
do-2SG.PRS/FUT-S
'What have you eaten? You are belching a lot.' (MNN)

(4.65) *ṭing b-íti ruph-í khyo*
straight become-PFV.PTCP stand-PFV.PTCP what.OBL
lał-ís-an
look.at-2SG.PRS/FUT-S
'What are you looking at standing so straight (and motionless)?' (MNN)

With a negative element, *kyaáγ* in (4.66) means 'any action', and *hiš khyó* (4.67) means 'any object'. With the dative postposition, *khyo* yields *khyóte* 'what for', 'why', illustrated in (4.68).

(4.66) *avá kyaáγ no k-om-án*
I anything NEG do-1SG-PF.S
'I am not doing anything.' (answer to 'What are you doing?') (MNN in Bashir 2023b)

(4.67) *markhán-a hiš khyo no poš-ít-am*
fog-LOC1 anything.OBL NEG see-PST.D-1SG
'I didn't (couldn't) see anything in the fog.' (DSAL)

(4.68) *khyó-te h-av*
what-DAT come.PST.D-2SG
'What have you come for/why have you come?' (MNN)

kí 'which' can function either pronominally (4.69), or adjectivally (4.70).

(4.69) *ma hisá kí*
my share which
'Which (one of these) is my share?' (MNN)

(4.70) *kí* *vóḷti* *rahí* *a-r-ú*
which direction departure AUG-do.PST.D-2SG
'In which direction have you set out? (In which direction are you going?)' (DSAL)

kiváli 'which one' implies a choice from among a finite set of possible referents, as in (4.71) and (4.72).

(4.71) *kiváli* *ta*
which.one yours
'Which one is yours?' (SWKA in Bashir 2023b)

(4.72) *hes* *kiváli* *o-š-óy*
DISTAL.SG.DIR who AUG-be-PST.D.3SG
'Which one/who was that?' (IWA in Bashir 2023b)

Stressed *kyá* 'what' functions pronominally in (4.73) with a strong negative implication. In (4.74) it is adjectival. In a yes–no question, unstressed *kya* means 'any' (4.75). With a negative element, *kya no* can mean 'not any' or 'nothing' (4.76).

(4.73) *lál-o* *xorá-i* *kyá* *š-er*
high.status.person-OBL mill-LOC2 what be(INAN)-PRS.3SG
Proverb. 'What does a *lal* have to do in a water-mill?' Sense: 'He has nothing to do there.' That is, high-status people shouldn't take part in low-level/status tasks. (DSAL)

(4.74) *má-te* *kya* *niṣán* *al-áv?*
me-DAT what gift bring.PST.D-2SG
'What gift have you brought for me?' (MS)

(4.75) *tu* *má-te* *kya* *niṣán* *al-áv-aá*
you me-DAT a(ny) gift bring.PST.D-2SG-Q
'Have you brought a/any gift for me?' (MS)

(4.76) *qašqár-a* *ma-t* *kya* *no* *a-r-ú,*
Qashqar-LOC1 me-DAT anything NEG AUG-do.PST.D-2SG

yarxún-a *ma-t* *kya* *salám*
Yarkhun-LOC1 me-DAT what greeting

Proverb. 'You did nothing for me in Qashqar (which is very far from home), what is the use of your salaam in Yarkhun (which is nearer to home)?' (IWA in Bashir 2023b)

The written forms of the indefinite and the interrogative meanings are identical, and the difference between them is signalled only by intonation. For example, written, sentence (4.77) can have meaning (a) or (b). In (a), with the indefinite meaning 'somewhere', the main sentence stress is on the verb *bayáy*, while in (b), with interrogative meaning 'where', the main sentence stress is on *kúy*, 'where?'.

(4.77) (a) *vóšun kuy bayáy* (b) *vóšun kúy bayáy*
broom somewhere went — broom where went
(a) 'The broom is lost somewhere.'
(b) 'Where did the broom go? (What happened to the broom?)'

Another type of indefinite meaning is conveyed by the word *falánki* 'such and such', as in example (4.78).

(4.78) *avá xabár gan-ík-o hasé falánki*
I information take-INF-OBL REM.SG.DIR such.and.such
móš-o havál-o pr-ay
man-OBL mention-OBL give.PST.D-3SG
'When I asked (about something), s/he mentioned such and such a person.' (MNN)

4.2.3 Reflexive pronoun

The reflexive pronoun is *tan* 'self' (4.79).[10] It also functions adjectivally (see Chapter 7 for examples of its adjectival use), and is also frequently used, stressed, with an emphatic sense (4.80). Used as a direct object, *tan* is followed by *soró*, originally the OBL of *sor* 'head', which now participates in an oblique form for 'self' (4.81).

(4.79) *har iváli tan-te gan-úr*
each person self-DAT take-IMP.2PL
'Everyone take for themselves!' (DSAL)

[10] This appears to be a direct heritage from Vedic Sanskrit, in which both *tanū́* < 'body' (T5656) and an adjectival element *svá* (Kulikov 2007: 83) appear in the reflexive and the emphatic functions. In later Indo-Aryan languages, reflexive meanings are usually expressed with reflexes of *ātmán-* Vedic 'self', later 'breath', 'soul' (T1135), for example, Urdu *apnā* 'self's'.

(4.80) *reéni kół-o na tán çač̣h-ír na*
dog bone-OBL NEG self.EMPH gnaw-3SG.PRS/FUT.NS NEG
xur-ó-t d-oy
other-OBL-DAT- give-3SG.PRS/FUT.NS
'A/the dog neither gnaws the bone itself nor gives it to anyone else.' (DSAL)

(4.81) *tan sor-ó ḍonḍ-á-ve*
self's head-OBL go.away-CAUS-IMP.SG
'Get away! Get out of here!' (IWA in Bashir 2023b)

4.2.4 Reciprocals

Reciprocal elements *iγó* 'each other', lit. 'one-OBL' (4.82), and *ivál iválo* 'each other' (4.83) are followed by the postposition *sum* ~ *su* 'with'.

(4.82) *iγó sum gramkháłi kor-ík-ar γayr*
each.other with mutual.help do-INF-ABL without
déh-a hal.b-in no bo-y
village-LOC1 live-POT.PTCP NEG be.able-3SG.PRS/FUT.NS
'One cannot live in a village without helping each other.' (RKB)

(4.83) *zindagí-a ivál ivál-o su kuṭhú di-élik*
life-LOC1 one.person one.person-OBL with shoulder give-NEC
'In life (people) should help one another.' (lit. 'give a shoulder to each other') (DSAL)

iγó can appear in other contexts involving contact (4.84) or comparison (4.85) of one thing with another.

(4.84) *dar-án ṣúng-a iγó sóra d-et*
wood-OBL.PL corner-LOC1 each.other on.top.of put-IMP.SG
'Stack the wood in the corner.' (lit. 'Put the pieces of wood on top of each other.')

(4.85) *ponǰ çamúṭ iγó báhrki noh*
five finger each.other equal.to are.not
'The five fingers are not equal in size.' (DSAL)

5
Deictic elements

Deictic elements—pronominal, adjectival, and adverbial—in concert with the rich system of locative case endings, permeate the grammar of Khowar.

5.1 Demonstrative pronouns

Khowar has a three-term deictic system, based on the parameters of distance and visibility—proximal (+ near, + visible), distal (Ø near, Ø visible), and remote (− near, − visible). The demonstrative pronouns serve as third-person pronouns for both animates and inanimates. They occur either in their basic forms or in extended forms with an emphatic/specifying element *h(a)*.[1] In general, the extended forms occur the first time something is mentioned in a conversation or text, and subsequent mentions often appear with the basic (unextended) forms. The short excerpt from a folk text shown in (5.1) illustrates this. For this reason, extended forms tend to show up in individual (contextless) sentences like the examples in dictionaries or this book, while basic forms occur much more frequently in connected discourse or texts.[2]

[1] This *h(a)-* is cognate with the specificity/emphasis markers found with similar functions in several other Far-Northwestern Indo-Aryan languages. These include *š(a)-* in Kalasha (see Trail & Cooper 1999: 278 for examples) and Wakhi, where all demonstratives may take emphatic *(h)a-* (cf. Persian *ham-* 'same'), as in *ha-ya vaxt* 'that same, that very time' (Bashir 2009: 824). *(h)a-* ~ *ee-* also occur with similar functions in Palula (Bashir 2003: 885; Liljegren 2016: 130−1). Liljegren calls the two forms 'weak' and 'strong' and considers the weak form to be the default choice. A similar marker in Pashai has the shape (*e-*) (Bashir 2003: 828).

[2] Strikingly, in Bashir (2023b), a dictionary, there are 93 pronominal occurrences of *hasé* but none of *se* and 24 of *hayá* but only one of *ya*.

(5.1) *hamít-an* *dos-í* *ul-áʋ-ur* *ré-ni-an*
PROX.PL-OBL catch-PFV.PTCP fly-CS-IMP.PL say-3PL.PRS/FUT-S
mít-an *kíca.korí* *ul-eé-isi* *ré-t-ay.ki*
PROX.PL.OBL how fly-CS-1PL.PRS/FUT.NS say.PST.D-3SG
'They are saying, "Catch them and fly them (make them fly)," 'He said, "How can we make them fly?"' (oral text, Village Bang)

The demonstrative/deictic pronouns are shown in Table 5.1.

Table 5.1 Demonstrative pronouns

Proximal (+ near, + visible)	Singular	Plural
Direct	*(ha)yá* 'he', 'she', 'it'; 'this person/thing'	*(ha)mít* 'they', 'these people/things'
Oblique	*(ha)mó* 'him', 'her', 'it'; 'his', 'hers', 'its'	*(ha)mítan* 'them'; 'theirs'
Distal (Ø near, Ø visible)		
Direct	*(h)es* 'he', 'she', 'it', 'that one'	*(h)et* 'they', 'those people/things'
Oblique	*(h)oró* 'him', 'her', 'it'; 'his' 'hers', 'its'	*(h)étan* 'them'; 'theirs'
Remote (− near, − visible)		
Direct	*(ha)sé* 'he', 'she', 'it'; 'that one'	*(ha)tét* 'they'
Oblique	*(ha)toγó* ~ *(ha)toó* 'him', 'her', 'it'; 'his', 'hers', 'its'	*(ha)tétan* 'them'; 'theirs'

When the singular proximal form *hayá* 'this one' refers to an inanimate entity, the instrumental case ending *-en* 'with', 'by' and ablative *-ar* 'from' follow the oblique form *hamó*, with a hiatus-filling /γ/, yielding *hamoγén* and *hamoγár*. With the distal form *hes*, however, the instrumental and ablative case endings attach to the demonstrative singular base, *he*, again with the hiatus-filling consonant *γ*, giving *(h)eγén* 'by that' and *(h)eγár* 'from that'. The remote forms are built on the third-person adjectival base *(ha)t-*, giving instrumental singular *(ha)teγén* 'by that' and ablative *(ha) teγár* 'from that'. Instrumental and ablative plurals are formed with the postpositions *sóra* (INS) and *sar* (ABL): *hatét-an sóra* 'with (by means of) them' and *hatét-an sar* 'than them'.

The oblique forms, both singular and plural, function as objects of postpositions, direct objects, and genitives. The genitive pronominal forms are adjectival in function, as seen in examples (5.2) and (5.6) below. The pronominal and adjectival forms (Section 5.2) are constructed on the same bases, but their forms differ somewhat.

5.1.1 Proximal forms

The proximal form refers to entities which are visible and/or are within the range of the speech act. The proximal oblique plural form appears in example (5.1) above. The proximal forms *hayá*, *hamó*; *hamít*, *hamítan* 'this, s/he'; 'his, him, her, hers'; 'these', 'them' are often accompanied by a pointing gesture, as in (5.2), in which *hayá* refers to land being pointed out by the speaker, SG. Examples (5.2) and (5.3) illustrate proximal forms as subjects; (5.4) shows a proximal form as direct object; (5.5) has a dative-marked indirect object; and (5.6) shows the proximal oblique singular form with a genitive meaning.

(5.2) *hayá* *ma tát-o* *bumc̣húti*
PROX.SG.DIR my father-OBL ancestral.land
'This is my father's ancestral land.' (SG in Bashir 2023b)

(5.3) *hamít* *ma kórm-a* *no há-ni*
PROX.PL.DIR my work-LOC1 not come.PST.D-3PL
'These things weren't useful to me.' (lit. 'These things did not come into my work.') (DSAL)

(5.4) *hamó* *gan-í* *ma-t* *kyaáγ*
PROX.SG.OBL take-PFV.PTCP me-DAT something
d-os-aá
give-2SG.PRS/FUT.NS-Q
'Will you give me something for this?' (lit. 'Will you take this and give me something?') (oral text, Village Bang)

(5.5) *xodáy-á:* *hamó-te* *žan no* *d-os-aá*
God-VOC PROX.SG.OBL-DAT life NEG give-2SG.PRS/FUT.NS-Q
'O, God, won't you give her life?' (oral text, Village Bang)

(5.6) *hamó* *braár* *ma peç̣* *dust*
PROX.SG.OBL brother my warm friend
'His/her brother is my close friend.' (MNN)

5.1.2 Distal forms

The use of the distal forms is more complex. Since they are Ø-marked for both distance and visibility, they can refer either to entities which are visible but somewhat removed from the speaker, as in (5.7) and

(5.8), or to entities not physically visible but known or within the scope of the context of the (extended) speech act (5.9). The distal form *hes* can function both exophorically, referring to something in the environmental context rather than something in the discourse, as in (5.7) and (5.8), and anaphorically, as in (5.9) if the sentence is in reply to a question like 'What did X do?'. In cases without sufficient context, it is difficult to determine which type of reference is involved. For instance, in (5.10) *horó* could refer either to a person visible to both speaker and interlocutor, or to someone recently mentioned but not/no longer visible; without further context, it is not clear whether the referent of *horó* is present or not. In (5.11), however, the referent of *hes*, a woman disguised as a man, is (clearly) not present with the king and his minister.

(5.7) *hes ma-sár dudéri niš-í as-úr*
DIST.SG.DIR me-from far sit-PFV.PTCP be(ANIM)-PRS.3SG
'S/he is sitting far from me.' (SWKA in Bashir 2023b)

(5.8) *hes zom-ó čurčułík-en kas-ír-an*
DIST.SG.DIR cliff-OBL edge-INS walk-3SG.PRS/FUT-S
'He is walking right on the edge of the cliff.' (SWKA in Bashir 2023b)

(5.9) *hes pyal-ó čhin-ít-ay*
DIST.SG.DIR cup-OBL break-PST.D-3SG
'S/he broke the cup.' (MNN in Bashir 2023b)

(5.10) *keł-í keł-í horó γeč koš*
weep-PFV.PTCP weep-PFV.PTCP DIST.SG.OBL eye swollen
birú
become.I.3PL
'From weeping continuously his/her eyes swelled up.' (DSAL)

(5.11) *háte xotbá kor-í wezeén bík-o háte baço-ó*
the nikah do-PFV.PTCP evening become.INF-OBL the king-OBL
vazír rárdu.ki é: mó:š, hes
minister say.PST.PTCP hey man, DIST.SG.DIR
avrát kyá– hes avrát
woman EMPH – that/she woman.

'After doing the nikah[3], when it was evening the king's minister said, "Hey, man, that is a woman, that is a woman!"' (oral text, Village Kari)

As with the proximal forms, the oblique distal forms refer to direct objects, objects of postpositions, or genitive arguments 'him/her, his/her, his/ hers/its'. In (5.10), *horó* has genitive meaning; in (5.12) and (5.13) *horó* is the direct object; and in (5.14) it is the object of the postposition *sóra* 'with'.

(5.12) *horó çiçh-é-k asqán*
DIST.SG.OBL learn-CAUS-1NF easy
'It is easy to teach him/her.' (SWKA in Bashir 2023b)

(5.13) *i skoṭ rét-ay.ki avá horó al-óm*
one scout say.PST.D-3SG I DIST.SG.OBL take-1SG.PRS/FUT.NS
'One Scout said, "I will marry her."' (oral text, Village Kari)

(5.14) *tu pušúr-o hayá čaqú-o sóra čhin-ís-aá noh*
you meat-OBL this knife-OBL with cut-2SG.PRS/FUT.NS-Q if.not
horó sóra
DIST.SG.OBL with
'Will you cut the meat with this knife, (or if) not, with that one?' (SWKA in Bashir 2023b)

hes can also refer anaphorically to an entire predication; in example (5.15) it functions as a resumptive pronoun referring to the embedded question 'how s/he did it'.

(5.15) [*hasé kiča.kóri a-r-ér*] *hes má-te maálúm*
REM.DIR how AUG-do.PST.D-3SG DIST.SG.DIR me-DAT known
'I know [how s/he did it].' (SWKA in Bashir 2023b)

Deictic forms can refer to elements of an image, like a picture on television. In (5.16) a child is explaining a TV image to her mother, in which *hes* 'that one' refers to the person in the background of the picture (farther away from an imaginary observer located in the scene being portrayed), and *hamó* 'this one' refers to the person in the foreground of the picture (closer to the observer).

[3] Marriage ceremony, at which a marriage contract is signed.

(5.16) *he* *vóṣki hes* *hamó-te*
DIST.SG.DIR side DIST.SG.DIR PROX.SG.OBL-DAT
h-ay – *na:n*
come.PST.D-3SG – mother
'The one on that side has come to (kill) this one, mother.' (TMFD)

Without the emphatic/specifying element *h(a)-*, distal *es* is used cataphorically, often when a speaker doesn't immediately recall a word, has misspoken and makes a correction, or is not yet ready to use the precise term intended, as in examples (5.17) and (5.18). The English translations of these sentences attempt to capture the discourse effect of *es*. In (5.19) *es* functions to catch the attention of the addressee, indicating something to follow that needs to be paid attention to.

(5.17) *múł-a* *es* *dreé*
ground-LOC1 DIST.SG. DIR spread.PFV.PTCP
š-er – *tarpál*
be(INAN)-PRS.3SG – tarpaulin
'On the ground a (what-do-you-call-it) has been spread—a tarpaulin.' (MS in Bashir 2023b)

(5.18) *má-te* *es* *ʦadár ang-yé*
me-DAT DIST.SG.DIR shawl bring-IMP.2SG
'Bring me a (you know) a shawl.' (oral text, Village Kari).

(5.19) *é:* *braár* *tu* *es* *kor-é* – *ta* *braár* *sağád-o*
hey brother you DIST.SG.DIR do-IMP.2SG your brother Sajjad-OBL
gan-ír *tu* *laṭén-o* *gan-é*
take-3SG.PRS/FUT you lantern-OBL take-IMP.2SG
'Hey, brother, do (like this): your brother will take Sajjad, you take the lantern.' (MS in Bashir 2023b)

In (5.20), *es* functions as an abbreviation for a description of a series of actions presumed to be shared cultural knowledge understood by the listeners. The oblique form of *es*, *oró*, refers to a direct object in (5.21).

(5.20) *af* *es* *a-r-éni*
outside necessary.preparations AUG-do.PST.D-3PL
'Outside, they made the necessary preparations.' (oral text, Village Bang)

(5.21) *oró* *mat* *det* – *karadíny-o*
DIST.OBL.SG me-DAT give.IMP.2SG – earphones-OBL
'Give me (that thing)—the earphones.' (RAKR in Bashir 2023b)

I have not encountered *es* used alternatively with *hes*, as, for example *ya* can appear instead of *hayá*. The difference in function between the basic and the extended distal forms, *es* and *hes*, is different from that between proximal *ya* and *hayá* or remote *se* and *hasé*.

The plural direct distal form, *het*, is seen in (5.22) and the plural oblique in (5.23).

(5.22) *het* *tan* *múži* *bo* *palapúṭ* *dy-av*
DIST.PL.DIR REFL among much quarrelling give-IPFV.PTCP
o-š-óni
AUG-be-PST.D.3PL
'They were quarrelling among themselves (were not as close as they had been).' (MAK in Bashir 2023b)

(5.23) *avá vesor-í* *kór-i* *hét-an* *bard-é-t-am*
I widow-hood do-PFV.PTCP DIST.PL-OBL grow-CS-PST.D-1SG
'I brought them up enduring widowhood.' (IF in Bashir 2023b)

5.1.3 Remote forms

Entities referred to with remote forms are far away—neither visible nor in the scope of the speech act. Remote forms function anaphorically; for instance, example (5.24) shows *hasé* in an exchange where the unseen referent, Ahmad, has been previously mentioned in the discourse context. In (5.25), *hatoó* is the direct object 'him'; and in (5.26) and (5.27) it functions adjectivally, carrying the genitive meaning 'his' (vicinity, wife).

(5.24) Question: *ahmát* *ta* *sum* *no* *h-ay-aá*
Ahmad you.OBL with NEG come.PST.D-3SG-Q
'Didn't Ahmad come with you?'

Answer: *hasé* *áči* *as-úr*
REM.SG.DIR behind be(ANIM)-PRS.3SG
'He is behind (me).' (SWKA in Bashir 2023b)

(5.25) *hat-oó* *yií* *qoyá-ve*
REM.SG-OBL here call-IMP.2SG
'Call him here.' (oral text, Village Bang)

(5.26) *hat-oó* *gón-i* *i* *zarú bap* *aás-t-ay*
REM.SG-OBL vicinity-LOC2 one aged old.man be(ANIM)-PST.I-3SG
'There was a very old man with him.' (oral text, Village Bang)

(5.27) *hat-oγó* *boók petsh-í* *b-aγ-áy*
REM.SG-OBL wife leave-PFV.PTCP go-PST.D-3SG
'His wife left (him) (temporarily).' (DSAL)

Examples (5.28) and (5.29) illustrate the remote plural, direct and oblique case forms.

(5.28) *hatét* *iυál iυály-o-te* *niṣán tar-é-t-ani*
REM.PL.DIR one one-OBL-DAT gift reach-CS-PST.D-3PL
'They presented each other with gifts.' (SWKA in Bashir 2023b)

(5.29) *hatét-an* *múži* *saf-o-sár* *čan* *hasé*
REM.PL-OBL among all-OBL-ABL poor REM.SG.DIR
o-š-óy
AUG-be-PST.D.3SG
'Among them, he was the poorest of all.' (IF in Bashir 2023b)

5.2 Demonstrative adjectives

This section treats deictic adjectives, which are similar but not identical to the pronominal forms. Like the demonstrative pronouns, demonstrative adjectives constitute a three-level system—proximal, distal, and remote. They have a base (short) form, or an extended form with an *h*-initial prefix; the extended forms tend to occur when an entity is first mentioned in a discourse and can impart an emphatic or specifying sense. Like other adjectives, they do not inflect for case; the proximal forms, however, have distinct singular, (*ha*)*yá* 'this', and plural, (*ha*)*mí* 'these' forms, a feature not found with other adjectives. The distal and remote forms, however, have only one form for direct and oblique, singular and plural: *he* 'that', 'those' and *haté* 'that', 'those'. Table 5.2 displays the singular and plural, direct and oblique forms of the demonstrative adjectives.

Table 5.2 Demonstrative adjectives

	Singular	Plural
Proximal (+ near, + visible)		
Direct	(*ha*)*yá* 'this'	(*ha*)*mí* 'these'
Oblique	(*ha*)*yá* 'this'	(*ha*)*mí* 'these'
Distal (Ø near, Ø visible)		
Direct	(*h*)*e* 'that'	(*h*)*e* 'those'
Oblique	(*h*)*e* 'that'	(*h*)*e* 'those'
Remote (– near, – visible)		
Direct	(*ha*)*té* 'that'	(*ha*)*té* 'those'
	(*ha*)*sé* 'that'	
	háte 'the'	*háte* 'the'
Oblique	(*ha*)*té* 'that'	(*ha*)*té* 'those'
	háte 'the'	*háte* 'the'

5.2.1 Proximal forms

Examples (5.30) and (5.31) illustrate the proximal singular and plural direct forms; (5.32) and (5.33) exemplify oblique singular and plural contexts, respectively.

(5.30) *ma hayá droç̣ bim d-íti*
my PROX.SG.DIR grapevine wilting.disease strike-PFV.PTCP
š-er
be(INAN)-PRS.3SG
'This grapevine of mine has wilting disease.' (AR in Bashir 2023b)

(5.31) *hamí zap bo girán*
PROX.PL.DIR clothes very expensive
'These clothes are very expensive.' (RKB in Bashir 2023b)

(5.32) *hayá pay-ó xáʦum ká*
PROX.SG.OBL goat-OBL owner who
'Who is the owner of this goat?' (DSAL)

(5.33) *hamí lú-an xur kúra b-i mo*
prox.pl.obl word-obl.pl other where go-pfv.ptcp proh
det
give.imp.2sg
'Don't go and say these things anywhere else.' (DSAL)

5.2.2 Distal forms

Example (5.34) shows the distal singular in a direct context and (5.35) in an oblique singular context; (5.36) shows the distal plural in an oblique context.

(5.34) *he ṭikadár gadáy b-íti baɣ-áy*
dist.sg.dir contractor homeless become-pfv.ptcp go.pst.d-3sg
'That contractor became homeless and left.' (oral text, Village Kari)

(5.35) *he ḍaq-ó samlát g-íti*
dist.sg.obl boy-obl moustaches come-pfv.ptcp
š-éni
be(inan)-prs.3pl
'That boy's moustaches have appeared.' (DSAL)

(5.36) *ispá he boík-an ǰam no lołíru*
we dist.pl.obl bird-obl.pl well neg see.pst.ptcp
b- irét- am
become-pst.i-1pl
'We didn't see those birds properly.' (oral text, Village Uthul)

5.2.3 Remote forms

Like all the deictic adjectives, the direct singular form *hasé* can modify either animates (5.37) or inanimates (5.38). The direct plural form *haté* appears in (5.39). Oblique singular *haté* appears in a locative context in (5.40) and with a direct object in (5.41). Example (5.42) shows oblique plural *haté* with direct objects.

(5.37) *hasé moóš ma su ǰur*
rem.sg.dir man I.obl with connected
'That man is an acquaintance of mine.' (MS in Bashir 2023b)

(5.38) *ta hasé lu sahí*
your REM.SG.DIR word right
'What you (previously) said is right.' (SWKA in Bashir 2023b)

(5.39) *sírfi haté ḍaq hanún skúl-o-te há-ni*
only REM.PL.DIR boys today school-OBL-DAT come.PST.D-3PL
'Only those boys came to school today.' (SWKA in Bashir 2023b)

(5.40) *haté žaγa-á baγ-áυ-aá*
REM.SG.OBL place-LOC1 go.PST.D-2SG-Q
'Did you go to that place?' (DSAL)

(5.41) *ta háte šahr-ó i ṣohrt kó-m-an*
your REM.SG.OBL city-OBL one swallow do-1SG.PRS/FUT-S
'I will swallow that city of yours in one gulp.' (oral text, Village Bang)

(5.42) *haté kirkóṭ-an gan-í haté*
REM.PL.OBL skin.legging-OBL.PL take-PFV.PTCP REM.PL.OBL
bistar-án leçh-í maydá.kor-í
bedding-OBL.PL trample-PFV.PTCP spoil-PFV.PTCP
náx-i nis-áy
sleeping.nook-LOC2 emerge.PST.D-3.SG
'Taking those skin leggings, trampling and dirtying that bedding he went into the sleeping nook.' (oral text, Village Bang)

Demonstrative forms also function in reference tracking. In example (5.43), the remote form *hasé* refers to the second boy mentioned, the victim of beating (direct object), while the distal form *horó* refers to the first boy mentioned, the aggressor (subject).

(5.43) *i ḍaq i ḍaq-ó dík-o hasé ḍaq horó*
one boy$_{a}$ one boy$_{b}$-OBL beat-OBL REM.SG.DIR boy$_{b}$ DIST.SG.OBL
tát-o nás-a xaυs-ít-ay
father-OBL near-LOC1 complain-PST.D-3SG
'When one boy hit another boy, that boy (the victim) complained to his (the aggressor's) father.' (RAKR in Bashir 2023)

With the remote singular form *haté* stressed on the pronominal element *té*, this form means demonstrative 'that', as in (5.40). When unstressed, or slightly stressed on the first syllable, remote forms can function like a definite article 'the' with either inanimate (5.44), (5.45) or animate referents (5.46). Examples (5.47) and (5.48) demonstrate clearly the contrast between weakly initially stressed *háte* 'the' in (5.47) and finally stressed *haté* 'that' in (5.48).

(5.44) *é: brá:r qalám-o avá hay-íi ku-kúra*-LOC1
O brother pen-OBL I here-LOC2 or other-where-LOC1

lakh-í as-tá:m, háte žaγ-oó abathá
put-PFV.PTCP be-PST.I.1SG the place-OBL lost

kor-í as-úm
do-PFV.PTCP be(ANIM)-PRS.1SG

'Brother, I put (my) pen here somewhere or other, (but) I have forgotten the place.' (MS in Bashir 2023b)

(5.45) *háte gól-tu b-i háte ṭék-a*
the gully-LOC3 go-PFV.PTCP the top-LOC1

nis-át-am
emerge-PST.D-1SG

'Going up into the gully, I came out on the top.' (AK in Bashir 2023b)

(5.46) *háte durzán ḍaq ušṭur-í b-aγ-áy*
the mischievous boy run.away-PFV.PTCP go-PST.D-3SG
'The mischievous boy ran away.' (SWKA in Bashir 2023b)

(5.47) *háte moóš ma lú-o maán-t-ay mágar*
REM.SG.DIR man my words-OBL accept-PST.D-3SG but

háte kiméri-o no maán-t-ay
REM.SG.DIR woman-OBL NEG accept-PST.D-3SG

'The man accepted my words, but he didn't accept the woman's (words).' (MNN)

(5.48) *haté moóš ma lú-o maán-t-ay mágar*
REM.SG.DIR man my word-OBL accept-PST.D-3SG but

hayá moóš no maán-t-ay
PROX.SG.DIR man NEG accept-PST.D-3SG

'That man accepted my words, but this man did not accept (them).' (MNN)

(5.49) *haté* *ǰu* *brȧr-gíni* *hayrán* *o-šó-ni*
REM.PL.DIR two brother-PL amazed AUG-be.PST.D-3PL
'Those two brothers were amazed.' (oral text, Village Bang)

5.3 Adverbial forms

The singular deictic bases of the pronominal (Table 5.1) and adjectival (Table 5.2) systems are shown here in Table 5.3. From these are formed locative, quantitative, and manner adverbs.

5.3.1 Locative adverbs

Basic locative adverbs have three sets of forms, constructed on the proximal, distal, and remote bases. Forms consisting of the base plus the LOC1 case ending *-a* include the stative locative element *-r-* seen in *kúra* 'where'. Forms including LOC2 *-i*, and LOC4 *-o* ~ *uú*,[4] both of which, in contrast with *-a*, include a directional component of meaning, do not include the stative locative element *-r-*. I have not found the deictic bases combined with the LOC3 case ending *-tu*. These forms are displayed in Table 5.4.[5] As with deictic pronouns and adjectives, a facultative (*ha-*) ~ (*h-*) can appear in the extended forms.

The basic proximal directional forms *yaá* (*y*+*a*) 'here'; *yií* (*y* + *i*) 'hither'; *yuú* (*y* + *o* ~ *u*) 'down here' indicate direction toward the speaker, with the punctual, horizontal, or vertical semantic component supplied by the locative case element. Example (5.50) lays out these choices.

Table 5.3 Demonstrative singular bases

Degree of distance	Singular base
Proximal (+ visible, + near)	*(ha)yá* 'this (one)'
Distal (Ø visible), (Ø near)	*(h)e* 'that (one)'
Remote (– visible) (– near)	*(ha)té* 'that (one)'
	(ha)sé 'that (one)'

[4] With the deictic bases, the LOC4 ending is *-uú*, rather than *-o*.
[5] The Khowar system bears a close structural resemblance to that of Wakhi, where fusion of the basic locative prepositions expressing the parameters of verticality and horizontality with the deictic/demonstratives yields a complex series of locative adverbials (Bashir 2009: 832). Grjunberg and Steblin-Kamensky (1976: 582–7) has full paradigms for these forms.

Table 5.4 Locative adverbs constructed on the deictic bases

	LOC1 *-a*	LOC2 *-i*	LOC4 *-o* ~ *-u*	LOC3 *tu*
Proximal (+ visible, + near)	*(ha-)yára* ~ *(ha-)yéra* > *(ha)yaá* 'here'	*(ha-)y-ií* 'in here'	*(ha-)y-uú* 'down here'	?
Distal (Ø visible), (Ø near)	*(h-)ér-a* 'there'	*(h-)é-i* 'in there'	*(h-)oó* ~ *(h)úu* 'down there'	?
Remote (– visible),(– near)	*(ha-)tér-a* 'there'	*(ha-)té-i* 'in there'	*(ha-)t-uú* 'down there'	?

(5.50) a. *yaá gyé* 'Come here (to me)' (motion to a point location near speaker)
b. *yií gyé* 'Come (up) here.' (motion upward or horizontally toward speaker).
c. *yuú gyé* 'Come down here.' (motion downward toward speaker)

The extended proximal, pointlike locative *hay-aá* 'here' appears in (5.51)

(5.51) *nadír xán-o qalám haya-á behč-íru*
Nadir Khan-OBL pen PROX.SG-LOC1 remain-PST.PTCP
bir-áy
become.MIR-3SG
'Nadir Khan's pen got left here (in this place); (just noticed it).' (MNN in Bashir 2023b)

The proximal, downward form *hayuú* 'down here' is illustrated in (5.52). The proximal, horizontal form *hayií* 'in here' is illustrated in (5.53), which also illustrates the indefinitising element *ku-*, as in *kukaá* 'someone or other'.

(5.52) *hayá pón-tu b-ími-an-aá hay-uú*
PROX.SG.DIR road-LOC3 go-2PL.PRS/FUT-S-Q PROX.SG-LOC4
b-ími-an
go-2PL.PRS/FUT-S
'Are you going up this road (or) down here?' (spoken at a junction offering the choice of ascending and descending paths) (oral text, Village Sorech)

(5.53) *hay-ií* *ku-kúra* *š-er*
PROX.SG-LOC2 somewhere.or.other be(INAN)-PRS.3SG
'It is in here somewhere or other.' (MS in Bashir 2023b)

The extended distal, pointlike LOC1 is illustrated in (5.54), and the extended remote LOC1 form in (5.55).

(5.54) *ayh hér-a* *he* *gilás-o* *uúγ* *š-er-aá*
up DIST-LOC1 DIST.SG.DIR glass-LOC4 water be(INAN)-PRS.3SG-Q
'Is there any water in that glass up there?' (MNN in Bashir 2023b)

(5.55) *hatoγó* *çak-é-i* *hat-éra* *dr-á-ve*
REM.SG.OBL adhere-CAUS-PFV.PTCP REM-LOC1 put-CAUS-IMP.SG
'Get him/her to put them there.' (RAKR in Bashir 2023b)

Finding examples of the base (unextended) deictic forms, like remote *téra* 'there' requires that we examine connected texts, like those found in oral tellings of folk tales; *téra* in (5.56) and *téi* in (5.57) are such examples.

(5.56) *ṭék-a* *nis-áy* *ki* *haté* *ṣapík haṣ*
top-LOC1 emerge.PST.D-3SG when REM.PL.DIR bread just.like.that
tan *tér-a* *š-éni*
EMPH REM-LOC1 be(INAN)-PRS.3PL
'When he emerged on the top (of a hill), those breads are there just as they were before.' (oral text, Village Bang)

(5.57) *lo-í* *uγ* *gan-í* *b-aγ-áy,* *té-i*
look-PFV.PTCP water take-PFV.PTCP go-PST.D-3SG REM-LOC2
as-ít-ay *asmán parí*
be(ANIM)-PST.D-3SG sky fairy
'She (a woman who had come to get water) looked, took the water and left—she, the sky fairy, was in there (the previously mentioned fort).' (oral text, Village Bang)

5.3.2 Quantitative adverbs

Deictic adverbs of quantity also display three degrees of distance; their forms are given in Table 5.5. Like the spatial forms, they can be combined

Table 5.5 Quantitative adverbials constructed on the deictic bases

	Base form	Base form + *-a*
Proximal	*(ha)múni* 'this much', 'by now'	*(ha)múnya (hamúni+-a)* 'by this time', 'meanwhile'
Distal	*háni* 'that much', 'so much'	*hánya (háni + -a)* 'by that time'
Remote	*(ha)rúni* 'that much', 'so much'	*(ha)rúnya (harúni + -a)* 'by that time'

with the LOC1 case ending. Example (5.58) illustrates the proximal form, (5.59) the distal form, and (5.60) the remote form.

(5.58) *hamún-i tan dúr-a tor-ít-ay*
PROX-LOC2 REFL home-LOC1 reach-PST.D-3SG
'By this time s/he$_{a}$ has reached her/his$_{a}$ home.' (DSAL)

(5.59) *hán-i badtabyát b-íti hán-i tang*
DIST-LOC2 upset become-PFV.PTCP DIST-LOC2 unhappy
b-íti tu khyóte šar.istoón-t-av
become-PFV.PTCP you why sigh-PST.D-2SG
'Why did you sigh, so upset and sad?' (oral text, Village Bang)

(5.60) *hat-oó harún-i oráru gy-av*
REM.SG-OBL REM-LOC2 sleepiness come-IPFV.PTCP
o-š-óy ki drung anús zome-áv
AUG-be-PST.D.3SG that long day yawn-IPFV.PTCP
o-š-óy
AUG-be-PST.D.3SG
'S/he was so sleepy that s/he was yawning all day long.' (MYS in Bashir 2023b)

5.3.3 Manner adverbs

Basic adverbs indicating manner or type are formed from the deictic bases + *ṣ* (Table 5.6).

Table 5.6 Manner adverbials constructed on the deictic bases

Proximal	*(ha)móṣ* 'like this'
Distal	*haṣ* 'like this', 'like that', 'thus'
Remote	*(ha)róṣ* 'like that'

These forms are illustrated in examples (5.61) *(ha)móṣ* 'like this', (5.62) *haṣ* 'like this' ~ 'like that', and (5.63) *haróṣ* 'like that'. They can also function adjectivally, as does *haróṣ* 'like that' in (5.63).

(5.61) *hamóṣ kór-i zayá mo ko*
prox.adv do-pfv.ptcp waste proh do.imp.2sg
'Don't waste it like this!' (DSAL)

(5.62) *armán haṣ ki b-es-ír*
wish dist.adv that become-sbjv-3sg
'Would that it be thus!' (MK in Bashir 2023b)

(5.63) *haróṣ kórum ko a-r-ú*
rem.adv deed why aug-do.pst.d-2sg
'Why did you do something like that?' (MNN)

With *hamóṣ* 'like this' and *haróṣ* 'like that', the base forms *moṣ* and *roṣ* without the initial *ha-* are frequently heard, adverbially as in (5.64) and adjectivally as in (5.65).

(5.64) *prúšṭi xur lu pr-av haníse xur – roṣ ko*
before other word give.pst.d-2sg now other – rem.adv why
'You said one thing before, now (you are saying) something else. Why (have you done) like that?' (MNN)

(5.65) *roṣ roy o-br-ít-ani*
rem.adj people aug-die-pst.d-3pl
'Such (good) people have died.' (SWKA in Bashir 2023b)

6
Verbs

6.1 Introduction: verbal categories

Khowar has lost inherited Indo-Aryan gender, which was primarily based on biological sex, and has developed animacy-based gender. Existential 'be' has separate forms for animate and inanimate entities—*as-* for animates and *š̌-* for inanimates. These are the only basic verbs strictly specified for animacy, although some verbs co-occur mainly or only with animates or inanimates. However, since all finite verbs agree with the subjects of their sentences in person, number, and animacy when they include a form of *as-* or *š̌-*; and perfect tenses—present and past, both direct and indirect—are formed from a participle plus an animacy-agreeing finite form of 'be', this distinction pervades the verb system.

Evidentiality status (direct or indirect) is expressed with all finite forms. Direct forms are those which express information or events directly witnessed by the speaker, or which are established knowledge. Indirect forms express events not witnessed by the speaker, like things which happened in the distant past, or legendary/mythological events. Evidentiality status sometimes overlaps with mirativity, as illustrated in the next paragraph.

Mirativity is a grammatical category which morphologises information about the mind of the speaker rather than about the source of information. Thus, it is distinct from evidentiality, which grammaticises the source of information. Mirative forms convey that a predication is new information for a speaker—it impinges on an 'unprepared mind' (Slobin & Aksu 1982: 196–8).[1] As Delancey (1977: 33) put it: "Mirative meanings reflect the status of the proposition with respect to the speaker's overall knowledge structure." Mirativity always indicates new information for a speaker, whereas indirectivity only indicates that the event referred to was not directly observed by the speaker. Thus, an event reported with a mirative form may be either direct or indirect. For instance, if a person unexpectedly hears another person speaking Khowar, he could say *hes khovár korák biráy* 'S/he can speak Khowar'. This is both newly acquired and directly acquired knowledge; that is, it is both mirative and direct. If, on the other hand, someone just notices that a shovel has rusted, he might say *bel bulyaná birú biráy* 'The shovel has rusted', which is both indirect and mirative, since it is both new information and reports an event (rusting) that was not witnessed by the speaker.

Regular finite verb forms can carry the categories of animacy (animate or inanimate), evidentiality (direct or indirect), mirativity (new or old knowledge), aspect (perfective or imperfective), mood (realis or irrealis), person (first, second, or third), number (singular or plural), tense (present/future or past), and specificity (specific or non-specific). Specificity is marked in the present/future only. The existential/locative verbs *as-* and *š̌-* 'be' are not marked for specificity and have a simple present tense, not a present/future. Present/future meanings for *as-* and *š̌-* are supplied by forms of *b-* 'become', which is marked for specificity and has a present/future form.

Non-finite forms include perfective, imperfective, past, resultative, and potential participles; necessitative (modal) constructions; and the deverbal nominals agent noun, infinitive, and a causative/desiderative noun.

Finite forms are constructed on the present stem, past stem, transitive/causative stem, past participle, perfective participle, imperfective participle, and with the agent noun.

[1] Mirativity and the unprepared mind in Kalasha are discussed in Bashir (1988a: 73–7). At that time, the term 'mirativity' had not yet achieved widespread use. Mexas (2016) is a recent cross-linguistic study, bringing together what has been learned about mirativity since the initial work of Delancey.

6.2 Root structure

Most Khowar verb roots are consonant-final. A few roots consist of a single consonant or consonant cluster. They include:

C	*d-* 'give', 'strike/beat'; *b-* 'become', *b-* 'be able', *b-* 'go'; *g-* 'come'; *š-* 'be (inanimate existential)'
CC	*br-* 'die'

Monosyllabic consonant-final patterns are:

CVC	*kor-* 'do'; *por-* 'lie down'; *niš-* 'sit'; *ǰoṣ-* 'consider', 'judge'; *nis-* 'emerge', *gan-* 'take', 'buy'; *žib-* 'eat'; *ç̣ok-* 'adhere to'
CVCC	*bord-* 'grow larger'; *behč-* 'remain', 'be left behind'; *čang-* 'tell falsehood'; *šoxts-* 'pass', 'die'
CVCCC	*behrč-* 'remain', 'be left behind'; *lohrt-* 'roll around'
CCVC	*bren-* 'shear (sheep)', 'cut hair (human)'; *blay-* 'fade'
CCVCC	*braxč-* 'talk nonsense'; *vreṇj-* 'sizzle'
CCVCCC	*threnç̣k-* 'stretch one's body'
VC	*as-* 'be (animate existential)'; *až-* 'be born'; *ut-* 'enter'
VCC	*ang-* 'bring'; *avr-* 'ride'; *amk-* 'sprinkle earth or ashes on a snow-covered field to hasten melting'
VCCC	*oxtr-* 'be frightened'

Disyllabic consonant-final root patterns are:

CVCVC	*búç̣hur-* 'open up', 'come untied'; *kížib-* 'move'
CVCVCC	*búlunǰ-* 'be scattered'; *nuhúnǰ-* 'stop moving'
CVCCVC	*párvez-* 'send off (someone on a journey)'; *bírpon-* 'irrigate a field before ploughing'; *núšṭuts-* 'rush out of a gap (water)'
VCVC	*áver-* 'snatch away'; *úbul-* 'increase'
VCCVC	*ávsek-* 'wean'; *ándoz-* 'walk carefully'; *ískuṭ-* 'shrink'
VCCCVC	*íštrux-* 'sneeze'
VCCVCC	*ístavs-* 'say bad things about someone'

Vowel-final root patterns include monosyllabic:

CV	*ra-* 'bark'; *ru-* 'grow long'; *re-* 'speak'; *ro-* 'dye'; *ri-* 'leak'; *bo-* 'sow', 'plant'; *le-* 'find', 'harvest'; *su-* 'sew'; *phu-* 'blow'; *thi-* 'stay firmly in place'; *čhi-* 'break (intransitive)'
CCV	*dreé-* 'put', 'place'; *kru-*'be annoyed with someone'

Disyllabic vowel-final patterns include:

CVCV	*zomó-* 'yawn'; *púlu-* 'burn'
CVCCV	*búhtu-* 'fear'
VCV	*oré-* 'sleep'; *oxó-* 'swell up'; *úzu-* 'freeze (living things)'; *alé-* 'let slip away (opportunity, animal)'
VCCV	*usneé-* 'swim'
VCCCV	*úndru-* 'separate from one another'

6.3 Present stem and forms based on it

Present stems consist of the (sometimes altered) root, and a thematic vowel: /u/, /o/, or /i/. Present/future conjugations are formed from the present stem + the personal endings shown in Table 6.1.

Table 6.1 Present/future personal endings with thematic vowel

Person	Singular	Plural
1	V́-*m*	V́-*si*
2	V́-*s*	V́-*mi*
3	V́-*r*, V́-*i*	V́-*ni*

Most monosyllabic *o*-root verbs change /o/- to /a/ in the present stem. Many of these verbs have /i/ as their thematic vowel.[2] For example, *poš-* 'see' has the present stem *paš-* with thematic i; its present/future non-specific forms are shown in Table 6.2. Present/future specific forms are the present/future non-specific forms + suffixed *-an*.

Table 6.2 Present/future non-specific of *poš-* 'see'

Person	Singular	Plural
1	*paš-ím* 'I see/will see'	*paš-ísi* 'We see/will see'
2	*paš-ís* 'You see/will see'	*paš-ími* 'You see/will see'
3	*paš-ír* 'S/he, it sees/will see'	*paš-íni* 'They see/will see'

Other basic verbs that follow this pattern include *kos-* 'walk', *boṣ-* 'rain', *b-* 'go', *tor-* 'reach', 'arrive at', and *por-* 'lie down'. Their present/future non-specific forms are: *parím* 'I lie down/will lie down', *baṣír* 'it rains/will rain', *bir* 's/he, it goes/will go', and *kasír* 's/he, it walks/will walk'.

[2] However, this does not hold for all such *-o-* root verbs; for example, *ç̣hom-* 'pain' changes *-o-* to *-a-* but has thematic *-u-* in the present stem, as in *ma buk ç̣hamúran* 'My throat hurts'.

With some verbs, there is variation among speakers in which thematic vowel appears; for instance, both the third-person singular forms *tarúr* and *tarír* 's/he will arrive' are attested.

However, not all o- root verbs change /o/ to /a/ in the present stem. Notable is the most frequently appearing transitive verb, *kor-* 'do', as in *koróm* > *koóm* 'I do/will do', with thematic vowel o, the paradigm of which is shown in Table 6.3. The forms including r from the root have now been mostly replaced by the r-less forms.

Table 6.3 Present/future non-specific of *kor-* 'do'

Person	Singular	Plural
1	*kor-óm* > *kom* 'I do/will do'	*kor-ósi* > *kósi* 'We do/will do'
2	*kor-ós* > *kos* 'You do/will do'	*kor-ómi* > *kómi* 'You do/will do'
3	*korói* > *koi* 'He, she, it does/will do'	*kor-óni* > *kóni* 'They do/will do'

Other important verbs with thematic /o/ in the present stem are: *b-* 'become'; *b-* 'be able'; *g-* 'come'; *ang-* 'bring'; *al-* 'take away'; and *d-* 'give', 'strike'.

Some verbs with thematic /u/ are: *ri-* 'leak', *ç̣hom-* 'pain', *no-* 'appear', *łeng-* 'sway', and *br-* 'die'.[3]

Some, but not all, verbs with root vowel /o/ change /o/ to /a/ in both the present and transitive/causative stems, for example *poš-* 'see' with present stem *paš-* (Table 6.2) and transitive/causative stem *pašé-* 'show'. Others retain /o/ in the transitive/causative stem, for example *por-* 'lie down', 'fall' (vi) has *par-* as present stem with thematic i, seen in (6.1), but /o/ in the transitive/causative *poréik* 'put to sleep', *poráve* 'put to sleep! (IMP.SG)', and the past stem *porítay* 's/he, it lay down'.

(6.1) *bizbár bizbár-o d-ík-o ḍom-ó-te poç̣*
eagle eagle-OBL beat.INF-OBL Dom-OBL-DAT feather
par-ír
fall-3SG.PRS/FUT.NS
Proverb. 'When eagles fight among themselves, feathers fall to the Dom.'[4]
Sense: 'When two persons quarrel among themselves, a third party gets the benefit.' (NKN in Bashir 2023b)

[3] For historical discussion of the origins of these thematic vowels, see Morgenstierne (1947: 19–20).

[4] A Dom is a person belonging to the hereditary caste of musicians.

Some o-root verbs appear to change /o/ to /u/ in the derived transitive/causative, for example *drox-* ~ *drux-* 'itch' (vi) and *druxé-* (vt) 'scratch an itch'. This may, however, reflect the alternation between unstressed /o/ and /u/, as in *mux* ~ *mox* 'face', rather than a change of the root vowel.

Regular monosyllabic verbs with /e/, /i/, /u/, or /a/ in the root retain these vowels in all tense-aspect forms, yielding present and past stems identical with the root. A few such verbs are *keł-* 'cry', 'weep', *thi-* 'remain still/quiet', *ut-* 'enter', *až-* 'be born'. For example, present/future, past direct, perfective participle, and past participle forms of *keł-* 'cry', 'weep' are: *kełím(an)* 'I weep (am weeping)', *keł-ítam* 'I wept', *keł-í* 'having wept', and *keł-íru* 'wept (unseen)'.

Some intransitive verbs with the root pattern C*u*C*u*(C) retain that pattern in the present/future tenses and the past direct but change it to C*a*C*e*(C) in the derived transitive/causative. For example, ***púlu***- 'burn (vi)', ***palé***- 'burn' (vt); *rúkhuṣ-* (vi) 'crawl, drag oneself along the ground', *rakhéṣ-* (vt) 'drag (something) along'; *rúmbur-* (vi) 'be crushed or crumbled', *rámber-* 'crush or crumble (vt)'; and *púłγučh-* 'get tangled in something', *páłγečh-* 'tangle in something (vt)'.

For most other regular, underived verbs, the present stem is the same as the root for basic intransitives, like *niš-* 'sit' *niš-ím* 'I (will) sit', and transitives, such as *axl-* 'comb' *axl-ím* 'I (will) comb'.

6.3.1 Present/future forms of some important verbs

Present/future non-specific forms consist of the present stem with its thematic vowel + the personal endings, as in Table 6.1. This section lays out present/future non-specific paradigms of some frequently used basic verbs. A few of the most frequently appearing verbs have *-i* as the third-person singular personal ending; they include *kor-* 'do' (*koi* <*korói* 's/he, it does') (Table 6.3), *b-* 'become' (*boi* 's/he, it becomes') (Table 6.5), *g-* 'come' (*goi* 's/he, it comes') (Table 6.6), and *d-* 'give, strike' (*doi* 's/he, it gives, strikes') (Table 6.9). Most other verbs have *-r* as the third-person singular ending; important among them are *š-* 'be(INAN)' (*šer* 'it is'); *por-* 'lie down' *parír* ('s/he, it lies down, falls'); and *b-* 'go' (*bir* 's/he, it goes').

The three homophonous roots *b-* 'go', *b-* 'become', and *b-* 'be able' share some but not all forms. The verb *b-* 'go' has regular present/future forms with thematic vowel /*i*/ (Table 6.4). The present/future forms of *b-* 'become' and *b-* 'to be able' both have thematic /o/ in the present/future; they are shown here in Table 6.5. Their past tense forms, however, differ (see Tables 6.28 and 6.29 below).

Table 6.4 Present/future non-specific of *b-* 'go'

Person	Singular	Plural
1	*bim* 'I go, will go'	*bísi* 'We go, will go'
2	*bis* 'You go, will go'	*bími* 'You go, will go'
3	*bir* 'S/he, it goes, will go'	*bíni* 'They go, will go'

Table 6.5 Present/future non-specific of *b-* 'become' and 'be able'

Person	Singular	Plural
1	*bom* 'I become, will become'; 'I am able, will be able'	*bósi* 'We become, will become'; 'We are able, will be able'
2	*bos* 'You become, will become'; 'You are able, will be able'	*bómi* 'You become, will become'; 'You are able, will be able'
3	*boi* 'S/he, it becomes, will become', 'is'; 'S/he, it is able, will be able'	*bóni* 'They become, will become', 'are'; 'They are able, will be able'

Present/future non-specific forms of *g-* 'come' are regular (Table 6.6), but the past direct is irregular (Table 6.18 below).

Table 6.6 Present/future non-specific of *g-* 'come'

Person	Singular	Plural
1	*gom* 'I come, will come'	*gósi* 'We come, will come'
2	*gos* 'You come, will come'	*gómi* 'You come, will come'
3	*goi* 'S/he, it comes, will come'	*góni* 'They come, will come'

The present/future non-specific forms of *ang-* 'bring' and *al-* 'take away' are presented in Tables 6.7 and 6.8. Their past direct forms are given in Tables 6.14 and 6.15 below.

Table 6.7 Present/future non-specific of *ang-* 'bring'

Person	Singular	Plural
1	*angóm* 'I bring, will bring'	*angósi* 'We bring, will bring'
2	*angós* 'You bring, will bring'	*angómi* 'You bring, will bring'
3	*angói* 'S/he, it brings, will bring'	*angóni* 'They bring, will bring'

Table 6.8 Present/future non-specific of *al-* 'take away'

Person	Singular	Plural
1	*alóm* 'I take away, will take away'	*alósi* 'We take away, will take away'
2	*alós* 'You take away, will take away'	*alómi* 'You take away, will take away'
3	*alói* 'S/he, it takes away, will take away'	*alóni* 'They take away, will take away'

The verb *d-* 'give', 'strike', has regular present/future forms (Table 6.9) but an irregular past direct (Table 6.19 below).

Table 6.9 Present/future non-specific of *d-* 'give', 'strike/beat'

Person	Singular	Plural
1	*dom* 'I give, beat, will give, will beat'	*dósi* 'We give, beat, will give, will beat'
2	*dos* 'You give, beat, will give, will beat'	*dómi* 'You give, beat, will give, will beat'
3	*doi* 'S/he it gives, beats, will give, will beat'	*dóni* 'They give, beat, will give, will beat'

6.3.2 Functions of the present/future non-specific

Present/future non-specific (PRS/FUT.NS) forms are used with future meaning (6.2)[5] and in the sense of a generic (6.3) or habitual (6.4) present.[6] They can also function with hortative meaning, as in (6.119) and (6.120) below.

(6.2) *avá angár-o až-é-m*
I fire-OBL be.born-CAUS-1SG.PRS/FUT.NS
'I will light the fire.' (MNN in Bashir 2023a)

(6.3) *púši no vax-ír*
cat NEG bark-3SG.PRS/FUT.NS
'A cat doesn't bark.' ('Cats don't bark.') (Chitral Town)

(6.4) *avá hamíš čhúči rayéšṭi ruph-óm*
I always morning early get.up-1SG.PRS/FUT.NS
'I always get up early in the morning.' (Chitral Town)

6.3.3 Present/future specific

The present/future specific (PRS/FUT-S) consists of the present/future non-specific + *-an*, for example *kóm-an* 'I am doing'.[7] Its sense is like that of the English present progressive, which can be used to report either an

[5] For this reason, some authors refer to this form as 'future'.
[6] Morgenstierne (1947: 21) calls my PRESENT/FUTURE.NS an aorist, which "is used as an indefinite present and as a future". My analysis of the function of this form agrees with this statement; however, since the term 'aorist' is not widely understood today, I have chosen to use the more transparent present/future.non-specific.
[7] Some writers call this form 'present'.

action or event in progress at the present time, as in (6.5) and (6.6), or an event known to be happening in the near future (6.7).

(6.5) *ta* *braár* *haníse* *kyaγ* *k-óy-an*
you.OBL brother now what do-3SG.PRS/FUT-S
'What is your brother doing now?' (EB field notes)

(6.6) *kú-i* *b-ís-an*
Where-LOC2 go-2SG.PRS/FUT-S
'Where are you going?' (EB field notes)

(6.7) *pač̌hambe-én* *noγ* *dúr-i* *b-íni-an*
Thursday-INS new house-LOC2 go-3PL.PRS/FUT-S
'On Thursday they are going to their new home.' (DSAL)

6.4 Past stem

The past stem is the base of the past direct forms, which consist of the past stem + the past tense morpheme -*(i)(s)t*- + the past direct personal endings, shown in Table 6.10.[8]

Table 6.10 Past direct personal endings

Person	Singular	Plural
1	*-am*	*-am*
2	*-au*	*-amí*
3	*-ai*	*-aní*

6.4.1 Regular past stem

This section treats the regular past direct and displays the regular paradigm of *poš*- 'see'. For most verbs, the past stem consists of the root + -*(i)(s)t*-. Past direct forms add the past direct personal endings (Table 6.10) to the past stem. Today, *-ist-* has become abraded in most Khowar dialects, becoming *-it-*, *-t-*, or even Ø. In Lotkuh and Ishkoman, which are farther from the main Chitral valley, some older forms retaining the augment and *-s-* persist, notably *aréstam* 'I did'.

[8] In Laspur, the second-person singular ending of the PST.D is sometimes heard as *-á*, instead of *-áu*. For example, *nišá* 'You sat down' (cf. '*nišítau* or *nišáu*').

For most verbs, the past stem is the same as the root, for example *por-* 'lie down' *por-ítam* 'I lay down'. The past direct paradigm for the regular verb *poš-* 'see' is given in Table 6.11. Example (6.8) illustrates its use.

Table 6.11 Past direct of *poš-* 'see'

Person	Singular	Plural
1	*pošítam* 'I saw'	*pošítam* 'We saw'
2	*pošítau* 'You saw'	*pošítami* 'You saw'
3	*pošítai* 'S/he, it saw'	*pošítani* 'They saw'

(6.8) *avá kitáb-o poš-ít-am*
I book-OBL see-PST.D-1SG
'I saw the book.'

A second past stem, for most verbs identical to the root, is the base of the past participle. A few verbs ('do', 'die', 'eat', 'break (vi)', and 'go') have irregular second past stems.

6.4.2 Irregular past stems

This section introduces some important verbs with irregular past stems. A few frequently used verbs retain the preterital augment *o-* ~ *a-* inherited from OIA *a-* in their past stems. Some of these appear in Table 6.12 ('do', 'die', 'eat', 'be(INAN)', 'break (vi)', 'be able').[9] Other frequently occurring verbs, like *g-* 'come' and *d-* 'give', 'strike', also have irregular, suppletive, past stems (Table 6.12).

Table 6.12 Verbs with irregular past stems

Root and gloss	Present stem, including thematic vowel	Past stem	Second past stem	Past participle	Perfective participle
		Verbs with augment in past stem			
kor- 'do'	*koró-*	*a-r-*	*kar-*	*kardu*	*kori*
br- 'die'	*briú-*	*o-br-*	*bir-*	*birdu*	*bihrti*
žib- 'eat'	*žibó-*	*o-yó-*	*žir-* ~ *žur-*	*žirdu* ~ *žurdu*	*žuti*

[9] *b-* 'be able' still retained the augment *o-* (< *a-*) in 1902, when the Khowar translation of the *Ganj-i-Pakhto* (Khan 1902) was published, but it has since gone out of use. The form *obéstam* 'I was able' (< *b-* 'be able'), which shows both the augment and the past tense formative *-ést-*, both of which are no longer in use in the main varieties of Khowar, is multiply attested in that work, as well as in Morgenstierne (1947) and (1973b), which also have the form *oléstam* 'I found' (← *le-* 'find'). This indicates that loss of the augment in that verb was fairly recent, that it has proceeded by individual lexical items, and that it continues today.

Table 6.12 (continued)

Root and gloss	Present stem, including thematic vowel	Past stem	Second past stem	Past participle	Perfective participle
		Verbs with augment in past stem			
čh- 'break' (vi)	*čhiú-*	*o-čh-*	*čhir-*	*čhirdu*	*čhiti*
b- 'be able'	*bo-*	*(o)-be-*	*bir-*	*biru*	*biti*
š- 'be(INAN)'	*še-*	*o-šo-*	*šir-*	*širu*	–
		Verbs with suppletive past stems			
g- 'come'	*go-*	*ha-*	*g-*	*giru*	*giti*
d- 'give', 'strike'	*do-*	*phr- ~ pr-*	*d-*	*diru*	*diti*
b- 'become'	*bo-*	*h-*	*b-*	*biru*	*biti*
b- 'go'	*bi-*	*bayá-*	*boy-*	*boydu*	*bi*
		Verbs with other irregular past stems			
al- 'take away'	*aló-*	*avá- ~ avé-*	*al-*	*aldu*	*alti*
ang- 'bring'	*angó-*	*alá- ~ alé-*	*ang-*	*angíru*	*angiti*

Forms of *al-* 'take away' and *ang-* 'bring' overlap interestingly to a certain extent. Their present stems, past stems, and past participles are compared in Table 6.13, and their past direct paradigms are given in Tables 6.14 and 6.15.[10]

Table 6.13 Present and past stems of *ang-* 'bring' and *al-* 'take away'

Root and gloss	Present stem	Past stem	Past participle
ang- 'bring'	*angó-*	*al-*	*angiru*
al- 'take away'	*aló-*	*av-*	*aldu*

Table 6.14 Past direct of *ang-* 'bring'

Person	Singular	Plural
1	*alétam* 'I brought'	*alétam* 'We brought'
2	*aláu* 'You brought'	*alétami* 'You brought'
3	*alái* 'S/he brought'	*aláni* 'They brought'

[10] The final *-u* of the sequence *-áu* is pronounced as consonantal *v*, thus *-áv*, and final *-i* in *-ái*, is pronounced as consonantal *y*. In the main text, forms and examples involving these sounds will be written as *-ay* and *-av*; however, when they appear as personal endings in paradigms or tables, they will be written as *-au* and *-ai*. This is done to preserve continuity with earlier works on Khowar and historical forms.

Table 6.15 Past direct of *al-* 'take away'

Person	Singular	Plural
1	*avétam* 'I took away'	*avétam* 'We took away'
2	*aváu* (< *avétau*) 'You took away'	*avétami* 'You took away'
3	*avái* 'S/he, it took away'	*avání* 'They took away'

The past direct first-person and second-person plural forms of *ang-* 'bring'; *al-* 'take away'; *žib-* 'eat'; *b-* 'go'; *g-* 'come'; and *d-* 'give', 'strike' retain the *-t-* of the old past tense formative *-ist-*, while the second-person singular and third-person forms do not (see Tables 6.14 and 6.15 above and 6.18 below in the following section).[11] The past direct forms of the regular verbs *poš-* 'see' (Table 6.2 above) and *por-* 'lie down', 'fall', on the other hand, retain this *-t-* in all three persons, singular and plural.

6.4.3 Irregular past direct paradigms

This section lays out past direct paradigms of some of these important and frequently used verbs. Table 6.16 shows the past direct forms of *žib-* 'eat'; Table 6.17 gives the past direct forms of *b-* 'go'; the past direct paradigm of *g-* 'come' is shown in Table 6.18; the past direct forms of *d-* 'give', 'strike', appear in Table 6.19; the past direct of *b-* 'be able' appears in Table 6.20; and that of augment-retaining *kor-* 'do' is shown in Table 6.21. The forms in Table 6.21 are those used in conservative dialects. Increasingly, though, regularised and sometimes shortened forms without the augment, like *korítay* or *koórtay* 's/he, it did', are being used.

Table 6.16 Past direct of *žib-* 'eat'

Person	Singular	Plural
1	*oyótam* 'I ate'	*oyótam* 'We ate'
2	*oyóu* 'You ate'	*oyótami* 'You ate'
3	*oyói* 'S/he, it ate'	*oyóni* 'They ate'

Table 6.17 Past direct of *b-* 'go'

Person	Singular	Plural
1	*bayátam* 'I went'	*bayátam* 'We went'
2	*bayáu* 'You went'	*bayátami* 'You went'
3	*bayái* 'S/he, it went'	*bayáni* 'They went'

[11] Some older or dialectal forms have *bayétam*.

Table 6.18 Past direct of *g-* 'come'

Person	Singular	Plural
1	*hátam* 'I came'	*hátam* 'We came'
2	*hau* 'You came'	*hátami* 'You came'
3	*hai* 'S/he, it came'	*háni* 'They came'

Table 6.19 Past direct of *d-* 'give', 'strike', 'beat'

Person	Singular	Plural
1	*p^{h}rétam* 'I gave, struck'	*p^{h}rétam* 'We gave, struck'
2	*prau* 'You gave, struck'	*p^{h}rétami* 'You gave, struck'
3	*prai* 'S/he, it gave, struck'	*práni* 'They gave, struck'

Table 6.20 Past direct of *b-* 'be able'

Person	Singular	Plural
1	*bétam* 'I was able'	*bétam* 'We were able'
2	*bétau* 'You were able'	*bétami* 'You were able'
3	*bétai* 'S/he, it was able'	*bétani* 'They were able'

Table 6.21 Past direct of *kor-* 'do' (conservative varieties)

Person	Singular	Plural
1	*arétam* 'I did'	*arétam* 'We did'
2	*arú* 'You did'	*arétami* 'You did'
3	*arér* 'S/he, it did'	*arétani* 'They did'

Shortened forms of past direct forms are frequently heard; for example, instead of *torítay* 'reached' or *γerítay* 'turned into', *toórtay* and *γeértay* are heard. In these forms the *-i-* of the second syllable has been elided and the vowel of the first syllable lengthened. This does not happen with all verbs, however. For instance, I have not heard **uluúṣtai* instead of *uluṣítai* 'it tore'. With some verbs the past tense morpheme is sometimes entirely elided, for example with *ut-* 'enter' *utáy* instead of *utítay* 's/he, it entered' is heard; and with *niš-* 'sit' there is *nišáy* as well as *nišítay*.[12]

[12] What difference(s) in meaning, if any, may exist between the full forms like *nišítay* and short forms like *nišáy* is a topic that remains to be explored.

6.4.4 Functions of the past direct

The past direct (PST.D) is built on the past stem. Past direct paradigms for several important or irregular verbs have been given in Section 6.4.3. This section focuses on the functions of the past direct.

The past direct is used (1) to report directly witnessed or experienced events which occurred before the moment of speech in the recent past, as in (6.9),[13] (2) for actions known to be taking place in the imminent future (6.10), (3) in the protasis of realis conditionals (6.11) (see also Section 9.5.3.1), and (4) as a performative verb,[14] as in example (4.20) above. The second function occurs almost exclusively with the first person (singular), since one is privy only to one's own thoughts and in control only of one's own actions.

(6.9) *hasé* *lahúr-o-te* *baγ-á-y*
REM.SG Lahore-OBL-DAT go-PST.D-3SG
'S/he went/has gone to Lahore.' (first-hand knowledge) (EB field notes)

(6.10) *avá* *baγ-át-am*
I.DIR go-PST.D-1SG
'I'm off (I'm leaving right now).' (EB field notes)

(6.11) *vexík-o-t* *biyár* *ki pr-av*
Wakhani person-OBL-DAT behind.in.saddle if put.PST.D-2SG
hun-ó-t *xaṣáp kor-óy*
saddle-OBL-DAT grab do-PRS/FUT.3SG
Proverb. 'If you seat a person from Wakhan behind you in the saddle, he will grab the saddle (from you).' (IWA in Bashir 2023b)

6.5 Derived transitive/causative stem

Derived transitive/causative stems consist of root + *-é-* (< *á-i*), as in *por-ék-* 'to lay down (to sleep) [of an animate entity]' (vt) and *korék* 'to

[13] As can be seen from the glosses of (6.9), the PST.D can sometimes refer to the very recent past, having the force of the English 'hot news' present perfect.
[14] A performative verb is one which, by its very utterance, accomplishes the action it reports. In English, this is accomplished with a simple present tense; for example, "I pronounce you husband and wife", spoken by a religious or legal functionary.

cause to be done' (vc).[15] Causative past direct forms from *kor-* 'do' and *žib-* 'eat' are formed without the augment, as in *korétam* 'I caused to be done' and *žibétam* 'I caused to be bitten/eaten (by an animal secondary agent)'. The transitive/causative stem of *b-* 'go' is formed on the second past stem *boγ-*, as in *boγéik* 'to cause to go out (light, fire)', 'erase (writing)'.

Many Indo-Aryan languages have two distinct layers of causative morphology. For instance, Urdu *kaṭnā* 'to be cut' (vi), *kāṭnā* 'to cut' (vt), and *kaṭānā* or *kaṭvānā* (vc) 'to have something cut by someone'. Khowar's close relative Kalasha has both first and second causative formations, a first causative in *-é-* and a second causative in *-a-vá-*, as in *ḍúḍik* 'to sleep' (vi), *ḍuḍék* (< *ḍuḍáik*) 'to put someone to sleep' (vt), *ḍuḍ-a-vá-ik* 'to have someone be put to sleep by a secondary agent' (vc) (Trail & Cooper 1999: 476).

In contrast, Khowar has only one layer of causative morphology, formed with *-é-*, which functions as either a direct causative/derived transitive (6.12) and (6.14) or an indirect causative involving a secondary agent (6.13). Causatives can be formed on basic intransitives or transitives. Causative/derived transitives from basic intransitives include posture verbs like: *nišík* 'to sit' (vi), *nišé(y)k* 'to seat' (vt); *ruphík* 'to stand up' (vi), *ruphé(y)k* 'to cause to get/stand up' (vt); and *porík* 'to lie down' (vi), *poré(y)k* 'to lay down (animate object)' (vt). Typical causative derivations from basic transitives include: *ṭhurík* 'to sip' (vt) and *ṭhuré(y)k* (vc) 'to cause/help to sip' (6.5); *pošík* (vt) 'to see' and *pašé(y)k* (vc) 'to show (6.12) (6.13); or *çiçhík* 'to learn' (vt) and *çiçhé(y)k* (vc) 'to teach', 'to send a message', 'to have taught by someone' (vc), but not **çiçavéik*.

(6.12) *avá kitáb-o ta paš-é-t-am*
I book-OBL you.OBL see-CAUS-PST.D-1SG
'I showed the book to you.'

[15] Derived transitives have *-é(y)k* infinitives, usually pronounced as *-ék*. The development is: *áik* > *-ék*. Infinitives of derived transitives are variously romanised with *-éik*, *-ék*, or *-éyk*. These differences arise because of variability in the pronunciation of the trace of the *-í* from the underived infinitives. The spellings with *éi* and *éy* both represent the perception by some speakers that there is something besides a simple /é/ in these forms. The spelling with *-éy* reflects the perception that this is a vowel with a consonantal off-glide rather than a diphthong; that with *éi* attempts to preserve the /i/ of the infinitive ending of the underived verb.

(6.13) *hat-oγó* *çak-é-i* *kitáb-o* *ta*
REM.SG-OBL adhere-CAUS-PFV.PTCP book-OBL you.OBL
paš-é-t-am
see-CAUS-PST.D-1SG
'I got him/her to show you the book.'

(6.14) *uγ* *ma* *ṭhur-á-ve*
water I.OBL sip-CAUS-IMP.2SG
'Give me a sip of water.' (DSAL)

The derived formation in (6.13) has causative semantics, since the conception includes, in addition to a primary agent, a direct object (book), a person who is caused or helped to do the action of seeing (you), and a secondary agent/causee (*hatoγó* 'him/her'). In (6.14) the agent is understood to be the addressee, 'you'. If a secondary agent (causee) is mentioned, it can be followed by *poyár* 'through, by' (6.15) or *çakéi* 'having attached', the perfective participle of *çakéik* 'to attach', 'to put to work', the transitive/causative of *çokík* 'to adhere to' (6.13) (6.16).

(6.15) *kos* *poyár* *ma-t* *çiçh-á-ve*[16]
someone.OBL through I.OBL-DAT convey.message-CAUS-IMP.2SG
'Send me a message through someone.' (DSAL)

(6.16) *avá* *yardóy-an* *kórm-a*
I member.of.working.party-OBL.PL work-LOC1
çaké-i *asúm*
put.to.work-PFV.PTCP be(ANIM)PRS.1SG
'I have put the cooperative working party to work.' (MNN in Bashir 2023b)

Causative/transitive derivations from basic intransitives pattern like *poč-* 'ripen', 'be cooked' (vi) and *pačé(y)-* 'cook' (vt); they are also formed from intransitive conjunct verbs, like *ṭhor b-* 'to fall' (vi) and *ṭhoré(y)-* 'cause to fall', 'push down (animate object)' (vt). These forms can have the sense of either transitives or causatives.

Some formally transitive/causative derivations form semantically intransitive verbs, notably onomatopoetic verbs for the characteristic

[16] *çiçhéik* lit. 'to teach' is the derived causative of *çiçhík* 'to learn'. The [ʋ] in the Imperative singular of derived causative verbs is a hiatus-filling consonant between the causative morpheme *-á-* and the *-e* of the singular Imperative form.

sounds produced by various animals, such as *brayeék* (vt) 'to bleat (sheep, goat)', *ḍoyeék* (vt) 'to moo', 'low (cow)', *mayeék* (vt) 'to mew', 'meow (kid, lamb, cat)'; or other onomatopoetic formations like *žiryeék* 'to cry loudly', 'shriek', 'scream' (vt) (← *žriy* 'a cry, shriek'), *froṣeék* 'to breathe noisily through the mouth or nostrils' (vt). The semantics of the transitive/causative morpheme in these forms seems to be 'MAKE(SOUND)'.

6.6 Verbs of 'being'

6.6.1 *as*- and *š*-, existential/locative 'be'

Both of these verbs assert existence, in a specific place or at a specific time, not identity. They do not refer to non-specific, generic, or habitual situations or events, which are expressed with a present/future non-specific form of *b*- 'become'.[17] The present tense of *as*- and *š*- appears in locative or existential sentences, or as the auxiliary in a present perfect form. These two verbs carry information on animacy, person, number, tense, and evidentiality. They are not marked for specificity in the present tense. Additionally, their past indirect forms are not identical to past participial forms, as they are for other verbs. Paradigms of the present direct of *as*- 'be (ANIMATE)' and *š*- 'be (INANIMATE)' appear in Tables 6.22 and 6.23, respectively.

Table 6.22 Present direct of *as*- 'be (ANIMATE)'

Person	Singular	Plural
1	*as-úm* 'I am'	*as-úsi* 'We are'
2	*as-ús* 'You are'	*as-úmi* 'You are'
3	*as-úr* 'S/he, it(ANIM) is'	*as-úni* 'They (ANIM) are'

Table 6.23 Present direct of *š*- 'be (INANIMATE)'

Person	Singular	Plural
1	–	–
2	–	–
3	*šer* 'It (INAN) is'	*šéni* 'They (INAN) are'

[17] Compare the use of the present imperfective of *ho*- 'become' in Urdu to express generic statements, like *seb mīṭhā hotā hæ* 'Apples are (generally) sweet', as opposed to *ye seb mīṭhā hæ* 'This apple is sweet', referring to a specific apple.

The use of animate and inanimate 'be' in the present direct tense is illustrated in (6.17) and (6.18), respectively. Indirect counterparts of these sentences are formed with the mirative of *b-* 'become' and the agent noun, as shown in (6.19) and (6.20).

(6.17) *ma braár dur-i as-úr*
My brother house-LOC2 be(ANIM)-PRS.3SG
'My brother is in the house (direct, first-hand knowledge).'

(6.18) *ma dur hayaá š-er*
my house here be(INAN)-PRS.3SG
'My house is here.' (direct, first-hand knowledge)

(6.19) *ma braár dur-i as-ák bir-áy*
My brother house-LOC2 be(ANIM)-AG become.MIR-3SG
'(I have just found out that) my brother is at home.'

(6.20) *salím-o dur hayaá š-ak bir-áy*
Salim-OBL house here be(INAN)-AG become.MIR-3SG
'(I have just learned that) Salim's house is here.'

The present tense of both *as-* and *š-* in both existential (6.21) and locative (6.22) meanings is negated with *níki* ~ *néki.* Mirative counterparts are formed with *no asǻk bir-* or *no šak bir-* (6.23).

(6.21) *dar-ó čóṫing níki*
wood-OBL small.piece is.not
'There isn't even a scrap of wood.' (ZHD in Bashir 2023b)

(6.22) *kulánu dúr-a níki*
husband/man home-LOC1 is.not
'(My) husband is not at home.' (IF in Bashir 2023b)

(6.23) *hay-ií no š-ak bir-áy*
here-LOC2 NEG be(INAN)-AG become.MIR-3SG
'It isn't (in) here (implied that speaker has looked for it and not found it).' (Chitral Town)

Past direct and past indirect forms of *as-* are given in Tables 6.24 and 6.25, respectively.

Table 6.24 Past direct of *as-* 'be (ANIMATE)'

Person	Singular	Plural
1	*asítam* ~ *ástam* 'I was'	*asítam* ~ *ástam* 'We were'
2	*asítau* ~ *ástau* 'You were'	*asítami* ~ *ástami* 'You were'
3	*asítai* ~ *ástai* 'S/he was'	*asítani* ~ *ástani* 'They were'

Table 6.25 Past indirect of *as-* 'be (ANIMATE)'

Person	Singular	Plural
1	*astétam* ~ *astátam* ~ *astá:m* 'I was' (unwittingly)	*astétam* ~ *astátam* ~ *astá:m* 'We were' (unwittingly)
2	*astá:u* 'You were' (unwitnessed by speaker)	*astétami* ~ *astátami* ~ *astá:mi* 'You were' (unwitnessed by speaker)
3	*astá:i* 'S/he, it was' (unwitnessed by speaker)	*astá:ni* 'They were' (unwitnessed by speaker)

Tables 6.24 and 6.25 show that the main difference between the past direct and past indirect forms of *as-* is stress placement.[18] The stress in the past direct of this verb is on the first syllable or the *i* of the past tense formant *-ist-*, while in the past indirect stress is on the final syllable, with some elongation of the vowel of that syllable. Use of the past direct and indirect forms of *as-* 'be(ANIM)' is illustrated in (6.24).

(6.24) *avá oré-i* *as-ít-am* *angáh*
I sleep-PFV.PTCP be(ANIM)-PST.D-1SG awake
hó-t-am *ki* *xur* *kos*
become-PST.D-1SG when other someone's
dúr-a *as-tét-am*[19]
house-LOC1 be(ANIM)-PST.I-1SG
'I had gone to sleep/was asleep. When I awoke (I realised that) I was at someone else's house.' (MNN)

Past direct forms of *š-* 'be' are shown in Table 6.26. The past direct of *š-* retains the OIA augment. However, the animacy distinction has become neutralised in its past direct tense, whether it is the main verb in a sentence or a tense-bearing auxiliary in complex tense-aspect forms

[18] The forms in Table 6.25 were supplied by Maula Nigah Nigah and have also been attested in the speech of other persons from Upper Chitral. It appears, however, that the evidentiality distinction in this verb may be weakening, and that perhaps not all speakers still use these forms in 2025.
[19] The translation of (6.24) suggests that perhaps the form *astétam* ~ *astátam* had/has mirative as well as indirect senses.

(Section 6.8.3). Hence, in Table 6.26 *š-* is not specified as INANIMATE and its use is not restricted to inanimate subjects, first- and second-person forms appearing in this table. In forms other than the past direct, however, it appears only with inanimates. In the speech of many people, and in rapid speech, the first and second-person forms are reduced, as shown in Table 6.26. In some people's speech, an older third-person singular form *oóštay* < *ošótay* is heard instead of *ošóy*.

Table 6.26 Past direct of *š-* 'be'

Person	Singular	Plural
1	*ošótam* ~ *óštam* 'I was'	*ošótam* ~ *óštam* 'We were'
2	*ošóu* 'You were'	*ošótami* ~ *óštami* 'You were'
3	*ošói* ~ *oóštai* 'S/he, it was'	*ošóni* 'They were'

Just as the formally past indirect of *b-* 'become' functions as a semantically present mirative for *as-*, the formally past indirect of *š-* 'be (INANIMATE)' supplies a semantically present mirative for *š-*. The forms *širáy* 'it is (and was)' and *širáni* 'they are (and were)' are formally past tense forms, but they convey present mirative meaning. These forms are shown in Table 6.27.

Table 6.27 Mirative of *š-* 'be (INANIMATE)'

Person	Singular	Plural
1	-	-
2	-	-
3	*širái* 'It is/there is' (and was, just realised now)	*širáni* 'They are/there are' (and were, just realised now)

The use of the mirative of *š-* is illustrated in (6.25). There is a subtle difference between this meaning and that of (6.26); in (6.25) the speaker has just discovered the book himself, while in (6.26) he may have discovered it himself or learned about its presence from some other source.

(6.25) *kitáb laybréri-a širáy*
book library-LOC1 be(INAN)-PST.I.3SG
'The book is (and was) in the library.' (I just found it there myself.) (RKB)

(6.26) *kitáb laybréri-a š-ak bir-áy*
book library-LOC1 be(INAN)-AG become.MIR-3SG
'(I have learned that) the book is in the library.' (I may have actually found it myself or been told about its presence by someone else.) (RKB)

Since the past direct tense of both *as-* and *š-* can be used with animate entities, the difference in sense between these two forms is important. In (6.27) *ošóy* forms a past tense counterpart for the present tense nominal sentence *hasé ma ʦeq žuúr* 'She is my younger daughter'. The past tense sentence implies that my daughter is no longer present in the discourse context or is no longer living. In (6.28), on the other hand, *asítay* is a past tense counterpart of the present tense locative predication *ma žuúr hayaá asúr* 'My daughter is here.'

(6.27) *hasé ma ʦeq žuúr o-š-óy*
she my younger daughter AUG-be-PST.D.3SG
'She was my younger daughter.' (MNN)

(6.28) *ma žuúr hayaá as-ít-ay*
I.OBL daughter here be(ANIM)-PST.D-3SG
'My daughter was here (but is now somewhere else).' (MNN)

6.6.2 *b-* 'become'

The verb *b-* 'become' is not specified for animacy; its semantic oppositions in the present/future tense are like those of other regular verbs, distinguishing between specific and non-specific, in contrast with those of *as-* and *š-*, which do not distinguish specific and non-specific. Present/future non-specific forms of *b-* 'become' provide present/future meanings for *as-* 'be(ANIM)' and *š-* 'be(INAN)', which do not have these forms. They are shown in Table 6.5.

Present/future non-specific forms of *b-* 'become' (Table 6.5) convey general, present tense statements about non-specific entities (6.29), permanent truths (6.30), gnomic statements (6.31), or future meanings (6.32).

(6.29) *čók-o rang zemín-o ráng-a*
small.owl-OBL colour earth-OBL colour-LOC1

b-oy
become-3SG.PRS/FUT.NS

'The colour of a small owl is like the colour of earth.' (MA in Bashir 2023b)

(6.30) *ç̣hoy-ó ǰú-o sóra božík-o troy b-oy*
six-OBL two-OBL with divide-OBL three become-3SG.PRS/FUT.NS
'Six divided by two is three.' (SWKA in Bashir 2023b)

(6.31) *šum ałók-o bi bo b-oy,*
bad pumpkin-OBL seed many become-3SG.PRS/FUT.NS
šum roy-ó lu bo b-oy
bad person-OBL words many become-3SG.PRS/FUT.NS
Proverb. 'A bad pumpkin has lots of seeds; a bad person talks too much.' (MAK in Bashir 2023b)

(6.32) *pisá ki ma halé-mi pisá-te hóst-a*
you(PL) if me let.stay-2PL.PRS/FUT.NS you.PL-DAT hand-LOC1
uγ dreé-m khanízek
water pour-1SG.PRS/FUT.NS serving.woman
b-om pisá-te
become-1SG.PRS/FUT.NS you.PL-DAT
'If you will let me stay, I will pour water on your hands (before eating); I will be your maidservant.' (oral tale, Village Chapali)

In sentences like (6.31), x is an indefinite NP, 'a bad pumpkin', 'a bad person'. This is a very frequent usage; it contrasts with equational sentences with the meaning x = y, where x denotes a definite or specific entity, and which are expressed as nominal sentences with no copula, for example (6.33). For further discussion of nominal sentences, see Section 9.2.1.

(6.33) *díšul kor-ík šum adát*
verbal.abuse do-1NF bad habit
'Verbally abusing is a bad habit.' (DSAL)

As with other verbs, present/future specific forms of *b-* 'become' suffix *-an* to the non-specific forms.[20] They express actions either in progress at the time of speech (6.34) or known to be occurring in the immediate future.

[20] This is structurally parallel to the same process in Kalasha, where *-dai* is the marker of the present/future specific form (Bashir 1988a: 42). As in *parím* 'I go/will go' versus *parĭm-dai* 'I am going' (Bashir 1988a: 60).

(6.34) *hayá dar phat no b-oy-án bohrt-ó*
this wood split NEG become-3SG.PRS/FUT-S rock-OBL
žav díya
son EMPH
'This wood isn't splitting—it's hard as a rock.' (SWKA in Bashir 2023b)

Past direct, past indirect, and mirative forms of *b-* 'become' are given in Tables 6.28, 6.29, and 6.30, respectively.[21]

Table 6.28 Past direct of *b-* 'become'

Person	Singular	Plural
1	*hótam* 'I became'	*hótam* 'We became'
2	*hou* 'You became'	*hótami* 'You became'
3	*hoi* 'S/he, it became'	*hóni* 'They became'

Table 6.29 Past indirect of *b-* 'become'

Person	Singular	Plural
1	*birétam* ~ *birátam* 'I became, am' (unwittingly)	*birétam* ~ *birátam* 'We became, are' (unwittingly)
2	*birú* 'You became'	*birú* 'You became'
3	*birú* 'S/he, it became'	*birú* 'They became'

Table 6.30 Mirative of *b-* 'become'

Person	Singular	Plural
1	*birétam* ~ *birátam* 'I became, am' (unwittingly)	*birétam* ~ *birátam* 'We became, are' (unwittingly)
2	*biráu* (< *birétau*) 'You became, are' (just learned)	*birétami* ~ *birátami* ~ *birámi* 'You became, are' (just learned)
3	*birái* 'S/he, it became, is' (just learned)	*biráni* 'They became, are' (just learned)

The mirative forms of *b-* 'become' (Table 6.30) supply mirative counterparts for direct nominal predications; compare (6.35) direct and (6.36) mirative; (6.37) direct and (6.38) mirative; and the locative/existential sentences (6.39) direct and (6.40) mirative. The mirative sentences in (6.36), (6.38), and (6.40) could be either direct (first-person observations by the speaker), or indirect (information told by someone else).

[21] Grierson (1919) and Morgenstierne (1947) show the older first singular *hostam* and third singular *hor* forms.

(6.35) *hasé naháng-o dur*
REM.SG dragon-OBL house
'It is a/the dragon's house.' (established knowledge)

(6.36) *hasé naháng-o dur bir-áy*
REM.SG dragon-OBL house become.MIR-3SG
'It is a/the dragon's house.' (new knowledge) (Endresen & Kristiansen 1981: 223)

(6.37) *hasé khovár kor-ák*
REM.SG Khowar do-AG
'S/he is a Khowar speaker'. (established knowledge)

(6.38) *hasé khovár kor-ák bir-áy*
REM.SG Khowar do-AG become.MIR-3SG
'(Apparently/I have just learned that) s/he speaks Khowar.'

(6.39) *ma braár skúl-i as-úr*
my brother school-LOC2 be(ANIM)-PRS.3SG
'My brother is in school.' (established, first-hand knowledge)

(6.40) *ma braár skúl-i as-ák bir-áy*
My brother school-LOC2 be(ANIM)-AG become.MIR-3SG
'(I have just learned that) My brother is in school.'

6.7 Non-finite verbal forms

Non-finite forms are not specified for person or number. Khowar has the following adverbial, adjectival, and nominal forms.

6.7.1 Perfective participle

The regularly formed perfective participle (PFV.PTCP) consists of root + *-i*, as with *kor-í* ~ *kór-i* 'having done', *su-í* ~ *sú-i* 'having stitched'. A few very common verbs with consonant-final roots form this participle with *-iti*; these include: *b-* 'become', *bíti* ~ *bití* 'having become'; *g-* 'come', *gíti* ~ *gití* 'having come'; *ang-* 'being' *angíti* ~ *angití* 'having brought'; and *d-* 'give', 'strike', *díti* ~ *dití* 'having given', 'having struck'. A few form the perfective participle with *-ti*, including *žib-* 'eat', *žutí* ~ *žútí* 'having eaten'; *al-* 'take away', *altí* ~ *álti* 'having taken away'; *br-* 'die', *birtí* ~ *bihtí* 'having died'.[22] The perfective participles of a few verbs, for example, *re-* 'read', 'recite', 'say'; *reé* or *raá* 'having read/said', are irregular. The two existential verbs *as-* and *š-* 'be' do not have perfective participles.

Stress placement on the perfective participle varies; it is sometimes on the stem vowel, as *bíti*, and sometimes on the suffix *-i*, as *bití*. When the participial phrase denotes an adverbial, like *kíča bíti* 'how?', *kíča kóri* 'how?', or *phik bíti* 'quietly'; or an adjectival modification, as *ç̣hutk kor-i* 'fallow' in example (6.135) below, stress is on the stem vowel; but when the participle is an auxiliary in a perfective verb form reporting the completion of an action, especially when that result is anticipated, the stress is on the participial suffix, the final *-í*, as in (6.41). Also compare the examples in Section 6.8.3.

(6.41) *alú mu‡ kor-í š-éni*
potato root do-PFV.PTCP be(INAN)-PRS.3PL
'The potatoes have formed tubers (and are ready to be harvested).' (MNN in Bashir 2023b)

The perfective participle functions in several ways. Together with finite auxiliary elements, it is the base of four perfect tenses—present perfect direct, *korí asúr* 'S/he has done'; perfect mirative, *korí asák biráy* '(I have learned that) s/he has done', past perfect direct, *korí asítai* > *koríastai* 'S/he had done/did', and past perfect indirect, *korí astá:i* 'S/he had done/did' (unwitnessed by speaker). When the past direct of *as-* appears as an auxiliary in the past perfect direct, it is usually pronounced with close juncture with the perfective participle, as *koríastam* 'I did/had done', and people with whom I have discussed this feel that the participle plus auxiliary are perceived as a single word. However, in this book they are written separately for the sake of analytical clarity for linguists and non-Khowar-speaking readers.

In construction with finite forms of the vectors *b-* 'go'; *laák-* 'leave', 'release', and sometimes *niš-* 'sit', the perfective participle forms a compound verb in the usual South Asian sense;[23] for example, *tu puluí bis* (you burn.PFV.PTCP go.2SG.PRS/FUT.NS) 'You will get burned

[22] This form (Morgenstierne's 'absolutive') goes back to *-(i)ya*, Prakrit *-ia*, and to Vedic *-tvaya*. (Morgenstierne 1947: 27). See Morgenstierne (1947 passim) for further historical discussion.

[23] The commonly accepted understanding of compound verb in South Asianist linguistics is a V1 V2 sequence in which V1, in a non-finite form, is the 'main verb' and a finite form of V2 is a 'vector verb'. Verbs which function as vector verbs come from a limited set, including verbs which have a motion component in their meaning; 'go', 'come', 'give', 'take' are the most frequently appearing. Compound verbs convey a single action or event with various semantic nuances, not a sequence of two actions.

(be careful!)' (see Section 6.9.2). It functions to link two or more clauses (6.42)[24] or to express various adverbial meanings (6.43). The use of the perfective participle in clause chaining is discussed in more detail in Section 10.10.1.2. With the transitive verb *khuleé-* 'finish off' it forms a complement (see Section 10.9.5).

Some frequently occurring polymorphemic perfective participial expressions have become lexicalised and function as simple adverbs. With intransitives, noun, adjective, or adverb + *bíti*, the perfective participle of *b-* 'become', yields an adverb, as in *i.bíti* 'together' (lit. 'having become one'), *phik.bíti* 'quietly', and *kíča.bíti* 'how?'. With transitive concepts, noun, adjective, or adverb plus the perfective participle of *kor-* 'do' yield adverbs like *kíča.kóri* 'how?', *zor.kóri* 'insistently', 'forcefully', *ḍang.kóri* 'tightly' (6.43).

(6.42) *hes* *ma poš-í* *avǰí* *b-ití*
DIST.SG.DIR me meet-PFV.PTCP persuaded become-PFV.PTCP
as-úr
be(ANIM)-PRS.3SG
'Having met me, s/he has been persuaded.' (MNN in Bashir 2023b)

(6.43) *małáγ-o* *ḍang.kór-i* *bot-é*
bundle-OBL tight do-PFV.PTCP tie-IMP.SG
'Tie the bundle tightly.' (RKB in Bashir 2023b)

6.7.2 Imperfective participle

The regularly formed imperfective participle (IPFV.PTCP) consists of root + *-áv*, as *kor-áv* 'doing'.[25] Some verbs have irregular imperfective participles, for example *b-* 'go', of which the imperfective participle *boγ-áv* 'going', is built on the second past stem *boγ-*. The imperfective participle occurs in the following constructions. It is the base of imperfective tenses: past imperfective direct, *koráv ošótam* (~ *korávoštam*) 'I was doing'; past imperfective indirect *koráv astá:m* ~ *astétam* 'I was doing (reportedly; unintentionally)'; past habitual direct *korávtam* 'I used to do'; and a past habitual indirect, which has only 3SG and 3PL forms

[24] 'Conjunctive participle' is the term used for this form in this function in much contemporary descriptive or comparative literature on South Asian languages. Recently the term 'converb' has come into use. In this book, however, I refer to this form as the 'perfective participle'.
[25] Some writers on Khowar refer to this form as a 'present participle'.

(*koráu-r*) 's/he used to do (reportedly)' and *koráu-ni* 'they used to do (reportedly)'.

When not participating in a finite verb form, the imperfective participle is adverbial; some examples of its use are shown in (6.44), (6.45), (6.46), and (6.47). It also appears in purpose clauses (see Section 9.5.2.4).

(6.44) *γerd-í áči gy-av ma*
turn-PFV.PTCP back come-IPVF.PTCP me
bezár a-r-ér
annoyed AUG-do.PST.D-3SG
'Turning and coming back repeatedly, s/he has annoyed me.' (DSAL)

(6.45) *pon pón-a niš-áv baγ-át-am*
road road-LOC1 sit-IPFV.PTCP go-PST.D-1SG
'I went along sitting (resting) at many places on the road.' (DSAL)

(6.46) *roy ḍal b-av g-óni-an*
people group become-IPFV.PTCP come-3PL.PRS/FUT-S
'People are coming in groups.' (DSAL)

(6.47) *ḍaq̣ keł-áv b-aγ-áy*
boy weep-IPFV.PTCP go-PST.D-3SG
'The boy went away weeping.'

The imperfective participle, like the past participle, displays the nominal property of taking a case ending. With *-a* (LOC1) it forms a temporal adverbial expression, as in (6.48). In (6.49) and (6.50), the imperfective participle has a stative sense, and when followed by *-a* (LOC1) yields an adjectival sense, attributive as in (6.49), and predicative in (6.50).

(6.48) [*bathán-o petsh-áv-a*] *pays-án*
country-OBL leave-IPFV.PTCP-LOC1 money-OBL.PL
bož-ít-ani
divide-PST.D-3PL
'[As they were leaving their country] they divided the money.' (SWKA in Bashir 2023b)

(6.49) *hayá* [*lav* *kor-áv-a*] *kan*
this fruit make-IPFV.PTCP-LOC1 tree
'This is a tree [in its fruit-bearing stage].' (MNN)

(6.50) *hayá ḍaq* [*bord-áv-a*] *as-úr*
This boy grow-IPFV.PTCP-LOC1 be(ANIM)-PRS.3SG
'This boy is [in his growing stage].' (MNN)

6.7.3 Past participle

The past participle (PST.PTCP), resultative participle (RES.PTCP), and potential participle (POT.PTCP), along with some uses of the present perfect, yield patient-oriented constructions.

The past participle is constructed on the second past stem. The regular second past stem of verbs with infinitives in *-ík* is identical to the root. These verbs have past participles in *-íru*, for example *gan-íru* 'taken' (← *gan-* 'take'). For verbs with infinitives in *-é(i)k*, it is root + *-é*, for example *bardé(iru)-* 'nurtured', 'brought up' (← *bardé-* 'nurture'), 'bring up'. A few verbs, for instance 'do', 'die', 'eat', and 'break (vi)', have irregular second past stems ending in *-r*. These have past participles in *-du*: *kardú* 'did', 'done' (← *kor-* 'do'); *rardú* 'said' (← *re-* 'say'); *lardú* 'found' (← *le-* 'find'); and *žúrdu* 'ate', 'eaten' (← *žib-* 'eat'). The second past stem of *b-* 'go', *boɣ-*, is quite irregular, giving the past participle *boɣdú* 'went', 'gone'.

The past participle expresses anterior and/or resultative meanings. It can function as verb, adjective, or noun. As a verb, it is a past indirect. As an adjective, it is 'patient-oriented', referring to the subject of an intransitive verb (6.51), or the patient of a transitive verb (6.52).[26] When the past participle of a transitive verb forms part of a complex verb form like the past indirect mirative, its subject can be an agent, like the fly in (6.53), or a patient, like the bricks in (6.54). The PST.PTCP of an intransitive in a complex verb form refers to the subject, like the calf in (6.55). Past participles also form semi-lexicalised participial relative clauses (6.56). They sometimes are fully lexicalised as nouns; for example, *peṣíru* 'flour' (← 'ground') is the lexicalised past participle of *peṣ-* 'grind'.

(6.51) *hasé* *kos-íru* *moóš*
REM.SG walk-PST.PTCP man
'He is a well-travelled person.' (IF in Bashir 2023b)

[26] ul-Mulk (1966: 24) calls this the 'patient noun'.

(6.52) *ves-íru sayúrǰ-o sar dos-íru kiṣípi ǰam*
await-PST.PTCP falcon-OBL than catch-PST.PTCP magpie good
Proverb. 'A caught magpie is better than an awaited falcon.' (TMF, MNN) (Compare the English proverb 'A bird in the hand is worth two in the bush.')

(6.53) *magás pušúr-a bis dré-ru bir-áy*
fly meat-LOC1 eggs put-PST.PTCP become.MIR-3SG
'Flies have laid eggs on the meat.' (just observed now) (DSAL)

(6.54) *havl ǰu ušṭú lakh-íru bir-áy*
only two brick place-PST.PTCP become.MIR-3SG
'Only two bricks have been laid.' (just observed now) (RAKR in Bashir 2023b)

(6.55) *baċhół pułyoč̌h-íru bir-áy*
calf become.entangled-PST.PTCP become.MIR-3SG
'The calf has got entangled (in ropes).' (resultant state just observed) (DSAL)

(6.56) *avá tan [kȧr-a-tor-íru] lú-o ta-te*
I REFL ear-LOC1-reach-PST.PTCP word-OBL you-DAT
d-óm-an
give-1SG.PRS/FUT-S
'I am telling you something [that I have heard].' (hearsay) (MNN in Bashir 2023b)

Some verbs have past participial formations both in *-du* and in *-íru* or *-éru*, for example *réik* 'to speak', with both *réru* (rare) (perhaps < *raíru*) and *rárdu*; *puluík* 'to burn (vi)'; *puluídu* and *pulíru*; *poŕík* 'to lie down', which has the forms *poríru* and *pardú* (6.48); and *koŕík* 'to do', with *kárdu* and *koríru* (rare). Other (dialectal/idiolectal) variation can arise from alternation of stem /u/ and /i/, for example *žurdú* and *žirdú*. The form *pardú* appears to refer to the theme/location of the action of lying down (6.57).[27]

[27] However, differences between the meanings of the *-du* and *-iru* or *-eru* forms remain to be explored.

(6.57) *xur-ó pardú žén-a avá no*
other-OBL lie.down.PST.PTCP charpai-LOC1 I NEG
par-ím
lie.down-1SG.PRS/FUT.NS
'I won't sleep on a charpai[28] where somebody else has slept.' (MNN)

As a verb, the past participle focuses on the resultant state of some event or action which occurred in the absence of the speaker/observer. The following forms are based on it: (i) past indirect (PST.I), as in *tat boγdú* '(someone's) father left/is gone' (event not witnessed by speaker); (ii) past indirect mirative, as in *tat boγdú biráγ* '(someone's) father has left (just learned now)', *kardú birétam* 'I did/have done (just learned, reportedly, unintentionally)', (iii) past incompletive (PST.INC), as in *kardú ošótam* 'I would have done/was about to do (but didn't)'.

It functions as an adjective, either attributive, *hayá čhirdú išnári* 'This is a broken thing', or predicative, as in *bápo pirán utruçíru* 'The old man's shirt is torn'. It frequently forms participial relative clauses, like *hayá [hanise ažíru] haté žav* 'This is the son [that was born now]'. It also functions as a noun, for example *birdú* 'dead person', and *peṣíru* 'flour' (lit. 'ground grain'). Its nominal nature allows it to take case markers: oblique, as in the postpositional phrase in (6.58); LOC1 to form an irrealis construction (6.59); and ablative *-ar* (6.60). Examples (6.58) and (6.61) illustrate the fluid nature of this form. In the idiomatic expression in (6.58), it is in the past indirect verbal form and states that an agent did something unobserved, while in (6.61) it functions as a noun referring to a patient (the deed(s) done).

(6.58) *kaá/*kos kyaáγ kardú-o γon*
someone.DIR/*someone's.OBL something do.PST.PTCP-OBL like
'as though someone has done something (unseen by speaker) to someone' (MNN)

(6.59) *ma γoš birú-a avá boγ-es-ám vá*
my free.time be.PST.PTCP-LOC1 I go-SBJV-1SG EMPH
'If I had had time, I definitely would have gone.' (MNN in Bashir 2023b)

[28] A charpai is a bed consisting of a wooden frame which is filled in by woven rope or string of some sort. I retain this word because no English gloss, for example 'cot', captures the specific meaning of charpai.

(6.60) *tayár kar-dú-ar póya*
ready do-PST.PTCP-ABL after
'after preparing it' (MA in Bashir 2023b)

(6.61) **avá/ma kardú šum no b-óy*
*I/my do.PST.PTCP bad not become-3SG.PRS/FUT.NS
'[That which I have done] will not be bad.' (MNN)

6.7.4 Resultative participle

The resultative participle (RES.PTCP) is another patient-oriented form. It consists of the (sometimes altered /o/ > /a/) verb root + *-ónu*, for example, *korónu* 'done' (root *kor-*), or *çakónu* 'attached' (root *çok-*). A resultative patient-oriented sentence involves the resultative participle and a finite form of 'be' or 'become'. Subjects of resultative participial sentences, which are semantic patients, appear in either the direct (6.62) or oblique case (6.63). As with direct objects, oblique case appears with specific or definite entities, which may be either inanimate (6.62) (6.63) (6.64) or animate (6.65). In (6.64) we see both a lexicalised resultative participle, 'song', and a syntactic resultative construction, 'was sung'. Although most resultative constructions occur with transitive verbs, they can also be used with intransitives, for example from *br-* 'die' in (6.66) and *ǰoṣ-* 'consider' in (6.67). For this reason, and since other usages, such as *našónu* 'worsened', 'deteriorated in condition (of a healing wound)', seen in (6.68), suggest a resultative meaning with a wider sense than the traditional transformational understanding of 'passive' which involves an agent in the conceptualisation, I call this form a 'resultative participle' rather than a 'passive participle', which some of the glosses might suggest.

(6.62) *noγór petsh-ónu b-íti š-éni*
fort abandon-RES.PTCP become-PFV.PTCP be(INAN)-PRS.3PL
'The forts have been abandoned.' (DSAL)

(6.63) *boxt-ó haya-á lakh-ónu b-íti*
stone-OBL this-LOC1 put-RES.PTCP become-PFV.PTCP
š-er
be(INAN)-PRS.3SG
'The stone has been placed here.' (MNN)

(6.64) *bašónu baš-e-ónu ho-y*
song sound-CAUS-RES.PTCP become.PST.D-3SG
'The song was sung.' (SWKA in Bashir 2023b)

(6.65) *ma žav bapdúr-i sat-ónu*
my son grandfather's house-LOC2 nurture-RES.PTCP
b-íti as-úr
become-PFV.PTCP be(ANIM)-PRS.3SG
'My son has been brought up in his maternal grandfather's house.' (MS in Bashir 2023b)

(6.66) *ma bap unnís so unnís-o žáng-a bri-ónu*
my grandfather 19 hundred 19-OBL war-LOC1 die-RES.PTCP
h-oy
become.PST.D-3SG
'My grandfather died in the 1919 war.' (MS in Bashir 2023b)

(6.67) *adráx-o mroy-án pari-án-an pay*
mountain.slope-OBL ibex.DIR.PL fairy.PL-OBL.PL goat
ǰoṣ-ónu b-oy
consider-RES.PTCP become-3SG.PRS/FUT.NS
'Mountain ibexes are considered to be goats belonging to the fairies.' (RAKR)

The resultative participle is also used substantively, as 'burn' in (6.68) and in (6.69), where *apáki.dyónu*, 'morsel' (lit. '(to be) put in the mouth'), referring to the hero about to be eaten by a demon, is the subject of the clause. Some originally resultative formations have become lexicalised as nouns or adjectives; for example *bašónu* 'song' ← *bošík* 'to sound' (6.70); adjectival phrases like *hardiçakónu* 'attractive' (lit. 'heart adhered') ← *hardí* + *çakónu* (resultative participle of *çok-* 'adhere to'), *amištónu* 'a cheese-based dish', and *kramónu* 'a specific number of sheaves put on the threshing floor at a single time for threshing by animals'.

(6.68) *akbár-o žav-ó pulu-idú naš-ónu*
Akbar-OBL son-OBL burn-PST.PTCP deteriorate-RES.PTCP
h-oy
become.PST.D-3SG
'Akbar's son's burn became worse (after starting to heal).' (MS in Bashir 2023b)

(6.69) *máte kur-ár es rétay.ki haníse apák-i*
me-DAT where-ABL this, say.PST.D.3SG now mouth-LOC2
dy-ónu g-ití as-úr - losnúku
put-RES.PTCP come-PFV.PTCP be(ANIM)-PRS.3SG - morsel
'He said, now where has this [thing-to-be-put-in-the-mouth] come from—this morsel?' (oral text, Village Sorech)

(6.70) *paránu bašónu roxts-ónu b-íti*
old song forget-RES.PTCP become-PFV.PTCP
š-éni
be(INAN)-PRS.3PL
'The old songs have been forgotten.' (DSAL)

6.7.5 Potential participle

A form consisting of root + *-ín* yields a potential participle (POT.PTCP). In construction with *b-* 'be able' it conveys potentiality, as seen in examples (6.71), (6.72), (6.73), (6.74), (6.75), (6.76), and (6.77). As with the resultative participle (6.63), a subject can be oblique marked, as is 'stone' in (6.71). This form appears with both transitives (6.71) (6.72) (6.73) and intransitives, like 'walk' in (6.74), 'be' in (6.75), 'stop moving' in (6.76), and 'become' in (6.77).

(6.71) *boxt-ó hayaá lakh-ín b-óy-an*
stone-OBL here put-POT.PTCP be.able-3SG-PRS/FUT-S
'The stone can be placed here.' (MNN)

(6.72) *kíča kor-ín b-oy*
how do-POT.PTCP be.able-3SG.PRS/FUT.NS
'What can be done?' (Chitral Town)

(6.73) *huṣ kor-ín no b-av*
recognition do-POT.PTCP NEG be.able-IPFV.PTCP
o-š-óy
AUG-be-PST.D.3SG
'(S/he) couldn't be recognised.' (Ishkoman)

(6.74) *baréki pon-én čhuy-ó kos-ín no*
narrow path-LOC.PL night-OBL walk-POT.PTCP not
b-oy
be.able-3SG.PRS/FUT.NS
'One can't walk on narrow paths at night.' (DSAL)

(6.75) *ki no h-oy di as-ín*
if NEG become.PST.D-3SG even be(ANIM)-POT.PTCP
b-oy
be.able-3SG.PRS/FUT.NS
'Even if it doesn't happen, one can go on living.' (RKB)

(6.76) *hér-a bi thi-ín*
DIST-LOC1 go.PFV.PTCP stop.moving-POT.PTCP
b-oy
be.able-3SG.PRS/FUT.NS
'It will go there and stop moving.' (a stone rolling downhill) (MNN in Bashir 2023b)

(6.77) *kya korm-ó ki tałxí-a kor-ín*
REL work-OBL that enthusiasm-OBL1 do-POT.PTCP
hoy kamyáb b-in
become.PST.D.3SG successful become-POT.PTCP
b-oy
be.able-3SG.PRS/FUT.NS
'Work which is done with enthusiasm and concentration can be successful.' (SWKA in Bashir 2023b)

6.7.6 Necessitative constructions[29]

6.7.6.1 -élik

One necessitative form (NEC) consists of root + *-élik*, ~ *-éli* in Lower Chitral.[30] It conveys a sense of necessity arising from within or affecting the agent. Often it conveys a sense of moral (deontic) necessity as well. Examples (6.78) and (6.79) illustrate its use.

[29] These two particles have close parallels in Kalasha (Bashir 1988a: 91–9).
[30] Bashir (1988a: 403–4) discusses the likely Turkic origin of *-élik*.

(6.78) *uzui-dú-o-te* *angár kor-élik*
freeze-PST.PTCP-OBL-DAT fire make-NEC
'We should make a fire for the (nearly) frozen person.' (MNN in Bashir 2023b)

(6.79) *ham-ó* *sum muhabát kor-í* *ham-ó*
PROX.SG.OBL with love do-PFV.PTCP PROX.SG-OBL
behí-o *áča* *ç̣ok-élik*
welfare-OBL behind attach-NEC
'We must cherish it and pursue its welfare.' (MYS in Bashir 2023b)

It can also be used adjectivally (6.80) (6.81) and nominally (6.82) in the sense of some person or animal in a specific condition.

(6.80) *hayá* *roči.drélik* *moóš*
PROX.SG.DIR fast.keeping man
'He is a man keeping fasts.' (IF in Bashir 2023b)

(6.81) *hes* *aželi.korélik bití* *as-úr*
DIST.SG.DIR pregnant become-PFV.PTCP be(ANIM)-PRS.3SG
'She has become/is pregnant.' (MNN in Bashir 2023b)

(6.82) *darélik-an-te* *baṣ* *det*
animal.being fattened-OBL.PL-DAT feed give.IMP.2SG
'Give good feed to the animals being fattened for slaughter.' (SWKA in Bashir 2023b)

6.7.6.2 *baṣ*

A second necessitative construction (NEC2) consists of the oblique infinitive + *baṣ*. The word *baṣ* has a range of meanings: it is a noun meaning 'share' or 'food', as in (6.82) above, and the modal particle discussed in this section.[31] It usually expresses necessity arising from outside the agent/speaker—from the nature of the situation, the potential action, or its objects. Examples (6.83) and (6.84) illustrate its use in a predicate, and (6.85) shows it used as an attributive adjective in a functional relative clause equivalent.

[31] The multiple meanings of *baṣ* in Kalasha are discussed in Bashir (1988a: 94–5).

(6.83) *ḍóngu mevá no žib-ík-o baṣ*
unripe fruit NEG eat-INF-OBL NEC2
'Unripe fruit should not be eaten.' (MNN in Bashir 2023b)

(6.84) *ma theštú xaṣké-ik-o baṣ*
my onions hoe-INF-OBL NEC2
'My onions need to be hoed.' (SWKA in Bashir 2023b)

(6.85) *hayá [no kor-ík-o baṣ] kórum*
PROX.SG.DIR NEG do-INF-OBL NEC2 action
'This is something [which should not be done].' (IF)

6.7.7 Deverbal nominals

6.7.7.1 Infinitive

The infinitive (INF) is a verbal noun formed from the root + *-ík* for intransitives, as *poník* 'to lie down' and basic (underived) transitives like *kor-ík* 'to do'. Derived transitive/causatives consist of the root + the causative morpheme *-á-* + infinitive ending *-ik*, as with **kor-á-ik > kor-é-(i) k > koré(y)k ~ korék* 'to have done (by someone)' or *poré(y)k* 'to lay down/cause to lie down (an animate entity)'. Since the stress in these derived transitives/causatives is on the causative morpheme, the /i/ of the infinitive ending loses its stress, weakening to a consonantal /y/ or being entirely elided. Some writers use roman spellings of these derived transitives/causative infinitives with a /y/ representing a trace of the now unstressed /i/ of the infinitive ending in *-éik*, thus *koré(y)k*; others retain the unstressed /i/, writing *-éik*; still others write simply *-ék*.

As a noun, the infinitive can take some of the singular case endings of other inanimates: OBL *-o*, LOC1 *-a*, ABL *-ar*, and INS *-en*; but not LOC2 *-i*, LOC3 *-tu*, LOC4 *-o*, or plural case endings. The oblique is the most frequently occurring case ending with the infinitive.

The direct case infinitive can function as the subject of a sentence (6.86) (6.87) or as a direct object (6.88).

(6.86) *lav-éri kan bo-ík svab dí*
fruit-bearing tree plant-INF meritorious.act indeed
'To plant a fruit tree is indeed an act of (religious) merit.' (MNN)

(6.87) *af kiméri d-ik band h-oy*
down.country woman give-INF stopped become.PST.D-3SG
'Giving women downcountry (in marriage) has stopped.' (TMF)

(6.88) *avá behč-é-ik maṣk-ím-an*
I remain-CAUS-1NF want-1SG.PRS/FUT-S
'I want to help (it/them) remain (alive).' (RAKR in Bashir 2023b)

The oblique marked infinitive appears with specific infinitival direct objects (6.89). The context in example (6.89) is that a very specific message was to be conveyed but was forgotten.

(6.89) *hasé hatoó-t lu d-ík-o roxts-ít-ay*
REM.SG.DIR REM.OBL-DAT word give-INF-OBL forget-PST.D-3SG
'He forgot to tell her.' (oral text, Village Chapali)

One of most frequent uses of the oblique infinitive is to indicate a change of subject in a clause chain, as in (6.90), where the subject of the first clause is *tat* 'father' and that of the second clause is *hasé* 'he'.

(6.90) *hatoγó tat g-ík-o hasé*
REM.SG.OBL father come-INF-OBL REM.SG.DIR
gónǰ-i khóšt hoy
storeroom-LOC2 hidden become.PST.D.3SG
'When his$_j$ father$_i$ arrived, he$_j$ hid in the storeroom.' (SWKA)

The oblique infinitive occurs with postpositions, for instance *báče* ~ *báčen* 'for' (6.91), dative *-t(e)(n)(e)* (6.92), *sum* ~ *su* 'with' (6.93).

(6.91) *host-án nig-ík-o báče peç uγ-ó sum*
hand-OBL.PL wash-INF-OBL for hot water-OBL with
uṣák uγ binǰ-á-ve
cold water mix-CAUS-IMP.SG
'For washing (your) hands, mix cold water with hot water.' (RAKR in Bashir 2023b)

(6.92) *trupoóγ bukh-ó çhom-ík-o-t ǰam*
salty.water throat-OBL pain-INF-OBL-DAT good
'Salty water is good for a sore throat.' (SWKA in Bashir 2023b)

(6.93) *tat br-ik-o sum ži-žáv nur-ít-ani*
father die-INF-OBL with REDUP.PL-son separate-PST.D-3PL
'When their father died, the sons separated.' (SWKA in Bashir 2023b)

It participates in several complement structures, some of which are: expression of ability (6.94) and (6.95); expression of propriety, suitability, necessity, or obligation (6.96); and the complement of 'allow' (6.97).

(6.94) *avá garmí-a tab.ang-ík-o no bé-t-am*
I heat-LOC1 tolerate-INF-OBL NEG be.able-PST.D-1SG
'I couldn't tolerate the heat.' (GMKH)

(6.95) *hes hayá korm-ó korík-o*
DIST.SG.DIR PROX.SG work-OBL do.INF-OBL
b-oy
be.able-3SG.PRS/FUT.NS
'S/he will be able to do this work.' (EB field notes)

(6.96) *ma pešáur-o-t b-ík-o baṣ*
1SG-OBL Peshawar-OBL-DAT go-INF-OBL NEC2
'I have to go to Peshawar.' (EB field notes)

(6.97) *nathán b-ík-o ka laák-oy-an*
disobedient be-INF-OBL who allow-3SG.PRS/FUT-S
'Who will let (anyone) be disobedient.' (rhetorical question with negative implication; that is, no one will let anyone be disobedient) (MNN)

The oblique infinitive of *b-* 'become', *bíko*, frequently serves as a quasi-lexicalised conjunction, 'and then', 'so', 'in that case' (6.98).

(6.98) *bíko avá kyaní ko-m*
so I what do-1SG.PRS/FUT.HORT
'So what should I do?' (MNN)

Examples of the infinitive with other case endings are given below: LOC1 (6.99), ABL (6.100), and INS (6.101).

(6.99) *host pong çok-ík-a pat*
hand foot attach-INF-LOC1 until
lit. 'until one's hands and feet catch on' Sense: 'until one is able to work and earn' (MYS in Bashir 2023b)

(6.100) *br-ík-ar kyáwat.di xalás b-in no*
die-INF-ABL ever free become-POT.PTCP NEG
b-óy
be.able-3SG.PRS/FUT.NS
'One can never escape death.' (MAK in Bashir 2023b)

(6.101) *hayá žuṫí xál-a ǰam mágam ċokónu b-ík-en*
PROX.SG apricot taste-LOC1 good but clinging be-INF-INS
d-íti žib-ík-o-t ǰam noh
give-PVF.PTCP eat-INF-OBL-DAT good not
'This (variety of) apricot tastes good, but because its flesh sticks to the seed it isn't good for eating.' (MS in Bashir 2023b)

6.7.7.2 Agent Noun

An important deverbal nominal is the agent noun (AG) consisting of root + *-ák*, for example *korák* 'a doer', 'one/something who/which is able to do'. The agent noun functions as an ordinary noun, as in (6.102), where it appears with the oblique plural case ending, and (6.103); or an adjective (6.104) (6.105) (6.106). It participates in a series of tense-aspect forms which, in addition to their tense-aspect meanings, carry the meaning of 'a V-er', 'one who is able to V'. Some of its uses can be analysed as functional relative clauses, as in (6.106).

(6.102) *avá ta čang-ím čhuí rošt-ó*
I you.OBL lie-1SG.PRS/FUT.NS night day-OBL
čang-ír kaá.ki čang-ít-ay
lie-3SG.PRS/FUT.NS whoever lie-PST.D-3SG
čang-ák-an gerdán-a
lie-AG-OBL.PL neck-LOC1
'I lie to you, the night lies to the day, whoever lies, it is on the neck of the liars.' (the liar is responsible) (formulaic opening of traditional tales)

(6.103) *tu hamó žan-ák b-os*
you PROX.OBL know-AG become-2SG.PRS/FUT.NS
'You will become acquainted with him/her/this.' (MNN)

Agent nouns usually refer to animate agents, as in (6.102) and (6.103), but not necessarily, for example, if the agency of natural forces or characteristic properties of an object is involved (6.104) (6.105) (6.106). However, they cannot refer to an object requiring a human agent for its use (6.107); nouns denoting such objects require the instrumental noun/adjective in *-íni*, as in (6.108).

(6.104) *buní bo boṣ-ák žayá*
booni very rain-AG place
'Booni is a very rainy place.' (Booni)

(6.105) *phéting him kor-ák mas*
Pheting snow do-AG month
'Pheting is a snowy month.' (Booni)

(6.106) [*namí ǰazáb kor-ák*] *išnári*
moisture absorbed do-AG thing
'A thing [which absorbs moisture]' (AKM)

(6.107) **zap nig-ák mašín*
clothes wash-AG machine
* 'clothes washing machine'

(6.108) *zap nig-íni mašín*
clothes wash-INS machine
'clothes washing machine'

6.7.7.3 Causative/desiderative nominal

A deverbal nominal which has causative (CAUS) and desiderative (DES) meanings (CAUS.DES) consists of root + *-áru*, for example *piyáru* 'thirst', 'desire to drink'. This form appears with the oblique case of the experiencer. For example, *ma uy piyáru góyan* 'I am thirsty' (lit. 'my desire/need to drink water is coming'). Sometimes the meaning is more causative than desiderative, as in *ma oráru góyan* 'I feel sleepy.' (lit. 'to me sleepiness is coming'). This form originates in a causative formation (Bashir 2015).[32] Thus *uy pi-á-ru* (water drink-CAUS-NMLZ), 'something which causes one to drink', 'thirst', and *oráru* as 'that which causes one to sleep'. Example (6.109) shows the causative sense clearly. These forms mostly seem to refer to bodily functions or emotions, as with *žibáru* 'desire to eat', *miyáru* 'urge to urinate', *buhtuáru* 'feeling of fear',

[32] This is cognate in form and meaning with the Kalasha causative/desiderative construction in *-álak*.

or *guṫe-áru* 'desire to rotate something in the ear' (6.110). This morphological process is completely productive.

(6.109) *ma keł-áru g-óy-an*
me weep-CAUS.DES come-3SG.PRS/FUT-S
'I can't help weeping.' (SWKA in Bashir 2023b)

(6.110) *kár-o ki drux-ít-ay guṫe-áru*
ear-LOC4 if itch-PST.D-3SG rotate-CAUS.DES
g-oy
come-3SG.PRS/FUT.NS
'If one's ear itches inside, it makes one feel like rotating something in the ear (to relieve the itching).' (SWKA in Bashir 2023b)

This form can take OBL (6.111), ABL (6.112), LOC1 (6.113), and LOC2 (6.114) case endings.

(6.111) *hasé ma orár-o čhin-ít-ay*
REM.3SG my sleep.CAUS.DES-OBL break-PST.D-3SG
'S/he woke me up.' (lit. 'broke my sleep') (SWKA)

(6.112) *ma orár-ar nez-ít-ay*
me sleep.CAUS.DES-ABL take.out-PST.D-3SG
'S/he didn't let me sleep.' (lit. 'took me out of sleep') (SWKA)

(6.113) *orár-a xošp poš-ít-am*
sleep.CAUS.DES-LOC1 dream see.PST.D-1SG
'In (my) sleep I had a dream.' (SWKA)

(6.114) *moóš huṣ kárdu ki hamít bót-a*
man understanding do.PST.I that these night-LOC1
ma xesmát kor-í orár-i dreé
me tired do-PFV.PTCP sleep-LOC2 put.PFV.PTCP
istor-ó žib-óni čhúchi ruph-í
horse-OBL eat-3PL.PRS/FUT.NS morning get.up-PFV.PTCP
hási-a ma tan žib-óni
breakfast-LOC1 me EMPH eat-3PL.PRS/FUT.NS
'The man understood that tonight they will tire me out, make me sleep, and eat my horse. In the morning they will get up and eat me for breakfast.' (MH in Appendix)

6.8 Finite forms

Finite verb forms can carry information for tense (present/future, past); aspect (imperfective, perfective); specificity (specific, non-specific); modality (indicative, non-indicative); evidentiality (direct, indirect); mirativity (old knowledge, new knowledge); person (first, second, third); and number (singular, plural). Evidentiality is obligatorily indicated in all tenses and aspects. Forms here called 'direct' report established knowledge or first-hand experience. Those labelled 'indirect' convey indirect (non-first-hand or reported knowledge), glossed as 'unwitnessed' or 'unseen'. Mirative meanings, glossed as 'I have just learned that', 'it turns out that', or 'reportedly' are indicated by the use of the mirative forms of *b-* 'become', most frequently *biráy*, the third-person singular form (see Table 6.30 above).

6.8.1 Forms constructed on the root

The non-indicative forms hortative, imperative, and optative urge or state that something should be done. Hortatives are forms urging first persons (me or us) to do something; imperatives instruct or order a second-person addressee (you) to do something; and optatives state or question the desirability of some third-person entity (s/he, it, they) doing something. These forms consist of the root + the endings in Table 6.31.

Table 6.31 Hortative, imperative, and optative endings

Person	Singular	Plural
1 Hortative	*-ím, -óm, -ám*	*-si*
2 Imperative	*-é(h) ~ -én*	*-ór, -úr*
3 Optative	*-ár, -úr*	*-áni*

6.8.1.1 Hortative

Example (6.115) illustrates the first-person plural hortative (HORT) of *b-* 'go', and (6.116) a negated first-person singular hortative. See also example (8.93) below.

(6.115) *gy-e* *bí-si*
come-IMP.2SG go-HORT.1PL
'Come on, let's go.' (EB field notes)

(6.116) *šum b-íti* *bathán-a* *mo*
bad become-PFV.PTCP native.country-LOC1 PROH
as-ám
be(ANIM)-HORT.1SG
'Let me not live a bad life in my own country!' (MNN in Bashir 2023b)

6.8.1.2 Imperative

Regular second-person singular imperatives (IMP) consist of root + *-é*. A few frequently used verbs have irregular singular imperatives. *d-* 'give', 'strike' has an irregular singular form *det* 'give!' 'strike!', but a regular plural form *dyor*. The singular imperatives of *b-* 'become', *bos*, and *al-* 'take away', *alós* 'take it away' are irregular, being identical to the second-person singular present/future non-specific. The verb *ẓeék* 'to call a falcon' has *ẓaá* as its singular imperative. Shortened forms of the singular imperative of *kor-* 'do' and *lołé-* 'look at', *koó* 'do!' and *loó* 'look!' instead of *koré* and *lołé*, are frequently heard.

Second-person plural imperatives are formed from root + *-ór* or *-úr*. Some verbs with present/future thematic vowel /í/ have *-úr* in the plural imperative, among them *nišúr* 'sit!'; *ganúr* 'take!'; *marúr* 'kill!'; *dosúr* 'grab!', 'seize!'; and *boγúr* 'go away!'. A few verbs with thematic /ú/ in the present/future also take *-úr*; they include *briúr* 'die!', *γerúr!* 'revolve', and *ṣirǰúr!* 'propitiate'. Verbs with thematic *-ó-* have *-ór*; some *-ór* forms are *žibór* 'eat!', *gyór* 'come!', *angyór* 'bring!', and *bór* 'become!'.[33] The imperative forms of *b-* 'go' are irregular, being formed on the second past stem *boγ-*. Plural imperatives in context are illustrated in (6.117) and (6.118).

Imperatives of derived transitive/causatives include the causative morpheme *-á-* with hiatus-filling *-υ-* preceding the singular ending *é*, yielding singular *-áve* (6.119). Plural forms in *-áur* are illustrated in (6.120).

(6.117) *yíi* *gy-or*
hither come-IMP.PL
'Come here!' (EB field notes)

(6.118) *pisá* *boγ-úr*
you.PL go-IMP.PL
'You (PL) go away!' (EB field notes)

[33] *kor-* 'do' is an exception, its plural imperative form being *korúr*.

(6.119) *angár-o boγ-á-ve*
fire-OBL go-CAUS-IMP.SG
'Put out the fire!' (MNN in Bashir 2023b)

(6.120) *tan čatír-an zraṭh-á-ur*
REFL tent-OBL.PL dismantle-CAUS-IMP.PL
uláγ-an-te bar-án bar-á-ur
pack.animal-OBL.PL-DAT load-OBL.PL load-CAUS-IMP.PL
'Take down your tents. Load the loads on the pack animals.' (oral text, Village Bang)

6.8.1.3 Optative

Examples (6.121) and (6.122) exemplify the third-person singular optative (OPT).

(6.121) *horó babú as-ík-a kor-ár*
DIST.SG.OBL clerk be-INF-LOC1 do-OPT.3SG
'It should be done while the clerk is present.' (SWKA in Bashir 2023b)

(6.122) *ahmát as-ár ispá b-ísi*
Ahmad be(ANIM)-OPT.3SG we go-HORT.PL
'Ahmad should stay; we will go.' or 'Let Ahmad stay, let's go.' (SWKA in Bashir 2023b)

The forms of *b-* 'go' are irregular. Its hortatives are built on the present stem and are identical to the present/future non-specific (see 6.122). Its singular and plural imperatives and third-person singular optative are formed on the second past stem *boγ-*; the third-person plural optative is formed on the past stem *baγ-*. These forms of *b-* 'go' are shown in Table 6.32; examples of the first-person plural hortative and second-person plural imperative appear in (6.122) and (6.120) above, respectively.

Table 6.32 Hortative, imperative, and optative forms of *b-* 'go'

Person	Singular	Plural
1 Hortative	*bim* 'I should/can go'	*bísi* 'Let's go!'
2 Imperative	*boγé* 'Go!'	*boγúr* 'Go!'
3 Optative	*boγár* 'S/he, it should go'; 'let her/him, it go'	*baγáni* 'They should go'; 'let them go'

6.8.1.4 Subjunctive

The regularly formed subjunctive (SBJV) consists of the root + *-es-* + subjunctive personal endings (Table 6.33).[34] It is spelled out for *kor-* 'do' in Table 6.34 and its use exemplified in (6.123). Some verbs form their subjunctive irregularly on the second past stem, for example *b-* 'go', with subjunctive *boγ-es-án* 'I would go'. Subjunctive forms appear mostly in irrealis conditional sentences like (6.123). See also the examples in Section 9.5.3.2.

Table 6.33 Subjunctive personal endings

Person	Singular	Plural
1	*-án* ~ *-ám* 'I would V'	*-án* ~ *-ám* 'We would V'
2	*-ú* 'You would V'	*-ími* 'You would V'
3	*-ír* 'S/he, it would V'	*-íni* 'They would V'

Table 6.34 Subjunctive of *kor-* 'do'

Person	Singular	Plural
1	*koresán* ~ *koresám* 'I would do'	*koresán* ~ *koresám* 'We would do'
2	*koresú* 'You would do'	*koresími* 'You would do'
3	*koresír* 'S/he, it would do'	*koresíni* 'They would do'

(6.123) *avá baáčhá biru-á γarib-án-an su madát kor-es-án*
I king be.IRR poor-PL.OBL.PL with help do-SBJV-1SG
'If I were a king, I would help the poor.' (MNN in Bashir 2023b)

6.8.2 Forms constructed on the past participle (PST.PTCP)

6.8.2.1 Past indirect

The bare past participle functions as a simple past indirect (PST.I) form for second- and third-person subjects. This form reports the result of an action which took place in the past, unseen by the speaker. Past indirect forms of *b-* 'go' are given in Table 6.35. First-person forms are not shown in this table, since first-person actors would usually know first-hand about their own actions. In cases when they don't, as in unwitting actions, their actions are reported by the past indirect mirative (see Table 6.37).

[34] According to Rahmat Karim Baig, the first-person subjunctive endings in *-án* are found in Upper Chitral; in Lower Chitral, they are *-ám*. Morgenstierne (1947) also discusses *-án*. Some early published sources (O'Brien 1895: 17; Grierson 1919: 137) have *-ám*.

Actions by second-person or third-person actors, however, can be either observed (direct) or unobserved (indirect) by a speaker/observer.

Table 6.35 Past indirect of *b-* 'go'

Person	Singular	Plural
1	-	-
2	*boγdú* 'You went'	*boγdú* 'You went'
3	*boγdú* 'S/he, it went'	*boγdú* 'They went'

Table 6.36 gives the past indirect forms of *kor-* 'do'. For example, *se kárdu* 's/he, it did, (unobserved by speaker)'. Examples (6.124) and (6.125) illustrate this. For this reason, it frequently appears with events that happened in the distant past, and in the narration of traditional folk tales. See also example (9.131) below for an example with the past indirect of *b-* 'become'.

Table 6.36 Past indirect of *kor-* 'do'

Person	Singular	Plural
1	-	-
2	*kárdu* 'You did'	*kárdu* 'You did'
3	*kárdu* 'S/he, it did'	*kárdu* 'They did'

(6.124) *ma gík-ar prúšṭi roy bóγ-du*
my come.INF-ABL before people go-PST.I
'Before my arrival, people had left (unseen by me).' (RKB)

(6.125) *ruṣk g-íti ma biskóṭ-an žir-dú*
rat come-PFV.PTCP my biscuit-OBL.PL eat-PST.I
'A rat came and ate my biscuits (unseen by me).' (RKB)

6.8.2.2 Past indirect mirative

The past indirect mirative (PST.I.MIR) forms in Table 6.37 consist of the past participle + the mirative forms of *b-* 'go', which impart their mirative sense. Thus, these forms are both indirect and mirative, which is not necessarily the case with all indirect forms or all mirative forms. Actions by first-person agents of which they were not aware at the time but learned of later are reported with the past indirect mirative forms.[35]

[35] A form consisting of the past participle + the agent noun of *as-* 'be' + PST.I of *b-* 'become', as in *avá kardu asák birétam* '(I now realise that) I am one who has done it (unwittingly)' is sometimes encountered. However, Rahmat Karim Baig thinks that although it is sometimes heard, it is characteristic of the usage of non-native speakers.

Table 6.37 Past Indirect mirative of *b-* 'go'

Person	Singular	Plural
1	*boydú birétam* 'I went' (unwittingly)	*boydú birétam* 'We went' (unwittingly)
2	*boydú biráu* 'You went' (just learned)	*boydú birétami* 'You went' (just learned)
3	*boydú birái* 'S/he, it went' (just learned)	*boydú biráni* 'They went' (just learned)

The past indirect mirative differs from the past indirect in that an event may not have been observed by a speaker, but he may have known about it for some time, thus making it old, established knowledge. Such situations are reported with the past indirect. The past indirect mirative, on the other hand, reports events that are both unobserved by the speaker and new knowledge for him. See examples (6.126), (6.127), and (6.128) for first-, second-, and third-person examples.

(6.126) *ohó: tonǰé-iru birét-am*
oh ruin-PST.PTCP become.MIR-1SG
'Oh, (I see that) I have (unwittingly/mistakenly) ruined it.' (RKB)

(6.127) *tu hatéra as-íru bir-áv*
you there be(ANIM)-PST.PTCP become.MIR-2SG
avá ta no poóš-t-am
I you not see-PST.D-1SG
'(I have found out that) you were there, (but) I didn't see you.' (MNN)

(6.128) *γarúdi kár-du bir-áy*
spoiled do-PST.PTCP become.MIR-3SG
'It (the field) has been ruined.' / 'Someone/something has ruined (the field).' (unseen by speaker, just learned now) (ZMZ in Bashir 2023b)

6.8.2.3 Past incompletive

The past participle + past direct of *š-* 'be' yields a form that means 'was about to V but (did not complete the action)', a past incompletive (PST.INC), for example *kardú ošótam* 'I was about to do/have done, would have done'.[36] This meaning is illustrated in (6.129) and (6.130).

[36] The same meaning development takes place in English. For example, 'I was going to London but couldn't get a ticket.'

(6.129) *ayí ma d-irú o-š-óy ǰambélut*
snake me strike-PST.PTCP AUG-be-PST.D.3SG fortunately
tu h-áv
you come.PST.D-2SG
'A snake was about to bite me; fortunately, you came.' (MNN in Bashir 2023b)

(6.130) *avá úγ-o boγdú o-š-ót-am*
I water-LOC4 go.PST.PTCP AUG-be-PST-1SG
'I was about to drown in the water (but was saved).' (RKB)

6.8.2.4 Irrealis

The past participle + LOC1 yields an irrealis (IRR) construction, for example, *avá kardú-a* 'if I had done' or 'would that I had done.' Example (6.131) illustrates the use of both the subjunctive and the irrealis forms in an irrealis conditional. The irrealis form appears in the protasis ('if clause') and the subjunctive in the apodosis ('then clause'). The irrealis form also expresses wishful thinking, as in (6.132).

(6.131) *žang birúa tabahí b-es-ír*
war become.IRR destruction become-SBJV-3SG
'If war had happened, there would have been destruction.' (DSAL)

(6.132) *avá océ ma dinár khał i barabár birúa*
I and my beloved both one equal become.IRR
'Would that I and my beloved were of like mind.' (MNN) (line from song of Sher-e-Mulk)

6.8.3 Forms constructed on the perfective participle

Tense-aspect forms constructed on the perfective participle include the present perfect direct (PRS.PRF.D), present perfect mirative indirect, the past perfect direct (PST.PRF.D), and the past perfect indirect (PST.PRF.I).

6.8.3.1 Present perfect direct

The present perfect direct (PRS.PRF.D) consists of the perfective participle + the present tense of *as-* or *š-* 'be', depending on the animacy of the subject. Examples (6.133), (6.134), and (6.135) illustrate the form with a transitive verb and an animate subject, yielding an active agentive meaning. With an inanimate subject and a transitive verb affecting an animate object, the present perfect direct conveys a patient-oriented meaning, as in (6.136).

(6.133) *avá noy muxén kor-í as-úm*
I.DIR new verandah do-PFV.PTCP be(ANIM)-PRS.1SG
'I have made a new verandah.' (DSAL)

(6.134) *b-ití he lú-o pr-av-aá no*
become-PFV.PTCP DIST.SG utterance-OBL give.PST.D-2SG-Q NEG
b-ití
become-PFV.PTCP
'Did you say that intentionally or not?' (MNN in Bashir 2023b)

(6.135) *hayá sal ċhetr-ó ċhutk kór-i as-úm*
this year field-OBL fallow do-PFV.PTCP be(ANIM)-PRES.1SG
'This year I have left the field fallow.' (MNN in Bashir 2023b)

(6.136) *drox-ík ma-t saxtí kór-i š-er*
itch-1NF me-DAT intense.trouble do-PFV.PTCP be(INAN)-PRS.3SG
'Itching has tormented me.' (DSAL)

(6.137) *čumr-ó łováki kór-i š-ér*
iron-OBL round do-PFV.PTCP be(INAN)-PRS.3SG
'The (piece of) iron has been made round.' (IF in Bashir 2023b)

Stress differs on the perfective participle between (6.133) (6.134) above and (6.135) (6.136) (6.137). In (6.133) the sentence states the accomplishment of an action, and in (6.134) the intentionality of an accomplishment is questioned, hence the stress on the participial ending (*-í*). In (6.135), (6.136), and (6.137), on the other hand, an adjectival modification results, hence stress on the verb stem. In (6.136), *saxtí koríik* 'to cause trouble' is (like) a conjunct verb with *saxtí*, the resultant state of *kor-* 'do'.

An animate subject which is the patient of the action(s) described, as in (6.138), gives this construction a passive-like sense.

(6.138) *haté istor-án ǰér-a bot-í as-úni,*
REM.PL horse-PL row-LOC1 tie-PFV.PTCP be(ANIM)-PRS.3PL
bot-í petsh-í as-úni
tie-PFV.PTCP leave-PFV.PTCP be(ANIM)-PRS.3PL
'Those horses have been tied in a row, tied and left (there).' (oral text, Village Bang)

6.8.3.2 Present perfect mirative indirect

A present perfect mirative indirect (PRS.PRF.MIR.I) form consists of the perfective participle + the agent noun of *as-* or *š* 'be' + the mirative of *b-* 'become'. The meaning of this form is necessarily both mirative and indirect, since the speaker has not witnessed the action/event and has just learned about it. An example of this form in context is (6.139).

(6.139) *hamóṣ šáhar-a paáčá tan žav-ó-te nam lakh-í*
such.a city-LOC1 king REFL son-OBL-DAT name put-PFV.PTCP
as-ák bir-áy rétai.ki
be(ANIM).PST.I-3SG become.MIR-3SG say.PST.D
'He said "(I have heard that) in such a city the king has named his son."' (oral tale, Village Bang)

6.8.3.3 Past perfect direct

The past perfect direct (PST.PRF.D) consists of the perfective participle + the past tense of *š-* or *as-* 'be'. With animate subjects, this form yields an active sense of volitional action (6.140) (6.141) (6.142). Example (6.143) illustrates it with an impersonal intransitive verb, and (6.144) shows an inanimate subject, 'hunger', as subject/agent of a transitive verb. The Khowar past perfect direct can be glossed as an English simple past, or an English past perfect, with the simple past reading more frequent.[37]

(6.140) *avá boík-an-te phaší dar-í as-t-am*
I bird-OBL.PL-DAT trap set-PFV.PTCP be(ANIM)-PST.D-1SG
'I set/had set a trap for birds.' (MNN in Bashir 2023b)

(6.141) *ang-ití as-ít-am*
bring-PFV.PTCP be(ANIM)-PST.D-1SG
'I brought/had brought it.' (RKB)

(6.142) *avá oštánu toníṣu mar-í as-t-am*
I 8.year.old ibex kill-PFV.PTCP be(ANIM)-PST.D-1SG
'I killed/had killed an eight-year-old ibex.' (SWKA in Bashir 2023b)

[37] That is, the Khowar 'past perfect' does not function in the same way as the English form with the same name.

(6.143) *ohtíri* *boṣ-í* *o-š-óy*
day.before.yesterday rain-PFV.PTCP AUG-be-PST.D.3SG
'It rained/had rained the day before yesterday.' (witnessed by speaker) (DSAL)

(6.144) *ç̣huí* *kor-í* *o-š-óy* *paxtí-o*
hunger do-PFV.PTCP AUG-be-PST.D.3SG rice-OBL

ǰam *o-yó-t-am*
well AUG-eat-PST.D-1SG

'I was hungry (so) I ate a lot of rice.' (lit. 'Hunger had afflicted me, so …') (DSAL)

6.8.3.4 Past perfect indirect

The perfective participle of the main verb + the past indirect form of *as-* 'be' yields a past perfect indirect (PST.PRF.I) form, which is used to report unwitnessed actions. Notice that the stress in the past indirect form falls on the final syllable and the vowel of the final syllable is somewhat elongated, whereas in the past direct form it is either on the penultimate or the initial syllable. In examples (6.145) and (6.146), both of which have second-person subjects in interrogative sentences, the context makes it clear that the speaker did not witness the actions referred to. In (6.147), the speaker (tripod, personified) signals its lack of knowledge of going anywhere, hence the indirect verb form.

(6.145) *kúi* *bi* *as-t-á:v*
where go.PFV.PTCP be(ANIM)-PST.I-2SG
'Where did you go (not seen by speaker)?' (Sense: 'Where have you been?') (DSAL)[38]

(6.146) *xuk kuṣ-í* *as-t-á:v-aá*
pig slaughter-PFV.PTCP be(ANIM)-PST.I-2SG-Q
'Did you slaughter a pig?' (id. Sense (sarcastic): 'You have eaten something secretly and not given any to us' (it must be a pig, which is forbidden to Muslims)) (DSAL)

[38] Endresen and Kristiansen (1981) in their text *ǰu rafeqán* 'Two comrades' have the sentence *e brar, kúri bi asítav*, glossed as 'Eh, brother, where were you going?', uttered when encountering a traveller on the road, apparently in the sense of 'Where did/had you set out for?' This may represent a different sense from that in (6.137), which shows contemporary usage.

(6.147) *čidín ma phan sórum ré-k-o didáng-o rárdu*[39]
pot my bottom gold say-INF-OBL tripod-OBL say.PST.PTCP
ki avá kúi bi ast-á:m
that I where go.PFV.PTCP be(ANIM)-PST.I.1SG
Proverb. 'When the pot said, "My bottom is gold", the tripod's reply was, "Where was I?"' (lit. "Where had I gone?") (Sense: 'You are lying.') (MNN in Bashir 2023b)

A first-person subject reporting an unintentional action is shown in (6.148). Since people are assumed to normally be aware of their own actions, use of an indirect form with a first-person subject signifies unwitting, or sometimes mistaken action.

(6.148) *avá orár-o múži kapál-o sasíri kór-i*
I sleep-OBL in head-OBL uncovered do-PFV.PTCP
as-té:t-am
be(ANIM)-PST.I -1SG
'In my sleep I (had) uncovered my head (unwittingly, unintentionally).' (MNN)

6.8.4 Forms constructed on the imperfective participle

6.8.4.1 Past imperfective direct

The past imperfective direct (PST.IPFV.D) is formed as follows: imperfective participle + past direct of *š-* 'be'. Since the animacy distinction is neutralised in the past direct of *š-* 'be', both animate and inanimate subjects appear in this tense form, like the first-person subject in example (6.149) and the two third-person subjects in (6.150), one inanimate (*oráru*) and the other understood animate (*hasé*, 3SG.REM.DIR 's/he').

(6.149) *avá ta γeč kor-áv o-š-t-am*
I you eye do-IPFV.PTCP AUG-be-PST.D-1SG
'I was waiting for you.' (SG in Bashir 2023b)

[39] The oblique marker on *didáng* 'tripod' is interesting. According to today's synchronic grammar, no subject is oblique marked, hence *rárdu* should not be a verb. Thus, it appears that in this sentence *rárdu* is functioning as a noun, with the sense 'what the tripod said (is)'. I have translated it here as 'the tripod's reply'.

(6.150) *hat-oó harúni oráru gy-av*
3SG.REM-OBL so.much sleepiness come-IPFV.PTCP
o-š-óy ki drung anús
AUG-be-PST.D.3SG that long day
zome-áv o-š-óy
yawn-IPFV.PTCP AUG-be-PST.D.3SG
'S/he was so sleepy that s/he was yawning all day long.' (MYS in Bashir 2023b)

6.8.4.2 Past imperfective indirect

The imperfective participle + the past indirect of *as-* 'be(ANIM)' forms a past imperfective indirect (PST.IPFV.I), which is used to express unwitnessed actions in the past. For example, *koráv astá:m* 'I was doing (unwittingly, reportedly)'.[40] Since this is an indirect form, it is naturally compatible with reported actions or events in the distant past, as in (6.151). With first-person subjects, who are normally assumed to be aware of their own actions, this form conveys the sense of unwitting or mistaken action, as in (6.152).

(6.151) *bázi žaγa-á roy ṣapík no leé łółu*
some place-LOC1 people bread not find.PFV.PTCP *łółu*
žú-ti hal.b-áv as-tá:ni
eat-PFV.PTCP live-IPFV.PTCP be(ANIM)-PST.I.3PL
'In some places people couldn't get bread and were living by eating *łółu*.'[41] (hearsay information, unseen actions)

(6.152) *tu haníse no girúa avá γalát kor-áv*
you now not come.IRR I wrong do-IPFV.PTCP
as-tá:m
be(ANIM)-PST.I.1SG
'If you hadn't come now, I would have been (unwittingly) doing it wrong.' (but you corrected me, so I stopped) (RKB)

[40] In normal conversational speech the medial /i/ of the past tense morpheme is elided and forms including *š-* and *as-* as auxiliaries are pronounced as [*korávoštam*], [*korávastam*], [*koravastám*], for example.
[41] *łółu* is a dish made from a small amount of rice mixed with leafy greens and boiled. It was eaten in former times when food was scarce (ZHD, p.c.).

A typical example of the past imperfect indirect is (6.153), which occurs in a traditional tale about supernatural beings, the main narrative of which therefore appears with indirect verb forms.

(6.153) *ještan-án haté záyla tan phon-áv*
jeshtan-PL that manner EMPH dance-IPFV.PTCP
ast-á:ni
be(ANIM).PST.I-3PL
'The jeshtans were dancing in that very same manner.'[42] (MH in Appendix)

Examples (6.154) and (6.155) show the expression of indirect (6.154) versus direct (6.155) knowledge about a third-person subject. Example (6.154) reports indirect knowledge, for example as acquired from hearing elders talk, while in (6.154) direct knowledge of someone who witnessed these events himself is conveyed.

(6.154) *qadím-a bol g-íti dur-án*
old.times-LOC1 armies come-PFV.PTCP house-OBL.PL
talán kor-áv as-tá:ni
plundering do-IPFV.PTCP be(ANIM)-PST.I.3PL
'In the old days (it is said that) armies used to come and plunder the houses.' (indirect knowledge) (DSAL)

6.8.4.3 Past habitual direct

A past habitual direct (PST.HAB.D) form consists of the imperfective participle + *-ta-* + personal endings. The *-t-* indicating past tense is an abraded remnant of the past tense marker *ist-*, which survives only in the first- and second-person plural past direct forms of *š-* 'be(INAN)', but is present in all three persons and both singular and plural forms of the past direct of *as-* 'be(ANIM)' and the past habitual direct. The personal endings are the same as those of the past direct. These endings are shown in Table 6.38. For example, *koráv-tam* 'I used to do'.

[42] See the Appendix for discussion of the meaning of *ještan*.

Table 6.38 Past habitual direct endings

Person	Singular	Plural
1	*-tam*	*-tam*
2	*-tau*	*-tami*
3	*-tai*	*-tani*

The use of this form is illustrated in (6.155), (6.156), (6.157), and (6.158). Compare (6.154) with (6.155).

(6.155) *qadím-a bol g-íti dur-án*
old.times-LOC1 armies come-PFV.PTCP house-OBL.PL
talán koráv-tani
plunder do-IPFV.PTCP-PST.HAB.D.3PL
'In the old days armies used to come and plunder the houses.' (direct knowledge) (DSAL)

(6.156) *prúšṭ-i kimeri-án sór-a khóy*
before-LOC2 woman-PL head-LOC1 cap
dy-áv-tani
put-IPFV.PTCP-PST.HAB.D.3PL
'In previous times women used to wear caps on their heads.' (direct knowledge) (RKB)

(6.157) *hasé noɣór-a payrá kor-áv-tay*
REM.SG fort-LOC1 watch do-IPFV.PTCP-PST.HAB.D-3SG
'He used to do sentry duty at the fort (and no longer does).' (direct knowledge) (RKB)

(6.158) *him dy-áv-tay haníse no*
snow strike-IPFV.PTCP-PST.HAB.D.3SG now NEG
d-oy-an
strike-3SG.PRS/FUT-S
'It used to snow; now it doesn't.' (direct knowledge) (Chitral Town)

6.8.4.4 Past habitual indirect

A past habitual indirect (PST.HAB.I) form consisting of the imperfective participle + *-r* (third-person singular) or *-ni* (third-person plural) is an indirect counterpart to the past habitual direct (PST.HAB.D). This form is found only for the third person and occurs infrequently: *koráur, koráuni* 'S/he, they used to do', as in (6.159).[43]

(6.159) *hasé noɣór-a payrá kor-áu-r*
REM.SG fort-LOC1 watch do-IPFV.PTCP-PST.HAB.I.3SG
'He used to do sentry duty at the fort.' (hearsay, unwitnessed) (RKB)

6.8.4.5 Complex continuous constructions

With finite forms of *g-* 'come' and *al-* 'bring', the imperfective participle forms complex aspectual constructions, like *koráv hátam* 'I have been doing (starting in the past and continuing into the present)'. Forms like *koráv hátam* are considered by some to be calques of Urdu constructions like *kartā āyā hū̃* 'I have been doing'. However, numerous spontaneous examples are attested, indicating that for some speakers at least these forms have become naturalised in Khowar. Examples (6.160), (6.161), and (6.162) show this construction with intransitive verbs and *g-* 'come'; examples (6.163) and (6.164) show it with transitives and *ang-* 'bring'.[44]

(6.160) *alú loṭ b-av g-óni-an*
potato big become-IPFV.PTCP come-3PL.PRS/FUT-S
'The potatoes are becoming big.' (SWKA in Bashir 2023b)

(6.161) *haníse čhuy-ó drungí kam b-av*
now night-OBL length less become-IPFV.PTCP
g-óy-an
come-3SG.PRS/FUT-S
'These days the length of the nights is decreasing.' (SWKA in Bashir 2023b)

(6.162) *hasé roxts-ónu b-av g-óy-an*
it forget-RES.PTCP become-IPFV.PTCP come-3SG.PRS/FUT-S
'It is being forgotten.' (referring to one of the old words under discussion) (MNN)

[43] The meaning of this past habitual indirect form seems very close to (or the same as?) that of the past imperfective indirect. This question remains to be explored.
[44] One might think that similar constructions would also occur with *b-* 'go', as they do in Urdu, but I have not found any occurrences of them. Thus, it appears that these constructions are not entirely parallel with similar Urdu constructions, probably because of their relatively recent introduction into the language.

(6.163) *avá dałe-áv alé-t-am mágar het*
I drive.away-IPFV.PTCP bring-PST.D-1SG but DIST.PL.DIR
γerd-áv áči há-ni
turn-IPFV.PTCP back come.PST.D-3PL
'I kept on driving (them) away, but they kept on turning around and coming back (by another way).' (RKB in Bashir 2023b)

(6.164) *ta šaytaní-o avá noṭ kor-áv ang-óm-an*
your mischief-OBL I note do-IPFV.PTCP bring-1SG.PRS/FUT-S
'I have been observing your bad behaviour (for some time).' (MNN in Bashir 2023b)

6.8.5 Forms constructed with the agent noun

The agent noun + the mirative form of *b-* 'become' generates a series of forms with mirative meaning of present tense sentences with *as-* and *š-*, and present/future forms for other verbs. Table 6.39 presents these present mirative forms for *as-* 'be(ANIM)'. Similar forms exist for *š-* 'be(INAN)'.

Table 6.39 Mirative of *as-* 'be (EXISTENTIAL, ANIMATE)'

Person	Singular	Plural
1	*asák birétam* 'I turn out to be'	*asák birétam* 'We turn out to be'
2	*asák biráu* 'You turn out to be'	*asák birétami* 'You turn out to be'
3	*asák birái* 'S/he, it(ANIM) turns out to be'	*asák birétani* 'They(ANIM) turn out to be'

6.8.5.1 Present/future mirative

The present/future mirative (PRS/FUT.MIR) is a mirative counterpart of the present/future direct. It consists of the agent noun + the mirative of *b-* 'become'. In the present/future mirative the specific versus non-specific distinction is neutralised, and it functions as a mirative counterpart of the present tense of *as-* 'be(ANIM)' and *š-* 'be(INAN)'; or of the present/future direct, either specific (6.165) or non-specific (6.166), of other verbs. So, for example, (6.168) is the mirative counterpart of (6.167). Example (6.169) shows that, depending on context, the tense distinction can also be neutralised, since this sentence refers to something that happened in the past. Example (6.170) shows a mirative counterpart of a present tense nominal sentence. Sentence (6.171) is the mirative counterpart of *níki* 'it isn't (here)'.

(6.165) *ifáḍ mestúč-o pon-ó paká kor-ák biráy*
IFAD Mastuj-OBL road-OBL paved do-AG become.MIR-3SG
'IFAD is reportedly going to pave the Mastuj road.'[45] (RKB in Bashir 2023)

(6.166) *zemín yor-ó nas-én γerd-ák bir-áy*
earth sun-OBL side-LOC.PL turn-AG become.MIR-3SG
'(I have just learned that) the earth revolves around the sun.' (SWKA in Bashir 2023b)

(6.167) *hasé masrúf as-úr*
REM.SG busy be(ANIM)-PRS.3SG
'S/he is busy (now).' (direct knowledge)

(6.168) *hasé masrúf as-ák bir-áy*
REM.SG busy be(ANIM)-AG become.MIR-3SG
'S/he turns out to be busy (now).' (new information/hearsay) (MNN in Bashir 2023b)

(6.169) *noγór-a menú gík-o tup petsh-ák bir-áni*
fort-LOC1 guest come.INF-OBL cannon fire-AG become.MIR-3PL
'When guests came to the fort, they would fire cannons (in salute).' (reportedly) (DSAL)

(6.170) *hes khowár kor-ák bir-áy*
DIST.SG Khowar do-AG become.MIR-3SG
'S/he speaks Khowar.' (new knowledge, just realised)

(6.171) *no š-ak bir-áy*
NEG be(INAN)-AG become.MIR-3SG
'It isn't here.' (implied: 'I have looked but not been able to find it.')

6.8.5.2 Past direct of nominal predicates

The past direct of *š-* 'be' with the agent noun forms a past tense counterpart (6.171) of a present tense nominal sentence like *avá γał korák* 'I am a polo player'. With additional material, like the purpose phrase *γał koráv* 'to play polo', it can yield a past imperfective sense (6.172).

[45] IFAD = International Fund for Agricultural Development.

(6.171) *avá γał kor-ák o-š-ót-am*
I polo do-AG AUG-be.PST.D-1SG
'I was a polo player (but no longer am).' (MNN)

(6.172) *avá γał kor-áv boγ-ák ó-š-t-am mágam haníse*
I polo do-IPFV.PTCP go-AG AUG-be-PST-1SG but now
petsh-í as-úm
leave-PFV.PTCP be(ANIM)-PRS.1SG
'I used to go to play polo, but now I have given it up.' (MNN in Bashir 2023b)

6.8.5.3 Perfect mirative

The perfective participle + the agent noun of *as-* or *š-* 'be' + the mirative of *b-* 'become' yields a mirative counterpart of either the present perfect or past perfect direct. It refers to actions that were done or happened in the past, but of which the speaker has only become aware now. It can carry the sense of unintended consequences, especially with a first-person agent (6.173). Example (6.174) shows the form with an inanimate subject.

(6.173) *korí as-ák bir-ét-am*
do.PFV.PTCP be(ANIM)-AG become(PST.I)-PST-1SG
'(It turns out that) I am/was the one who did/has done it (mistakenly).' (RKB)

(6.174) *ohó ma hayá pirán uluṣ-í š-ak bir-áy*
oh, my this shirt rip-PFV.PTCP be(INAN)-AG become-PST.I-3SG
'Oh, this shirt of mine is ripped.' (just noticed now) (EB field notes)

6.9 Complex predicates

6.9.1 Conjunct verbs

Conjunct verbs are complex predicates consisting of a nominal (noun or adjective) element plus a verbaliser (light verb). Like Iranian, Turkic, and many other Indo-Aryan languages, Khowar has numerous conjunct verbs, and, with increased borrowing, the proportion of them in the verbal lexicon is increasing.[46] There are several distinct types of conjunct verbs, including the following.

[46] For an extensive discussion of conjunct verbs in Palula, see Liljegren (2010).

6.9.1.1 Adjective + verbaliser

A frequently occurring intransitive–transitive pair involves *b-* 'become' forming intransitives and *kor-* 'do' making grammatically formal transitives.[47] This pattern occurs with stage-level adjectives, which combine to form temporally bounded predicates. Stage-level adjectives name properties that are only temporarily true of an entity, for example 'I am sick today.'[48] All of the 75 conjunct verbs consisting of adjective + *b-* in Bashir (2023b) involve stage-level adjectives. A few such adjectives are: *avǰí* 'persuaded', *broól* 'numb', *čhin* 'broken', *c̣hutk* 'fallow', *fel* 'failed (in an examination)', *verán* 'bored', *zran(d)* 'startled'. For example, from the adjective *abathá* 'forgotten', 'mistaken' are formed *abathá b-* 'be mistaken' 'go astray' (6.175) and a corresponding transitive *abathá kor-* 'mislead someone', 'cause someone to go astray' (6.176).

(6.175) *avá abathá hó-t-am*
I lost become-PST.D-1SG
'I have strayed from the (right) path.' ('I have gotten lost.') (MS in Bashir 2023b)

(6.176) *tu ma abathá a-r-ú*
you me misled AUG-do.PST.D-2SG
'You have misled me.' (MS in Bashir 2023b)

6.9.1.2 Noun + verbaliser

Some noun + verbaliser combinations, however, do not participate in intransitive–transitive pairs like those formed from adjective + verbaliser discussed in Section 6.9.1.1. Several such conjunct verbs involve nouns denoting body parts + *kor-* 'do' and express simplex verbal concepts. For example, *bits kor-* 'carry on the breast and front of the shoulder (usually a child)', *ḍok kor-* 'carry on the shoulders and back', *kar kor-* 'listen' (6.177), and *γeč kor-* 'wait for' (6.178).

Transitive conjunct verbs can take a direct object external to the conjunct verb, which can be either direct or oblique case-marked, and either animate or inanimate, for example inanimate *lú-o* in (6.177) and animate *ta* in (6.178). The nominal component of the conjunct verb itself, however, is not a direct object of the conjunct verb and cannot take

[47] This is similar to the pattern found in other IA languages.

[48] For detailed discussion of stage-level predicates, see Marín (2009) and other references including Jäger (2001), Fernández Leborans (1995), and Luján (1981).

oblique marking. This generalisation holds with all types of transitive conjunct verbs.

(6.177) *é: ma ç̣e:k, ma lú-o kar.kor-é*
o my dear.one my words-OBL listen.to-IMP.2SG
'O, my dear, listen to what I am saying.' (SG in Bashir 2023b)

(6.178) *tu albát ǰošpóṇǰ taríq-a go-s*
you probably fifteen date-LOC1 come-2SG.PRS/FUT.NS

avá ta γeč.k-om
I you.OBL wait.for-1SG.PRS/FUT.NS

'You'll probably come on the fifteenth; I'll wait for you.' (MS in Bashir 2023b)

Other noun + *kor-* collocations express specific types of behaviour or action. Some of these are: *γormútu kor-* 'regurgitate and ruminate', 'chew a cud'; *γošnaγóši kor-* 'search for leftover walnuts', 'glean'; *išṭók kor-* 'play', 'dance'; *lašṭáv kor-* 'write a prayer on paper, soak the paper in water to dissolve the ink, and then give the water to a patient to drink in hope of curing his ailment' (NKN); and *γečári kor-* 'give the evil eye' (6.179). Some collocations of this type, however, do have intransitive counterparts in *b-* 'become'; for instance, along with *γečári kor-* 'give the evil eye' there is *γečári bik* 'to be affected by the evil eye'. In such cases they refer to an occurrence of the action or behaviour.

(6.179) *γečári kor-ík bo šum adát*
evil.eye do-1NF very bad habit
'Giving the evil eye is a very bad habit.' (MS in Bashir 2023b)

Other noun + verb combinations involve the basic verb *d-* 'give', 'strike', which combines with numerous nouns to yield meanings which range between clearly transitive and clearly intransitive. They yield both literal and non-literal meanings. For example, *uγ d-* 'irrigate'; 'water (livestock)', and *uγ kor-* 'irrigate' are quite literal, with *uγ* 'water' as a conceptual (but not syntactic) direct object of *d-*. The same applies to *dast d-* 'shake hands' (6.180).

(6.180) *má-su dast pr-ay*
me-with hand give.PST.D-3SG
'S/he shook hands with me.' (MNN in Bashir 2023b)

Other such collocations involve *d-* in an intransitive sense of 'strike' (move in such a way as to impact or affect something). For example, *asmánar lášṭa dik*, literally 'to strike the ground (having fallen) from the sky', has the idiomatic sense 'to be upset and helpless'. In this expression, *d-* refers only to a falling motion with a locative expression (6.181). Many other collocations involving *d-* are semantically intransitive; for example, *çuqumbíẓ d-* 'swing on a swing', *ṭhúxi d-* 'doze off with head falling forward', *łay d-* 'begin to ripen', 'take on colour (fruit)', *ónḍoγ d-* 'dive', *pon d-* 'be pleasing to'.

(6.181) *salím-o tat brík-o asmán-ar lášṭ-a*
Salim-OBL father die.INF-OBL sky-ABL ground-LOC1

pr-ay
strike.PST.D-3SG

id. 'When Salim's father died, he fell from the sky to the earth.' (Sense 'He became upset and helpless.' (SWKA in Bashir 2023b)

It is important to note that most of the numerous transitive meanings that develop from *d-* 'give' 'strike' involve physical, abstract, or metaphorical motion away from a deictic centre or agent. The meanings 'give' and 'beat', 'strike' show this particularly clearly.

Numerous transitive collocations are formed with *dreé-* 'put', 'place'. Many of these have a literal or concrete meaning; for example, *ačár dreé-* 'put onions in the sun to dry'; *ayúkun dreé-* 'lay an egg'; *batín dreé-* 'put a rope on an animal in order to lead it'; *łay dreé-* (lit. 'design put') 'carve designs in wood', 'embroider'. With these, the noun component is the semantic object of *dreé-* but, as with other transitive conjuncts, it is non-specific and is not oblique marked.

Other collocations with *dreé* include a locative or ablative case-marked noun. The meaning of these is less concrete and often quite specific. A number of them involve causing an animate entity to be affected by a mental or physical state (often negative). Some of these are formed with the LOC1 case of the noun component. They include *baláha dreé-* 'involve someone in trouble'; *qáhra dreé-* 'intentionally make someone angry', lit. 'put into anger'; *γáma dreé-* 'make trouble for someone', 'cause grief for someone'; *nanγería dreé-* id. 'punish so severely that one remembers one's mother'; *ṭiríka dreé-* 'persecute', 'terrify someone' (*ṭirík* 'to defecate', 'shit'); *nánga dreék* 'to flatter'.

Some consist of the ABL of the noun + *dreé*, some of which have intransitive counterparts with *b-* 'become'; for example, *pongár dreék* 'to make thinner and weaker to the point of death (an animal by a negligent owner)' and *pongár bik* 'to be weak to the point of death (animal)'; *ḍongár dreék* 'to upset someone extremely, causing confusion and disorientation' and *ḍongár bik* 'to become upset and confused'; and *halár dreék* 'to annoy someone' (*hal* 'condition').

Others consist of the LOC2 of the noun + *dreék*. Some of these are: *póngi dreék* 'to put grain which has fallen outside the threshing floor back under the animals' feet', id. 'to persuade'; *yádi dreék* 'to remind'; and *hardií dreék* 'to remind' (lit. 'put into the heart') (6.182).

(6.182) *ǰam a-r-ú ma hardi-í dreé*
good AUG-PST.D.do-2SG my heart-LOC2 put.PFV.PTCP
'You did well to remind me.' (SWKA in Bashir 2023b)

Some refer to commencing an important traditional activity; these include *khol dreé-* 'begin threshing', *kiṣ dreé-* 'ready the plough to start ploughing', *xoraá dreé-* 'start to grind grain in a water mill', and *tav dreé-* 'start cooking bread for a specific function or celebration' (lit. 'put the cooking iron [on the fire]') (6.183).

(6.183) *g-íti baáčaí frosk h-oy*
come-PFV.PTCP kingdom straight become-PST.D-3SG
zéri-o-te tav dré-t-ani murát
celebration-OBL-DAT cooking.iron put-PST.D-3PL desire
drust h-oy
complete become.PST.D-3SG
'He came and the kingdom was set right; they put on the cooking iron for a celebratory feast; his desire was fulfilled.'[49] (oral tale, Village Bang)

Other intransitive–transitive pairs are formed with an intransitive conjunct verb in *b-* 'become' and a morphologically derived transitive/causative form; for example, *bas b-* 'to spend the night' and *basé-* 'invite or give permission to spend the night', 'put hens in their coop for the night', as in *kahákan basáve* 'put the hens in their coop for the night'. The pair *ṭhor b-* 'fall down (animate entity)' (6.184) and *ṭhoré-* 'cause to fall' (6.185) are similarly related.

[49] Holding a celebratory feast is a typical ending of a traditional tale.

(6.184) *ṭhor b-ós-an kyá*
fallen become-2SG-PRS/FUT-S EMPH
'You are going to fall down!' (spoken to a child running carelessly) (SWKA in Bashir 2023b)

(6.185) *hamít no ṭhor-é-ni-an*
PROX.DIR.PL NEG fallen-CAUS-3PL.PRS/FUT-S
'These (shoes) don't make one fall (aren't slippery or too loose).' (SWKA in Bashir 2013b)

6.9.2 Compound verbs

The definition of compound verb used by South Asianist linguists is a complex verbal construction consisting of a non-finite verb form (V1) plus a finite verb which bears tense, aspect, and person-number marking (V2).[50] These finite verbs come from a very limited set—basic verbs of motion or those with a strong directional component in their meanings. Because of the motion or directional component common to the meanings of these verbs, I use the term *vector* to refer to them. GO, COME, THROW, LEAVE BEHIND, PUT, SIT DOWN, GIVE, and TAKE are among the verbs most commonly encountered as vectors in South Asian languages and more widely cross-linguistically.

In Khowar, compound verbs are formed with only a small number of vectors: *b-* 'go' in (6.186), (6.187), (6.188), and (6.189); *laák-* 'release' in (6.190); and *niš-* 'sit' in (6.191) (Bashir 1988a: 249).[51] Compound verbs with *b-* 'go' in non-past tenses often refer to anticipated events and can act as warnings, as in (6.186). In the past tense they report events that cannot be undone (6.187) (6.188) (6.189). It seems that compound verbs with *b-* 'go', like Khowar *bihtí bayáy* 'died' in (6.187), for example, are 'stronger' (the vector verb is more literal and less 'bleached') than, for instance, Urdu *mar gayā* 'died'.[52]

[50] In the literature on Iranian languages, 'compound verb' refers to what in the South Asianist literature is called a 'conjunct verb'. More recently, both of these constructions are subsumed under the category of complex predicates.
[51] They appear not to be formed with PUT, GIVE, RISE, FALL, THROW, TAKE, and SEE. This tentative conclusion is based on rejection by my consultants of test sentences incorporating such constructions, leading me to think that compound verbs are recent additions to the language.
[52] This is consistent with a hypothesis that compound verbs in Khowar belong to a newer stratum of the language than do those of Hindi or Urdu and are thus less semantically 'bleached'.

(6.186) *tu pulu-í b-is*
you burn-PFV.PTCP go-2SG.PRS/FUT.NS
'You will get burned.' (Bashir 1988a: 250)

(6.187) *ma ṭhak i léšu as-ít-ay. hasé*
my only one cow be(ANIM)-PST.D-3SG REM.SG.DIR
doṣ bih-tí baγ-áy
yesterday die-PFV.PTCP go.PST.D-3SG
'I had only one cow. Yesterday it died.' (MNN in Bashir 2023b)

(6.188) *harén čh-ití baγ-áy*
mirror break-PFV.PTCP go.PST.D-3SG
'The mirror broke.' (MNN)

(6.189) *γeč ç̣hom-í ç̣hom-í kánu b-íti*
eye hurt-PFV.PTCP hurt-PFV.PTCP blind become-PFV.PTCP
baγ-áy
go.PST.D-3SG
'His/her eyes having hurt continuously, s/he went (permanently) blind.' (MNN)

Used as vector in a compound verb construction, *laák-* 'release' can convey a sense of unforeseen negative consequences (6.190).

(6.190) *thúu palóγ-an bezem-í laák-it-am*
alas apple-OBL.PL sell-PFV.PTCP release-PST.D-1SG
'Alas, I sold the apples (mistakenly).' (RKB)

As a vector, *niš-* 'sit' indicates completeness and finality of an action (6.191). When used as a vector, the past direct form of *niš-* 'sit' is the shortened form *niš-áy* instead of *niš-ít-ay.*

(6.191) *hasé bók-o laákh-i niš-áy*
REM.SG.DIR wife-OBL release-PFV.PTCP sit.PST.D-3SG
'He divorced his wife (the action has been completed).' (RKB)

7
Adjectival modification

7.1 Introduction

Adjectival modification in Khowar is accomplished with basic, monomorphemic adjectives like *loṭ* 'big'; participial words or phrases, for example *boγdú* 'gone', 'past'; oblique noun phrases, such as *šaḍál khanǰó* 'of (that is, 'who makes') uncut stone walls'; oblique pronominal forms, as in *ma zuúr* 'my daughter'; *baṣ* phrases, *ṭhuríko baṣ* 'able to be sipped'; deictic adjectives (see Chapter 5); and relative clauses of several types (see Section 9.5.1).

This chapter is concerned with adjectival function, rather than form class.

7.1.1 Simplex adjectives

Khowar has a large inventory of simplex adjectives. Bashir (2023b), a collection of words encountered in my fieldwork, lists 908 adjectives. During that work I did not attempt to collect as many adjectives as possible, and Bashir (2023b) makes no claim to be a complete dictionary, making it virtually certain that many more simplex adjectives exist. Some of the ones I have found are basic, monomorphemic adjectives which encode meanings from several of Dixon's semantic types (Dixon 2009: 73) (see Table 7.1).

These 908 adjectives also include past participial forms like *blaydú* 'faded, wilted' (← *blay-* 'wilt'), or adjectives derived from nouns with the suffix *-i*, for example *anús* 'day' *anúsi* 'daily'. Some are compound words, like *apakṣúṣi* 'dry-mouthed', that is, 'extremely thirsty'. A significant number of indigenous Khowar adjectives denote highly specific

Table 7.1 Semantic types of Khowar adjectives

Semantic type	Examples
colour	*išpéru* 'white', *ṣa* 'black', *kruy* 'red'
size	*loṭ* 'big', *tseq* 'small'
quality/value	*ǰam* 'good', *šum* 'bad'
speed	*pin* 'fast', 'intense' (< Bur.), *tez* 'fast', 'intense' (< Prs., Ur.), *γuúz* 'slow- moving', 'lazy'
age	*noóγ* 'new', *paránu* 'old', 'of long standing', *zarú* 'old' (inanimates) 'aged' (animates), *avgáv* 'very old' (animal), 'senile' (human)
quantity	*bo* 'many'; *çhik* 'all'; *kam* 'less', 'few'
cardinal numerals	see Section 7.3.1
position	*ẓang* 'high', *past* 'low'
physical property	*phox* 'soft'; *ḷang* 'hard'; *ámu* 'undercooked', 'raw'; *počíru* 'cooked'
human qualities	*baxíl* 'miserly', 'stingy'; *gadéri* 'mad', 'crazy'; *γoṭ* 'feeble-minded', 'dumb' (unable to speak); *učútu* 'intelligent

attributes or behaviours of things, animals, or persons, for example, *daržát* 'excessive', 'annoying', 'unpleasant' (talk); *bingíri* 'splaying to the left and right (horns)'; or *guúẓ* 'sniffing around with head down and sneaking away without being seen (animal or person)'.

7.1.2 Properties of adjectives

Adjectives are invariant; they do not inflect for animacy, number, or case. For some adjectives, plurality can be indicated by reduplication, as in *ǰu ǰamǰám žižáv* 'two good (REDUP.PL) sons', where the adjective *ǰam* 'good' is reduplicated. This is a commonly used mechanism. Adjectives can function attributively, where they precede the noun they modify (7.1), or predicatively (7.2) (7.3). In predicative function, they can appear in nominal sentences (7.2) or in verbal sentences including a copula, *as-* 'be(ANIM)' (7.3).

(7.1) *hasé ṣiéli lugár o-š-óy*
he beautiful speaker AUG-be-PST.D.3SG
'He was a fine speaker.' (no longer a good speaker, or dead) (SWKA in Bashir 2023b)

(7.2) *het tan múži ǰam*
3PL.DIST REFL between good
'They are on good terms with each other.' (MA in Bashir 2023b)

(7.3) *ǰam as-ús-aá*
good be(ANIM).PRS.2SG.-Q
'How are you?' (lit. 'Are you okay?') (DSAL)

Oblique forms of nouns, such as *nán-o* 'mother's' (7.4), and pronouns like *kos* 'whom', 'whose', the oblique singular of *ka* 'who' (7.5), function as adjectives.

(7.4) *ṣa góγu di tan nán-o γéč-a ṣieéli*
black beetle also REFL mother-OBL eye-LOC1 beautiful
Proverb. 'Even a black beetle is beautiful in its mother's eyes.' Sense: 'Even an imperfect child is beautiful to its mother.' (IF in Bashir 2023b)

(7.5) *hayá kitép kos*
this book whose
'Whose book is this?' (EB field notes)

Most adjectives function freely as nouns. For example, in (7.6) *γoṭ* 'mute', 'feeble-minded' is a noun referring to a person having that quality and is the subject of the sentence. In (7.7) and (7.8) the adjectives *krémaḍuk* 'hunchbacked' and *γečén.tukhúnu* 'sharp-eyed' refer to persons already known by those physical characteristics, and function like quasi proper names. The adjective *ʦeq* 'small' is frequently used in the meaning of 'child', which is pluralised by reduplication, giving *ʦeʦéq* 'children'. Similarly, the adjective *loṭ* 'big', the plural of which is *lilóṭ*, is used in the sense of 'elders'. Some past participles become lexicalised as nouns, for example *peṣíru* 'grind.PST.PTCP' → 'flour' (7.9).

(7.6) *γoṭ kú-i baγ-áy*
feeble-minded.one where-LOC2 go.PST.D-3SG
'Where has the feeble-minded person gone?' (EB field notes)

(7.7) *krėm-a.ḍúk h-ay-aá*
back-LOC1.hump come.PST.D-3SG-Q
'Has the hunchback come?' (refers to a specific person usually known by this attribute) (EB field notes)

(7.8) *γeč-én.tukhúnu*
eye-LOC.PL.sharp
'a/the sharp-eyed one' (character in a traditional folk tale)

(7.9) *peṣír-o purun-í ṣapík kor-é*
flour-OBL sift-PFV.PTCP bread make-2SG.IMP
'Sift the flour and (then) make bread.' (DSAL)

7.1.3 Stage-level versus individual-level adjectives

The distinction between stage-level and individual-level adjectives is centrally important in Khowar. Stage-level adjectives refer to properties that are only temporarily true of something, for example, *laház* 'sick', *khoṭ* 'angry'. Such adjectives participate in conjunct verb pairs formed with *b-* 'become' and *kor-* 'do', as in (7.10). They are also found in sentences with copulas which assert existence in a temporary state, as in (7.11). Individual-level adjectives, on the other hand, describe permanent qualities of a person or place and do not occur with a present tense copula. Examples (7.12) and (7.13) describe such permanent qualities, like being a miser or being cold (a place).[1]

(7.10) *ma tat khoṭ b-íti as-úr*
my father angry become-PFV.PTCP be(ANIM)-PRS.3SG
'My father has become angry.' ('is angry now') (MNN in Bashir 2023b)

(7.11) *hayá ḍaq bord-áv-a as-úr*
this boy grow-IPFV.PTCP-LOC1 be(ANIM)-PRS.3SG
'This boy is in a growing phase.' (MNN in Bashir 2023b)

(7.12) *hasé kós-te kyaáγ no d-oy-*
REM.SG anyone-DAT anything NEG give-3SG.PRS/FUT.NS
bohrt-ó žav
stone-OBL son
'He doesn't give anything to anyone—(he is) a real miser.' (lit. 'son of a rock') (SWKA in Bashir 2023b)

(7.13) *ispá žaγá bo uṣák*
our place very cold
'Our place is very cold.' (DSAL)

[1] For detailed discussion of stage-level and individual-level predicates in Khowar, Kalasha, and other neighbouring languages, see Bashir (2023a).

7.2 Interrogative elements

7.2.1 Interrogative/indefinite adjectives

The most general interrogative adjective is *kyá* ~ *kya*, which, depending on stress, can have interrogative or indefinite meaning. Stressed *kyá* can mean 'what?' (7.14), 'what kind of?' (7.15), and 'no' in rhetorical WH-questions (7.16). Unstressed *kya* can mean 'some' (7.17) or 'any' in negative contexts (7.18).

(7.14) *kyá ʣah kó-s-an*
what moist.dish make-2SG.PRS/FUT-S
'What moist dish are you making?'[2] (DSAL)

(7.15) *c̣hayák kyá hál-a as-úr*
patient what condition-LOC1 be(ANIM).PRS-3SG
'How is the patient?' (DSAL)

(7.16) *ẓoγ keły-ó kutér-ar kyá šang*
thin sheep-OBL knife-ABL no danger
Proverb. 'A thin sheep has nothing to fear from the knife.' Sense: 'A desperate person doesn't fear anything.' (DSAL)

(7.17) *ʋa di kya lu det*
more also some utterance give.IMP.2SG
'Say something else/more!' (DSAL)

(7.18) *má-te kya mağbúri néki*
me-DAT any obligation is.not
'I am not under any obligation.' (MS in Bashir 2023b)

Stressed *kí* 'which?' asks for something to be picked out of a defined set; its use is exemplified in (7.19) and (7.20). *kíča* 'what kind of' is used as in (7.21).

(7.19) *kí vólṭi rahí a-r-ú*
which direction departure AUG-do.PST.D-2SG
'In which direction have you set out?' (DSAL)

[2] *ʣah* 'moist dish' means any dish served in small quantities for added taste along with the main dish of bread or rice. It is sometimes glossed as 'curry', but it can also be a milk product or stewed fruit.

(7.20) *kí dukán-a anz-ém*
which shop-LOC1 send-1SG.PRS/FUT.NS
'To which shop should I send it?' (MS in Bashir 2023b)

(7.21) *hasé kíča moóš*
REM.SG.DIR what.kind.of man
'What kind of man/person is he?' (MNN in Bashir 2023b)

7.2.2 Quantitative interrogatives

Quantitative interrogatives include *kandúri* 'how much?' (sometimes 'how many?') and *kamaá* 'how many?' *kandúri* 'how much' is used mostly with mass nouns like 'grain', as in (7.22) or 'money' (7.23). In (7.24) and (7.25) it has a rhetorical sense 'so many' rather than functioning as an interrogative. In (7.24) it appears with the less highly individuated count nouns *uláγ* 'beast of burden' and *roy* 'people'. In (7.25) it is seen in a formulaic recitation of the quest of the protagonist in many traditional tales; in this rhetorical usage, *kandúri* appears with both the count nouns 'year' and 'day'; and the mass nouns *vaxt* 'time' and *ṭem* 'time'.

(7.22) *hayá sal ta kandúri žoó h-óni*
this year your how.much grain become.PST.D-3PL
'This year how much was your grain crop?' (DSAL)

(7.23) *dur savz-ék-o báče kandúri paysá haǰát*
house make-INF-OBL for how.much money necessary
b-oy
become-3SG.PRS/FUT.NS
'How much money will be needed to make a house?' (RKB in Bashir 2023b)

(7.24) *kandúri uláγ-an-te bar a-r-éni kandúri*
so.many animals-OBL.PL-DAT load AUG-do.PST.D-3PL so.much
kyaáγ aréni kandúri roy toó-su
whatever did so.many people REM.OBL.SG-with
pr-áni
give.PST.D-3PL
'They loaded so many animals, did so much whatever, and sent so many people with him.' (oral text, Village Bang)

(7.25) *kandúri sal bay-áy, kandúri vaxt bayáy*
how.many year go.PST.D-3SG how.much time passed

kandúri anús bayáy kandúri ṭem bayáy
how.many day passed how.much time passed

kandúri noh
how.much not

'So many years passed, so much time passed, so many days passed, how much time passed, how much didn't …' (oral text, Village Bang)

With highly individuated count nouns, like 'son', *kamaá* 'how many?' consistently appears, as in (7.26).[3]

(7.26) *ta kamaá ži-žáv as-úni*
your how.many RED.PL-son be(ANIM)-PRS.3PL
'How many sons do you have?' (DSAL)

Preceded by *i* 'one', these words yield approximating terms, *i kandúri* 'about', 'approximately' and *i kamaá* 'a few' (7.27).

(7.27) *i kamaá ḍaq skúl-o-te h-áni*
a.few boy school-OBL-DAT come.PST.D-3PL
'A few boys came to school.' (MNN in Bashir 2023b)

7.3 Quantitative expressions

7.3.1 Numerals

The cardinal numerals are listed in Table 7.2.

Notice that the form of the teen numerals 11–19 is 10 + n rather than the inherited Indo-Iranian pattern n + 10, seen, for example, in Urdu *pandarah* '15' (5 + 10).[4] The traditional Khowar number system was vigesimal, based on multiples of 20; thus *ǰu.bíšir* '40' was/is expressed as 'two 20s'. This system is/was also found in Kalasha, partially in several other languages of the Hindukush area (Liljegren 2017), and

[3] It seems, however, that the distinction between mass and count nouns is weakening in some people's speech.
[4] The 10 + n pattern is found also in some of the Iranian Pamir languages, Tibeto-Burman, Burushaski, and marginally in Tirahi (Bashir 1988a: 413). Liljegren (2023) contains a recent discussion of numeral patterns in an areal context.

Table 7.2 Cardinal numerals

1	*i*	11	*ǰoš.í*	21	*bišir.í*	75	*troy.bíšir.ǰoš.pónǰ*
2	*ǰu*	12	*ǰoh.ǰú*	30	*bišir.ǰóš*	80	*čor.bíšir*
3	*troy*	13	*ǰoš.tróy*	32	*bišir.ǰoh.ǰú*	86	*čor.bišir.çhóy*
4	*čor*	14	*ǰoh.čór*	40	*ǰu.bíšir*	90	*čor.bišir.ǰóš*
5	*ponǰ*	15	*ǰoš.pónǰ*	42	*ǰu.bišir.ǰú*	97	*čor.bíšir.ǰoš.sót*
6	*çhoy*	16	*ǰoh.çhóy*	50	*ǰu.bišir.ǰóš*	100	*ponǰ.bíšir, šor*
7	*sot*	17	*ǰoh.sót*	53	*ǰu.bišir.ǰoš.tróy*	101	*i.šor.í*
8	*õšṭ*	18	*ǰoš.ő̃šṭ*	60	*troy.bíšir*	200	*ǰu.šór*
9	*nyoh*	19	*ǰoš.nyóh*	64	*troy.bišir.čór*	1,000	*i hazár*
10	*ǰoš*	20	*bíšir*	70	*troy.bišir.ǰóš*	50,000	*ǰu.bišir.ǰoš hazár*

over a wide swath of South Asia, including in Panjabi and Saraiki (Bashir & Conners 2019: 164). Recently, in the late twentieth and twenty-first centuries, Urdu numerals are rapidly replacing the Khowar numerals, especially for those greater than 20.

Though basically adjectival, the cardinal numerals frequently act as nouns. Thus, the adjective *i* 'one', functioning as a noun, can take the case suffixes *-a* (LOC1), *-tu* (LOC3), and *-ó* (OBL), yielding *íya* (*i* + *a*) (7.28), *ítu* (*i* + *tu*) (7.29), and *iyó* (*i* + *-ó*) (7.30). With vowel-initial suffixes, a [y]-glide appears between /i/ and /a/, and [y] between /i/ and /o/.

(7.28) *he ǰu ang-íru – muxtalíf zom-ár*
DIST.PL.DIR two bring-PST.PTCP – different mountain-ABL
ang-íru – ṣáyoz, laš.bíti laš.bíti he
bring-PST.PTCP – glacier slowly slowly DIST.SG.OBL
him-ó tan qésma savzé-i ṣáyoz
snow-OBL own type make-PFV.PTCP glacier
çok-í í-ya
become established-PFV.PTCP one-LOC1
tar-úni
reach-3PL.PRS/FUT.NS
'Those two ice masses brought from different mountains—very very slowly turn the snow (into ice) like themselves, and join together to form a glacier.' (MNN, text in Bashir 2008)

(7.29) *daryá í-tu d-íti samandár*
rivers one-LOC3 strike-PFV.PTCP sea
yer-úni-an
turn.into-3PL.PRS/FUT-S
'Rivers come together and turn into a sea.' (DSAL)

(7.30) *i-γó-te* *ṣoy-é-i* *niš-úr*
one-OBL-DAT near-CAUS-PFV.PTCP sit-IMP.2PL
'Sit close to each other.' (DSAL)

The ablative suffix follows *sot* 'seven' in (7.31); *çhoy* 'six' and *ǰú* 'two' have the oblique in (7.32).

(7.31) *sot-ár-i* *ǰošpónǰ minúṭ* *b-i* *š-er*
seven-ABL-LOC2 fifteen minute go-PFV.PTCP be(INAN)-PRS.3SG
'It is 7:15.' (lit. 'from seven, fifteen minutes have gone') (Sloan 2006: 106)

(7.32) *çhoy-ó* *ǰú-o* *sóra* *bož-ík-o* *troy*
six-OBL two-OBL by divide-INF-OBL three
b-oy[5]
become-3SG.PRS/FUT.NS
'Six divided by two is three.' (SWKA in Bashir 2023b)

Ordinal numerals are formed from the cardinal numeral by suffixing oblique *-ó*; thus *ǰuó* 'second' (7.33) *troyó* 'third'. The word for 'first', *aveló*, is an exception, being based on the Arabic-origin root *avval* 'first'.

(7.33) *avá* *ǰuó* *nambár-a* *hát-am*
I second number-LOC1 come.PST.D-1SG
'I came in second place.' (TMFD in Bashir 2023b)

7.3.2 Quantifiers

Quantifiers are a type of determiner which express quantity with respect to some whole. Words for 'all' include original Khowar *pɫik* 'all', 'complete', as in *pɫik korík* 'to completely finish off' (7.34), *çhik*, and *khaɫ*. From Persian are *duht* (with variants *duhrt* and *drust*) (7.35), *thamám*, *khul*, and *saf*. 'Each' and 'every' are often expressed with *har* (7.36). 'Both' or 'all' can be expressed with *khaɫ*, depending on the context, as seen in (7.37). *som* 'both' is used only with things that occur in inherent sets of two, like paired body parts: eye, ear, hand, leg, knee, foot, arm, as in (7.38).[6]

[5] Note the stress in *ǰú-o* 'two-OBL' compared with that in *ǰuó* 'second'.
[6] Baig (1997: 209).

(7.34) *haté davlát-o no behč-é-i pɫik*
REM.SG.OBL treasure-OBL NEG remain-CAUS-PFV.PTCP complete
kor-í gaán-t-ay
do-PFV.PTCP take-PST.D-3SG
'Not leaving any of that treasure, (he) gathered it all and took it.' (oral text, Village Bang)

(7.35) *duht roy ǰáma bíti*
all people gathered become-PFV.PTCP
duá a-ré-ni
prayer AUG-do.PST.D-3PL
'All the people gathered and said a prayer.' (DSAL)

(7.36) *har ivál-o-t no loɫ-élik*
each one-OBL-DAT NEG look-NEC
lit. 'One should not look at everyone.' Sense: 'One shouldn't do as everyone else does; one should do what is right.' (MNN in Bashir 2023b)

(7.37) *khaɫ troy*
all three
'all three'

(7.38) *som host çaɫ k-óni i host çaɫ no*
both hand clapping do-3PL.PRS/FUT.NS one hand clapping NEG
k-oy
do-3SG.PRS/FUT.NS
Proverb. 'Both hands clap; one hand doesn't clap.' Sense: In order to get something from someone, one has to give something. (DSAL)

Piece or part is expressed with *nas* 'edge', 'piece' as in (7.39). To indicate partial amounts, *pháti* 'some (but not all of)', 'part of' is used, as in (7.40) and (7.41). For discussion of referentiality distinctions between *pháti* and *phat*, both meaning 'some of', see Section 10.1. When a possessive pronoun occurs with a quantifier, the order of elements within the noun phrase is Possessive pronoun–Quantifier–Noun, as in (7.40). Incompleteness is expressed by *phatúki* 'partial', 'incomplete'. 'Some but not many' is expressed with *baz* (< Ar.), and 'a little' can be expressed by *phuk*, as in (7.42). Fractional parts are expressed with an ordinal numeral plus the noun *hisá* 'part', as in (7.43).

(7.39) *pyalá čh-ití ǰu nas h-oy*
cup break-PFV.PTCP two piece become.PST.D-3SG
'The cup broke into two pieces.' (MYS in Bashir 2023b)

(7.40) *ma pháti birú pišávar-a abád*
my some.of relative Peshawar-LOC1 settled
'Some of my relatives are settled in Peshawar.' (DSAL)

(7.41) *pháti čalayγár iskuṭ-ák bóni*
some cloth shrink-AG become-3PL.PRS/FUT.NS
'Some kinds of cloth are liable to shrink.' (SWKA in Bashir 2023b)

(7.42) *uγ-ó báče phuk him bir-é-m*
water-OBL for a.little snow melt-CAUS-1SG.PRS/FUT.NS
'I will melt a little snow for water.' (MNN in Bashir 2023b)

(7.43) *čhor-ó hisá*
four-OBL share
'one fourth (of something)'

'A few (as opposed to none, all, or many)' is expressed with *i.kandúri* (7.44) or *i.kamaá* (7.45) and (7.27); *kam* '(too) few', 'little', 'rare' (7.46) is opposed to 'enough', 'plenty'.

(7.44) *sal koós-t-ay, bas koós-t-ay, yurán*
year walk-PST.D-3SG day walk-PST.D-3SG year
kos-ít-ay i.kandúri vaxt koós-t-ay
walk-PST.D-3SG some time walk-PST.D-3SG
'He walked for a year, he walked for a day, he walked for a year, he walked for some time' (oral tale, village Kari)

(7.45) *i.kamaá žun numá g-óni*
a.few person not.yet come-3PL.PRS/FUT.NS
'A few persons have not yet come.' (will come after a while) (DSAL)

(7.46) *menuíti koók-o*[7] *menuíti-a ṣapík kam*
invitation do.INF-OBL invitation-LOC1 food little

o-š̌-óy
AUG-be-PST.D.3SG

'When (he, they) invited guests, there was too little food.' (oral text, Village Parwak)

To indicate large quantities or numbers, *ṭip* 'much', 'many', 'lots of', 'full of' appears in an exchange like:

Q: *kandúri pai asúni*? 'How many goats are there?'
A: *ṭip* 'Lots.' (see also (7.47)).

(7.47) *več̌h-ák šahr-én ṭip*
beg-AG city-LOC.PL very.many
'Cities are full of beggars.' lit. 'Beggars are numerous in cities.' (MNN)

dunyá also means 'very many', 'a huge number of', as in *dunyá pay asúni* 'There are a huge number of goats'; *zyad* 'more', 'much', as in (7.48). *ambóh* ~ *ambóx* 'many', 'much' also indicates a large quantity (7.49).[8]

(7.48) *sin griṣpó bík-o bo zyad b-óy-an*
river summer become-OBL very more become-3SG.PRS/FUT-S
'Summer has come and the river is rising a lot.' (DSAL)

(7.49) *i sal muzdúri a-r-ér paysá ambóx*
one year labour AUG-do.PST.D-3SG money much

h-óni to-γó
become.PST.D-3PL REM.SG-OBL

'He laboured for a year … His money increased greatly.' (oral text, Village Kari)

Absence of any, 'no', is expressed with *kaá* 'anyone' or *kya* NP 'any NP' as subject plus a negative word—*níki* ~ *néki*, the negative of existential 'be' (7.50), a negated verb (7.51), or *kya* 'no' (4.42).

[7] = *koríko*.
[8] /h/ often changes to /x/, especially in Lower Chitral.

(7.50) *xur kaá níki*
other anyone is.not
'There is no one else.' (EB field notes)

(7.51) *kaá to-γó dúr-i no b-íni*
anyone REM.SG-OBL house-LOC2 NEG go-3PL.PRS/FUT.NS
'No one goes to his house.' (RKB in Bashir 2023b)

With numerals, two classifier (CLF) particles are commonly employed: *daná* 'item', 'unit' is used for countable non-human entities, animate or inanimate; for example, *sot daná áłi* 'seven ducks', *ponǰ daná thuék* 'five rifles', *ǰoš daná* 'ten (of them)' (7.52) (7.53); and *nafrí*, a noun meaning 'individual (human)', 'person', as a classifier for humans, as in *ponǰ nafrí* 'five persons', *ponǰ nafrí kimerián* 'five women'. These are of Persian origin.

(7.52) *avá hanún ǰoš daná birmóγ-o phordú bo-ít-am*
I today ten CLF walnut-OBL plant plant-PST.D-1SG
'Today I planted ten walnut trees.' (MNN in Bashir 2023b)

(7.53) *boht-ó múž-a i daná láγal lé-t-am*
rock-OBL interior-LOC1 one CLF spinel find-PST.D-1SG
'Inside the rock I found one spinel crystal.' (DSAL)

The morpheme *-łínǰi* '-fold', 'occurrence', added to cardinal numeral names, forms words like *ǰułínǰi* 'two-fold', 'doubled', 'twice' or *troyłínǰi* 'thrice', as in (7.54).

(7.54) *avá hayá kitáb-o troyłínǰi r-aá*
I PROX.SG.OBL book-OBL thrice read-PFV.PTCP
as-úm
be(ANIM)-PRS.1SG
'I have read this book three times.' (MS in Bashir 2023b)

7.4 Comparative and superlative constructions

Comparative expressions consist of the oblique form of a noun or pronoun denoting the standard of comparison followed by the postposition *sar* 'than', a development of the ablative case ending *-ar*, followed by the adjective, as in (7.55).

(7.55) *ves-íru sayúrǰ-o sar dos-íru kiṣípi ǰam*
await-PST.PTCP falcon-OBL than catch-PST.PTCP magpie good
Proverb. 'A caught magpie is better than an awaited falcon.' (compare the English 'A bird in the hand is worth two in the bush.') (DSAL)

Superlative meaning is expressed by the phrase *sáf-o sar* + ADJ (7.56) or *sáf-an sar* + ADJ, 'of/from all' followed by the adjective (7.57).

(7.56) *hatét-an múži sáf-o sar čan hasé*
REM.PL-OBL among all-OBL.SG ABL poor REM.SG.DIR
o-š-óy
AUG-be-PST.D.3SG
'Among them, he was the poorest of all.' (IF in Bashir 2023b)

(7.57) *basmatí grinǰ sáf-an sar aslí*
basmati rice all-OBL.PL ABL real
'Basmati rice is the best (lit. 'most genuine') of all (kinds of rice).' (DSAL)

7.5 Reflexive adjective

The element *tan* 'self' is used as a reflexive adjective (7.58), as an emphatic with adjectives (7.59), and, with an expressively stressed and lengthened vowel, it conveys strong emphasis and exclusivity, as in (7.60). This element functions both adjectivally and pronominally (see Section 4.2.3).

(7.58) *baxtavár roy tan maqsát-i tar-ír*
fortunate person REFL objective-LOC2 reach-3SG.PRS/FUT.NS
'A fortunate person reaches his objectives.' (MNN)

(7.59) *hayá ma tan kitáb*
PROX.SG.DIR my EMPH book
'This is my own book.'

(7.60) *avá tá:n k-om*
I EXCL do-1SG.PRS/FUT.NS
'I will do it myself.' (not anyone else) (MNN)

7.6 Intensifiers

Some adjectives occur frequently with specific intensifying terms. Some of these are: *ṭungṭáng čhuy* 'completely dark (of a thick dust cloud)', *tuq phłis* 'completely naked', *ṭiír maáyz* 'completely insane' (*ṭiír* 'unconscious', 'deeply asleep' is a meaningful word on its own), *čir baríki* 'very thin' (Naji 2008: 190), *lim lašṭ* 'completely flat' (Naji 2008: 417), *lim limít* 'completely quiet' (Naji 2008: 417). *giír* intensifies 'dark': *giír čhuy* 'extremely dark (of night)' (7.61). Colour terms have their own intensifiers. They include *ṣung* 'extremely (black)'; *ṣung ṣa* 'pitch black', 'dark black'; *phuk* 'bright', 'intensely (white)', as in *phuk išpéru* 'snow white'. *taq* added to some colour names (*oç* 'green', 'blue', 'grue';[9] *savz* 'green', *ʣehč* 'yellow'), indicates an intense or darker hue, for example *taq savz* 'dark green'. 'Red' is intensified with *trax*: *trax kruy* 'dark red'.[10]

(7.61) *giír čhuy-ó laṭén-ar γayr kos-ín no*
dark night-OBL lantern-ABL without walk-POT.PTCP NEG
b-oy
be.able-3SG.PRS/FUT.NS
'One can't walk on a dark night without a lantern.' (DSAL)

In many colloquial (often idiomatic) expressions, the idea of completeness is inherent in the expression. For example, *čoók bik*, lit. 'to be(come) a small earth-coloured owl', has the idiomatic senses of 'to be completely unavailable', 'to be completely unaffected by anything', 'not to come under anyone's influence' (SWKA in Bashir 2023b). The expression *iváki khar kiṣík*, literally 'to plough up someone's roots', has the idiomatic sense 'to completely destroy someone'. A compound of *dar* 'wood' + *bohrt* 'stone', *darabóhrta* means 'broken up', 'completely separated'. There are also the Perso-Arabic-origin terms *bilkhúl*, *faqát*, and *sarasár*, all meaning 'completely'.

[9] In some languages, the same word refers to colours which in English are differentiated as 'blue' and 'green'. The term 'grue' was coined by the philosopher Nelson Goodman (1955) for such colours. For discussion in the literature on basic colour terms, see Berlin and Kay's seminal treatment (1969) and later discussions, for example Saunders (2000) and Levinson (2000).
[10] Turkish makes much use of intensive adjectives formed by partial reduplication which "assigns to the modifiers 'fullness' or 'perfectness' of the sense expressed by the base" (Demircan 1987: 25). In these examples, the partially reduplicated element is in upper-case letters, as *SAP-sari* 'fully yellow', *KAP-kara* 'black', *MOS-mor* 'violet', *SIP-siyah* 'black', *MAS-mavi* 'blue'. Tajik Persian also forms intensive adjectives like *zab-zard* 'very bright yellow'; *sap-safed* 'very white', 'ultra-white'; *sip-siyah* 'pitch black'; *sup-surx* 'bright red'. The Persian pattern is: s~z V p/b-ADJ depending on the voiceless/voiced initial consonant of the adjective (Mamatov et al. 2005).

7.7 Past participle in adjectival function

The past participle functions as a past indirect verb form (Section 6.8.2.1), as an adjective, or as a noun. Past participles used as simple attributive adjectives, *kárdu* 'closed' and *uríru* 'opened' appear in (7.62).

(7.62) *kár-du darvaz-oó ur-é*[11] *ur-íru*
do-PST.PTCP door-OBL open-IMP.2SG open-PST.PTCP
darvaz-oó kor-é
door-OBL do-IMP.2SG
'Open the closed door; close the opened door!' (oral text, Village Sorech)

Bare past participles do not occur alone as predicative adjectives; they occur in attributive position as simple adjectives (7.62), or as part of complex verb forms (see Section 6.4.2). Like other adjectives, they can function as nouns, and they frequently function to form relative clauses (see Section 9.5.1.1.2).

[11] Alternate pronunciation of *huré*, with initial /h/ elided.

8
Adverbial modification

8.1 Introduction

Adverbials express adjunct relationships—temporal, spatial, quantitative, degree, manner, or causal relationships—that is, elements of a predication other than the core arguments, subject, direct object, and indirect object. Adverbial functions are expressed in Khowar with several types of elements—simple adverbs which are sometimes monomorphemic and sometimes a nominal root + a case ending (locative, ablative, or instrumental case endings of inanimates); sets of forms constructed on the deictic bases; postpositional phrases; participial phrases; and subordinate clauses. Adverbials can modify single words like verbs, adjectives, other adverbs; phrases; or entire clauses (sentence adverbs).

8.2 Spatial adverbs

For adverbial forms built on the deictic bases, see Section 5.3.

8.2.1 Pre-verbal directional particles

In addition to adverbs formed on the deictic bases with the locative cases, important directional elements associated with verticality are *ayh* 'up' (T249) and *af* 'down', 'away' (T726), which have an absolute sense relative to the vertical/horizontal dimension, either geographical or gravitational, both large and small scale. *ayh* indicates location or motion upward (and usually away from the speaker/deictic centre) (8.1) (8.3); *af* indicates location or motion downward (normally away from the speaker/deictic centre) (8.4) (8.5). *ayh* (< OIA *ádhi* ‘up’, ‘above’ (T249)) and *af* (< OIA áva ‘away’, ‘down’ (T249) usually appear immediately pre-verbally. With verbs of motion they almost always appear and seem almost obligatory.[1]

The forms *yií*, *yuú*, and *yaá*, formed from the proximal element *-y-* plus the LOC2, LOC4, and LOC1 endings, indicate motion toward the speaker—upward or at the same level (8.2), downward (8.6), or horizontal (8.7). Together with *phar* ‘over there’ (8.8), these basic adverbs constitute a paradigm as shown in Table 8.1.

(8.1) *bohrt-ó horó-t {ayh/*yií}*
rock-OBL 3SG.DIST.OBL-DAT {(up) there/*up here}
tar-á-ve
reach-CAUS-IMP.2SG
‘Hand the stone (up) to him/her.’ (Bashir 2000b: 23)

(8.2) *bohrt-ó ma-t {yií/*ayh} tar-á-ve*
rock-OBL me-DAT {(up) here/*up there} reach-CAUS-IMP.2SG
‘Hand the stone (up) to me.’ (Bashir 2000b: 23)

(8.3) *ayh zóm-tu b-ím-an*
up mountain-LOC3 go-1SG.PRS/FUT-S
‘I am going up (to) the mountain.’ (Bashir 2000b: 23)

(8.4) *af ṣotár-o b-ím-an*
down river.bed-LOC4 go-1SG.PRS/FUT-S
‘I am going down to the riverbed.’ (Bashir 2000b: 23)

(8.5) *žo-ó γoʦh-í γeryér-an*
grain-OBL clean-PFV.PTCP broken.grains.and.stones-OBL.PL
af uláv-e
away throw-IMP.2SG
‘Clean the grain and throw out the broken grains and stones.’ (Bashir 2023b)

Table 8.1 Basic pre-verbal directional adverbs

	Vertical dimension		Horizontal dimension
Speaker deixis	Upward	Downward	
Toward	*y-ií* ‘up here’	*y-uú* ‘down here’	*y-aá* ‘over here’
Away from	*ayh* ‘up there’	*af* ‘down there’	*phar* ‘over there’

[1] These directional particles are reflexes of the Sanskrit ‘verbal prefixes’ (Whitney 1981[1889]: 414–5) ~ ‘preverbs’ (Casaretto and Schneider 2015, passim), and (Papke 2010, passim).

(8.6) *paloóɣ yuú ɣer-ít-ay*
apple down (here) fall-PST.D-3SG
'The/an apple fell down here (toward me).' (RKB in Bashir 2023b)

(8.7) *yaá lołé hayá i rupayá gi*
here look-IMP.2SG PROX.SG.DIR one rupee note/coin
'Look here; this is a one-rupee note/coin.' (IF in Bashir 2023b)

Location or motion away from a deictic centre at approximately the same level as the speaker is expressed with *phar* 'over there'; *ayh* 'up(ward)' usually means motion away from the speaker, 'go', as in (8.3) above. With imperative utterances, however, the deictic centre changes to the addressee, who is the implied agent/subject of the instruction or command. In such cases, *g-* 'come' can be used with *ayh*, as in (8.9), meaning motion away from the agent (the addressee) and toward the speaker.

(8.8) *avá phar g-om*
I over come-1SG.PRS/FUT.NS
'I'll come over (away from where I am over to where you are).' (MNN in Bashir 2023b)

(8.9) *ayh g-yé, ma dur-ó-te*
up come-IMP.2SG my house-OBL-DAT
'Come up to my house.' (Bashir 2000b: 23)

The particles *ayh, af,* and *phar* usually appear immediately preceding the verb and function adverbially, but they can also be used adjectivally, as in (8.10), (8.11), (8.12), and (8.13). When adjectival, they precede a noun (phrase) rather than the verb.

(8.10) *ma tat ayh ċhétr-ar g-óy-an*
my father up field-ABL come-3SG.PRS/FUT-S
'My father is coming from the upper field.' (SWKA in Bashir 2023b)

(8.11) *ma tat af ċhétr-ar g-óy-an*
my father down field-ABL come-3SG.PRS/FUT-S
'My father is coming from the lower field.' (SWKA in Bashir 2023b)

(8.12) *af dur-ó braár xatán-o uyur-éru*
below house-OBL brother house-OBL roof.with.mud-PST.PTCP
bir-áy
become.MIR-3SG
'The man of the house below has roofed his house with mud (learned by speaker upon being told about this or seeing the roofed house).' (ZMZ in Bashir 2023b)

(8.13) *phar dúr-i*
over.there house-LOC1
'in the house next door' (MNN in Bashir 2023b)

Both *ayh* and *af* often combine with basic verbs like *d-* 'give', 'strike', or *b-* 'go' to yield a lexicalised meaning which can contrast with the meaning of the forms used separately. For example, *af dik* lit. 'strike downward', 'to close (a door)' contrasts with *afdík* 'to become old and worn out (for example, clothes)'. The literal meaning of *ayh néik* 'take up' appears in (8.14), but with an idiomatic sense in (8.15) with the phrase *khakó ayh. néik* 'to spoil someone's mind/mood'.

(8.14) *šiáq ayh néy-k-o sanǰír af draz-úr*
mud up take.out-INF-OBL beam down be.pressed-3SG.PRS/FUT.NS
'When mud is taken up (onto the roof), the main beam is pressed down.' (MNN in Bashir 2023b)

(8.15) *hányi drungár lu pr-ay ki khak-ó*
such long talking give.PST.D-3SG that head-OBL
ayh.né-t-ay
up.take.out-PST.D-3SG
'S/he talked for so long that s/he spoiled (my) mind (mood).' (IF in Bashir 2023b)

These adverbs can also be used as sentence adverbs, as in (8.16).

(8.16) *ayh moóš haté daryáh-an múž-a*
up.there husband REM.PL.OBL river-OBL.PL middle.LOC1
beéč-t-ay
remain-PST.D-3SG
'Up there, (her) husband was left between those rivers.' (oral text, Village Chapali)

8.2.2 *tóri* and *múłi*

The adverbs *tóri* 'upper', 'upward' (T1779) and *múłi* 'lower', 'downward' (T10250), which consist of the roots *tor-* 'upper' and *muł-* 'low' plus the LOC2 case ending *-i*, have a comparative sense relative to each other.[2] Their basic use is with reference to location or motion on a slanted surface, which inherently has a higher and a lower side. For example, two major side valleys of the main Chitral Valley are Torkhow and Mulkhow; Torkhow is higher than Mulkhow in terms of the large-scale geographical gradient of elevation. With reference to Figure 8.1, which represents two houses located on a slope, speaker A would say (8.17) to refer to house number 1 and (8.18) to refer to house number 2.

(8.17) *ma-sar múłi he dur*
I.OBL-ABL below DIST.SG.DIR house
'the house below me.' (Bashir 2000b: 23–4)

(8.18) *ma-sar tóri he dur*
I.OBL-ABL above DIST.SG.DIR house
'the house above me' (Bashir 2000b: 23–4)

The basic sense can be extended to apply to a surface which is both physically and conceptually flat, in such a way that *tóri* 'upper' comes to mean 'farther away', 'ahead of', as in (8.19).[3]

Figure 8.1 Basic sense of *tóri* and *múłi*. Created by Dale Mertes, Media Application Specialist at the University of Chicago.

[2] *tor-* appears only as a bound morpheme, as far as I am aware, while *muł* is an unbound morpheme, meaning 'thing below', for instance 'root'.

[3] This development has also been noted for the Mayan language Tzeltal: "… what is curious is that there is an additional use of the same terms: 'uphill' refers to a region further away from the speaker, 'downhill' as closer to the speaker …" (Levinson 1994: 844). Levinson explains this as a result of the equivalence of the two-dimensional retinal projections of both higher and more distant objects.

(8.19) *tór-i-roó* *lołé*
upward-LOC2-somewhat look-IMP.2SG
'Look a little ahead (of you).' (Bashir 2000b: 24)

Functioning as a noun meaning, for example 'root (of plant)', 'sole (of foot)', or 'bedding', *muł-* can take LOC1 (8.20), LOC3 (8.21), and LOC4 (8.22) case endings.[4]

(8.20) *múł-a* *zemín ḍang - sór-a* *asmán ẓang*
bottom-LOC1 land hard top-LOC1 sky high
Proverb. 'Below, the ground is hard; above, the sky is high.' Sense: Refers to a situation when one has no good alternative and can do nothing. (SWKA in Bashir 2023b)

(8.21) *hon-ár* *nis-í* *rešṭ-ó* *múł-tu*
flood-ABL come.out-PFV.PTCP avalanche-OBL bottom-LOC3
Proverb. 'getting out of the flood then being buried underneath an avalanche' Sense: 'to escape from one trouble and find oneself in a worse one' (SWKA in Bashir 2023b), (compare the English idiom, 'out of the frying pan into the fire')

(8.22) *tuṣ-ó* *múł-o* *uγ* *h-oy*
straw-OBL bottom-LOC4 water become.PST.D-3SG
id. 'There was water under the straw (which is not visible).' Sense: Applies to a situation when a wrongdoing is not visible. (MNN in Bashir 2023b)

From the root *muł-* is also derived *mułonéški* 'downward (diagonally)'. Other terms in the system of spatial representation are *biašépi* 'upward diagonally', *ҫók-tu* 'upward, vertically or diagonally', and *thróski* 'horizontally, ahead or back'.

8.2.3 Other spatial roots

Some spatial adverbs develop temporal senses; see Section 8.3.1 for discussion of these. Most, however, do not. This section discusses some of the most important adverbs with mainly spatial meanings. The nominal root *muúž* 'middle', 'inside' takes LOC1 *-a* (8.23), LOC2 *-i* (8.24), LOC3 *-tu* (8.25), LOC4 *-o* (8.26), OBL *-ó* (8.27) and (8.28), INS *-én* (8.29), and ABL *-ar* (8.30). In (8.25) LOC3 *tu* appears because of the vertical

[4] As far as I am aware, *tor-* 'upper' takes only the LOC2 ending.

orientation of the sword. Another example illustrating the relevance of the orientation of an object is *ḍaq tan nán-o áč-tu ruph-ít-ay* 'The boy stood directly behind his mother', in which the boy's orientation with respect to his mother is vertical and close.

(8.23) *salím ahmát očé akbár-o múž-a ruph-í*
Salim Ahmad and Akbar-OBL middle-LOC1 stand-PFV.PTCP
as-úr
be(ANIM)-PRS.3SG
'Salim is standing between Ahmad and Akbar.' (SWKA in Bashir 2023b)

(8.24) *ispá múž-i ká ǰam*
we.OBL middle-LOC2 who good
'Who among us is good?' (implied: no one is) (DSAL)

(8.25) *hat khongór-o tan očé hat kumór-o múž-tu*
REM.3SG sword-OBL REFL and REM.3SG girl-OBL middle-LOC3
lakh-ít-ay
place-PST.D-3SG
'He placed the sword between himself and the girl.' (oral text, Village Sorech)

(8.26) *zemín-o múł-a ki bay-áni, va het*
soil-OBL below-LOC1 when go.PST.D-3PL again DIST.3PL.DIR
ç̣hutí-o múž-o yer-úni
soil-OBL inside-LOC4 turn.down-3PL.PRS/FUT.NS
'When they go beneath the earth, they again turn downward through the soil …' (MNN on artificial glaciers, in Bashir 2008).

(8.27) *ǰu darvaz-án tóri peést-ay, ǰu darvaz-án múłi*
two door-OBL.PL above leave.PST.D-3SG two door-OBL.PL below
peést-ay, muž-ó darvazá-tu ut-í
leave.PST.D-3SG middle-OBL door-LOC3 enter-PFV.PTCP
hal.hoy
stay.PST.D.3SG
'He left two doors above, he left two doors below, he entered the middle door and stayed there.' (oral text, Village Bang)

(8.28) *haté muž-ó ʦaréni-a bík-o*
REM.3SG middle-OBL doorway-LOC1 go.INF-OBL
af haté pong-ó ʦaréni-a
downward REM.3SG foot-OBL doorway-LOC1
h-áy
come.PST.D-3SG
'When he$_i$ went to that middle doorway, then he$_j$ came to the lowermost doorway.' (oral text, Village Sorech)

(8.29) *áči háte t-oó havlí-o muž-én*
afterwards 3SG.REM his courtyard-OBL middle-INS
gy-av o-š-t-áy haté žoy
come-IPFV PTCP AUG-be-PST-3SG 3SG.REM water.channel
'Afterwards, it was coming through his courtyard—that water channel.' (oral text, Village Kari)

The senses developed from *muž* are mainly concrete and spatial, but in (8.30) we see an abstract sense. From this root also develops *mužγéšṭi* 'middle (son, daughter, brother, sister)' (8.31).

(8.30) *avá di xodáy-o bandá … adém-o muž-ár*
I too God-OBL person Adam-OBL middle-ABL
'I too am a slave/person of God—from Adam.' (oral text, Village Sorech)

(8.31) *loṭhoró žav toó-t xodayí pr-ay mužγéšṭi di*
elder son REM-DAT alms give.PST.D-3SG middle also
toó-t pray ʦiroó di toó-t pray
him-DAT gave youngest also him-DAT gave
'The eldest son gave him alms, the middle (son) also gave him (alms), (and) the youngest also gave him (alms).' (oral text, Village Bang)

Several adverbs express interiority and exteriority. The root *niṣ-* 'out', 'outside (of some container or enclosure), which includes a directional component, can take the LOC2 ending (8.32), or the LOC2 + ABL, as in (8.33). Another word for 'outside' is *béri* (T9227), 'outside of a bounded area', e.g. 'house' or 'country', as in (8.34).

(8.32) *čay níṣ-i h-ay*
tea out-LOC2 come.PST.D-3SG
'The tea boiled over (lit. 'came out (of the pot)').' (SWKA in Bashir 2023b)

(8.33) *hasé má-te níṣ-i-ar huy pr-ay*
3SG.REM.DIR me-DAT outside-LOC2-ABL call give.PST.D-3SG
'S/he called to me from outside.' (EB field notes)

(8.34) *čhuy-ó béri mo kos-é*
night-OBL outside NEG walk-IMP.2SG
'Don't walk around outside at night.' (DSAL)

The root *andrén-* 'in(side)' concerns relationships to a closed space. *andrén-* 'inside' can take all four locative case endings: with LOC1 *andrén-a* 'inside' (a largeish permanently or inherently closed thing)' (8.35), LOC2 *andrén-i* 'inside, (horizontal/extended relation)' (8.36), LOC3 *andrén-tu* '(up vertically) inside' (8.37), and LOC4 *andrén-o* '(down) inside (a deep thing)' (8.38). In (8.37) LOC3 appears because nostrils are oriented vertically.

(8.35) *xarbuz-oó andrén-a uɣ ṭip bir-áy*
melon-OBL interior-LOC1 water full become.MIR-3SG
'The watermelon turned out to be full of juice.' (Bashir 2000b: 22)[5]

(8.36) *salím andrén-i as-úr*
Salim interior-LOC2 be(ANIM).PRS.3SG
'Salim is inside (the room or the house).' (Bashir 2000b: 21–2)

(8.37) *naskár-o andrén-tu zaxmí b-íti*
nose-OBL interior-LOC3 wounded become-PFV.PTCP
š-er
be(INAN)-PRS.3SG
'The inside of (someone's) nose is wounded.' (Bashir 2000b: 21–2)

[5] Since a watermelon is inherently closed, the amount of juice inside it can only be determined once it is opened/cut. Hence the appearance of the mirative form *biráy*.

(8.38) *sabún almarí-o ṭék-a baltí-o andrén-o*
soap cabinet-OBL top-LOC1 bucket-OBL interior-LOC4

š-er
be(INAN)-PRS.3SG

'The soap is inside the bucket on top of the cabinet.' (Bashir 2000b: 21–2)

Words expressing verticality include *past* 'low', 'down' and the nominal element *sor-* 'top' (← 'head'), which takes LOC1 (8.39), LOC2 (8.40), and LOC3 (8.41), as well as ablative endings. These forms from *sor-* have grammaticised into postpositions, which follow the oblique case. The noun *sor* 'head' is also used with its original nominal meaning, as in (8.42). The LOC1 form of *sor* 'head' has developed into an instrumental postposition *sóra* 'with', as in (8.43).

(8.39) *sanǰír ṭhun-án sór-a thi-úr*
main.beam pillar-OBL.PL top-LOC1 rest-3SG.PRS/FUT.NS
'The main roof beam rests on the pillars.' (DSAL)

(8.40) *gol-ó sór-i ser né-i as-úni*
stream-OBL top-LOC2 bridge build-PFV.PTCP be(ANIM)-3PL.PRS
'They have built a bridge over the stream.' (DSAL)

(8.41) *yúru host-ó sór-tu nay-úni-an*
vein hand-OBL top-LOC3 be.visible-3PL.PRS/FUT-S
'Blood vessels are visible on the top of (someone's) hand.' (DSAL)

(8.42) *sor póng-an lažék dr-aá as-úni*
head foot-OBL.PL *lažék* put-PFV.PTCP be(ANIM)-PRS.3PL
'They have put a dish of head and feet cooked with split wheat (*lažék*) (on to cook).' (DSAL)

(8.43) *ṭhongí-o sóra dar čhin-ím-an*
small.axe-OBL with wood cut-1SG.PRS/FUT-S
'I am cutting wood with a small axe.' (DSAL)

The words *phar* (location) and *phári* (direction) 'over there', 'across (away from, at a distance)' indicate location or direction away from a deictic centre. Examples (8.44) and (8.45) illustrate static goal and dynamic directional senses, respectively; and (8.13) above has a static locative meaning.

(8.44) *hes* *mahmezé-i* *žóy-a*
DIST.3SG.DIR jump-PFV.PTCP water.channel-LOC1
phar nis-áy
over emerge-PST.D.3SG
'S/he jumped over the water channel (in direction away from speaker).' (DSAL)

(8.45) *avá kúr-i* *b-im* *phár-i* *b-oγé*
I where-LOC2 go-HORT.SG over.there-LOC2 go-IMP.2SG
Q: 'Where should I go?' A: 'Go over there.' (MS in Bashir 2023b)

The basic terms *dudéri* 'far', 'distance' (8.46) and *ṣoy* 'near', 'closeness' (8.47) refer to distance but are not specified for direction and do not include a motion component. These words function both as adverbs and as nouns. Examples (8.46a) (8.46b), and (8.47a) (8.47b) illustrate their adverbial (a. sentences) and nominal functions (b. sentences).

(8.46)
a. *zom* *bo* *dudéri š-éni*
mountains very far be(INAN)-PRS.3PL
'The mountains are very far away.' (MNN in Bashir 2023b)

b. *zom* *dudéri-ar* *γéč-i* *g-óni-an*
mountain distance-ABL eye-LOC2 come-3PL.PRS/FUT-S
'The mountains are visible from a distance/afar.' (RKB in Bashir 2023b)

(8.47)
a. *ta* *dur* *ṣoy* *š-er-aá*
your house near be(INAN)-PRS.3SG-Q
'Is your house nearby?' (SWKA in Bashir 2023b)

b. *hasé* *ṣóy-a* *g-íti* *di* *no*
REM.SG.DIR near-LOC1 come-PFV.PTCP even NEG
paš-ír
see-3SG.PRS/FUT.NS
'S/he can't see even having come close.' (SWKA in Bashir 2023b)

8.3 Temporal adverbs

8.3.1 Spatio-temporal adverbs

Some spatial adverbs with a horizontal motion component also develop temporal senses. I consider the spatial senses as primary, temporal senses secondary, and other metaphorical or abstract senses tertiary. The nominal root *nast* has the spatial meanings 'before', 'ahead of', 'in front of' (8.48) (8.49). Temporal senses include *nást-a*, 'a few moments before', and *na:st-a* 'quite a while before' with LOC1 *-a*.[6] *nast* can also function as a noun 'past', as in (8.50).

(8.48) *reéni sáf-o sar nast rahí a-rer*
dog all-OBL than ahead departure AUG-do.PST.3SG
'The dog set off ahead of everyone.' (DSAL)

(8.49) *nast b-os*
ahead go-IMP.2SG
'Go ahead/in front (of me).' (MNN in Bashir 2023b)

(8.50) *nast-ó roy ǰam o-š-óni*
past-OBL people good AUG-be-PST.D.3PL
'The people of the past were good (implied: better than people today).' (MNN in Bashir 2023b)

The bound nominal morpheme, *ač-* 'back' combines with LOC1-*a*, LOC2 *-i*, LOC3 *-tu*, LOC4 *-o*, INS *-én*, and OBL *-ó*. This yields the postpositions *áč-a* 'behind (pointlike location)' (8.51) (8.52); *áč-i* 'afterwards', 'back' (8.53), and 'after', which follows the ABL of a NP, as in *korík-ar áči* 'after doing'; *áč-tu* 'behind (in vertical orientation)' (8.54); *áčo* 'behind (and low)' (8.55); *ač-én* 'by (way of) the back' (8.56); and nominal *ač-hó* 'the future', 'that coming afterward', as in (8.57).[7] In example (8.51) the difference between *áči*, involving horizontal direction of the gaze, and *áča*, involving a pointlike location of the horsemen, is clear.

[6] According to MNN, the difference in sense, with *na:sta*, indicating a longer interval, is produced iconically by elongating the vowel.
[7] Secondary aspiration develops on /č/ before the stressed oblique ending *-ó*.

(8.51) *áč-i* *loóɫ-t-ay* *ki* *ǰoš istorí* *toó*
back-LOC2 look-PST.D-3SG when ten horsemen REM.3SG.OBL

áč-a *as-úni*
behind.LOC1 be(ANIM)-PRS.3PL

'When he looked back (he saw that) ten horsemen are behind him.' (oral text, Village Bang)

(8.52) *ta* *áč-a* *ka* *g-óy-an*
you.OBL behind-LOC1 who come-3SG.PRS/FUT-S
'Who is coming behind you?' (SWKA in Bashir 2023b)

(8.53) *ma gaɫí* *áč-i* *nis-í* *š-er*
my watch back-LOC2 emerge-PFV.PTCP be(INAN)-PRS.3SG
'My watch is behind/slow.' (MNN in Bashir 2023b)

(8.54) *hayá dar-ó* *anṭen-oó* *áč-tu* *det*
this wood-OBL antenna-OBL back-LOC3 put.IMP.2SG
'Put this piece of wood up behind the antenna.' (Bashir 2000b: 16)

(8.55) *ma poš-í* *khanǰ-ó* *áč-o* *khošṭ*
me see-PFV.PTCP wall-OBL behind-LOC4 hidden

h-oy
become.PST.D-3SG

'Seeing me, s/he hid (on the ground) behind the/a wall.' (MYS in Bashir 2023b)

(8.56) *boík kan-ó* *ač-én* *ulu-ít-ay*
bird tree-OBL behind-INS fly-PST.D-3SG
'The bird flew behind the tree.' (RKB in Bashir 2023b)

(8.57) *ǰam zun-ík-o* *ač-hó* *báče thobá*
well be.beaten-INF-OBL future-OBL for forswearance

a-r-ér
AUG-do.PST.D-3SG

'When he was soundly beaten, he forswore for the future (never to repeat the action which had caused him to be beaten).' (DSAL)

prušṭ 'in front of' (T8820) functions adverbially, adjectivally, and nominally. *prušṭ bik* 'to go out to receive guests' (8.58) illustrates the adverbial use. Example (8.59) illustrates the LOC1 form of *prúšṭ*; and (8.60), (8.61), and (8.62) the LOC2 form. In *prúšṭ-i zamána* 'previous times' we see an adjectival use of *prúšṭi*. When *prúšṭi* is used postpositionally, it follows the ABL (8.61). The ABL appears in *prušṭ-ár bik* 'to vanish from right in front of someone', as in example (8.63). Example (8.64) with the OBL of *prušṭ* illustrates the idiomatic sense of *prušṭ-ó-te gik* 'to be accomplished easily'.

(8.58) *hanún pisá prušṭ hoó-te mo boγ-úr*
today you in.front.of DIST.OBL-DAT PROH go-IMP.2PL
očh-ór
wait-IMP.PL
'Today (you) don't go out to receive him! Wait' (oral text, village Chapali)

(8.59) *ta prúšṭ-a ka as-úr*
you.OBL ahead-LOC1 who be(ANIM)-PRS.3SG
'Who is ahead of you?' (SWKA in Bashir 2023b)

(8.60) *ma gałí prúšṭ-i b-i š-er*
my watch ahead-LOC2 go-PFV.PTCP be(INAN)-PRS.3SG
'My watch is fast.' (has gone ahead of the actual time).' (MNN)

(8.61) *kor-ík-ar prúšṭ-i*
do-INF-ABL before-LOC2
'before doing'

(8.62) *prúšṭ-i hay-uú čókul gy-áv-tani*
before-LOC2 PROX-down rockslide come-IPFV.PTCP-HAB.D.3PL
'Previously rockslides used to come down here.' (SG in Bashir 2023b)

(8.63) *ma poč-íru pondí ma prušṭ-ár baγ-áy*
I.OBL cook-PST.PTCP waybread I.OBL front-ABL go.PST.D-3SG
Proverb. 'The waybread I cooked for my journey has vanished from in front of me.' Sense: 'My grown son has died before me.' (MS in Bashir 2023b)

(8.64) *davlát prušṭ-ó-te h-ay*
wealth front-OBL-DAT come.PST.D-3SG
'(We) have come into wealth.' (lit. 'wealth has come in front of us') (RAKR in Bashir 2023b)

8.3.2 Temporal adverbs 'now' and 'then'

To refer to the present time (moment of the speech act), *(ha)níse(n)* 'now' (8.65) (8.66) and *thésu* ~ *thesum* 'just now', 'right now' (8.67) are used.

(8.65) *é:i, g-ití as-ús he báče tu*
hey, come-PFV.PTCP be(ANIM)-PRS-2SG 3SG.DIST for you

haníse khyóte es no ko-s-án?
now why it NEG do-2SG.PRS/FUT-S

'Hey, you have come for that, now why aren't you doing it?' (oral text, Village Parwak)

(8.66) *avá yał kor-áv boy-ák ó-š-t-am mágam*
I polo do-IPFV.PTCP go-AG AUG-be-PST.D-1SG but

haníse petsh-í as-úm
now leave-PFV.PTCP be(ANIM).PRS-1SG

'I used to go to play polo, but now I have given it up.' (MNN in Bashir 2023b)

(8.67) *dadá thésu g-ití as-úr*
father just.now come-PFV.PTCP be(ANIM)-PRS.3SG
'Father has just come.' (Village Zondrangram)

Stressed *dí* 'now', 'so' appears in contexts like *dí bísi* 'now let's go!' and example (8.68). This word appears clause initially, as opposed to unstressed *di* 'also', 'too', which immediately follows the word or phrase to which it applies.

(8.68) *é: brargíni-á:n ma khamánd ayh ç̣ak-é-t-ay*
hey brothers-VOC.PL my bow up attach-CAUS-PST.D-3SG

dí avá ayh nis-ím
now I up go.out-1SG.PRS/FUT.NS

'Hey, brothers, my bow has hit its mark, now I will go up there.' (oral text, Village Bang)

'Then', 'at that time', as opposed to 'now', is expressed with *haté waqt* or *hatóvat*, as in (8.69) and (8.70). Both *the* (8.71) and *théki* (8.72) mean 'then', in the sense of 'then', 'next', 'after that'.

(8.69) *avá haté váqt-a badtabyát as-ít-am*
I that time-LOC1 sad be(ANIM)-PST.D-1SG
'I was feeling sad at that time.' (MNN in Bashir 2023b)

(8.70) *the áči ki h-áni, hatóvat ta*
then back when come.PST.D-3PL at.that.time you.OBL
kós-te ki dy-áru h-ay
who.OBL-DAT that give-CAUS.DES come.PST.D-3SG
d-os
give-2SG.PRS/FUT.NS
'Then when they come back, at that time you will give (her) to whomever you feel like.' (oral text, Village Bang)

(8.71) *the se grinǰ gaán-t-ay the se čalayyár gaántay*
then REM.3SG rice buy-PST.D-3SG then he cloth bought
the šoxór gaántay the grinǰ gaántay the šu
then sugar bought then rice bought then handloom.cloth
gaántay – h-ay dur-ó-ten
bought – come.PST.D-3SG home-OBL-DAT
'Then he bought rice, then he bought cloth, then he bought sugar, then he bought rice, then he bought handloom woollen cloth—he came home.' (oral text, Village Kari)

(8.72) *théki baǰaxána boš-ít-ay théki doól boš-ít-ay*
then band sound-PST.D-3SG then drum sound-PST.D-3SG
théki ḍázi kor-ík-a prá-ni
then firing do-INF-LOC1 beat.PST.D-3PL
'Then the band played, then drums played, then they began to fire in the air.' (oral text, Village Bang)

8.3.3 Divisions of time

Basic terms for times of day include: *čhúči* 'morning'; *graníš* 'noontime', 'early afternoon'; *pišín* 'afternoon (approximately 12.30–4.00 p.m.)'; *čhaγonás* 'late afternoon', 'early evening (from about 4.00 p.m. to 6.00 p.m.)' (lit. 'edge of shade'); *šam* 'evening'; and *čhuí* 'night', 'darkness'.

Words for the sequence of days preceding and following the current day are: *(ha)-nún*, 'today', 'these days'; *čhúči* 'in the morning', 'tomorrow'; *pingačhúy* 'tomorrow'; *pingáh* 'the day after tomorrow'; *šupingáh* 'third day from now', 'day after *pingáh*'; *walóγun* 'fourth day from now, the day after *šupingáh*'; *doṣ* 'yesterday'; *ohtíri* 'the day before yesterday'; *očóhti* 'the third day before now, the day before *ohtíri*'.[8] Examples (8.73) and (8.74) show two senses of *čhúči*. *γerdí anús* means 'the next day', with the reference point the current day in the world of a narrative or story, not the current day in the world of the speaker/storyteller (8.75). With days of the week, *uxtí* expresses 'next', as in *uxtí adin-én* 'on next Friday' (from the actual time of speech) (4.29) above. With days of the week, instrumental *-én* is used for temporal location.

(8.73) *avá har anús čhúči ċhoy bağa-á ruph-óm*
I every day morning six o'clock-LOC1 arise-1SG.PRS/FUT.NS
'I get up every day at six o'clock in the morning.' (MNN)

(8.74) *čhúči pišávur-o-te b-ím-an*
tomorrow Peshawar-OBL-DAT go-1SG.PRS/FUT-S
'Tomorrow I am going to Peshawar.' (EB field notes)

(8.75) *γerd-í anús-o háte vav baγ-áy*
turn-PFV.PTCP day-OBL REM.3SG old.woman go.PST.D-3SG
'On the next day the old woman left.' (oral text, Village Kari)

Words for the present year and numbers of years before and after the present year include: *hayá sal* 'this year', *sóra sal* 'following year', *uxtí sal* 'next year', *por* 'last year' (8.76), *poržér* 'two years ago', *γoržér* 'three years ago'.

(8.76) *por boṣík no b-íti zemín pulu-ít-ay*
last.year rain NEG become-PFV.PTCP land burn-PST.D-3SG
'Because there was no rain last year, the land dried up.' (DSAL)

The concept of a temporal interval beginning at a point in the past and continuing into the present, 'since', is expressed with NP-ABL + *yií* or *yíri* 'up to now', as in (8.77) and (8.78). Unbounded time is *hamíš* 'always'. Continuing action, 'still', is expressed by *haníse di*.

[8] These terms were supplied by Maula Nigah Nigah of Village Zondrangram in Terich, who pointed out that there is some regional variation in their meanings within Chitral. For example, *doṣ* means 'yesterday' in Torkhow, Mulkhow, and Chitral Town, but in Laspur and Yarkhun it means 'day before yesterday' (MNN, SWKA, and IF in Bashir (2023b)).

(8.77) *por-ár* *y-ií* *ma γeč* *khur* *b-íti*
last.year-ABL here-LOC2 my eyes dim become-PFV.PTCP
š-éni
be(INAN)-PRS.3PL
'My eyesight has become weak since last year.' (DSAL)

(8.78) *avá* *haté* *vaxt-ár* *yír-i* *niš-í* *as-ít-am*
I that time-ABL now-LOC2 sit-PFV.PTCP be(ANIM)-PST.D-1SG
'I was sitting (someplace) from that time until now.' (MNN)

Repetition at temporal intervals is signalled by reduplicative expressions like *yorán-a yorán-a* 'each year', where *-a* is the LOC1 case ending.

Words referring to timeliness include *gur* 'late (in absolute sense, with reference to time of day or season)' (8.79), which contrasts with the meaning of *malál* 'late', 'delay' (in relative sense, with reference to proper or appointed time for something)' (8.80). The most common word for 'early' is *rayéšṭi*; *ẓ̌ot* has the additional senses of 'early in the morning', 'previously', 'already' and 'some time ago'. *darbát* 'for a little while' and *zamán-a* 'in a while' both refer to limited periods of time, with *zamán-a* 'in a while' indicating a longer time than *darbát-a* 'in a little while (today)', 'soon'.

(8.79) *dáłum* *šor-ó* *gur* *pač-úr*
pomegranate autumn-OBL late ripen-3SG.PRS/FUT.NS
'Pomegranates ripen late in the autumn.' (DSAL)

(8.80) *malál-a* *g-ík-o* *tat* *žav-ó* *buł-ít-ay*
delay-LOC1 come-INF-OBL father son-OBL scold-PST.D-3SG
'When he$_i$ came late, the father$_j$ scolded his son$_i$.' (DSAL)

8.4. Interrogative adverbs

8.4.1 Spatial interrogatives

The root *kur-* [*k(u)-* (interrogative) + *-r-* (locative element)] 'where?' refers to unspecified locations. It combines with the locative case endings LOC1 *-a* and LOC2 *-i*, yielding *kúr-a* 'where (pointlike location)?', as in *kúr-a paydá hov* 'What's up?' (lit. 'Where (why) have you turned up?'), and *kúr-i* and its short form *kúi* 'where (+ motion component)', 'whither?', as in *tu kúi bi astá:v* 'Where did you go?' (Sense: 'Where have you been?'). The simple, literal meaning of *kúra* 'where?' appears in (8.81). *kur* also takes the ABL *-ár*, giving *kur-ár* 'from where?', 'whence?' (8.82).

(8.81) *ham-ó kúr-a lé-t-av*
PROX.SG-OBL where-LOC1 find-PST.D-2SG
'Where did you find this/it?' (DSAL)

As with other WH-question words in Khowar and other languages, *kúra* 'where?' is also used in rhetorical questions which convey a strong negative implication, as in (8.82) and (8.83).

(8.82) *kałák-a pay-ó po níki šetú kur-ár*
Kałak-LOC1 goat-OBL footprint is.not buttermilk where-ABL
g-oy
come-3SG.PRS/FUT.NS
Proverb. 'In Kalak there isn't even a goat's footprint; where will buttermilk come from?' Sense: refers in general to misguided efforts. (GNK in Bashir 2023b)

(8.83) *báγ-a niš-ík-o γoš kúra š-er*
garden-LOC1 sit-INF-OBL free.time where be(INAN)-PRS.3SG
'I don't have time to sit in the garden.' (lit. 'Where is there free time to sit in the garden?' (MNN)

8.4.2 Temporal interrogative

The element *vat* (< Ar., Prs., and Ur. *vaqt* 'time') appears in some compound temporal adverbs, including the basic interrogative temporal adverb *kyávat* 'when?' (8.84). The reduplicated expression *kyávat kyávat* means 'from time to time', 'sometimes'; and *kyávat ki* 'when(ever) (relative)' is used as in (8.85). When *vaxt* 'time' occurs as a separate word, /x/ (< /q/) remains (8.86).

(8.84) *tu kyávat b-ís-an*
you when go-2SG.PRS/FUT-S
'When are you going?' (DSAL)

(8.85) *avá kyávat.ki g-óm-an tu kórum tan*
I whenever come-1SG.PRS/FUT-S you work EMPH
kó-s-an
do-2SG.PRS/FUT-S
'Whenever I come you are always working.' (MNN)

(8.86) *grisp-oó váxt-a γarí-tu šáru*
summer-OBL time-LOC1 high.pastures-LOC3 coolness
b-oy
become-3SG-PRS/FUT.NS
'In the summertime it is cool in the high pastures.' (DSAL)

The OIA-origin elements *kal* 'when' and *-kal* 'time for a specific activity' (T3084) remain in several words belonging to the OIA stratum of the language, like *hasyákal* 'breakfast time', *češṭákal* 'lunch time', *botákal* 'supper time', and others referring to times for specific routine activities like *kiṣbotákal* 'ploughing time'.

8.4.3 Reason or purpose interrogatives

The basic word for 'why?' is *ko*, used as in (8.87). Reason or purpose is also often expressed by *khyóte* 'what for?', as in (8.88).

(8.87) *čay no pi ko b-imi-an*
tea NEG drink.PFV.PTCP why go-2PL.PRS/FUT-S
'Why are you leaving without drinking tea?' (DSAL)

(8.88) *ṣotár-i khy-ó-te kas-ís-an*
river.bed-LOC2 what-OBL-DAT walk-2SG.PRS/FUT-S
'What are you walking around in the dry riverbed for?' (DSAL)

When the reason or motivation for an act is questioned or challenged, *kyaní* or *kyam* 'what', 'why' often appear, as in (8.89) and (8.90). Lack of reason is expressed by *ingár* 'for nothing', 'uselessly', as in (8.91).

(8.89) *zap-án ʦop kor-í kyaní k-ós-an*
garment-OBL.PL heap do-PFV.PTCP what/why do-2SG.PRS/FUT-S
'Why are you piling up the clothes (in disorder).' (DSAL)

(8.90) *burbúr.d-ití kyám bo-s-án*
glare-PFV.PTCP why become-2SG.PRS/FUT-S
'Why are you glaring at (someone)?' (RAKR in Bashir 2023b)

(8.91) *hes ingár bazár-i yaẓé-r-an,*
3SG.DIST for.nothing bazaar-LOC2 roam-3SG.PRS/FUT-S
kya kórum níki
any work is.not
'He is just roaming aimlessly in the bazaar. He doesn't have anything to do (there).' (MNN in Bashir 2023b)

When a negative sentence with *ko* 'why' is questioned or challenged, the negative *no* sometimes precedes *ko*, as in (8.92).[9] For further discussion of this point, see Section 9.2.3.

(8.92) *avá no ko b-ím-an*
I NEG why go-1SG.PRS/FUT-S
'Why won't/wouldn't I go?' (oral text, Village Bang)

8.5 Degree adverbials

In addition to the deictic adverbs of quantity (Section 5.3.2), some basic forms refer to excess or deficiency. The basic term for a large quantity or excess is *bo* 'very', '(too) much', as in (8.93). Several other adverbs intensify the meanings of the terms they modify; they include *ṭip* 'full', 'lots of' (8.94); *pin* 'fast', 'intense' (8.94); *thafá* 'quite', 'very' (8.95); *diš* 'extreme(ly)'; *saxt* ~ *sax* 'extreme(ly)', 'very much' (8.96); *doł* 'loud', 'strong', 'forceful', 'strongly', 'forcefully'; *faqát* 'exactly', 'just', 'right', 'only' (8.97); and *zyat* 'more'.

(8.93) *bo niš-ít-am dí par-ísi*
much sit-PST.D-1PL now lie.down-1PL.HORT
'We have sat (talking) for a long time, now let's go to sleep.' (RAKR in Bashir 2023b)

[9] NEG-WHY is an unusual word-order pattern, which I have not found in other nearby languages. Palula has the opposite order, WHY NEG, lexicalised in the word *keéna* 'WHY.NEG' (Liljegren 2016: 239). Dameli has the sequence *ku ni* 'WHY NEG' (Perder 2013: 211). Wakhi has the order 'WHY.NEG'. In my materials, the sequence *no ko* is attested mainly in oral folk texts where natural conversation appears. Whether this is observed natural conversation in the other languages mentioned remains an open question.

The basic sense of *pin* is 'intense', so it can also mean 'too much', as in (8.94), a well-known tongue twister. The various senses of *pin* (< Bur., Lorimer 1938: 290) partially overlap with those of *tez* (< Prs.) (8.95), a later addition to the lexicon, an instance of semantic doublets.

(8.94) *ṭhósṭ-a ṭip trin trín-o trup pin*
bowl-LOC1 full yogurt yogurt-LOC4 salt intense
'The bowl is full of yogurt; the yogurt is too salty.' (IWA in Bashir 2023b)

(8.95) *tez g-íti thafá ǰam a-r-ú*
fast come-PFV.PTCP very good AUG-do.PST.D-2SG
'You did very well to come quickly.' (DSAL)

(8.96) *ʣaxmí ma saxt c̣ham-é-t-ay mágam*
wound me severely pain-CAUS-PST.D-3SG but
žiré-t-am
digest-PST.D-1SG
'The wound hurt me severely, but I tolerated it.' (lit. 'digested it') (MNN)

(8.97) *ma žav faqát he ḍaq-ó γon tán*
my son exactly that boy-OBL like EMPH
'My son is/looks exactly like that boy.' (DSAL)

Words referring to insufficiency include *hávl* 'very little', 'hardly' (8.98), 'barely' (8.99); *kam* '(too) little', 'less' (8.100); and *phuk* 'a little' (8.102). *kam* 'less', 'little', which functions either adjectivally or adverbially, appears either as an independent word (8.100) or as an adjective-forming prefix, as in *kamnasíb* 'unlucky', 'unfortunate', *kamzát* 'of low caste or class', *kamdást* 'poor'.

(8.98) *čéy-o trup havl b-íti š-er*
tea-LOC4 salt very.little be-PFV.PTCP be(INAN)-PRS.3SG
'There is hardly any salt in the tea.' (RAKR in Bashir 2023b)

(8.99) *havl ma kár-a pr-ay*
barely my ear-LOC1 strike.PST.D-3SG
'I barely heard it.' (RAKR in Bashir 2023b)

(8.100) *haníse čhuy-ó drungí kam b-av*
now night-OBL length less become-IPFV.PTCP
g-óy-an
come-3SG.PRS/FUT-S
'These days the length of the nights is decreasing.' (SWKA in Bashir 2023b)

A suffixal morpheme with attenuative senses '-ish', 'rather' is *-roó*, as in *phuk roó* 'smallish', 'rather small'; 'somewhat'; 'a little' (8.101) and (8.102). *darbát* 'a little while' refers to a short interval, as in *darbát niší bísi* 'Let's sit for a little while and (then) go.'

(8.101) *é ɣaríp vav, yií g-ye! yi-roó g-ye!*
hey, poor old.woman here come-IMP.SG here-a.little come-IMP.SG
'Hey, old woman, come here, come here a little.' (oral text, Village Bang)

(8.102) *bas kos-ít-ay sal kos-ít-ay phuk*
day walk-PST.D-3SG year walk-PST.D-3SG a.little
af-roó b-i noɣór-o póng-a baɣ-áy
down-a.little go-PFV.PTCP fort-OBL foot-LOC1 go.PST.D-3SG
'He walked for a day, he walked for a year, (then) going a little downward he went to the foot (entrance) of a fort.' (oral text, Village Kari)

Several basic adverbs express degrees of speed. They include *ṣav* 'quickly', 'soon' (8.103); *pin* 'fast', 'strong' (8.104); *téz* 'quickly'; and *laš* (8.105) 'slowly, 'gently', 'quietly'.

(8.103) *paxtúri žaɣa-á nyamát ṣav tar-ír*
sunny place-LOC1 crops soon ripen-3SG-PRS/FUT.NS
'Crops ripen quickly in sunny places.' (DSAL)

(8.104) *hes pin dé-r-an*
3SG.REM fast run-3SG.PRS/FUT-S
'S/he is running fast.' (IWA in Bashir 2023b)

(8.105) *ma ḍek çhom-ík-en laš ɣuzár lakh-óm-an*
my leg hurt-INF-INST slowly step place-1SG.PRS/FUT-S
'Because my leg hurts, I am stepping slowly.' (DSAL)

8.6 Adverbial relations expressed by postpositions

Some adverbial relations formerly expressed by case endings in OIA are expressed in Khowar by postpositional phrases. They include temporal, goal, source, instrumental, and accompaniment meanings.

8.6.1 Goal

The dative postposition *-t ~ -te, ~ -ten, ~ -tene ~tenen* expresses various GOAL relationships, including physical destination (8.106), indirect object (8.107), addressee (8.108), purpose (8.109), and beneficiary (8.110).

(8.106) *ayí b-ir b-ir mał-ó-te*
snake go-3SG.PRS/FUT.NS go-3SG.PRS/FUT.NS nest-OBL-DAT
Proverb. 'A snake goes only to its nest.' Sense: A person prefers to go to his own home, no matter what it is like. (DSAL)

(8.107) *rét-ay.ki paáč-oó žur-gíni-an osoéni-an*
say.PST.D-3SG king-OBL daughter-PL-OBL.PL handkerchief-OBL. PL
pisá-te phrét-am
you.PL-DAT give.PST.D-1SG
'He said, "I (hereby) give the king's daughters' handkerchiefs to you."' (performative statement) (oral text, Village Bang)

(8.108) *háte ḍaq-ó-ten nan rétay.ki tan nán-o*
3SG.REM boy-OBL-DAT mother said REFL mother-OBL
bulbúl-é:
nightingale-VOC
'(His) mother said to the boy, "O, your mother's darling …"' (oral text, Village Uthul)

(8.109) *bo-í láka toó-te ṣádar-mádar malí*
plant-PFV.PTCP like REM.SG-DAT servant-ECHO.REDUP gardener
malí peés-t-ay uγ laák-ík-o-tenen
ECHO.REDUP leave-PST.D-3SG water release-INF-OBL-DAT
xaṣké-ik-o-ten
cultivate-INF-OBL-DAT
'Having planted it, he left servants and gardeners to water and cultivate it.' (oral text, Village Uthul)

(8.110) *sot ži-žáv as-ít-ani haté žižáv-an-te*
seven REDUP.PL-son be(ANIM).PST.D-3PL REM.PL
boók no al-áy
sons-OBL.PL-DAT wife NEG bring.PST.D-3SG
'He had seven sons. He didn't bring wives for those sons.' (oral text, Village Bang)

8.6.2 Source

Concrete or abstract SOURCE concepts, like motion away from a physical location or cause by something abstract, are expressed with the ablative case ending *-ar* (8.111) or a postposition based on the ablative (8.112) and (8.113). Motion away from an animate entity is usually expressed with the postposition *sar*, as in (8.112) and (8.113).

(8.111) *ma véṣky-ar tá-te kya taklíf no b-oy*
my side-ABL you-DAT any trouble NEG become-3SG.PRS/FUT.NS
'You won't have any trouble from me.' (SWKA in Bashir 2023b)

(8.112) *hasé ma sar kitáb-o avér-t-ay*
REM.SG me from book-OBL snatch-PST.D-3SG
'S/he snatched the book away from me.' (SWKA in Bashir 2023b)

(8.113) *xatumán savzé-i brár-o sar tanhá*
rooms make-PFV.PTCP brother-OBL from separate
ho-y
become.PST.D-3SG
'He made a house and separated from his brother.' (DSAL)

The ablative-based postpositions *sar* ~ *sári* and *-γar* ~ *γári* also express various abstract SOURCE concepts including interlocutor (8.114) and source of or reason for an attitude or opinion (8.115) (8.116).

(8.114) *kíča as-ús no ré-ni bašár*
how be(ANIM)-2SG.PRS NEG say-3PL.PRS/FUT.NS question
no k-óni hat-oó sar
NEG do-3PL.PRS/FUT.NS 3SG.REM-OBL from
'They don't say, "How are you?" They don't ask about him.' (lit. 'from him') (oral text, Village Sorech)

(8.115) *ma sar baṣék no a-r-ér*
me from trust NEG AUG-do.PST.D-3SG
'S/he didn't trust me.' (DSAL)

(8.116) *avá hat-oγó sar verán hó-t-am*
I REM.REM.SG-OBL from bored become.PST.D-PST.D-1SG
'I got bored with him/her.' (RKB in Bashir 2023b)

Comparison is one of the most frequent functions of the ablative postposition *sar*, as in (8.117), (8.118), and (8.119).

(8.117) *kumóru he ḍaq-ó sar úmr-a loṭ*
girl that boy-OBL ABL age-LOC1 big
'The girl is older than that boy.' (DSAL)

(8.118) *maṣk-ík-o sar d-ik ǰam*
ask.for-INF-OBL ABL give-INF good
'It is better to give than to ask for (things).' (DSAL)

(8.119) *ma sar di zarú i kaγ rét-ay ma sar*
me ABL even aged one crow say.PST.D-3SG me ABL
çhík-o sar loṭ … hasé
all-OBL ABL old … that.one
'(There is) a crow even older than me, it said, (it is) older than me, older than everyone … that one.' (oral text, Village Sorech)

8.6.3 Instrument

In addition to the instrumental case ending *-én*, instrumental meaning is expressed with the postposition *sóra* 'with (instrumental)' ← 'head.on', as in (8.120), (8.121), and (8.122).[10]

[10] Lorimer (1937: 77ff) notes that in Burushaski, Dumaki, and sometimes Khowar, but not in Shina, the suffix or postposition which essentially means 'on', 'upon', 'above' is used to denote the instrument or manner 'with' or 'by' which something is done, as in Burushaski *tʌxt-aṭɛ hurúṭimi* 'He sat *on* the throne' and *tobʎq-aṭɛ dɛlimi* 'he shot (him) *with* a gun'. This seems to be a contact effect between Burushaski and Khowar, with extension from Burushaski to Dumaki, but whether the construction originates in Khowar or in Burushaski is unclear.

(8.120) *bel-ó sóra toq ma-t ang-yé*
spade-OBL with mud I.OBL-DAT bring-IMP.2SG
'Bring me some mud with the spade.' (DSAL)

(8.121) *tshondzúr-o sóra bax nez-é*
awl-OBL with hole take.out-IMP.SG
'Make a hole with the/a shoemaker's awl.' (DSAL)

(8.122) *axerí i tał behč-í o-š-óy hat-oyó*
finally one key remain-PFV.PTCP AUG-be-PST.D.3SG REM.SG-OBL
sóra háte duváht-o huúr-t-ay
with REM.SG door-OBL open-PST.D-3SG
'Finally one key remained. With it he opened the door.' (oral text, Village Uthul)

8.6.4 Accompaniment

The two variant forms of the postposition *sum* ~ *su* 'with' are sometimes, but not always, interchangeable. Example (8.123) shows both variants used in the same context. *su* ~ *sum* can indicate accompaniment (8.124) or joint participation in an action, such as in embracing (8.123) or receiving help (8.125).

(8.123) *prušṭ g-íti toó sum toór-t-ay*
ahead come-PFV.PTCP REMOTE.SG OBL with reach-PST.D-3SG
toó su çang.h-oy
him with embrace-PST.D-3SG
'He came to receive him, reached him, and embraced him.' (oral text, Village Bang)

(8.124) *ma af laák-e ma yar-án-an su i.korí*
me out release-IMP.2SG me friend-PL-OBL.PL with together
'Let me out, together with my friends!' (oral text, Village Kari)

(8.125) *ma sum madát kor-é*
me with help do-IMP.SG
'Help me.' (SWKA in Bashir 2023b)

8.7 Manner adverbial relations expressed with perfective participles

The basic word for 'how?' is *kíča*. It is often encountered in construction with *bíti*, the PFV.PTCP of *b-* 'become' (8.126) with intransitive verbs and *kóri*, the PFV.PTCP of *kor-* 'do' with transitives. For example, (8.126) asks how an intransitive event (coming alive) could happen, and (8.127) asks how a transitive act (opening a door) can be done. Many such manner expressions are formed from adjectives + *bíti*, for example, *phik biti* 'quietly' (8.128), *i biti* 'together' (8.129).

(8.126) *xá:y ... žúnu kíča.b-íti hó-t-am*
Ooh ... alive how.become-PFV.PTCP become-PST.D-1SG
'Oh, how did I come alive?' (oral text, Village Sorech)

(8.127) *kíča.kór-i hur-ín b-oy*
how.do-PFV.PTCP open-POT.PTCP be.able-3SG.PRS/FUT.NS
'How can it be opened?' (TMFD)

(8.128) *žav-ó-t ré-t-ay.ki tu ré-t-ay.ki*
son-OBL-DAT say-PST.D-3SG.that you say-PST.D-3SG.that
niš-é phik.b-íti
sit-IMP.SG silent.become.PFV.PTCP
'She said to (her) son, "You sit quietly!"' (oral text, Village Parwak)[11]

(8.129) *i.b-íti b-ísi*
one.become-PFV.PTCP go-1PL.PRS/FUT.NS
'We'll go together.' or 'Let's go together.'

Many common adjectives can also function as adverbs, for example *γalát* 'wrong', 'incorrectly' (8.130) and *namúti* 'barefoot' as in *namúti mo kosé* 'Don't walk barefoot!'

(8.130) *γalát kardú bir-ét-am*
wrong do.PFV.PTCP become-PST.I-1SG
'I have (unwittingly) done it wrong (and just realised it now).' (RKB)

[11] The exact wording of the storyteller has been retained. It shows the frequent repetition of *rétayki*. 's/he said', often used as a filler, which is characteristic of this genre.

8.7.1 Complex motion events: motion event, path, and manner

Complex motion events essentially involve a motion event, a path (trajectory), and a manner of motion. The lexicalisation patterns of such motion events have been studied for many languages, and a two-part typology has emerged: languages which lexicalise manner and motion event in the verb, like English, and those in which the manner expression is expressed in an adjunct phrase, like Spanish. An illustrative English example is: *The man is limping away*, in which motion and manner are lexicalised in the verb 'limping'. An oft-cited example from Spanish is *la botella entró a la cueva flotando* 'The bottle entered the cave floating' ('The bottle floated into the cave'), in which motion and path are combined in the verb *entró* and manner expressed with the participle *flotando* (Talmy 2007: 89).[12]

In Khowar, perfective participles often function as adverbs, as in (8.131), (8.132), (8.133), (8.134), and (8.135). In (8.131), (8.132), (8.133), and (8.134) the manner of motion is expressed as a participial phrase, the motion event as the verb, and the path as a pre-verbal locative expression. In (8.135), the manner 'on top of the water' is expressed in a postpositional phrase, while the motion event and path, *af bayáy* 'went down', is conveyed by the verb and its pre-verbal directional particle or locative expression. These examples illustrate how Khowar expresses motion events which include elements of manner and path. In the glosses for these examples, the literal gloss is presented first, with the normal English expression in parentheses. In Khowar, the motion event itself is expressed by the verb and the manner of motion is expressed by a participle or other adverbial expression. In this respect, Khowar is typologically similar to Spanish or Turkish (Özyürek & Kita 2020).

(8.131) *hes* *mahmezé-i* *žóy-a* *phar*
DIST.3SG jump-PFV.PTCP water.channel-LOC1 away
nis-áy
emerge-PST.D.3SG
'Jumping, s/he crossed the water channel.' ('S/he jumped over the water channel.') (DSAL)

[12] This typological characteristic is discussed in the linguistics literature in terms of a typology of *path* (or verb-framed) and *manner* (or satellite-framed) languages. Early presentation of this idea is to be found in Talmy (1975 and 1985), and more recently in Talmy (2007) and Levin et al. (2010).

(8.132) *moóš khúṭ-i phar b-ír-an*
man limp-PFV.PTCP away go-3SG.PRS/FUT-S
'Limping, the man is going over there (away from speaker).' ('The man is limping away.') (DSAL)

(8.133) *pin de-é ma gón-a h-ay*
fast run-PFV.PTCP I.OBL vicinity-LOC1 come.PST.D.3SG
'Running quickly, s/he came to me.' ('S/he ran quickly to me.') (DSAL)

(8.134) *haté durzán ḍaq ušṭur-í baγ-áy*
REM.SG.DIR mischievous boy run-PFV.PTCP go.PST.D-3SG
'That mischievous boy left running.' ('That mischievous boy ran away.') (SWKA in Bashir 2023b)

(8.135) *dar uγ-ó sór-a sór-a af baγ-áy*
log water-OBL top-LOC1 top-LOC1 down go.PST.D-3SG
'The log went down(stream) on top of (the water)' ('The log floated downstream.') (SWKA in Bashir 2023b)

The same construction is also found with manner expressions denoting types of action other than simple motion, as in (8.136).

(8.136) *hasé froṣké-i qohté-i toór-t-ay*
REM.SG.DIR pant-PFV.PTCP pant-PFV.PTCP reach-PST.D-3SG
'S/he reached (his/her destination) panting.' (IWA in Bashir 2023b)

8.7.2 Adverbial use of the imperfective participle

The imperfective participle has mostly adverbial characteristics. It does not appear attributively, usually appearing preceding the verb phrase. Examples are (8.137) and (8.138).

(8.137) *ḍaq keł-áv baγ-áy*
boy weep-IPFV.PTCP go.PST.D-3SG
'The boy left weeping.' (EB field notes)

(8.138) *tu ingár čang-áv ma fan d-ós-an*
you for.nothing lie-IPFV.PTCP me deception give-2SG.PRS/FUT-S
'You are lying and deceiving me for nothing.' (DSAL)

It also has the nominal characteristic of taking case endings. The LOC1 form of the imperfective participle functions to express the temporal relation 'while'. The difference in sense between the plain imperfective participle and its locative form in *-áva* can be seen by comparing (8.137) and (8.140). In (8.137) the sense is that the boy started crying simultaneously with leaving.[13] The LOC1 morpheme in (8.140), however, indicates an already ongoing action (crying), during which a punctual action (leaving) takes place.

(8.139) *hasé lu.dy-áv-a γeč.γéč-a ašrú*
REM.SG speak-IPFV.PTCP-LOC1 eye.eye-LOC1 tears
h-óy
become.PST.D-3SG
'While s/he was talking, tears came into his/her eyes.' (SWKA in Bashir 2023b)

(8.140) *ḍaq keł-áv-a b-aγ-áy*
boy weep-IPFV.PTCP-LOC1 go-PST.D-3SG
'The boy left while (already) crying.' (EB field notes)

8.7.3 Sentence adverbial functions

The scope of sentence adverbials is the entire sentence, as in example (8.16) above; some modal or quasi-modal expressions fall into this category.

8.7.3.1 Event realisation

Some adverbs refer to the realisation status of an action or event. Two words specifically refer to unrealised events: *dex* 'almost', 'nearly' (8.141), which can also be reduplicated, yielding *dexdéx* 'nearly', 'just about to' (8.142). The verb form in both these examples is the past incompletive, which consists of the past participle + the past direct of *š-* 'be', which conveys non-completion of an action (see Section 6.8.2.3).

[13] Perhaps the boy did not want to leave and started crying when he had to leave unwillingly. I am grateful to Maula Nigah Nigah for pointing out this distinction.

(8.141) *thuék-en dex ma d-irú o-š-óv mágam*
rifle-INS almost me hit-PST.PTCP AUG-be.PST.D-2SG but

má-su no toór-t-ay
me-with NEG reach-PST.D-3SG

'You nearly shot me with the rifle, but (the bullet) didn't hit me.' (MNN)

(8.142) *dexdéx hatoγó d-irú o-š-ót-am*
just.about REM.SG.OBL beat-PST.PTCP AUG-be-PST.D-1SG

hánya suvál-o nez-ít-ay
just.then question-OBL solve-PST.D-3SG

'I was just about to beat him; just then he answered the question.' (MNN in Bashir 2023b)

Incomplete realisation or completion with difficulty is expressed with *havl* 'barely', 'hardly' (8.143).[14]

(8.143) *havl ma kár-a pr-ay*
barely my ear-LOC1 strike.PST.D-3SG
'I barely heard it.' (RAKR in Bashir 2023b)

Questioning of the realisation status, or the truth value, of a predication is indicated with the sentence-final interrogative particle *-aá*, which expresses polar, or 'yes–no' questions (8.144), (8.145).

(8.144) *kya išnári mat d-ós-an-aá*
some thing me-DAT give-2SG.PRS/FUT-S-Q
'Do you want to give me something?' (DSAL)

(8.145) *benusí-aá*
health-Q
'Are you well?' (lit. 'Is there good health?') (MNN in Bashir 2023b)

8.7.3.2 Epistemic modality

Epistemic modality, pertaining, among other things, to the speaker's perception of the likelihood of an action or event, is expressed in Khowar

[14] Example (8.99) is repeated here as (8.143) for the convenience of the reader.

by a variety of means, including sentence adverbs. See Section 10.5 for discussion of several mechanisms for conveying epistemic modality.

8.8 Adverbial relations expressed by subordinate clauses

Several types of adverbial relations are expressed by subordinate clauses, including temporal, causal, and purpose relations. These are treated in Chapter 9.

9
Morphosyntax

9.1 Introduction

Khowar is a consistent but flexible SUBJECT–OBJECT–VERB (SOV) language, with ADJECTIVE–NOUN (ADJ-N), GENITIVE–NOUN (GEN-N), standard-ADJ comparative construction, and NOUN–POSTPOSITION word-order patterns. The default word order is SOV, but it is flexible, depending on topic and focus considerations in the same way as in other SOV languages. Sentence-initial position is topical (old information), while new (focal) information is (immediately) pre-verbal. Since finite verbs are marked for person and number, pronominal subjects are often not expressed with full pronouns. When full pronouns occur, they usually convey an emphatic or contrastive sense or are introducing an actor for the first time.

Khowar has NOMINATIVE–ACCUSATIVE (NOM-ACC) case alignment, all subjects of intransitives and agents of transitives appearing in the direct case in all tense-aspect-mood (TAM) forms, and verb agreement with the subject in all tenses. There is no trace of the split ergativity found in most other New Indo-Aryan (NIA) languages. Retention of distinctive Old Indo-Aryan (OIA) past tenses and the *a*-augment apparently prevented the development of the participle-based past tenses found in the NIA languages in the Indo-Gangetic plain, thus allowing the retention of the OIA NOM-ACC case-marking system.

Subordinate clauses are both left- and right-branching. Relative clause structures are of two types: finite and non-finite.

9.2 Simple sentences

Simple sentences can have a nominal predicate—noun, pronoun, or adjective—or have a finite verb as predicate.

9.2.1 Nominal sentences

Khowar's *š-* 'be(INAN)' and *as-* 'be(ANIM)' are existential and locative predicates which also serve as auxiliaries in some TAM forms. They do not, however, appear as copulas in nominal sentences in the present tense, like 'I am a doctor'. In non-present sentences, however, a copular verb is necessary as a carrier of tense information. There are three types of nominal sentences. (1) Equational sentences are of the form x = y, where x and y are definite nominals; (9.1) is an example of this type. If the nominal predicate is an interrogative pronoun, as in (9.2) the reply is normally expected to be a definite or specific NP. (2) Some nominal sentences, for example (9.3), are of the form 'x is a y', where x is a definite NP and y is an indefinite NP. Such sentences express permanent class membership. (3) Some have the form x is ADJ; in such sentences an individual-level adjective names a permanent or inherent property of the subject, as in (9.4) and (9.5). Example (9.5) also illustrates the negation of a nominal sentence with *nóh*.[1]

(9.1) *hayá ma žav*
this my son
'This is my son.' (DSAL)

(9.2) *hayá pay-ó xátsum ka*
this goat-OBL owner who
'Who is the owner of this goat?' (DSAL)

(9.3) *ma braár ḍakṭhár*
my brother doctor
'My brother is a doctor.' (EB field notes)

(9.4) *hes i ḍek-én khašál*
DIST.SG one leg-INS lame
'S/he is lame in one leg.' (RAKR in Bashir 2023b)

[1] See Bashir (2023a) for detailed discussion of these points.

(9.5) *šot čo-ík jam nóh*
oath swear-1NF good NEG
'Swearing oaths is not good.' (DSAL)

Indirect/mirative counterparts of nominal sentences are constructed with the mirative of *b-* 'become' (9.6). The sentence in example (9.6) conveys information new to the speaker and is thus mirative. It could be either direct, if the speaker observed the tree dropping fruit himself, or indirect, if he was told this fact about the tree by someone else. To see the semantic contribution of indirectivity/mirativity, compare (9.6) with its direct counterpart (9.7). Example (9.8) illustrates a mirative counterpart of a nominal adjectival predicate.

(9.6) *hayá paloóɣ çhoróku bir-áy*
PROX.SG.DIR apple.tree liable.to.drop become.MIR-3SG
'This apple tree turns out to be one that bears fruit that drop easily.' (I just learned this now.) (SWKA in Bashir 2023b)

(9.7) *hayá paloóɣ çhoróku*
PROX.SG.DIR apple.tree liable.to.drop
'This apple tree is one that bears fruit that drop easily.' (I have known this for some time.) (SWKA in Bashir 2023b)

(9.8) *pay-ó muúž ṣa bir-áy*
goat-OBL marrow black become.MIR-3SG
'The goat's marrow is black (observed after breaking the bones).' (MS in Bashir 2023b)

When a copula does appear in a present tense sentence, as in (9.9) and (9.10), it indicates that the attribute, for example, being alive in (9.9) or being in a specific condition in (9.10), is temporary and applies (only) at a specific time. In (9.11) the event is stated to be occurring at a specific time, and in (9.12) the state is said to exist at a specific time (this year). In (9.13) a specific locative relationship obtaining at a specific time is asserted.

(9.9) *žúnu as-úr váhum mo b-or*
alive be(ANIM)-PRS.3SG worried PROH become-IMP.2PL
'S/he is alive. Don't worry.' (DSAL)

(9.10) *çhay-ák kya hál-a as-úr*
be.sick-AG what condition-LOC1 be(ANIM)-PRS.3SG
'How is the patient (now)?' (lit. 'What condition is the patient in?') (DSAL)

(9.11) *pingačhúi yał š-er*
tomorrow polo be(INAN)-PRS.3SG
'Tomorrow (afternoon) there is a polo match.' (DSAL)

(9.12) *hayá sal góm-an yur ǰam š-er*
this year wheat-OBL.PL year good be(INAN)-PRS.3SG
'This year is a good year for wheat (crops).' (the yield is good) (MNN)

(9.13) *avá biyabán-a as-úm*
I desert-LOC1 be(ANIM)-PRS-1SG
'I am (wandering) in the wilderness' (stanza from Baba Sayyar) (MNN)

9.2.2 Verbal sentences

Verbal sentences can occur with any of the finite verb forms discussed in Chapter 6. They may be declarative (9.14), imperative (9.15), or interrogative (9.16) utterances.

(9.14) *ǰust b-íti bay-áni*
joined become-PFV.PTCP go.PST.D-3PL
'They left together.' (DSAL)

(9.15) *e: ma c̣e:k ma lú-o kar kor-é*
o my dear.one my word-OBL ear do-IMP.SG
'O, my dear, listen to what I am saying.' (SG in Bashir 2023b)

(9.16) *kúra šir-áy*
where be(INAN).PST.MIR-3SG
'Where was/is it?' (said when something turns up after being searched for) (SWKA in Bashir 2023b)

Interrogative sentences can be substantive questions, formed with WH-question words (*wh*-initial in English; *k*- initial in Khowar) like 'where' in (9.16), or polar 'yes–no' questions, with the sentence-final question particle *-aá* (9.17).

(9.17) *ispusár dúr-i as-úr-aá*
sister house-LOC2 be(ANIM)-PRS.3SG-Q
'Is (my) (younger) sister at home?' (DSAL)[2]

[2] This sentence need not refer to a speaker's actual sister; it is a polite conventional way to refer to a younger or same-age female resident of a house.

9.2.3 Negation

The negative particle in declarative or interrogative sentences is *no* 'not'. In verbal sentences it usually immediately precedes the verb (9.18) and (9.19). When a nominal sentence is negated, the negative particle *nóh* is sentence-final (9.5 above) and a strong aspirated release results from stress on the negative word, represented in examples (9.5) and (9.20). This also occurs when the negative particle occurs sentence-initially, as the exclamation 'no' in (9.19), or when a sentence-final negative means 'or not', as in (9.20).

(9.18) *phuk lú-o sóra qiłqíł no kor-élik*
small matter-OBL on quarrel NEG do-NEC
'One should not quarrel over small things.' (MNN)

(9.19) *nóh avá no gan-í as-úm*
NEG I NEG take-PFV.PTCP be(ANIM)-PRS.1SG
'No, I haven't bought it.' (DSAL)

(9.20) *bél-tu gon d-ití š-ér-aá nóh*
spade-LOC3 handle put-PFV.PTCP be(INAN)-PRS.3SG-Q NEG
'Has a handle been put on the spade (or) not?' (DSAL)

The present tense of the existential/locative 'be' verbs *as-* (animate) and *š-* (inanimate) is negated with *néki* ~ *níki* 'is/are not' (9.21) (9.22).

(9.21) *lángari hanún zamana-á kúra néki*
wooden.platter today time-LOC1 anywhere are.not
'These days there are no wooden platters (for food distribution) anywhere.' (MNN)

(9.22) *vez ma sum š-er muká néki*
gunpowder I.OBL with be(INAN)-PRS.3SG shot is.not
'I have gunpowder but no shot.' (DSAL)

Combined with pronominal or adverbial forms, *no* gives *kaá no* 'no one' (9.23), *kya no* 'nothing', *kya.vat no* 'never' (9.24), and other such combinations.

(9.23) *hayá zamana-á zohč šiméni kaá no k-óni-an*
this time-LOC1 goat.hair rope anyone NEG do-3PL.PRS/FUT-S
'These days no one is making goat-hair ropes.' (DSAL)

(9.24) *rény-o rum kyá.vat frosk no b-oy*
dog-OBL tail any.time straight NEG become-3SG.PRS/FUT.NS
Proverb. 'A dog's tail will never become straight.' Sense: A person's basic character cannot change. (DSAL)

The prohibitive negative *mo* occurs in negative hortatives, like the first-person singular hortative in *šum bíti bathána mo asám* 'Let me not live a bad life in my own country!' (MNN in Bashir 2023b), imperatives (9.25), and optatives (9.26).[3]

(9.25) *sasíri b-íti yór-i mo kos-é*
bareheaded become-PFV.PTCP sun.LOC2 PROH walk-IMP2SG
'Don't walk bareheaded in the sun.' (DSAL)

(9.26) *hatoó ley zemín-a mo çoṭ-ár*
REM.SG.OBL blood ground-LOC1 PROH drip-OPT.3SG
'Let his blood not drip on the ground.' (oral text, Village Parwak)

When *no* negates a verb, it usually occurs immediately pre-verbally, as in (9.23) and (9.24) above. However, when the reason for the non-occurrence of an action is questioned or challenged with *ko* 'why', the negative 'not' sometimes precedes 'why' instead of occurring immediately before the verb, as in *moṭéro band no ko kosán* 'Why don't you turn off the engine?' (implied, 'you should') and (9.27). Here, a small word order change adds an important element of modal meaning.[4] When *khyóte* is used for 'why', this does not happen (9.28).

(9.27) *ma-t lu no ko d-omi-án-é:*
I-DAT word NEG why give-2PL.PRS/FUT-S-VOC
'Hey, why aren't you telling me?' (you should) (oral text, Village Sorech)

[3] In Laspur, according to Inayatullah Faizi, *no* is sometimes used with negative imperatives instead of prohibitive *mo*, as in *yíi no gye*, 'Don't come here.'

[4] This is an unusual word-order pattern. I have not found it in the neighbouring languages Palula, where the phrase for 'why not' is *keéna* 'why.NEG' (Liljegren 2016: 239); Dameli, where it is *ku ni* 'why NEG' (Perder 2013: 211); Kalasha, which has *ko ne* 'why NEG' (Heegård Petersen 2015: 73, 109, 239), or in Wakhi, where it is *čir nəy* 'why NEG' (Mock 1998: 243, 249). But perhaps more attention to oral texts is required in order to find such usages. Finding such usages in neighbouring languages would be strong evidence for micro-areal influence. Burushaski sentence structure is so different from these IA languages that it is difficult to draw a comparison.

(9.28) *é: g-ití as-ús he*
hey, come-PFV.PTCP be(ANIM)-2SG.PRS DIST.SG.OBL
báče tu haníse khyóte es no k-os-án
for you now why it NEG do-2SG.PRS/FUT-S
'Hey, you have come for that, now why aren't you doing it?' (oral text, Village Parwak)

Negating a present perfect concept referring to an anticipated event employs the word *numá* 'not yet' or 'after some time'. Followed by a present/future non-specific form of a verb, *numá* regularly appears in sentences of the type 'X has not yet happened', when the expectation is that it will happen (fairly soon) (9.29) (9.30) (9.31). The present perfect negated with the usual negative particle *no* does not appear in this type of context.

(9.29) *gaderí ho-ó sor-ár numá b-ir*
madness DIST.SG-OBL head-ABL after.some.time go-3SG-PF.NS
'His madness has not yet left him.' (lit. 'His madness will leave after some time') (MNN)

(9.30) *ganṭá hoy-aá numá*
hour become.PST.D.3SG-Q not.yet
'Has it been an hour yet, or not?' (Ishkoman)

(9.31) *ḍaq sabáq-ar numá g-óni*
boys lesson-ABL later come-3PL.PRS/FUT.NS
'The boys haven't (yet) come (back) from school.' or 'The boys will come back from school after a while.' (DSAL)

However, when an event is not perceived as expected or anticipated, the regularly negated present perfect can occur, as in (9.32), (9.33), or (9.34). Such sentences convey the sense that the window for expecting the event is closed (9.32), or that it is not expected to happen (9.33) (9.34).

(9.32) *hasé hanún no g-ití as-úr*
REM.SG.DIR today NEG come-PFV.PTCP be(ANIM)-PRS.3SG
'S/he has not come today.' (RKB in Bashir 2023b)

(9.33) *ḍaq tan mux-ó no nig-í as-úr*
boy REFL face-OBL NEG wash-PFV.PTCP be(ANIM)PRS.3SG
'The boy has not washed his face.' (DSAL)

(9.34) *avá ʣoóy no poš-í as-úm*
I yak NEG see-PFV.PTCP be(ANIM).PRS.1SG
'I have not (ever) seen a yak.' (EB field notes)

9.3 Direct object marking

Pronominal direct objects, which are inherently specific or definite, are always in their oblique case form; (9.35), (9.36), and (9.37) show first-, second-, and third-person pronominal direct objects, respectively.

(9.35) *kłok kahák ma c̣af.pr-áy*
broody hen 1SG.OBL peck.PST.D-3SG
'The broody hen pecked me.' (SWKA in Bashir 2023b)

(9.36) *ta paš-é-m*
you.SG.OBL see-CAUS-1SG.PRS/FUT.NS
'I will show you.' (EB field notes)

(9.37) *zarú ǰoṣ-í kumóru toyó no av-áy*
old consider-PFV.PTCP girl REM.SG.OBL NEG take.PST.D-3SG
'Considering him (too) old, the girl did not marry (lit. 'take') him.' (DSAL)

Nominal direct objects can appear either in the direct case, as in (9.38), (9.39), and (9.40), or oblique.

(9.38) *kumóru ṣaváy bot-í as-úr*
girl beads.DIR tie-PFV.PTCP be(ANIM)-PRS.3SG
'The girl is wearing beads.' (lit. 'has fastened') (DSAL)

(9.39) *i cáłi moóš di poš-ít-am*
a pockmarked man.DIR also see-PST.D-1SG
'I also saw a man with a pockmarked face.' (DSAL)

(9.40) *šapír rék-o ḍaq buhtu-ír-an*
wolf.DIR say-OBL boy fear-3SG.PRS/FUT-S
'The boy is afraid of wolves.' (lit. 'If someone says "wolf", the boy is frightened.') (DSAL)

Oblique-marked direct objects appear in (9.41), animate and (9.42) (9.43), inanimate.

(9.41) *ḍaq šapír-o poš-í buhtu-ít-ay*
boy wolf-OBL see-PFV.PTCP fear-PST.D-3SG
'The boy saw the/a (specific) wolf and was frightened.' (DSAL)

(9.42) *ṣo.d-íti thuék-o neé-t-ani*
search-PFV.PTCP rifle-OBL find-PST.D-3PL
'They searched and found the rifle.' (DSAL)

(9.43) *uɣ-ó ka čhin-ít-ay*
water-OBL who cut-PST.D-3SG
'Who cut off the water?' (DSAL)

Animacy is not relevant to the appearance or non-appearance of the oblique case on objects, since both animate and inanimate objects can appear either in the direct case (9.38) (9.39) (9.40) or in the oblique (9.41) (9.42) (9.43). Volitionality, also, does not seem to be relevant, since the actions in (9.40) and (9.41) (fearing) are clearly not volitional. Neither is affectedness of the object, since neither the wolf in (9.40) or (9.41) nor the rifle in (9.42) is affected by the action of the agent.

In short, Khowar shows identified object marking (IOM), in that non-specific indefinite objects appear in the direct case (9.38) (9.39) (9.40) above, while definite or specific objects are oblique marked (9.41) (9.42) (9.43). To see this contrast clearly, compare (9.40) and (9.41) above.

9.4 Compounding

9.4.1 Compound noun phrases

Two or more nouns, both of which are either inanimate (9.44) or animate (9.45), or pronouns (9.46) can be combined into a compound noun phrase using the conjunction *očé* ~ *očén* ~ *očó* 'and'. When two postpositional phrases, as in (9.47), or two clauses are conjoined, as in (9.48) (see also Section 9.4.2) *va* 'and' is used. In general, *očé* ~ *očén* appears when the conjoined entities are concrete things or persons. Persian-origin *va* appears when they are non-concrete things like time expressions (9.47) or full predications (9.48). Compound noun phrases can be the subject of a sentence (9.44), the direct object (9.96) below, or the object of a postposition (9.45). When the first-person pronoun is conjoined with another person, as in (9.46) it comes first and the conjoined subject takes first-person plural verb agreement.

(9.44) *toó axlíni očé dazbé*[5] *hayá ṭhún-a*
REM.SG.OBL comb and prayer.beads this pillar-LOC1
çak-é-i š-éni
fasten-CAUS-PFV.PTCP be(INAN)-PRS.3PL
'Her [comb and prayer beads] have been fastened to this pillar.' (oral text, Village Bang)

(9.45) *salím akbár očé aslám-o khál-an sar drung*
Salim Akbar and Aslam-OBL both-OBL.PL ABL tall
'Salim is taller than both [Akbar and Aslam].' (SWKA in Bashir 2013)

(9.46) *avá očé tu hayií niš-í as-úsi*
I and you here sit-PFV.PTCP be(ANIM)-PRS.1PL
'[You and I] are sitting here.' (MNN and TMF in Bashir 2023b)

When two postpositional phrases (9.47) or two clauses (9.48) are conjoined, the meaning of 'and' is expressed with *va*, but not *očé*, *va* but not *očé* can also have the sense of 'else', 'additionally', as in (9.49) or 'again', as in (9.50).

(9.47) *pišín-o niméž [i baǰ-ár prúšṭi va*
afternoon-OBL prayer one o'clock-ABL before and
čor baǰ-ár áči] no b-oy
four o'clock-ABL after NEG become-3SG.PRS/FUT.NS
'The afternoon prayer is not said [before one o'clock and after four o'clock].' (DSAL)

(9.48) *hes haṣ no man-ír*
DIST.DIR.SG like.that NEG agree-3SG.PRS/FUT.NS
va ban žib-óy
and stick eat-PRS/FUT.NS.3SG
'He won't agree/submit just like that, and he will get a beating.' (MYS in Bashir 2023b)

(9.49) *va/*očé kyaγ h-oy*
else/*and what become-PST.D.3SG
'What else happened?' (RKB)

[5] Sometimes sandhi occurs between a vowel-final noun and the initial *o* of *očé*, for example *axlinyočé dazboót* 'to the comb and prayer beads', where final unstressed *-i* has become the semivowel *y*.

(9.50) *va/*očé no g-oy hasé – hasé*
again NEG come-3SG-PRS/FUT.NS REM.SG REM.SG
va no g-oy
again NEG come-3SG.PRS/FUT.NS
'He won't come again. … He won't come again.' (oral text, Village Kari)

Conjoining clauses one of which has an animate and the other an inanimate subject is discussed in Section 9.4.2.

9.4.2 Compound sentences

A compound sentence is one in which two finite clauses are conjoined, in a conjunctive ('and'), disjunctive ('but'), or alternative ('or') relation. Conjoining subjects in a compound subject requires that both conjuncts be either animate or inanimate. A locative or existential sentence conjoining an inanimate, like flowers, and an animate, like birds, as in (9.51), must be rendered with two separate clauses, each with its animacy-appropriate verb.[6] Also, a sentence like 'rain and hail are falling', or 'it is raining and hailing', must be constructed as in (9.52), where 'to rain' and 'to hail' are each expressed with the construction required for them. Notice that neither *očé* nor *va* 'and' appears in these examples. The sense of 'and' is conveyed in (9.52) by *di* … *di* 'also … also' ('both … and'). Sentences with conjunctive meaning involving sequences of events are typically expressed by clause-chaining constructions (Section 10.9.1).[7]

(9.51) *zóm-tu ṣiéli gambúri š-éni*
mountain-LOC3 beautiful flower be(INAN)-PRS.3PL
ṣiéli boyík as-úni
beautiful bird be(ANIM)-PRS.3PL
'On the mountains there are beautiful flowers and birds.' (ZHD)

[6] This is also the case in Ojibway, where animates and inanimates may not be conjoined (Corbett 1991: 305).
[7] I have found only one example of clauses conjoined with *očé*. It is shown here as (a1).

(a1) *maál phan-ír očé maál nahrt-ír*
Maal dance-3SG.PRS/FUT.NS and maal.song perform-3SG-PRS/FUT.NS
Traditional saying. 'Maal dances and performs.' (IF in Bashir 2023)

In (a1) *maál* is both the name of a song and the name of a poet; thus, the sentence means '*Maál* (the poet) sings and performs *maál* (the song).'

(9.52) *baṣ-ír-an di kuçhuní di d-óy-an*
rain-3SG.PRS/FUT-S also hail also strike-3SG.PRS/FUT-S
'It is raining and hailing.' (RKB)

On the other hand, compound sentences with contradictory meaning ('but'), like (9.53), in which the subject is the same but the nominal predicates contrast ('good' versus 'poor'), or (9.54), in which the verbal predicates ('driving away' and 'coming back') contrast, occur frequently.

(9.53) *he moóš the ǰam mágam γaríb*
DIST.SG.DIR man TOP good but poor
'That man is good, but (he is) poor.' (DSAL)

(9.54) *avá dałe-áv alé-t-am mágar het*
I drive.away-IPFV.PTCP bring-PST.D-1SG but DIST.PL.DIR
γerd-áv áči h-áni
turn-IPFV.PTCP back come.PST.D-3PL
'I kept on driving (them) away, but they kept on turning around and coming back.' (RKB in Bashir 2023b)

Alternative conjuncts 'or', in declarative or imperative sentences can be expressed with the Persian-origin *ya* 'or', as in (9.55).

(9.55) *ya ma baçaí-a tá-te žaγá no*
either my kingdom-LOC1 you-DAT place NEG
b-oy-án b-oγé ya ma
become-3SG.PRS/FUT-S go-IMP.2SG or me
alt-í hal.bos
take-PFV.PTCP stay.IMP.2SG
'Either here in my kingdom there is no place for you, go away, or else marry me and stay.' (oral text, Village Shotkhar)

Questions presenting a choice between two alternatives have a polar 'yes–no' question for the first alternative, with its verb marked by the question marker *-aá*, which is not repeated after the second alternative (9.56). Alternatively, the polar question can stand alone, with its *-aá* question marker, optionally followed by *kyaγ* 'or what?' (9.57).

(9.56) *hayá pón-tu b-ími-an-aá*
PROX.SG.OBL path-LOC3 go-2PL.PRS/FUT-S-Q
hay-uú b-ími-an
here-LOC4 go-2PL.PRS/FUT-S
'Are you going up this road (or) down here?' (spoken at a junction offering the choice between ascending and a descending paths) (oral text, Village Sorech)

(9.57) *tu kyaní b-os-án tu gadéri-aá kyaγ*
you how become-2SG.PRS/FUT-S you crazy-Q what
'What are you doing? Are you crazy—(or) what?' (oral text, Village Kari)

Often the ideas of conjunction ('and'), choice between alternatives ('or'), and disjunction ('but') are expressed by simple juxtaposition without any overt word, as in the proverb shown in (9.58), the gnomic utterance in (9.59), in which two nominal sentences with different subjects are conjoined by juxtaposition, or (9.60) in which a choice between the alternatives 'now' or 'later' is given.

(9.58) *asmán ẓang zemín ḍang*
sky high land hard
Proverb. 'The sky is high (and) the ground is hard.' Sense: Applies to a situation when a person has no viable alternatives. (DSAL)

(9.59) *lu d-ik asqán kor-ík girán*
speech give-INF easy do-INF difficult
'It is easy to talk, (but) to (actually) do something is hard.' (DSAL)

(9.60) *ta xyál-a hatét g-ík-o*
your opinion-LOC1 REM.PL.DIR come-INF-OBL
h-óni-aá numá?
become.PST-3PL-Q later
'Do you think they are ready to come now, (or) later?' (IWA in Bashir 2023b)

Whether a conjunctive, disjunctive, or alternative meaning emerges from the juxtaposition depends on the relationship between the two predicates. In (9.58) 'high' and 'hard' are not in semantic opposition, both indicating difficulty of one kind or another, hence 'and'; in (9.59) 'easy' and 'difficult' are opposites, hence 'but'; and in (9.60) the question marker *-aá* presents a choice between two alternatives, 'now' or 'later'.

9.5 Complex sentences

Complex sentences include a subordinate clause embedded in a main (matrix) clause. These subordinate clauses can contain either finite or non-finite verbs. They can be adjectival, adverbial, or nominal.

9.5.1 Relative clauses

Relative clauses (RCs) are typically adjectival and can either limit (restrictive) or add to (non-restrictive) the reference of a noun. In this work I will be using the widely accepted definition of a restrictive relative clause as a construction which delimits the potential reference of an NP (Comrie 1989: 143). A non-restrictive RC, in contrast, adds some element of meaning, rather than limiting a previously existing domain of reference. In this work I focus mainly on restrictive RCs. The larger sentence of which a RC is a part will be referred to as the matrix or main clause (MC). A free relative (headless relative) is a clause which neither modifies a head NP in the matrix clause nor includes an internal head, but *ex novo* specifies or constitutes an NP or an adverbial expression, which then plays a role in the matrix clause, as in the English 'I like [what I see]', or 'I'll go [wherever I have to]', in which the free relative clause establishes a new referent or specifies a location rather than referring to something previously specified. Such a new referent can be either definite or indefinite.

In Khowar, temporal, locative, manner, and quantitative relationships are frequently expressed as RCs. There are several types of Khowar RCs, none of which employ the historical IA *ǰ-* forms found in many other Indo-Aryan languages, like Urdu. They include both left- and right-branching structures. Left-branching constructions belong to older strata of the language, while right-branching ones are later developments (Bashir 1988a, chapter 5).

9.5.1.1 Left-branching constructions

9.5.1.1.1 Relative clauses with finite verbs

One left-branching structure has a sentence-initial finite relative clause followed by the MC, in which a demonstrative element representing the head noun appears. This class includes both nominal and verbal clauses. In this pre-nominal (relative) clause the verb is apparently not restricted for tense.[8] In this structure, the head noun may or may not appear (depending on context) in either the RC or the MC. In the typical case I have observed, the head noun is 'gapped' in the RC (represented here with Ø) and is represented in the MC by a resumptive demonstrative pronoun. Since there is always a prior or ambient conversational or cultural context for any real utterance, the specific identity of the referent is usually to be understood from context. I call this the V-FIN (finite verb) type, exemplified in (9.61).[9] In this construction, the distal demonstrative, *hes,* appears as a resumptive pronoun in the MC. In (9.62), a spontaneously uttered sentence, the head appears as a full NP internal to the RC and is recapitulated by the distal demonstrative element *hes* in the larger phrase. In this sentence the final vowel of the RC verb, *obrítá:y,* is elongated and maintained at a steady high pitch, signalling that this is a relative clause and that something else is to follow.[10] In (9.63) the RC, specifying the old man who is the subject of the MC, follows the MC.

(9.61) Ø [*páyp-a* *g-óy-an*] *hes* *ǰam* *va*
pipe-LOC1 come-3SG.PRS/FUT-S DIST.SG.DIR good EMPH
'(The water) [which is coming in the pipe] is really good.' (EB field notes)

(9.62) [*háte ḍaq eksiḍenṭ-a* *o-br-ít-á:y*] – *hes*
the boy accident-LOC1 AUG-die-PST.D-3SG – DIST.SG.DIR
'The boy who died in an accident' (lit. '[The boy died in an accident]—him') (EB field notes)

(9.63) *he* *bap* *ma móš-o* *sar* *ʦeq* –
DIST.SG old.man my man-OBL than small
[*Ø kiṣ-ír-á:n*] *he* *bap*
plough.3SG.PRS/FUT-S DIST.SG old.man
'That old man is younger than my husband—the old man [who is ploughing].' (EB field notes)

[8] This type is also treated as a coordinate structure, with the sentence-initial finite clause functioning as a topic (Hock 1989, passim).
[9] Similar left-branching relative structures are found in Gilgit Shina (Radloff and Shakil 1998: 149, 165).
[10] This expressive lengthening is represented in the spelling of examples (9.62) and (9.63).

In examples (9.64), (9.65), (9.66), and (9.67) the 'gapped' element is represented by Ø in the relative clause and 'resumed' in the MC with a remote pronominal (9.64), distal pronominal (9.65), or adverbial element (9.66) (9.67).

(9.64) *hayá* [*Ø haníse až-íru*] *haté žav*
PROX.SG now be.born-PST.I REM.SG son
'This is the son [that was born now].' (RKB)

(9.65) [*Ø o-yó-v*] *hes*
AUG-eat.PST.D-2SG DIST.SG.DIR
'[you ate it]—that one' ('the one [which you ate]') (EB field notes)

Temporal clauses are frequently cast as RCs, as in (9.66) and (9.67).

(9.66) [*sáyfula ǰan Ø thanedár as-úr*] *he vax*
Saifullah Jan police.head be(ANIM)-3SG.PRS DIST.SG.OBL time
'The time [when Saifullah Jan is (was) head of the police station]' (EB field notes)

(9.67) [*tu Ø g-ití as-t-áv*] *he anús-a*
you come-PFV.PTCP be(ANIM)-PST.D-2SG DIST.SG.OBL day-LOC1
'on the day [when you came]' (lit. '[you came] on that day') (EB field notes)

The left-branching V-FIN strategy in (9.68) is the usual and natural way to express this idea, especially in ordinary conversational discourse. Example (9.69), which employs a right-branching *ki* clause is an elicited counterpart of (9.68).

(9.68) [*Ø héra phar b-aγ-áy*] *hasé ma braár*
there over go-PST.D-3SG REM.SG.DIR my brother
'[(he) went over there] he is my brother.' ('The person who went over there is my brother.') (EB field notes)

(9.69) *hasé ma braár* [*kaáki héra phar b-aγ-áy*]
REM.SG.DIR my brother [who.REL there over go-PST.D-3SG]
'That is my brother [(the one) who went over there].' (elicited)

9.5.1.1.2 Relative clauses employing the past participle

The past participle (PST.PTCP) can function as a verb, adjective, or noun. Its protean nature complicates analysis of constructions and sentences where it occurs. When functioning adjectivally, it can be analysed as an attributive adjective, as in *čhírdu išnári* 'a broken thing', *rul díru kayás* 'lined paper', *don bóydu moóš* 'toothless man', or a relative clause depending on the amount of material preceding and/or following the participle. In addition to functioning as an adjective, it can be a noun, for example *birdú* 'dead person', *don boydú* 'person who has lost their teeth', and in participial RCs for example (9.70).

Since when functioning adjectivally, either as a simple adjective or as a relative clause, the PST.PTCP is patient oriented, if the verb of the PST.PTCP has an agent, like 'ministers' in (9.70), 'boy' in (9.71), 'you' in (9.72), 'I' in (9.73) and (9.74), or 'robbers' in (9.75), I analyse it as a PST.I verbal form. Note that the agent in such RCs—*ta* in (9.72), *ma* in (9.73), *ta* in (9.74), and *ḍaku-an* in (9.75)—appears in its oblique form.

(9.70) *háte [kumór-o angíru] vazir-án di*
REM.PL.DIR girl-OBL bring.PST.I minister-DIR.PL also
as-úni
be(ANIM)-PRS.3PL
'Those ministers [who had brought the girl] are (were) also there.' (oral text, Village Uthul)

(9.71) *avá [ta-té paysá d-irú] háte ḍaq-ó*
I you-DAT money give-PST.I REM.SG.OBL boy-OBL
huy phrét-am
call give.PST.D-1SG
'I called the boy [who gave money to you.]' (ZHD)

(9.72) *avá [ta haté paysá d-irú] ḍaq-ó huy phré-tam*
I you that money give-PST.I boy-OBL give-PST.D-1SG
'I called that boy [to whom you gave money].' (ZHD)

(9.73) *[ma poč-íru] pondí ma prušṭ-ár b-ay-áy*[11]
I.OBL cook-PST.I waybread I.OBL ahead-ABL go-PST.D-3SG
Proverb. 'The waybread [which I cooked (for my journey)] has gone ahead of me.' (Sense: used of the death of a young person in the prime of life, especially in the meaning of 'My grown son has died before me.') (MNN)

[11] Example (8.63) repeated here for convenience of the reader.

(9.74) [*ma und-íru*] *šiméni*
I.OBL hang-PST.I rope
'The rope [which I hung]' (MNN in Bashir 2023b)

(9.75) *hes* [*pór ḍakú-an mar-íru*] *mṓš-o*
DIST.SG.DIR last.year robber-OBL.PL kill-PST.I man-OBL
žuúr
daughter
'She is the daughter of the man [whom the robbers killed last year].' (IF)

In example (9.76) the verb of the PST.PTCP is intransitive, and there is no resumptive pronoun in the main clause, I interpret the participial phrase as adjectival, modifying 'woman'.

(9.76) [*zóm-o b-óγdu*] *kiméri-o lu*
mountain-LOC4 go-PST.PTCP woman-OBL word
dó-ni-an
give-3PL.PRS/FUT-S
'They are talking about the woman [who fell down the mountain].' (Bashir 2000a)

In RCs with *širú*, the PST.PTCP of *š-* 'be(INAN)', *širú* can function adjectivally (9.77) and (9.78) or substantively. In (9.77), in the phrase *bay širú* 'orchard having', *širú* agrees in animacy with its own inanimate subject *bay* 'orchard(s)' inside the relative clause, not with the animate head noun *pažál* 'shepherd', the 'possessor' in the matrix clause. Example (9.78) shows a similar agreement pattern.

(9.77) *ispá xayál-a kéłi he* [*bay š-irú*]
our thought-LOC1 sheep that orchards be(INAN).PST.I
pažál-o áča b-íni reé
shepherd-OBL after go-3PL.PRS/FUT.NS say.PFV.PTCP
xošán hót-am
glad become.PST.D-1PL
'Thinking that the sheep would follow the shepherd [who had orchards], we were happy.' (From *Kełivál kełítay* ['The shepherdess wept'], Faizi 1989)

(9.78) [*ḉav no š-irú*] *roy kyaáɣ*
status NEG be(INAN)-PST.PTCP person anything

kor-ík-o no b-oy
do-INF-OBL NEG be.able-3SG.PRS/FUT.NS

'A person [who has no status] can't do anything.' (DSAL)

When the past participle is used substantively, with no head noun in the matrix clause, the interpretation is that of a nominal free relative (9.79) (9.80) (9.81) (9.82). In these examples the PST.PTCP functions as a noun, in (9.79) and (9.82) showing oblique singular case. In (9.79) *širú* agrees in animacy with 'property', while the nominal free relative clause 'one who has property' refers to a human.

(9.79) [*ǰaydád š-irú-o*] *kya xač*
property be(INAN).PST.PTCP-OBL what problem
'[One who has property] has no (unsolvable) problems.' (DSAL)

(9.80) [*no kren-íru*] *ḍaq no b-oy,* [*no*
NEG buy-PST.PTCP boy NEG become-3SG.PRS/FUT NEG

iston-é-iru] *žav no b-oy*
scream-CAUS-PST.PTCP son NEG become-3SG.PRS/FUT.NS

Proverb. '[One that has not been purchased] cannot be a real slave; [one who has not caused the pains of childbirth] cannot be a real son.' Sense: 'Only one's own people are truly one's own.' (DSAL)

(9.81) *he* [*é-i as-íru*]*-aá*
DIST.SG.DIR DIST.SG-LOC2 be(ANIM)-PST.PTCP-Q
'(Do you mean) [the person who was in there]?' (Chitral Town)

(9.82) *haté* [*phur-én š-irú-o*] *mo*
REM.SG top-LOC.PL be(INAN)-PST.PTCP-OBL PROH

žib-é rét-ay
eat-IMP.SG say-PST.D-3SG

'"Don't eat [the one on the top]," he said.' (oral text, Village Bang)

In (9.83), however, *širú-an* functions adjectivally, modifying the head noun *durén* 'houses'. It agrees in animacy with both 'television', and 'houses', and in number with the head noun *durén* 'houses'. This is a puzzling behaviour, since adjectives are not marked for number, and the PST.I verb form does not take the *-an* ending.[12]

(9.83) [*ṭelivížan širú-an*] *dur-én*
television be(INAN).PST.PTCP-PL house-LOC.PL
'in the houses [which have television]' (EB field notes)

9.5.1.1.3 Relative clauses with deverbal nouns

Some deverbal nouns can act as functional RCs. The agent noun (root + *-ák*) (9.84), and the instrument noun (root + *-íni* ~ *-éni*) can function as simple adjectives, in forming RCs, or substantivally. The agent noun usually refers to an animate agent, as in (9.84). This is not always the case, however, and it can refer even to a temporal, as in *phéting him. korák mas* 'Pheting is a snowy month' or locative nominal (9.85). The instrument noun usually functions as a simple noun (9.86) but can also appear adjectivally in a figurative expression like (9.87) or in a relative clause equivalent (9.88).

(9.84) *kéłi he* [*baγ çak-e-ák*] *pažál-o*
sheep that orchard adhere.to-CAUS-AG shepherd-OBL
áča b-íni
after go-3PL.PRS/FUT.NS
'Sheep will follow that shepherd [who plants orchards].' (From *Kełivál kełítay* ['The shepherdess wept'], Faizi 1989)

(9.85) *buní bo boṣ-ák žaγá*
Booni very rain-AG place
'Booni is a very rainy place.' (heard in Booni)

(9.86) *kiṣ-íni*
ploughing-INS.N
'plough'

(9.87) [*ḍunḍ-íni*] *bap*
wool.fluffing-INS.N old.man
'an old man [bent over like a bow for fluffing wool]' (EB field notes)

[12] The only possible solution I can see is that *širú-an* is functioning both nominally and adjectivally simultaneously. But this would require explanation. This type of sentence needs further research.

(9.88) [*gordóγ-o* *ṭék-i* *d-íni*] *pandán*
donkey-OBL top-LOC2 put-INS.N matting
'a covering of mats [to put on a donkey's back]' (IF)

The necessitative construction consisting of the oblique infinitive plus *baṣ* (NEC2), for example *koríк-o baṣ* 'fit/needing to be done', can function in relative clause-equivalent formations (9.89).

(9.89) *hes* [*no* *kor-ík-o* *baṣ*] *kórum*
DIST.SG.DIR NEG do-INF-OBL NEC2 deed
'That is something [which should not be done].' (IF)

An adverbial word or phrase preceding a noun can also function like a short relative clause, as in (9.90).

(9.90) *hamó* [*phar*] *háte* *ḍaq-ó-t* *det*
PROX.OBL over.there REM.SG.OBL boy-OBL-DAT give.IMP2SG
'Give this to the boy [(who is) over there].' (Chitral Town)

9.5.1.2 k-word strategies

Followed by *ki*, interrogative/indefinite adjectives and adverbs yield relative elements (Table 9.1).[13] These *k*-word structures can be either sentence-initial in an overall left-branching sentence, or sentence-final. There are many sub-types of this structure; sentence-initial structures are illustrated in Section 9.5.1.2.1.

Table 9.1 Interrogative/indefinite → relative adjectives and adverbs

Interrogative/indefinite	Relative	Type of relative clause
kúra 'where?' (location)/'ever' (time)	*kúraki* 'where'	locative
kúri ~ *kúi* 'where?', 'whither?' (destination)	*kúriki* 'where'	
kyávat 'when?'/'ever'	*kyávatki* 'when'	temporal
kandúri 'how much/many?'/'so many'	*kandúriki* 'however much/many'	quantitative
kamaá 'how many?'	*kamaáki* 'however many'	

[13] The *ki* occurring in such elements is pronounced with close juncture to the preceding element. Hence in the Relative column in Table 9.1, *ki* is written together with the item it follows. This is different from *ki* functioning as a subordinating conjunction, when it is usually pronounced as a separate word.

Table 9.1 (continued)

Interrogative/indefinite	Relative	Type of relative clause
kíča 'how?'	*kíčaki* 'how', 'how(ever)'	manner
kíča kóri 'how (transitive)?'	*kíča kóriki* 'how(ever)'	manner
kíča bíti 'how (intransitive)?'	*kíča bítiki* 'how(ever)'	manner
kíča 'what kind of?'	*kíčaki* 'what(ever) kind of'	adjectival
kiváli 'which?', 'who?'	*kiváliki* 'which(ever)'	adjectival
kyaáy 'something'	*kyaáyki* 'what(ever)'	adjectival
kya 'what?'	*kyáki* 'which', 'that'	adjectival

9.5.1.2.1 Sentence-initial k-*word constructions*

Several variants of sentence-initial *k*-word structures are found, especially in formal oral or written discourse. One type, examples (9.91) and (9.92), has an internally right-branching RC, in which the RC is introduced with *kya* NP *ki*, with *ki* following the head noun. In (9.91) the head noun in the RC is *ḍaq* 'boy' and the remote demonstrative *hasé* 'he' in the MC is coreferential with it. In the RC the relative noun bears the case dictated by its role in the RC, subject, and in the MC the correlative pronominal *hasé* is treated according to its MC role, also subject.

(9.91) *hamo-γár* *áči* [***kya*** *ḍaq* ***ki*** *uštuúr-t-ay*] *hasé*
PROX.OBL-ABL after REL boy REL run.away-PST.D-3SG REM.SG.DIR
sax *ban* *žib-óy*
severely stick eat-3SG.PRS/FUT.NS
'After today, whichever boy runs away (from the classroom) will be severely beaten.' (lit. 'will eat a stick') (MS in Bashir 2023b)

This example shows an incipient relative-correlative strategy like that familiar from languages like Urdu. Although it utilises an interrogative/indefinite element rather than a historical IA relative *ǰ*- form, it employs the same case-marking strategies for the RC and MC and represents the head NP in the MC with a demonstrative pronominal element. This type occurs mainly in written or formal discourse. Example (9.92) occurred spontaneously in an explanation of the speaker's professional work in meteorology. The head NP, *vólṭi* 'side', is internal to the RC and also appears in the MC recapitulated by the remote demonstrative adjective *haté* 'that'. This sentence shows three layers of left-branching modification, indicated in the gloss by boldface type, and schematised here: [from which the wind flows] [that side] [that part].

(9.92) [***kya*** *vólṭi-ar* ***ki*** *gan o-š-óy*] ***haté***
rel side-abl rel wind aug-be-pst.d.3sg rem.sg
vólṭi ç̣hamúṭ-o ***haté*** *hisá ḍhé-ir*
side finger-obl rem.sg part feel.cold-3sg.prs/fut.ns
'**That** part of the finger on **that** side [**from which the wind blows**] feels cold.' (AKM)

The relative form can also occur as *kyáki* NP, as in (9.93), in which *kyáki* precedes the relativised noun and is recapitulated in the MC with the remote demonstrative adjective *haté* 'that'.

(9.93) *b-i va* [*ayh sór-a hasé* ***kyáki***
go-pfv.ptcp another up top-loc1 rem.sg.dir rel
noγór ošóy] ***haté*** *noγór-o*
fort was rem.sg.obl fort-obl
báhrki noγór-a toór-t-ay
equal.to fort-loc1 reach-pst.d-3sg
'He went and reached another fort, just as big as that fort [that was in the upper world].' (oral text, Village Uthul)

Sentence-initial free RCs in adverbial functions are common. Examples of spatial (9.92) above (9.94), and temporal (9.95) (9.96) RCs follow. Notice that there is no NP which can be considered a head noun in the MC or in the RC. The adverbial element and *ki* may appear immediately adjacent to one another (9.93) (9.94) (9.95) or separated by a noun (9.96). The entire RC in (9.95) defines a time *ex novo* and functions as a time adverbial in the MC. Clauses introduced with *kíčaki* 'how' are frequent; they too function as free manner adverbial relatives, as in (9.97).

(9.94) [*kúraki uγ š-er*] (*hatéra*) *goóm*
where.rel water be(inan)-prs.3sg (there) wheat
b-oy
become-3sg-prs/fut.ns
'[Where there is water], wheat will grow.' (Bashir 2000a)

(9.95) [*kyávatki tat h-ay*] *ta-t lu*
when.REL father come.PST-D-3SG you-DAT word

d-om
give-1SG.PRS/FUT.NS

'[When (your) father comes] I will tell you.' (Bashir 2000a)

(9.96) [*kya anús ki mal-án sóra šapír pr-ay*]
REL day REL livestock-OBL.PL on wolf strike.PST.D-3SG

deh-ó roy raǰúli očó toγó tát-o
village-OBL people Rajuli and her father-OBL

yad k-óni
memory do-3PL.PRS/FUT.NS

'[whenever a wolf would attack the livestock], the people of the village remember Rajuli and her father.' (From *Rajuli*, a short story by Yousaf Shahzad)

(9.97) [*kíčaki a-r-ú*] *haṣ paš-ís*
how.REL AUG-do.PST.D-2SG thus see-2SG.PRS/FUT.NS
Proverb. '[As you do (to others)], [so] you will see (the same thing being done to you.)' (Bashir 2000a)

When pronominal elements *kaáki,* 'whoever'; *kóski* 'whomever', 'whose ever'; *kyaáγki* ~ *khyóki* 'whatever'; and *kiváluki* ~ *kiváliki* 'whichever/ whoever (of a specified set)' occur sentence-initially, they form free relatives. In this structure, there is no head NP, either in the RC or in the MC, and the free relative defines *ex novo* a set of potential referents to which the demonstrative in the MC may refer. Examples are (9.98), (9.99), (9.100), and (9.101).

(9.98) [*kaáki nast h-áy*] *hasé gan-ír*
whoever ahead come.PST.D-3SG REM.SG take-3SG.PRS/FUT.NS
'[Whoever comes first] will get (it).' (RKB)

(9.99) [*kyaáγki bašár a-r-ét-ani*] *hét-an lu*
whatever question AUG-do-PST.D-3PL DIST-OBL.PL word

det
give.IMP.SG

'Tell (me) (about) [whatever (questions) they asked].' ('Tell me about whatever questions they asked.') (Chitral Town)

(9.100) *qalm-án múži [kiváliki ta xoš] gan-é*
pen-OBL.PL among which.REL you.OBL pleasing take-IMP.S
'Take [whichever] of the pens [you like].' (DSAL)

(9.101) *[kóski gan-í go-s-án] angy-é*
who.OBL.REL take-PFV.PTCP come-2SG.PRS/FUT-S bring-IMP.2SG
'Bring [whomever you want to].' (Bashir 2000a)

Since one of the meanings of *ki* is 'if' in conditional clauses, some sentence-initial free relatives are semantically very close to indefinite conditionals. In the two naturally occurring sentences (9.102) and (9.103), the verb form appearing in the subordinate clause is the past direct, the form usually occurring in realis conditionals. Example (9.102) is part of the formulaic opening for traditional oral tales; it recapitulates the RC not with a demonstrative element, but with a semantically equivalent agent noun. Examples (9.102) and (9.103) allow two interpretations, shown here as a. and b.

(9.102) *[kaáki čang-ít-ay] čang-ák-an gerdán-a*
who.REL lie-PST.D-3SG lie-AG-OBL.PL neck-LOC1
a. '[Whoever lies], (the responsibility) is on the neck of the liars.'
b. '[If anyone lies], (the responsibility) is on the neck of the liars.' (formulaic opening of traditional tales)[14]

(9.103) *[hamí kéłi kos áča ki bay-áni]*
PROX.PL sheep anyone after REL/IF go.PST.D-3PL
hét-an búk-i kutér tán b-oy
DIST-OBL.PL throat-LOC2 knife EMPH become-3SG.PRS/FUT.NS
a. '[Whoever these sheep follow], there will be only a knife at their throats.'
b. '[If these sheep follow anyone], there will be only a knife at their throats.' (From *Kełivál kełítay* [The shepherdess wept], Faizi 1989)

9.5.1.2.2 Sentence-final k-*word structures*

Example (9.104) shows a sentence-final RC. This sentence also includes a *ki*-clause complement of 'required', 'that we keep those words alive'.

[14] The pronunciations yielding these two senses differ. For sense (a) 'whoever', *ki* will have close juncture with *kaá,* while for sense (b), in which *ki* is the conjunction 'if', the juncture will be open, with *ki* as a separate word.

(9.104) *hanísen ispá sóra lazím š-er [ki haté*
now us on required be(INAN)-PRS.3SG that those
alfáz-an zindá behč-é-si]
words-OBL.PL alive remain-CAUS-1PL.HORT
[kyáaγki tonǰ bík-o b-ití
which.REL lost become.INF-OBL become-PFV.PTCP
š-éni]
be(INAN)-PRS.3PL
'Now it is incumbent upon us [that we keep those words alive] [which are about to be lost].' (Rahmat 1989)

9.5.1.2.3 Relative clauses formed with ki *alone*

In this structure, the relativising function is performed by the bare generalised complementiser *ki,* which introduces a variety of subordinate clauses, interpreted as 'if', 'when', 'that', or a relative element, depending on the nature of and relation between the clauses it links. This is like the relative clause structure found in Persian. In (9.105a) and (9.105b), clause-initial *ki* introduces a right-branching, sentence-final relative clause. The examples in my data suggest that this structure is used in Khowar for non-restrictive RCs.

(9.105a)
i haṣ thariqá di bir-áy [ki hat-oγó-te
a such method also become.MIR-3SG REL REM.SG-OBL-DAT
phyú-a łoł-ík ré-ni]
shoulder.blade-LOC1 look-1NF say-3PL.PRS/FUT.NS
'There was also such a method (of forecasting the weather) [which is called "looking at the shoulder blade"]' (AKM)

(9.105b)
hasé ma žuúr [ki t-oó
REM.SG I.OBL daughter that REM.SG-OBL
huú poóš-t-av]
down.there see.PST.D-2SG
'That is my daughter, [that you saw down there].' (MA in Bashir 2023)

9.5.2 Adverbial clauses

9.5.2.1 Temporal clauses

9.5.2.1.1 'if' ~ 'when' clauses

In addition to the temporal RCs shown above in examples (9.66) and (9.67), adverbial temporal clauses can be constructed with *ki* 'when' or 'if' immediately preceding the verb (9.106) (9.107). Usually, in temporal sentences in which the sense is close to conditional 'if', *ki* occurs in second position, following the subject of the clause, as in (9.106) and (9.107). In very short sentences like these two, this also puts *ki* in pre-verbal position.

(9.106) [*garmí ki bo a-r-ér*] *sin ṭip*
heat when/if much AUG-do.PST.D-3SG river full
b-óni
become-3PL.PRS/FUT.NS
'[When/if it is very hot], the rivers are full.' (MNN)

(9.107) [*ǰoš baǰá ki h-oy*] *the*
ten o'clock when become.PST.D-3SG then
par-ísi
lie.down-1PL.PRS/FUT.NS
'[When it is ten o'clock], then we go to bed.' (EB field notes)

9.5.2.1.2 Clause-final ki 'when' clauses

In many sentences consisting of two distinct clauses which express two distinct events in temporal sequence, the first of which often includes an agent (and an object), *ki* unambiguously meaning 'when' is clause-final in the subordinate temporal clause, as in (9.108) and (9.109). This produces a left-branching *ki*-final subordinate temporal clause.

(9.108) [*the haté peṭék-o dos-í y-ií*
then REM.SG.OBL shawl-OBL grab-PFV.PTCP hither
gaán-t-ay ki] *qay-é-ir-an*
take.PST.D-3SG when heavy-CAUS-3SG.PRS/FUT-S
'[Then when he seized that shawl and pulled it toward himself], (he felt that) it is heavy.' (oral text, Village Kari)

(9.109) [*te-γár múłi bakas-ó bil-ó ayh a-ré-r*
REM.SG-ABL below box-OBL lid-OBL up AUG-do.PST.D-3SG
ki] ʦhap ašrafí
when full.of gold.coins
'[When he lifted the lid of the box below that one], (he saw that) it was full of gold coins.' (oral text, Village Sorech)

9.5.2.2 Temporal relations between events

9.5.2.2.1 Simultaneity

When a punctual event intersects an ongoing event, as in (9.110), the ongoing event can be expressed with the LOC1 of the imperfective participle.

(9.110) [*avá boγ-áv-a] dukán band h-oy*
I go-IPFV.PTCP-LOC1 shop closed become.PST-D-3SG
'[While I was going (there)], the shop closed.' (EB field notes)

The LOC1 form of the infinitive of *as-* or *š-* can be used to refer to an ongoing state, 'while', as in (9.111).

(9.111) [*oré-i as-ík-a] har kaá*
sleep-PFV.PTCP be(ANIM)-INF-LOC1 every someone.INDEF
froṣ-ér
breathe.noisily-3SG.PRS/FUT.NS
'[While asleep] everyone breathes noisily.' (DSAL)

Intersection of a punctual event with an ongoing state can also be expressed with *hánya tan* or *harúnya tan* 'just then', 'suddenly' (9.112) or *xabár bíko* 'suddenly', 'immediately', 'just then' (lit. 'when awareness happened'), a frequently occurring semi-lexicalised phrase (9.113).

(9.112) *kaγáz ma prúšṭ-a o-š-óni hány-a*
paper my front.of-LOC1 AUG-be-PST.D.3PL this.much-LOC1
tan gan nis-áy
EMPH wind emerge-PST.D.3SG
'The papers were in front of me; suddenly, a wind sprang up.' (MNN in Bashir 2023b)

(9.113) *avá niš-í as-t-am xabár.bíko*
I sit-PFV.PTCP be(ANIM)-PST.D-1SG just.then

ma braár h-ay
my brother come.PST.D-3SG

'I had sat down/was sitting; just then my brother came.' (MNN in Bashir 2023b)

Simultaneity of two punctual events is expressed with the oblique infinitive of the first-clause verb when two different subjects are involved, as in (9.114), where the subject of the first clause is 'I' and that of the second clause is 'ibex'. In this sentence, the postposition *su* 'with' conveys the specific meaning of simultaneity. Precise simultaneity of two punctual events, 'as soon as', 'just as' can be further reinforced with *tan* 'EMPH' following the postposition *su*, as in (9.115).

(9.114) *dahár-a phar nis-ík-o su toníṣu ma*
ridge-LOC1 over emerge-INF-OBL with ibex I.OBL

róy-tu pr-ay
face-LOC3 strike.PST.D-3SG

'As (I) crossed over the ridge, an ibex came face to face with me.' (DSAL)

(9.115) *tu bík-o su tan hasé h-ay*
you go.INF-OBL with EMPH REM.3SG come.PST.D-3SG
'Just as you left, s/he came.' (MNN)

When the subjects of both clauses are the same, as is 'avalanche' in (9.116), the two clauses can be linked with the perfective participle.

(9.116) *rešṭ g-íti sin-ó bot-ít-ay*
avalanche come-PFV.PTCP river-OBL block-PST.D-3SG
'An avalanche came and blocked the river.' (DSAL)

9.5.2.2.2 Sequence

Temporal sequence is frequently expressed with postpositions. In reporting a marked sequence of events, the landmark event is expressed with an ablative-marked infinitive plus *prúšṭi* 'before' (9.117) (9.118) or *áči* 'after' (9.119) (9.120).

(9.117) *bayskóp ç̣ok-ík-ar prúšṭi prúšṭi hatéra toór-t-am*[15]
film begin-INF-ABL before before there reach-PST.D-1SG
'I reached there (the cinema) well before the film began.' (SWKA in Bashir 2023b)

(9.118) *frosk-é-k-ar prúšṭi kós-te kya no r-élik*
straight-CAUS-INF-ABL before anyone-DAT anything NEG give-NEC
'Before determining the truth, one shouldn't say anything to anyone.' (DSAL)

(9.119) *buçhuṣ-ík-ar áči gambúri-o bi savz b-óni*
bloom-INF-ABL after flower-OBL seeds made become-3PL.PRS/FUT.NS
'After blooming, a flower's seeds are formed.' (DSAL)

(9.120) *darbát çham-é-k-ar áči záxum broól h-oy*
a.while pain-CAUS-INF-ABL after wound numb become.PST.D-3SG
'After hurting for a little while, the wound became numb.' (DSAL)

The lexicalised oblique infinitive of *b-* 'become', *bíko*, 'so', 'then', 'given that', links an event with a preceding event or situation (9.121). This is a very frequently used discourse continuity mechanism.

(9.121) *bík-o avá kyaní ko-m*
become.INF-OBL I what do-1SG.PRS/FUT.NS
'So what can/should I do? (given what has happened)' (MNN in Bashir 2023b)

An event following, influenced by, caused by, or contingent on a preceding event can be introduced with *the* 'then', 'so' (9.122).

[15] This is an alternate pronunciation of *torítam*, in which the /i/ of the past direct morpheme has been elided and the stem vowel compensatorily lengthened, with transfer of stress from the elided /i/ to the second mora of the lengthened stem vowel.

(9.122) *tá-te xam-é-t-am the huṣ*
you-DAT descend-CAUS-PST.D-1SG then recognition
ko-s
do-2SG.PRS/FUT.NS
'If/when I beat you, then (only) will you understand.' (SWKA in Bashir 2023b)

In a sequence of two actions by the same agent, the first action is usually expressed with a perfective participle, as in (9.123). When different agents are involved, the first event is expressed with the oblique infinitive (9.124).

(9.123) *ṣapík-an šetú-o muré-i žib-é*
bread-OBL.PL buttermilk-LOC4 crumble-PFV.PTCP eat-IMP.2SG
'Crumble your bread into buttermilk and (then) eat it.' (IF in Bashir 2023b)

(9.124) *kéłi bray-ék-o xabár ho-t-am*
sheep bleat-INF-OBL alert become-PST.D-1SG
'When the sheep bleated, I became alert.' (DSAL)

Action up to a certain point, 'until' is expressed with the postposition *pat* 'up to', 'until' following the LOC1 case rather than the OBL, as in (9.125) and (9.126). In example (9.127) 'until when?', 'for how long?' is *kál-a pat*.

(9.125) *šám-a pat yií no tor-ít-ay*
evening-LOC1 until here NEG reach-PST.D-3SG
'Until evening, s/he didn't reach here.' (DSAL)

(9.126) *qužd a-ré-ni ki ispá af tor-ík-a*
shout AUG-do.PST.D-3PL that we down arrive-INF-LOC1
pat he qábr-a mo lakh-ór
until that grave-LOC1 PROH put-IMP.2PL
'They shouted, "Don't put (him) into that grave until we reach down there."' (oral text, Village Bang)

(9.127) *bo ma sust-é-t-av- kál-a pat*
much me weak-CAUS-PST.D-2SG – when-LOC1 until
phik b-om
quiet be.able-1SG.PRS/FUT.NS
'You have annoyed me a lot; how long can I keep silent?' (MNN in Bashir 2023b)

Several regional variants of a single word introduce sudden, unexpected actions, including *nagáh* 'unexpectedly', 'suddenly'; *vanagáh* (Zondrangram), *vahagamí* (Sorech) 'by chance'; *vȧnagahíut* (Sorech), *vahagamíote* 'possibly' (MNN). One variant is illustrated in (9.128). Another word for 'suddenly', 'unexpectedly' is *ḟlaq* (9.129). When reduplicated as *ḟlaqḟláq* this means 'continuously', 'repeatedly'. A partially reduplicated form *ḟlaqǰáq* is also attested, meaning 'suddenly', 'immediately' (Naji 2008: 350).

(9.128) *γarám-ar niš-í as-ít-am, vanagahíut thuék*
rest-ABL sit-PFV.PTCP be(ANIM)-PST.D-1SG suddenly rifle
nis-áy
discharge.PST.D-3SG
'I was sitting peacefully (when) suddenly a rifle went off.' (Village Sorech)

(9.129) *thuék-an tayar-áv-e ḟlaq zang-ó-te*
rifle-OBL.PL ready-CAUS-IMP.2SG suddenly war-OBL-DAT
maṣk-íni
summon-3PL.PRS/FUT.NS
'Get your rifles ready; they will call us to war suddenly.' (DSAL)

9.5.2.3 Reason or cause clauses (SOURCE)

Reasons or causes are situations or events which bring about or are the source of other events or situations. They are expressed in various ways. If the reason is an event or action, reason clauses can be formed with the conjunction *kóreko(ki)* 'because' (lit. 'why when/if one says') or an alternate form *kóki* (9.130). The cause is often expressed with a perfective participle, as in (9.131) and (9.132).

(9.130) *avá hanún ta sum kórum kor-ík-o no*
I today you.OBL with work do-INF-OBL NEG
b-óm-an kóki ma
be.able-1SG.PRS/FUT-S because I.OBL
phordú dík-o boγ-élik
sapling put-OBL go-NEC
'I can't work with you today because I have to go to plant saplings.' (IF in Bashir 2023b)

(9.131) *ǰip bax b-íti paysá tonǰ birú*
pocket hole become-PFV.PTCP money lost become.3SG.PST.I
'Because (my) pocket got a hole in it, (my) money was lost (unnoticed by me).' (RKB)

(9.132) *móš-o ḍek čh-íti kos-ík no*
man-OBL leg break-PFV.PTCP walk-1NF NEG
b-óy-an
be.able-3SG.PRS/FUT-S
'Because the man's leg broke, he is unable to walk.' (DSAL)

If the cause or reason is expressed with a noun (9.133) (9.134) or infinitive phrase (9.135), it takes the instrumental case ending. Reason clauses can also be expressed with the perfective participle of *re-* 'say', as in (9.136) (see also Section 9.6.1.1).

(9.133) *tat tan žav-ó nafarmaní-en γečh-ár né-i*[16]
father REFL son-OBL disobedience-INS eye-ABL remove-PFV.PTCP
as-úr
be(ANIM)-PRS.3SG
'The father has broken off relations with his son because of his disobedience.' (MNN)

(9.134) *hayá sal uṣakí-en šalí šadál bay-áni*
this year cold-INS rice unripe go.PST.D-3PL
'This year because of cold weather the rice was unable to ripen.' (lit. 'went unripened') (DSAL)

(9.135) *buk ç̣hom-ík-en uy-ó qłuč kor-ík-o no*
throat hurt-INF-INS water-OBL swallow do-INF-OBL NEG
b-óm-an
be.able-1SG.PRS/FUT-S
'Because of my sore throat, I cannot swallow the water.' (DSAL)

(9.136) *duniyá diš reé avá no há-t-am*
[weather bad say.PFV.PTCP] I NEG come-PST.D-1SG
'[Because the weather was bad], I didn't come.' (lit. 'Thinking "the weather is bad"') (Bashir 1996b: 226)

[16] Alternate form of *nez-í*.

9.5.2.4 Purpose clauses (GOAL)

In contrast with reason or cause, purpose is a type of goal or end point; hence, it can be expressed with the dative of the infinitive, as in (9.137) and (9.138), or with the oblique infinitive (9.139). It can also be expressed with a complementiser based on SAY (9.140),[17] or with the imperfective participle (9.141). Comparing (9.139) and (9.140), we see that (9.139) states a neutral fact, while (9.140) suggests the speaker's internal motivation to see Salim.

(9.137) [*lášt-i dr-ék-o-t*] *i častán gan-ít-am*
floor-LOC2 put-INF-OBL-DAT a mat take-PST.D-1SG
'I bought a mat [to spread on the floor].' (MNN)

(9.138) *buɫí dar* [*kiṣíni savzé-k-o-t*] *ǰam*
birch wood plough make-INF-OBL-DAT good
'Birch wood is good [for making ploughs].' (RKB)

(9.139) *avá* [*salím-o poš-ík-o*] *g-ití as-úm*
I.DIR Salim-OBL see-INF-OBL come-PFV.PTCP be(ANIM)-PRS.1SG
'I have come [to see/meet Salim].' (Bashir 1996b: 230)

(9.140) *avá* [*salím-o paš-ím reé*]
I Salim-OBL see-1SG.PRS/FUT.NS say.PFV.PTCP
g-ití as-úm
come-PFV.PTCP be(ANIM)-PRS.1SG
'I have come [to see/meet Salim].' (lit. 'I have come thinking, I will see Salim') (Bashir 1996b: 230)

(9.141) [*ta poš-áv*] *g-ití as-t-am*
you.OBL see-IPFV.PTCP come-PFV.PTCP be(ANIM)-PST.D-1SG
'I came/had come [to see you].' (MNN in Bashir 2023b)

9.5.3 Conditional clauses

There are two main types of conditional clauses: realis and irrealis (also called counterfactual or contrary-to-fact). A realis conditional presents an event as not yet realised, but (still) possible. An irrealis conditional

[17] See Section 9.6.1.1 for further discussion of the SAY complementiser and various examples.

presents an event as not having happened or presumed not to be going to happen. Closely related in meaning are concessives, that is, sentences with the pattern: 'Even if x is true, still y' (Section 9.5.3.3).

9.5.3.1 Realis conditionals

In a realis conditional referring to present or future time, the verb of the protasis ('if clause') is usually in the PST.D, and that of the apodosis ('then clause') in the PRS/FUT.NS. The conditional marker *ki* 'if' usually precedes the verb phrase of the protasis or is in second position (9.142) (9.143) (9.144) (9.145) (9.146). In many such clauses, *ki* means either 'if' or 'when'. Rarely, it is found sentence-initially, as in (9.147), where the subject is encoded in the verb but not expressed as an independent pronoun. Conditional *ki* is not found clause-finally.

(9.142) *žolá-i trup zyat ki h-oy ǰam*
nut.bread-LOC2 salt more if become.PST.D-3SG good
b-oy
become-3SG.PRS/FUT.NS
'If/when there is more salt in the nut bread, it is good.' (MNN)

(9.143) *hava-á ki kos-ít-ay taf no k-oy*
air-LOC1 if walk-PST.D-3SG heat NEG do-3SG.PRS/FUT.NS
'If one walks in a breeze, one doesn't feel hot.' (MNN)

(9.144) *muṣíč ki ambóh o-š-óni hayván halé-ik asqán*
alfalfa if much AUG-be-PST.D.3PL animal keep-INF easy
'If there is a lot of alfalfa, it is easy to keep animals.' (MNN)

(9.145) *yar ǰam ki o-š-óy zindagí-o mazá*
companion good if AUG-be-PST.D.3SG life-OBL enjoyment
b-oy
be-3SG.PRS/FUT.NS
'If one's companion/wife is good, life is enjoyable.' (DSAL)

(9.146) *malgíri ki no ás-t-ay γéži safár*
companion if NEG be(ANIM)-PST.D-3SG alone travel
kor-ík miškíl
do-INF difficult
'If one doesn't have a companion, it is difficult to travel alone.' (DSAL)

(9.147) *ki o-br-ít-am bri-úm*
if AUG-die-PST.D-1SG die-1SG.PRS/FUT.NS
'If/when I die, I (will) die.' (oral text, Village Parwak)

Note that when the condition refers to the existence of something, as in (9.146), the PST.D of *as-* 'be(ANIM)' occurs, but if the condition refers to a characteristic of something, as in (9.145), the PST.D of *š-* 'be(INAN) is found. When the condition refers to relationships between existing circumstances or uncontroversial statements, often with the sense of 'since', the protasis ('if clause') often appears in the present/future, specific and the apodosis ('then clause') in the present/future, non-specific form, as (9.148), (9.149), or optative (9.150).

(9.148) *tu ki ré-s-an avá ko-m*
you if say-2SG.PRS/FUT-S I do-1SG.PRS/FUT.NS
'If/since you are saying to (do it), I will do (it).' (RKB)

(9.149) *ta hayá lu ki sahí the horó lu*
your this statement if right then DIST.SG.OBL statement
γalát b-oy
wrong become-3SG.PRS/FUT.NS
'If/since this statement of yours is right, then his/her statement will be wrong.' (RKB)

(9.150) *žib-áru ki no g-óy-an the*
eat-CAUS.DES if NEG come-3SG.PRS/FUT-S then
š-ar
be(INAN)-OPT.3SG
'If/since (you) don't feel like eating, then don't.' (lit. 'let it be')' (RKB)

A conditional referring to location or existence in the past can have a past direct form in the 'if clause', and a present/future non-specific in the 'then clause' (9.151).

(9.151) *žang-ó múži hes ki parís-a as-ít-ay*
war-OBL during DIST.SG.DIR if Paris-LOC1 be(ANIM)-PST.D-3SG
the ma dust-ó žan-ák b-oy
then my friend-OBL know-AG be-3SG.PRS/FUT.NS
'If s/he was in Paris during the war, then s/he will/must know my friend.' (RKB)

A condition unlikely to be realised can appear with the past direct in the protasis and the subjunctive in the apodosis (9.152).

(9.152) *avá kúra ki sadár hó-t-am the hayá*
I ever if president become-PST.D-1SG then this
qanún-o čhin-es-án
law-OBL cut-SBJV-1SG
'If I were ever to become President, I would repeal this law.' (RKB)

If a condition refers to an event which has not yet happened, the outcome of which is uncertain and will not be known until after it has actually happened, the protasis will have a mirative form, often the indirect past mirative, and a present/future non-specific form in the apodosis, as in (9.153) and (9.155).

(9.153) *akbár ki no man-íru bir-áy …*
Akbar if NEG agree-PST.PTCP become.MIR-3SG
'(and) if Akbar doesn't (turns out not to) agree …' (MNN)

(9.154) *ki ǰam bir-áy tan dást-a lakh-óm*
if good become.MIR-3SG REFL hand-LOC1 keep-1SG.PRS/FUT.NS
'If it proves to be good, I will keep it with me.' (lit. 'in my own hands') (DSAL)

(9.155) *kúri ki pišávur-o-te b-oγdú birét-am*
ever if Peshawar-OBL-DAT go-PST.PTCP become.MIR-1SG
ta korm-ó zarúr k-om
your task-OBL definitely do-1SG.PRS/FUT.NS
'If I ever happen to go to Peshawar, I will definitely do your errand.' (MNN)

Stipulative conditionals can be expressed as in (9.156), with the conjunction *múnya ki* 'provided that', 'on condition that' and a verb in its optative form.

(9.156) *kitáb avá horó-te d-om, múnya.ki*
book I DIST.OBL-DAT give-1SG.PRS/FUT.NS provided.that
hes sabáq r-ar
DIST.DIR lesson read-OPT.3SG
'I will give her/him a book, provided that s/he study.' (MNN)

9.5.3.2 *Irrealis conditionals*

Irrealis conditionals referring to past time have the irrealis form, consisting of past participle + LOC1, in the 'if'-clause, and the subjunctive in the 'then clause', as in (9.157) and (9.158). When referring to present time, the subjunctive appears in both the 'if' and the 'then' clauses, as in (9.159).

(9.157) *ma yoš birúa avá boy-es-ám va*
I-OBL time become.IRR I go-SBJV-1SG EMPH
'If I had had time I would (surely) have gone.' (MNN)

(9.158) *ma páp-a çok-ít-av ma páp-a no*
I.OBL breast-LOC1 stick-PST.D-2SG I.OBL breast-LOC1 NEG
çokír-a ta pušúr ma-t losnúk no
stick.IRR you.OBL flesh I.OBL-DAT morsel NEG
b-es-ír ta ley ma-t ṭhur
become-SBJV.3SG you.OBL blood I.OBL-DAT sip
no b-es-ír
NEG become-SBJV.3SG
'You clung to my breast. If you hadn't clung to my breast your flesh wouldn't have been even a morsel for me, your blood wouldn't have been a sip.'[18] (oral tale, Village Bang)

(9.159) *avá quvatíng ki b-es-án the ma paysá vam*
I rich if become-SBJV-1SG then I.OBL money loan
gan-élik no b-es-ír
take-NEC NEG become-SBJV-3SG
'If I were rich, I would not have to borrow money.' (RKB)

Evidentiality values interact with the meaning of irrealis conditionals. Compare examples (9.160) and (9.161); both of these sentences have the same English gloss, yet there is a difference in meaning between them. In (9.160), with the subjunctive form in the 'then clause', the speaker knew at the time of administering the punishment that the boy would not have gone to school without it, while in (9.161), with the past indirect form in the 'then clause', he realised only afterwards, on the basis of something learned after administering the punishment, that the boy

[18] Clinging to the breast of a female demon (as a child would) is a plea to be under the protection of that demon.

only went to school because he was beaten. This difference results from the use of the subjunctive in (9.160) and the past indirect in (9.161).[19]

(9.160) *ta ban no dirú.a sabáq-o-te no boγ-es-ú*
you.OBL stick NEG beat.IRR lesson-OBL-DAT NEG go-SBJV-2SG
'If you had not been beaten, you would not have gone to school.' (IF in Bashir 1988b: 56)

(9.161) *ta bán no dirú.a sabáq-o-te no*
you.OBL stick NEG beat.IRR lesson-OBL-DAT NEG
boγ-áv as-táv
GO-IPFV.PTCP be-PST.1.2SG
'If you had not been beaten, you would not have gone to school.' (IF in Bashir 1988b: 56)

The same difference obtains between (9.162) and (9.163). In (9.162) the speaker knew at the time of making the decision to come from above the house that if we came from below, we would not be able to open the door, while in (9.163) he only discovered this after we in fact came from above and saw the situation of the gates and the locks.

(9.162) *ispá tor-én no girúa duváxt-o*
we above-INS NEG come.IRR door-OBL
hur-ík-o no b-es-ám
open-INF-OBL NEG be.able-SBJV-1PL
'If we hadn't come from above (as opposed to from below), we wouldn't have been able to open the door.' (IF in Bashir 1988b: 56)

(9.163) *ispá tor-én no girúa duváxt-o*
we above-INS NEG come.IRR door-OBL
hur-ík-o no b-av
open-INF-OBL NEG be.able-IPFV.PTCP
as-tám
be(ANIM)-PST.I.1PL
'If we hadn't come from above, we wouldn't have been able to open the door.' (IF in Bashir 1988b: 56)

[19] This analysis and explanation of examples (9.160) (9.161) and (9.162) (9.163) are due to Inayatullah Faizi.

If a certain condition does not obtain, *ki.no* 'otherwise' follows the negative statement and the verb is in the subjunctive (9.164).

(9.164) *ma su sṭemp níki – ki.nó avá kor-es-ám*
me with stamp is.not – otherwise I do-SBJV-1SG
'I don't have a stamp; otherwise, I would do it.' (ZHD)

9.5.3.3 Concessive relationships

The particle *di*, usually meaning 'also', can have the senses 'anyhow', 'nevertheless', 'even if' and, following a conditional clause, expresses concessive relationships, as in (9.165). Example (9.166) illustrates the use of *agárki* 'even if', combining both the usual *ki* and the Persian *agar* 'if', and *vá.di* in the sense of 'still', 'even so'.

(9.165) *phuk ki hoy di gan-ís-aá*
little if become.PST.D.3SG even.if take-2SG.PRS/FUT.NS-Q
'Even if there is only a little, will you take it?' (DSAL)

(9.166) *agárki ma lu γalát bir-áy vá.di*
even.if my statement wrong become.MIR-3SG still
háni noh
that.much NEG
'Even if my statement turns out to be wrong, still it is not so very wrong.' (MNN)

9.6 Complementation structures

The working definition of complement I employ is a word, phrase, or clause needed to complete the meaning of a verb. For instance, English 'want to' requires something stating what the speaker wants to do (a complement), as in 'I want [to go home].'; similarly, 'know' requires a statement of what the speaker knows, as in 'I know [(that) he is a good man]'.

9.6.1 Sentential complements

Sentential complements are those consisting of a complete clause with a finite verb. Three types of sentential complements are common in Khowar.

9.6.1.1 SAY complements

The first employs the complementiser *reé*, the perfective participle of *re-* 'say'. This is an older, left-branching construction which is found in many of the languages of the Hindukush and Karakoram area (Bashir 1996b). Examples (9.167) and (9.168) exemplify this construction used to report direct speech. Sentence (9.169) illustrates its extension to mental speech, thinking. The *reé-* complementiser construction is frequent in conversational Khowar.

(9.167) [*hoq* *hay* *reé*] *ma*
bogeyman come.PST.D.3SG say.PFV.PTCP I.OBL
buhtu-é-ni-an
fear-CAUS-3PL.PRS/FUT-S
'Saying "The bogeyman has come", they are frightening me.' (NKN)

(9.168) [*peṣíru angyé* *reé*] *yád-i*
flour bring-IMP.2SG say.PFV.PTCP memory-LOC2
dré-t-am
put-PST.D-1SG
'I reminded (him) to bring flour.' (lit. 'I reminded him, "Bring flour!"') (SWKA in Bashir 2023b)

(9.169) [*hanún baṣ-ír* *reé*] *váhum*
today rain-3SG.PRS/FUT.NS say.PFV.PTCP worried
as-úm
be(ANIM)-PRS.1SG
'I am worried that it will rain today.' (lit. 'thinking "it will rain today …"') (IF in Bashir 2023b)

The use of *reé* further develops into that of a complementiser roughly equivalent to English 'that', as in (9.170), where we see both *reé* and *ki*, in a mixed, transitional structure. In the spoken language, the complementiser *ki* has fused with *rétay* 's/he said' to form a single semantic/phonological unit *rétayki* 's/he said'. This occurs frequently in oral folk narratives, in the simple sense of 'said'.

(9.170) *azím haṣ ré-t-ay* *ki af* *bay-áni* *reé*
Azim thus say-PST.D-3SG that down go.PST.D-3PL say.PFV.PTCP
'Azim said that they have gone downcountry.' (MAK)

9.6.1.2 Sentence-initial finite complements

In a second type, the sentential complement is sentence-initial and is recapitulated in the MC with a pronominal form, in a structure similar to that of the left-branching V-FIN relative clause. This type is illustrated in (9.171) with a complement of 'know'.

(9.171) [*hasé kiča.kóri a-r-ér*] *hes má-te maálúm*
REM.SG how AUG-do.PST.D-3SG DIST.SG me-DAT known
'I know [how s/he did it.]' (SWKA in Bashir 2023b)

9.6.1.3 ki complements

A third complement type is the right-branching *ki*-clause, a construction found with many verbs of speech and extended concepts of mental speech. 'Think', 'know', 'hope', 'believe', 'tell', 'hear' now often occur with right-branching *ki*-clauses (9.172) (9.173) (9.174) (9.175); this type is more likely to occur in more formal or written registers, or with words of fairly recent Perso-Arabic origin, as in (9.175).

(9.172) *áči gy-áʋ-a pón-a ḍaq má-tene*
back come-IPFV.PTCP-LOC1 road-LOC1 boy me-DAT
lu pr-ay [*ki pón-a*
word give.PST.D-3SG COMP road-LOC1
ǰip eksiḍén ho-y]
jeep accident become.PST.D-3SG
'While (I was) coming back, a boy on the road told me [that a jeep (had) had an accident on the road].' (MAK in Bashir 2023b)

(9.173) *ma kár-a tór-i š-er* [*ki*
my ear-LOC1 reach-PFV.PTCP be(INAN)-PRS.3SG COMP
sádar g-óy-an]
president come-3SG.PRS/FUT-S
'I have heard [that the President is coming].' (SWKA)

(9.174) *uméd š-er* [*ki ispá širístu*
hope be(INAN)-PRS.3SG COMP us encouragement
kor-ós]
do-2SG.PRS/FUT.NS
'We hope/expect [that you will encourage us].' (ZMZ)

(9.175) *hokumát* *hókum pr-ay* [*ki* *ta*
government order give.PST.D-3SG COMP you.OBL
bandí *kor-ónu* *b-ay*]
imprisoned do-RES.PTCP become-OPT.3SG
'The government ordered [that you (should) be imprisoned].' (RKB)

In expressing reported speech, either with 'say' or with verbs of 'thinking', Khowar represents the reported speech with direct (as opposed to indirect) speech. That is, the wording of the complement clause remains that which the speaker or thinker used at the time he spoke or thought it, rather than as recast by a reporter with tense and person changes, as is done in English. In (9.176), the message is that the speaker has just been informed by person A that s/he (person A) has been told that person B is busy. Since for person A this is not direct or old knowledge, the mirative indirect form *biráy* appears. If person A were saying that s/he himself/herself is busy, s/he would employ direct speech, as in (9.177). In (9.177), since speaker A knows directly that s/he is busy, the direct form appears.

(9.176) *hasé* *má-te* *çiçhé-t-ay* [*ki* *hasé*
s/he$_a$ me-DAT send.message-PST.D-3SG COMP s/he$_b$
masrúf as-ák *bir-áy*]
busy be(ANIM)-AG become.MIR-3SG
'S/he$_a$ sent me a message that s/he$_b$ was busy.' (MNN)

(9.177) *hasé* *má-te* *çiçhét-ay* [*ki* *avá masrúf*
s/he$_a$ me-DAT send.message.PST.D-3SG COMP I$_a$ busy
as-úm]
be(ANIM)-PRS.1SG
'S/he$_a$ sent me a message that "I$_a$ am busy"'. (MNN)

An embedded question including direct reported speech appears in (9.178). The same applies in (9.179), in which direct speech appears, in the voice of the 'recogniser' rather than of the speaker/reporter (the woman recognised).

(9.178) *babá kya vat g-om ré-t-ay*
father what time come-1SG.PRS/FUT/NS say-PST.D-3SG
'What time did Father say he would come?' (lit. 'Father said, "I will come at what time?"')[20] (Chitral Town)

(9.179) *hes ma huṣ kor-í as-úr –*
DIST.SG me recognition do-PFV.PTCP be(ANIM)-PRS.3SG
[avrát] reé
woman say.PFV.PTCP
'He has recognised me—(that she is) a woman.' (i.e. 'I am is a woman') (oral text, Village Kari)

9.6.2 Non-finite complements

Sometimes verbs take an infinitival complement with the infinitive in the direct case, especially when the event mentioned is not specific, as in (9.180) and (9.181).

(9.180) *b-ik maṣk-ís-an-aá*
go-INF.DIR want-2SG.PRS/FUT-S-Q
'Do you want [to go]?' (DSAL)

(9.181) *ʦeq ḍaq deé-k žan-ír usní.d-ik noh*
little boy run-INF.DIR know-3SG.PRS/FUT.NS fall-INF.DIR NEG
Proverb. 'A little boy knows how [to run] (but) not how [to (fall and) rise (again)].' Sense: Used about an inexperienced person who undertakes something without understanding the possible consequences. (DSAL)

An oblique infinitive complement occurs when a specific event of being able to, allowing, agreeing, or forgetting is mentioned, in the same way as oblique marking appears with specific direct objects, as in the following examples: *b-* 'be able' (9.182), *laák-* 'allow' (9.183), *zo-* 'agree to' (9.184), *roxts-* 'forget' (9.185).[21]

[20] The English gloss, 'he would come' reflects the English 'sequence of tenses' in indirect speech, in which the tense of the reported discourse changes to match the tense of the verb of saying/reporting.
[21] *zo-* 'agree to' with a simple noun complement can take also LOC1, as in *ma lú-a no zoítay* 'S/he didn't agree to what I said' (DSAL).

(9.182)

hasé	*[kya paysá*	*ang-ík-o]*	*b-ét-ay-aá*
REM.SG.DIR	any money	bring-INF-OBL	be.able-PST.D-3SG-Q

'Was s/he able [to bring any money]?' (DSAL)

(9.183)

ma	*[b-ík-o]*	*laák-e*
I.OBL	go-INF-OBL	allow-IMP.2SG

'Allow me [to go]'/'Let me [go].' (RKB)

(9.184)

kumóru	*[ḍaq-ó*	*al-ík-o]*	*no*	*zo-ít-ay*
girl	boy-OBL	marry-INF-OBL	NEG	agree-PST.D-3SG

'The girl did not agree [to marry the boy].' (DSAL)

(9.185)

hasé	*[hatoó-t*	*lu*	*d-ík-o]*	*roxts-ít-ay*
REM.SG.DIR	REM.OBL.SG-DAT	word	give-INF-OBL	forget-PST.D-3SG

'He forgot [to tell her].' (oral text, Village Chapali)

In (9.186), 'want to' is expressed by the conjunct verb *ṣorxomár š-* 'intense desire exist', with an oblique infinitival complement which carries the genitive sense 'intense desire of eating'.

(9.186)

mraç̣	*žib-ík-o*	*ṣorxomár*	*š-er*
mulberry	eat-INF-OBL	intense.desire	be(INAN)-PRS.3SG

'(I) really want [to eat mulberries].' (crave mulberries) (Village Parwak)

10 Morphosemantics

This chapter is titled 'morphosemantics' because it considers the ways in which semantic parameters important in Khowar are expressed in its morphology. It treats several disparate topics on aspects of meaning which I understand to be central to how Khowar encodes a speaker's perception and understanding of the world. These topics have been mentioned in previous chapters, but here I single them out for more detailed focus. Referentiality, spatial concepts, modality, inferentiality, mirativity, expression of emotions, phasal constructions, self-referentiality and reduplication, and discourse particles are discussed in this chapter.

Three semantic parameters which I have found to be central to understanding the way Khowar structures and presents the world are: the temporal boundedness of states or events (temporary or permanent); whether knowledge is obtained directly or indirectly and whether it is old, established knowledge or new knowledge; and vertical and horizontal position and/or motion.

10.1 Referentiality

This section discusses the categories of specificity and definiteness in Khowar. Specificity plays an important role in both the nominal and verbal systems. My ordinary-language working definitions for these concepts are as follows. An entity is DEFINITE if both speaker and addressee know what is being referred to. For example, 'Where is *the book* I gave you?' assumes that the addressee knows which book the speaker is referring to. It is INDEFINITE SPECIFIC if the speaker knows what he is referring to but the listener cannot be assumed to know this.

For example, 'I am looking for *a book*.' in reply to someone who asks you what you are doing. The speaker knows which book he is looking for, but the listener probably does not. If the speaker does not have a specific entity in mind, just something which meets a general description, reference is INDEFINITE and NON-SPECIFIC. For example, 'I am looking for *a book* to read on the plane.' In this situation, any book which serves the purpose will do.

Khowar has no unique definite or indefinite articles like English indefinite 'a' or definite 'the'. Rather, definiteness is conveyed by a variety of mechanisms, distributed throughout the grammar—in the deictic system, in argument marking, in word order, and in selection of tense-aspect forms.

In the deictic system, the proximal third-person pronoun *hayá* 'this' is definite, since both speaker and listener are present in the speech-act situation. Proximal *hayá* is often accompanied by a pointing gesture. Distal *hes* may be definite or indefinite, depending on the degree to which a listener is privy to the prior context of an utterance. The normally stressed remote demonstrative pronouns *hasé* and *haté* 'he', 'she', 'it', 'that' are definite. With weak stress on the first syllable, *háse* and *háte* often function like a definite article 'the' (see Section 5.2.3). Specific indefinites can be indicated with *i*, lit. 'one', as in (10.1), where the speaker knows which old woman he is referring to but hasn't previously discussed her with the addressee. Non-specific indefinites can be indicated with *kya* 'any', as in (10.2), or be unmarked, as in (10.5) below.

(10.1) *ta i vav as-úr, hatoγó má-te*
your an old.woman be(ANIM)-PRS.3SG her me-DAT

det
give.IMP.2SG

'You have *an* old woman with you. Give her to me.' (oral text, Village Chapali)

(10.2) *ma-t kya tuγfá al-áv-aá*
me-DAT any gift bring.PST.D-2SG-Q
'Have you brought a/any gift for me?' (RKB in Bashir 2023b)

Marking of direct objects depends on specificity and definiteness. An oblique case marker on a direct object indicates definiteness or specificity. In (10.3), the direct object 'opportunity' is a specific indefinite, since the speaker clearly knows what it was but the addressee may not.

(10.3) *avá ǰam muqo-ó alé-t-am*
I good opportunity-OBL let.slip-PST.D-1SG
'I let slip a good opportunity.' (ZHD in Bashir 2023b)

Word order plays a role in indicating referential status. Sentence-initial position is associated with topicality and old information, which is usually definite, as in (10.4), where clearly both speaker and addressee know which money is being referred to. New information, usually indefinite, typically occurs immediately before the verb. Use of *as-* and *š̌-* 'be' in statements asserting the existence of something necessarily means that the subject is indefinite, as in (10.5).

(10.4) *pays-án tá-te áča d-om*
money-OBL.PL you-DAT later give-1SG.PRS/FUT.NS
'I will give you the money later.' (MYS in Bashir 2023b)

(10.5) *bron-ó ṭék-a boík as-úr*
ridge-OBL top-LOC1 bird be(ANIM)-PRS.3SG
'There is a bird on the top of the boundary ridge.' (MNN in Bashir 2023b)

The specificity status of an entity informs the choice of some verb forms. The present/future specific (PRS/FUT-S) form is associated with specificity of an action; in (10.6) the speaker is referring to an action ongoing at the time of speaking. The appearance of the PRS/FUT-S form usually correlates with specificity or definiteness of a core argument, as it does in (10.6), where the direct object, goats, is definite. The present/future non-specific (PRS/FUT.NS) third-person singular of *b-* 'become', *boy*, conveys the sense of a general, non-specific state of affairs, as in (10.7).[1] In sentences of this type, the subject is an indefinite NP. This is a very frequent usage and contrasts with equational sentences with the meaning x = y, where x denotes a definite entity, and which are expressed as nominal sentences without a copular verb.

(10.6) *pay-án gan-í adráx-tu*
goat-OBL.PL take-PFV.PTCP mountain.pasture-LOC3
bí-m-an
go-1SG.PRS/FUT-S
'I am taking the goats up to the mountain pastures.' (DSAL)

[1] Example 6.31 is repeated here as (10.7) for the reader's convenience.

(10.7) *šum ałók-o bíh bo b-oy,*
bad pumpkin-OBL seed many become-3SG.PRS/FUT.NS

šum róy-o lu bo b-oy
bad person-OBL words many become-3SG.PRS/FUT.NS

Proverb. 'A bad pumpkin has lots of seeds; a bad person talks too much.' (MAK in Bashir 2023b)

With some quantitative adverbs and some nouns, specificity and non-specificity are morphologically distinguished, with non-specific meaning indicated by a final unstressed *-i* added to the base (specific) form. For example, *drust* 'all (specific)' versus *drústi* 'all (non-specific)', *duht* 'all (specific)' versus *dúhti* 'all (non-specific)', *khul* 'all (specific)' versus *khúli* 'all (non-specific)', *phat* 'some (specific)' versus *pháti* 'some (non-specific)', *taklíf* 'trouble (specific)' versus *taklífi* 'trouble (non-specific)'. Examples follow as (10.8), (10.9), (10.10), and (10.11). In (10.8) a specific occasion is being discussed, while (10.9) is a general description of the population of Village Balim. Example (10.10) is an acknowledgement of a favour or a formulaic leave-taking expression apologising for giving trouble to a host on a specific visit, while (10.11) is a general statement about life experience.

(10.8) *ispá payp-ó korm-ó-te bi as-t-am*
we pipe-OBL work-OBL-DAT go.PFV.PTCP be(ANIM)-PST.D-1PL

ǰošpónǰ ǰun błats hóni mašvara-ár
fifteen persons collected become.PST.D-3PL consultation-ABL

áči phat ṭenkí-a kórum a-r-éni phat payp-án
after some tank-LOC1 work AUG-do.PST.D-3PL some pipe-OBL.PL

'We went to work on the pipe project; fifteen persons gathered. After consultation, some worked on the tank and some on the pipes.' (IF in Bashir 2023b)

(10.9) *balím-a troy qésma roy as-úni pháti*
Balim-LOC1 three kinds people be(ANIM)-PRS.3PL some

ǰam zeminvéni pháti kamgáłu pháti vedúru
big landowners some small.holders some without.houses

'There are three types of people in Balim. Some have lots of land, some have only small fields, and some are without homes.' (IF in Bashir 2023b)

(10.10) *ta* *taklíf* *aár-t-am*
you.SG.OBL trouble do-PST.D-1SG
'I have given you trouble/bothered you (on this occasion).' (IF in Bashir 2023b)

(10.11) *dunya-á* *avá* *bo* *taklífi* *poš-í*
world-LOC1 I much/many trouble see-PFV.PTCP
as-úm
be(ANIM)-PRS.1SG
'I have seen much trouble/many troubles in this world.' (MS in Bashir 2023b)

10.2 Patient-oriented meanings

There is no single form in Khowar which can be called 'passive' in the sense of the English passive. Several forms which convey meanings in which the subject is not active but is acted upon (a patient) have been discussed at various places in Chapter 6: the past participle (Section 6.7.3), the resultative participle (Section 6.7.4), the potential participle (Section 6.7.5), the present perfect (Section 6.8.3.1), and the causative/desiderative nominal (Section 6.7.7.3). If an agent or cause of an event affecting a patient is to be mentioned, *hósta* 'hand-LOC1' can follow the oblique of that agent, as in (10.12).

(10.12) *bo* *žun* *horó* *hóst-a* *tabáh* *h-óni*
many person DIST.SG.OBL hand-LOC1 ruined become.PST.D-3PL
'Many persons were ruined by him (financially, morally, their lives).' (RKB in Bashir 2023b)

Patient focus is inherent in certain lexical items. Many compound words consist of the name of some illness or negative force plus the element *-žúni* 'afflicted by'. Examples are: *ҫhekžúni* 'afflicted by a disease', *γamžúni* 'worried', *andȧvžúni* 'suffering from a fever', *buhtu̇ni̇žúni* 'possessed by a djinn', *balȧhžúni* 'possessed by an evil spirit'. These words name the cause/agent of the bad condition; they can be used both adjectivally, as in *ҫhekžúni moóš* 'man afflicted by a disease', and nominally, as in (10.13).

(10.13) *kučháy.žuní-o-te* *šunǰ* *çak-á-ve*
boil.afflicted.one-OBL-DAT needle adhere-CAUS-IMP.2SG
'Give an injection to the person suffering from boils.' (MNN in Bashir 2023b)

The suffix *-γári,* ~ *-γéri* ~ *-γíri* 'taken by or negatively affected by' appears with animate agents or natural forces, for example: *ganγíri* 'affected by a fairy or djinn' or 'distracted', *reniγári* 'bitten by a dog', *łovγári* 'taken by a fox', *ganγéri* 'taken by the wind', as in (10.16).

(10.16) *avá tan phost-ó muŕík-o-t hatoγó-t*
I REFL hide-OBL rubbing-OBL-DAT REM.SG.OBL-DAT
d-ití as-t-am toó gan.γéri
give-PFV.PTCP be(ANIM)-PST.D-1SG REM.SG-OBL wind.taken.by
kor-í tonǰ-éru bir-áy
do-PFV.PTCP ruin.PST.PTCP become.MIR-3SG
'I gave him my hide for softening. (I have now found out that) he let it be taken by the wind and ruined.' (IWA in Bashir 2023b)

10.3 Spatial concepts

Khowar has a highly elaborated system of representation of spatial concepts, based primarily on verticality and horizontality of position and trajectory, extent of the locus of the event, or the number of actants. These parameters interact in the selection from among four locative case suffixes, depending on the verticality or horizontality of position or direction (path), and on the shape, orientation, and extent of the actants. Thus, spatial extent also interacts with the category of number.[2]

The four locative case endings, which are used mostly with inanimates, and specific directional adverbs which specify verticality and direction combine to represent spatial concepts and their developments.

[2] The discussion in this section is primarily based on Bashir (2000b). Data in that paper are from fieldwork focused on the topic of spatial relations. I am grateful for these examples to Maula Nigah Nigah, at that time Headmaster, Government High School, Zondrangram, and to Inayatullah Faizi, at that time Lecturer, Government College, Booni.

10.3.1 Locative cases

Khowar has four locative case endings, all unstressed: *-a*, *-o*, *-i*, and *-tu*. Of these, *-tu*, *-o*, and *-i* are marked for verticality or horizontality, while *-a* is not (Table 10.1). Information given in Section 4.1.3.5 is summarised here.

LOC1 is the most general of the locative cases and indicates locations or directions not having a vertical–horizontal or motion component in their conceptualisation. See examples (10.17) – (10.22). As such, it has a wide range of extended meanings, applying to temporal as well as spatial location, functioning as a second oblique case, and in several grammatical functions.

(10.17) *bohrt-ó ṭék-a as-úr*
rock-OBL top-LOC1 be(ANIM).PRS-3SG
'S/he, it(ANIM) is on top of the rock.' (physical location)

(10.18) *háte łaγ-ó nás-a baγ-áy*
the shepherd-OBL side-LOC1 go.PST.D-3SG
'S/he went to the shepherd.' (physical location)

(10.19) *khovár-a*
Khowar-LOC1
'in Khowar' (abstract location)

(10.20) *to-ó g-ík-o váxt-a*
REM.SG-OBL come-INF-OBL time-LOC1
'at the time of his/her coming' (temporal location)

(10.21) *har vezén-a*
every evening-LOC1
'every evening' (temporal location)

Table 10.1 Locative cases

LOC1	*-a*	Ø vertical, Ø horizontal: point(like) location (spatial or temporal), − extent
LOC2	*-i*	+ horizontal (same level as agent): location, direction, motion (spatial or temporal), + extent
LOC3	*-tu*	+ vertical (upward): location, direction, motion, contact (Ø extent)
LOC4	*-o*	+ vertical (downward): location, direction, motion (Ø extent)

(10.22) *ʣox až-ík-a thukúnu*
thorn be.born-INF-LOC1 sharp
Proverb. 'A thorn is sharp at birth.' Sense: 'A clever person is clever from birth', extended to mean that a person's basic qualities are soon evident. (temporal location)

In addition to its locative functions, LOC1 performs several grammatical functions. Following the infinitive, it expresses the complement of *d-* 'give', 'strike' in an inceptive construction (10.23). This inceptive construction sometimes has the sense of 'began to be able to V'. The LOC1 forms a second oblique base, which precedes the postposition *pat* 'until' (10.24). Suffixed to an imperfective participle, it forms an adverbial participle with the sense 'while V-ing' (10.25). Suffixed to a past participle, it yields an irrealis meaning of wishful thinking or counterfactuality in irrealis conditionals (10.26).

(10.23) *phon-ík-a pray*
dance-INF-LOC1 strike.PST.D.3S
'S/he began to dance.'

(10.24) *qayamát-a pat*
doomsday-LOC1 until
'until doomsday'

(10.25) *boγ-áʋ-a*
go-IPFV.PTCP-LOC1
'while going'

(10.26) *b-irú-a*
be-PST.PTCP-LOC1
'if it had been' (irrealis conditional); 'would that it had been' (wishful thinking)

10.3.2 Interaction of locative case endings with nominal spatial morphemes

A number of basic nominal morphemes with spatial meaning combine with the different locative cases. They include the bound elements *andrén-* 'interior' and *ač-* 'back', and unbound nominals *muł* 'bottom', 'lowest part'; *nas* 'side'; 'vicinity', *sor* 'head', 'top'; *guç̣* 'base', 'intersection of the lowest point of a vertical object with a horizontal plane';

and *prušṭ* 'before', 'in front of'. The contrasting forms in (10.27), (10.28), (10.29), and (10.30), built on the base *andrén-* 'interior, inside', illustrate the interaction of the locative postpositions with the concept of interiority.

(10.27) LOC1: *andrén-a* 'inside (a largeish permanently/inherently closed thing)'
pay-ó andrén-a čhaní as-úr
goat-OBL interior-LOC1 kid be(ANIM)-PRS.3SG
'There is a baby (goat) inside the goat.' (SWKA in Bashir 2023b)

(10.28) LOC2: *andrén-i* 'inside' (extended horizontal location)
gor andrén-i kumáł-a ʣox
witch interior-LOC2 smoke.hole-LOC1 thorns
Proverb. 'A witch is inside (the house); there are thorn bushes on/over the smoke hole.' Sense: 'If people inside a house are making (bad-intentioned) plans, people on the outside can only speculate about what they are doing (because the smoke hole is blocked).' (NKN in Bashir 2023b)

(10.29) LOC3: *andrén-tu* 'up (vertically) inside'
noγór-o andrén-tu γer-úsi, salá
fort-OBL interior-LOC3 get.into-1PL.HORT consultation
k-óni-an ré-t-ay.ki
do.3PL.PRS/FUT-S say-PST.D-3SG
'He said, "Let's get up into the fort; they are planning something."' (oral text, Village Bang)

(10.30) LOC4: *andrén-o* '(down) inside' (a deep thing)
čhat-ó andrén-o bohrt š-éni
pond-OBL interior-LOC4 rocks be(INAN)-PRS.3PL
'There are rocks in the pond/lake.' (SWKA in Bashir 2023b)

Several factors determine which of the locative case endings appear in a given situation. One of these is the shapes of the actants involved in an event. In (10.31) *-tu* appears because a stick is a long object, striking the vertically oriented head; (10.32) is not good because a stick is a long object which would have either vertical or horizontal (not pointlike) impact on one's head. On the other hand, (10.33) is good because a rock is roundish and smaller than the head, so that the point of impact is like a point without vertical or horizontal extension. Similarly, (10.34) is good but (10.35) is not, because a rock is a pointlike rather than a long object. (10.38) would require an element of horizontal extension, either in the orientation of the impact or the shape of the impacting object, as illustrated in (10.36) and (10.37).[3]

(10.31) *ban ma khák-tu pr-ay*
stick my head-LOC3 strike.PST.D-3SG
'The stick hit me on the head.' (vertically)

(10.32) **ban ma khák-a pray*
*-LOC1

(10.33) *bohrt ma khák-a pr-ay*
rock my head-LOC1 strike.PST.D-3SG
'A rock hit me on the head.'

(10.34) *bohrt ma γéc-a pr-ay*
rock my eye-LOC1 strike.PST.D-3SG
'A rock hit me in the eye.'

(10.35) **bohrt ma γéc-i pray*
*-LOC2

(10.36) *ban ma khák-i pr-ay*
stick my head-LOC2 strike.PST.D-3SG
'A stick hit me on the head (with a horizontal motion and impacting my head with two-dimensional extent).'

(10.37) *ban ma khák-o pr-ay*
stick my head-LOC4 strike.PST.D-3SG
'A stick hit me on the head (descending from above and hitting my head vertically downward).'

Orientation of the actants also determines the choice of locative case ending. In (10.38), the glass is lying on its side in a horizontal position. In (10.39), however, it is standing vertically, occupying a more or less pointlike location, opposite the canonical front (spigot side) of the cooler (See Figure 10.1).

[3] Examples (10.31)–(10.49) are from Bashir (2000b: 18ff).

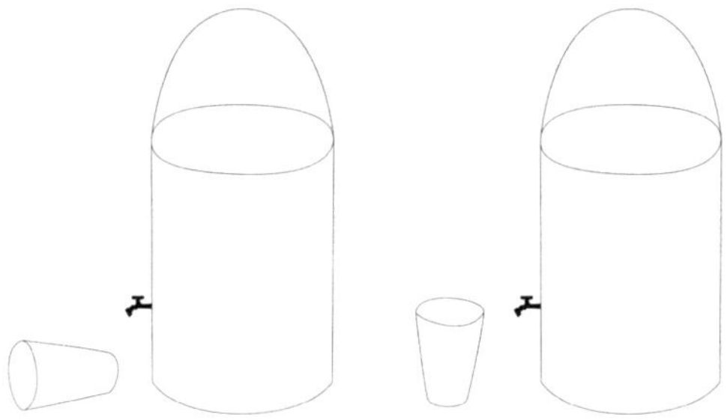

Figure 10.1 Orientation of actants. Created by Elena Bashir.

(10.38) *gilás kulér-o prúšṭ-i š-er*
glass cooler-OBL front-LOC2 be(INAN)-PRS.3SG
'The glass is (lying) in front of the cooler.'

(10.39) *gilás kulér-o prúšṭ-a š-er*
glass cooler-OBL front-LOC1 be(INAN)-PRS.3SG
'The glass is (standing) in front of the cooler.'

In (10.40) (10.41) and (10.42) (10.43) the difference between *-o* and *-i* encodes the difference in the trajectory of the moving actant.

(10.40) *hamó khanǰ-ó áč-o petsh-é*
PROX.SG.OBL wall-OBL back-LOC4 throw-IMP.2SG
'Throw this behind the wall.' (from in front of it and over it).' (The trajectory is up and down, with the final segment downward.)

(10.41) *hamó khanǰ-ó áč-i petsh-é*
PROX.SG.OBL wall-OBL back-LOC2 throw-IMP.2SG
'Throw this behind the wall.' (The addressee will have to go to a position from which the trajectory is horizontal.)

(10.42) *fuṭból mez-ó áč-o γeér-t-ay*
football table-OBL back-LOC4 fall-PST.D-3SG
'The football fell (down) behind the table' (if it was previously close enough to the table that its trajectory is downward)

(10.43) *fuṭból mez-ó áč-i γeér-t-ay*
football table-OBL back-LOC2 fall-PST.D-3SG
'The football fell behind the table' (if it came from far enough away that its total resultant trajectory was approximately horizontal).

The horizontal versus vertical line of sight from observer to object also helps select the appropriate locative case ending. Compare (10.44), with a potentially vertically downward line of sight, and (10.45), with a potentially horizontal line of sight.

(10.44) *hasé khanǰ-ó áč-o niš-í as-úr*
REM.SG wall-OBL back-LOC4 sit-PFV.PTCP be(ANIM)-PRS.3SG
'S/he is sitting (down) in back of the wall.' (if the wall is near and constitutes a noticeable vertical obstacle to the speaker's horizontal line of sight)

(10.45) *hasé khanǰ-ó áč-i niš-í as-úr*
REM.SG wall-OBL back-LOC2 sit-PFV.PTCP be(ANIM)-PRS.3SG
'S/he is sitting behind the wall.' (if the wall is farther away and line of sight is approximately horizontal)

The extent of the locus of an action or state also determines the choice of locative marking. In (10.46) the locus of the writing is conceptualised as pointlike, while in (10.47) its horizontal extent is emphasised.

(10.46) *kháňǰ-a niveš-í o-š-óy*
wall-LOC1 write-PFV.PTCP AUG-be-PST.D.3SG
'(It/something) was written on the wall.'

(10.47) *khánǰ-i niveš-í o-š-óy*
wall-LOC2 write-PFV.PTCP AUG-be-PST.D.3SG
'The wall was written on.' (over a large horizontal extent, implying that many things or a long text were written)

The choice of locative marking can also be influenced by the number of actants. Examples (10.48) and (10.49) illustrate the choice between *-a* and *-i*. In (10.48) the location of the singular actant (the boil) is pointlike, while in (10.49) the plurality of the actants (boils) imparts two-dimensional extension to the locus of the event.

(10.48) *múx-a kučháy nis-í š-er*
face-LOC1 boil emerge-PFV.PTCP be(INAN)-PRS.3SG
'A boil has come out on (someone's) face.'

(10.49) *múx-i kučháy nis-í š-éni*
face-LOC2 boils emerge-PFV.PTCP be(INAN)-PRS.3PL
'Boils have come out (all over) (someone's) face.'

In addition to its appearance with nouns and the basic spatial morphemes *ač-* and *prušṭ*, LOC2 also attaches to the ablative case ending *-ar*, giving an extended form *-ári*, which sometimes appears with other words having spatial or temporal meaning. When it occurs, it usually emphasises the extended duration or spatial extent of the state or event. Examples (10.50), (10.51), (10.52), and (10.53) illustrate this point.

(10.50) *vezen-ár-i baṣ-ír-an*
evening-ABL-LOC2 rain-3SG.PRS/FUT-S
'It has been raining (continuously) since (yesterday) evening.' (MAK in Bashir 2023b)

(10.51) *hoó i hamóṣ láka ḍaq yií neé-i*
DIST.SG.OBL a like.this like boy up.here bring.out-PFV.PTCP
as-úr, haté γar-ár-i
be(ANIM)-PRS.3SG REM.SG cave-ABL-LOC2
'A boy like this has brought her up here from out of that cave.' (oral tale, Village Uthul)

(10.52) *u̇γpiyáru gík-o hatéra šun d-íti, uγ-ó*
thirst come.INF-OBL there lips touch-PFV.PTCP water-OBL
p-ím-an r-av o-š-óy,
drink-1SG.PRS/FUT-S say-IPFV.PTCP AUG-be.PST-3SG
af-hár-i kyaáγ g-íti rigíṣ-o
down-ABL-LOC2 something come-PFV.PTCP beard-OBL
gaán-t-ay
grab-PST.D-3SG
'When he felt thirsty, touching his lips there to drink the water (lit. 'he was thinking "I want to drink water"'), from below something came and grabbed his beard.' (oral tale, Village Bang)

(10.53) *khošteér-ar poy-ári kandúri zamaná phár*
hide.PST.PTCP-ABL after-ABL-LOC2 so.much time past
baγ-áy,
go.PST.D-3SG
'A long time passed after (the body) was hidden.' (oral text, Village Parwak)

In example (10.54), *yíri*, an extended form of *yií* 'hither' consisting of the proximal element *y* + the locative element *r* + LOC2, indicates continuous temporal extent. In (10.55) we see the roots *kur-* 'where?' and *phar* 'over there', both with the LOC2 ending indicating motion with an approximately horizontal trajectory.

(10.54) *doṣ-ár yíri ṭhux-ér-an*
yesterday-ABL until.now cough-3SG.PRS/FUT-S
'S/he has been coughing lightly since yesterday until now.' (MNN in Bashir 2023b)

(10.55) *avá kúr-i b-im phár-i b-oγé*
I where-LOC2 go-HORT.1SG over there.LOC2 go-IMP.2SG
Question: 'Where should I go?' Answer: 'Go over there.' (MS in Bashir 2023b)

10.3.3 Association of spatial concepts with elements of the social world

The literal geographical or gravitational conceptualisation of verticality is mapped onto various aspects of the social world. The traditional Chitrali house was usually built on sloping land, with the entrance on the lower side of the slope and the interior parts of the house higher up the slope. This traditional house is conceptualised in terms of the vertical dimension, with the front parts of the house being lower and the parts farther away from the entrance being higher. Figure 10.2 is a simplified diagram of the main features of a traditional Chitrali house. In this scheme, the part of the house or a room closer to the door is 'downward' and the direction toward the interior of the room is 'upward'.

The terms *ayh* 'up' and *af* 'down' thus apply to regions of the house (10.56). Opening the door of a house is expressed in terms of moving the door upward or downward (10.57).[4]

[4] Examples (10.56)–(10.59) are also from Bashir (2000b: 18ff).

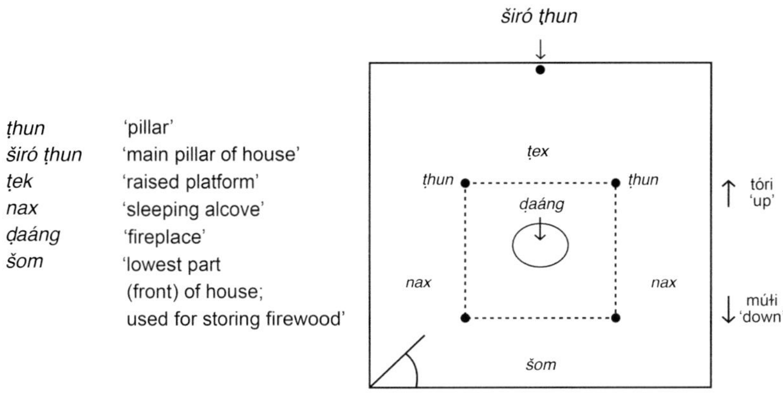

Figure 10.2 Diagram of a traditional Chitrali house. Created by Elena Bashir.

(10.56) a. *reéni af šóm-o bot-í*
dog down front.of.house-LOC4 tie-PFV.PTCP
as-úr
be(ANIM)-PRS.3SG
'The dog is tied (down) in the front part of the house.'

b. *ayh ṭék-tu nis-é*
up platform-LOC3 emerge-IMP.2SG
'Go up onto the platform.'

c. *dur-ár af nis-é*
house-ABL down emerge-IMP.2SG
'Go out of the house.'

(10.57) a. *duwáhrt-o ayh hur-é*
door-OBL up open-IMP.2SG
'Open the door.' (for a door which opens inward, that is, upward)

b. *duwáhrt-o af kor-é*
door-OBL down do-IMP.2SG
'Close the door.' (for a door which opens inward, that is upward)

This extended vertical conceptualisation correlates with the social dimension of status: the region of the main room farther away from the entrance is associated with higher status than the front part of the house; thus, honoured guests are always seated 'higher', as far away from the entrance as possible, and a host might say the sentence in (10.58) to a guest.

(10.58) *tóri* *niš-é*
upper.side sit-IMP.2SG
'Sit farther up.' (away from the entrance of the house)

The conceptualisation of going from the entrance of a house toward the interior as going from down to up is also generalised to other man-made enclosures. For example, a bus conductor, when telling passengers to 'move to the rear of the bus', farther from the door, says the sentence in (10.59).

(10.59) *ayh ç̣hó*
up go.on.IMP.SG
'Go on up.' (toward the back of the bus)

The directional term *yií* 'up here (toward speaker)' is also generalised to other situations where no physical elevation is involved. For example (10.60).

(10.60) *phuk* *yií laák-e*
a.little up let.go-IMP.2SG
'Turn it (TV) up a little.' (TMF)

10.3.4 Beginning and end

Beginning and end are typically conceptualised as *várz* 'top', 'head', 'origin', 'beginning' and *póng* 'foot', 'end'. So when telling a story, for example, one starts at the head and continues to the foot (10.61).

(10.61) *várz-a* *ç̣ak-é-i* *póng-a* *pat*
top-LOC1 adhere.to-CAUS-PFV.PTCP foot-LOC1 until
'Starting at the beginning (and continuing) to the end'

10.3.5 Typology of the Khowar spatial system

Much work has been done on the typology of spatial concepts, notably the research programme at the Max Planck Institute for Psycholinguistics. Levinson (1996) describes ABSOLUTE, INTRINSIC, and RELATIVE types of spatial reference. In the ABSOLUTE type, objects are located with reference to fixed directions, which can be either cardinal directions (north, south, east, west), or uphill/downhill gradients independent of speaker orientation. Speakers of a language with an absolute system based on cardinal directions will refer to an object as, for example 'to the north of x's house', while those who speak a language whose absolute system is based on uphill/downhill gradients will say 'uphill from x's house'. In the RELATIVE type, the left-right orientation of the human body (typically speaker's) is projected onto the scene to be described. In such a system, when one says, 'The chair is to the left of the tree', he means that as he faces the tree, the chair is on the same side as his left hand. In the INTRINSIC type, coordinates are determined by inherent features (front/back, sides or facets) of the figure object. For example, the front of a chair is the side that has the seat; the front of a water cooler is the side with the spigot. Thus, 'the cat is in front of the chair' means that the cat is on the seat-side of the chair, whether the seat-side of the chair is facing toward or away from the speaker.

With reference to this typology of linguistic/spatial systems, Khowar is primarily an absolute system, based on the geographical gradient of elevation, but also having some elements partaking of the intrinsic and relative systems.

First, let us look at considerations relevant to the absolute system. There are no indigenous words for cardinal directions in Khowar. Recently, Urdu words for north, south, east, and west have been adopted and are widely known, but they are not typically used for describing location or path in the Khowar-speaking area. In pre-twentieth-century Khowar, the closest approximation to cardinal directions was with the expressions in (10.62)–(10.65).

(10.62) *yor af yer-ík-o vóṣki*
sun down.there fall-INF-OBL direction
'the direction of the sun's setting' (west)

(10.63) *yor yií nis-ík-o vóṣki*
sun up.here emerge-INF-OBL direction
'the direction of the sun's rising' (east)

(10.64) *froskí-o vóṣki*
right-OBL direction
'the right(hand) direction' (sometimes used for north because Muslims in Chitral face west toward Mecca for prayers)

(10.65) *khołí-o vóṣki*
left-OBL direction
'the left(hand) direction' (sometimes used for south for the same reason)

Khowar's system is almost entirely based on the uphill versus downhill and horizontal parameters. Uphill/downhill and horizontal gradients have not, however, morphed into cardinal directions. The context for determining the specific interpretation of 'up' and 'down' varies according to geographical, cultural, or discourse context. The context can be large scale, like the scale involved in a trip from Chitral down to Peshawar, or small scale, for example the scale involved in asking someone to hand something up to the roof. If the large-scale and the small-scale gradients are in conflict, the smaller-scale gradient can override the larger-scale, as in example (10.59) above. In this case, the bus conductor would say *ayh ̦cho* 'go on up' ('move to the rear of the bus') even if the bus was headed uphill and the actual back of the bus was physically lower than the front. When the trajectory of an object is complex, the final segment of the trajectory appears to dominate, but these questions need much more study.

With regard to the RELATIVE system, words for 'left', *khółi*, and 'right', *fróski*, exist and are used commonly for body parts, like *fróski host* 'right hand'. They can also be used in giving directions which involve a person orienting himself relative to man-made structures with rectilinear elements like roads or bridges, as in (10.66).

(10.66) *sída hamoγ-én b-oγé- fróski bazú-o sóra tan ta*
straight this-INS go-IMP.SG right arm-OBL on REFL you.OBL
γéč-i g-oy
eye-LOC2 come-3SG.PRS/FUT.NS
'Go straight along this (road); you will see it automatically on your right side.' (MS in Bashir 2023b)

When specifying the locations of objects relative to one another, however, these terms are not used. Rather, most commonly one object is described as on the upper (*tóri*) or on the lower (*múłi*) side of the reference object; or the words *nas* 'side', 'vicinity', *praš* 'side', 'slope' are used. One would not specify one object as being to the left or right of another based on projecting the observer's body parts onto the scene.

The INTRINSIC system can sometimes operate for objects with a clearly identifiable front and back, like a water cooler with a spigot on its front; in such a case, another object can be specified as in front of or in back of it. This sentence applies to both of the configurations diagrammed in Figure 10.1, whether the front of the cooler is facing toward or away from the observer. For objects with no identifiable front or back, like a wall, being in front or in back of the wall is determined as in the RELATIVE system, so that something on the same side of a wall as the speaker is 'in front of' the wall, and something on the opposite side of a wall from the speaker is 'behind' the wall. See examples (10.40), (10.41), (10.42), and (10.43) above.

Though Khowar has some elements similar to those in the INTRINSIC type, and marginal usages resembling the RELATIVE type, by far the most pervasive parameter in Khowar is the upward versus downward and horizontal orientation and extent of location and direction/trajectory characteristic of the ABSOLUTE type.

10.4 Deontic modality

Two constructions express meanings of necessity or obligation: (1) a participle consisting of root + *-élik* ~ *-éli* (NEC),[5] and (2) a construction consisting of the oblique infinitive + *baṣ* (NEC2) in the modal meaning of *baṣ*. The *-élik* ~ *-éli* construction usually conveys deontic or moral necessity, usually associated with the agent, as in (10.67) and (10.68). The *baṣ* construction can express meanings of propriety, suitability, necessity, even ability, usually arising from some quality of the action or situation. Phrases with *baṣ* can be predicative, as in (10.69), or attributive adjectives, as in (10.70).

(10.67) *miskar.bázi-o očé qast lú-o huṣ kor-élik*
joking-OBL and truthful speech-OBL recognition do-NEC
'One must recognise joking and truthful words.' (MNN)

[5] The form with *-k* is usually found in Upper Chitral, while the form without *-k* is usually heard in Lower Chitral. The *k*-less form has also been borrowed into Kalasha.

(10.68) *hayá ispá sáf-o dur kyá – ham-ó sum*
PROX.SG.DIR our all-OBL home EMPH – PROX.SG-OBL with

muhabát kor-í ham-ó behí-o áča
love do-PFV.PTCP PROX.SG-OBL welfare-OBL behind

çok-élik
attach-NEC

'This is all of our home. We must cherish it and pursue its welfare.' (from short story *Rajuli*, Shahzad 1989)

(10.69) *díšul [no kor-ík-o baṣ]*
bad.speech NEG do-INF-OBL NEC2
'Verbal abuse is [not worthy of being done] (should not be done).' (DSAL)

(10.70) *hayá [no kor-ík-o baṣ] kórum*
PROX.SG.DIR NEG do-INF-OBL NEC2 deed
'This is something [that shouldn't be done].' (IF)

Modal *baṣ* has several other senses; it can sometimes express ability (10.71) or imminence of an event (10.72). One usage combines *baṣ* with the causative/desiderative nominal in *-áru*, conveying a sense of 'causing some action', as in (10.73).

(10.71) *hasé poš-ík-o baṣ noh*
REM.SG see-INF-OBL NEC2 is.not
'S/he is not able to see.' (SWKA in Bashir 2023b)

(10.72) *ḍaq d-ití d-ití faqát brík-o baṣ*
boy beat-PFV.PTCP beat-PFV.PTCP just die-OBL NEC2
'The boy was beaten so much that he is just about to die.' (MNN in Bashir 2023b)

(10.73) *hasé diš buhtu-áru g-ík-o baṣ moóš*
REM.SG very fear-CAUS.DES come-INF-OBL NEC2 man
'He is a very frightening man.' (RKB)

10.5 Epistemic modality

Epistemic modality involves ability, possibility, probability, certainty, or necessity determined not by moral, ethical, or social considerations, as is deontic modality, but by constraints related to a specific situation, or to knowledge and its acquisition.

10.5.1 Possibility and ability

Possibility and ability can be expressed in several ways: with the oblique infinitive + *b-* 'be able' (10.74), with the potential participle in *-ín* ~ *-én* (10.75) (10.76), and sometimes with the modal particle *baṣ̌* (10.77). In (10.77) we see *baṣ̌* in two different meanings—'liable to V' and 'should V'.

(10.74) *duváht-o hur-ík-o no bo-m*
door-OBL open-INF-OBL NEG be.able-1SG.PRS/FUT.NS
'I am not able to open the door (ever).' or 'I will not be able to open the door.' (MA in Bashir 2023b)

(10.75) *łay boík-o ç̣hiír di l-en*
speckled bird-OBL milk even find-POT.PTCP
b-oy
become-3SG.PRS/FUT.NS
Proverb. 'Even the milk of a speckled bird can be found (there).' Sense: Said about a place where even extremely rare things are available. (TMF in Bashir 2023b)

(10.76) *γoš no b-ík-o kúi b-ín no*
free.time NEG become-INF-OBL anywhere go-POT.PTCP NEG
b-oy-án
become-3SG.PRS/FUT-S
'Because (I) don't have time, (I) can't go anywhere.' (SWKA in Bashir 2023b)

(10.77) *čh-ík-o baṣ̌ išnáry-an sár-i axtyát*
break-INF-OBL NEC2 thing-OBL.PL ABL-LOC2 care
kor-ík-o baṣ̌
do-INF-OBL NEC2
'One should be careful with things which are liable to break.' (MNN in Bashir 2023b)

10.5.2 Probability

The word *albát*, when it occurs sentence-initially or in second position, indicates uncertainty or possibility, as in (10.78).[6] In (10.79) uncertainty is additionally expressed by *albát* plus the past indirect form, signalling the speaker's lack of direct knowledge. In (10.80) uncertainty is conveyed by the presence of *kya* and the sentence-final question marker *-aá*. Used sentence-finally, however, *albát* can convey epistemic necessity 'must be/must have', as in (10.81).

(10.78) *tu albát ǰošpónǰ taríq-a g-os*
you probably fifteen date-LOC1 come-2SG.PRS/FUT.NS
avá ta γeč.k-om
I you wait.for-1SG.PRS/FUT.NS
'You'll probably come on the fifteenth; I'll wait for you.' (MS in Bashir 2023b)

(10.79) *albát avá hatéra as-tá:m*
possibly I there be(ANIM)-PST.I.1SG
'Possibly I was there.' (MK in Bashir 2023b)

(10.80) *albát avá hatéra kya as-ít-am-aá*
maybe I there what be(ANIM)-PST.D-1SG-Q
'Maybe I was there.' (MK in Bashir 2023b)

(10.81) *g-ití as-úr albát*
come-PFV.PTCP be(ANIM)-PRS.3SG probably
'S/he must have come.' (RKB in Bashir 2023b)

Uncertainty, often expressed in English with 'might', can be expressed with *nagáh* or its variant *vánagah* 'lest', as in (10.82). These words tend to occur in contexts when an outcome is not desired.

(10.82) *nokhí savzé-i tayar-á-ve vánagah*
millrace fix-PFV.PTCP ready-CAUS-IMP.2SG lest
doł baṣ-ír
hard rain-3SG.PRS/FUT.NS
'Fix the millrace and make it ready, lest it suddenly (start to) rain hard.' (DSAL)

[6] Example 6.178 is repeated here as (10.78) for the convenience of the reader.

An utterance-final particle indicating uncertainty is *ko*; its use is illustrated in (10.83).

(10.83) Question: *axmát ṣapík žu-tí as-úr-aá?*
Ahmad meal eat-PFV.PTCP be(ANIM)-PRS.3SG-Q
'Has Ahmad eaten?'

Answer: *žu-tí as-úr-aá ko*
eat-PFV.PTCP be(ANIM)-PRS.3SG-Q UNCERT
'He may have eaten (but I am not sure).' (SWKA in Bashir 2023b)

A difference in likelihood between two situations shows up when (10.84) and (10.85) are compared. In (10.84), with the past direct of *b-* 'become', the sense is that my getting time is fairly possible; in (10.85), however, with the present/future non-specific of *b-*, the sense is that my getting time is less likely.

(10.84) *ma γoš ki h-oy avá bi-m*
my free.time if become.PST.D-3SG I go-1SG.PRS/FUT.NS
'If/when I get time, I will go.' (possible) (ZHD)

(10.85) *ma γoš ki b-oy avá bi-m*
my free.time if become-3SG.PRS/FUT.NS I go-1SG.PRS/FUT.NS
'If I (will) get time, I will go.' (less likely) (ZHD)

10.5.3 Certainty

A typical construction employing indigenous Khowar linguistic strategies to impart a sense of certainty is the stressed sentence-final particle *vá*, which adds a nuance of speaker commitment, something like 'definitely', as in the irrealis conditional in (10.86). Certainty can also be indicated by some adverbs, like *zarúr* 'definitely', 'surely' or *xamaxá* 'definitely', both of which are from Persian and Urdu. Example (10.87) illustrates this.

(10.86) *ma γoš birúa avá boγ-es-ám vá*
I.OBL time become.IRR I go-SBJV-1SG EMPH
'If I had had time, I definitely would have gone.' (MNN)

(10.87) *ṣapík-o su xamaxá khardačí žib-élik*
meal-OBL with definitely salad.greens eat-NEC
'One should definitely eat fresh greens with meals.' (DSAL)

10.6 Evidentiality

Expression of the evidentiality and mirativity status of an utterance is obligatory in Khowar. In each tense and aspect, a choice between a direct (D) and indirect (I) form must be made, as well as between expressing the predication as old or new knowledge (mirative). Table 10.2 lays out these correspondences illustrated with the third-person singular of the verbs *as-* 'be(ANIM)', š- 'be(INAN)', *b-* 'be(come)'and *kor-* 'do'. Mirativity is a separate category which, however, often coincides with indirectivity. Except for the past imperfect direct of *š-*, those

Table 10.2 Direct, indirect, and mirative forms of of *as- š-*, 'be', and of *b-* 'become', and *kor-* 'do'

Tense-aspect	Direct	Indirect	Mirative
		'be' verbs	
Present/future (*b-*)	*boi*	*birái*	*birái*
Present			
as-	*asúr*	*birai, asák birái*	*birái, asák birái*
š-	*šer*	*širai, šak birái*	*širái, šak birái*
Past			
as-	*asítai ~ aástai*	*astá:i, asíru*	*asíru birái*
š-	*ošói*	*šáur, širú*	*širú birái*
		kor- 'do'	
Present/future non-specific	*korói ~ koi*	*korák birái*	*korák birái*
Present/future specific	*koróyan ~ kóyan*	*korák birái*	*korák birái*
Past	*arér ~ korítai ~ koórtai*	*kardú*	*kardú birái*
Past imperfect	*koráv ošói* ANIM or INAN)	*koráv astá:i* (ANIM) *koráur*	*koráva birái*
Past perfect	*korí astai* (ANIM) *kóri ošói* (INAN)	*korí astá:i* (ANIM) *kóri šak birái* (INAN)	*korí asák birái* (ANIM) *kóri šak birái* (INAN)
Present perfect	*korí asúr* (ANIM) *kóri šer* (INAN)	*korí asák birái* (ANIM) *kóri šak birái* (INAN)	*korí asák birái* (ANIM) *kóri šak birái* (INAN)
Past habitual	*korávtai*	*koráur*	–

forms which include a form of *as*-, or *š*- 'be' as auxiliary show animacy agreement.

Evidentiality marking in Khowar grammaticises the source of information as direct (first-hand, personal, or established knowledge) or indirect (hearsay, non-witnessed, inference from observation of a result). These two information sources are even lexicalised in the terms *yečenpošíru* 'seen by the eyes' (direct) and *karatoríru* 'reached the ear' (indirect). In contrast, marking of mirativity grammaticises the state of a speaker's knowledge, and the sequence of its acquisition (old established or new knowledge), as in examples (10.88) and (10.89). It does not, however, imply speaker commitment or non-commitment to the truth of the utterance. Speaker commitment of various kinds is conveyed by sentence-final discourse particles (see Section 10.10.2.2).

(10.88) *hasé* *gy-áv-a* *avá niveš-áv*
REM.SG.DIR come-IPFV.PTCP-LOC1 I write-IPFV.PTCP
o-šót-am
AUG-be.PST.D-1SG
'When s/he came, I was writing.' (Bashir 1988b: 55)

(10.89) *hasé* *gy-áv-a* *avá niveš-áv*
REM.SG.DIR come-IPFV.PTCP-LOC1 I write-IPFV.PTCP
astá:m
be.PST.I.1SG
'When s/he came, I was writing.' (Bashir 1988b: 55)

The difference between (10.88) and (10.89) is that in (10.88) the speaker was himself aware that a visitor had come when he was writing; in (10.90) the speaker became aware only later of the fact that a visitor had arrived when he was writing, when it was reported to him by someone else.[7]

10.7 Involuntary experience

Like some other languages in the Greater Hindukush Karakoram region, Khowar expresses many involuntary actions, sensations, illnesses, emotions, or states with first-causative (derived transitive) verbs.[8]

[7] I am grateful to Inayatullah Faizi for the analysis and interpretation of examples (10.88) and (10.89).

[8] See Bashir (2015) for further cross-linguistic discussion of this point.

In these constructions, the experiencer is the patient/object and the transitive verb expresses the state, sensation, or affliction and implies that it is/was caused by some agent other than the experiencer. It is important to note that these constructions are different from the 'dative subject' construction widely discussed for South Asian languages (Bashir 1988a: 197ff). The agent of the verbal notion can be expressed, unexpressed, or impersonal. In the following examples the formally causative/transitive sentence expresses an involuntary (– control) action or event caused by some agent, animate or inanimate. Example (10.90) simply reports the fact of coughing, unmarked for volitionality/control status; in (10.91), in contrast, an agent/cause, though not explicitly named, is part of the conceptualisation, and the statement is marked for non-volitionality. Such an agent can be mentioned, as in (10.92).

(10.90) *avá khaph-ím-an*
I.DIR cough-1SG.PRS/FUT-S
'I am coughing.' (Ø control) (Bashir 2015: 6)

(10.91) *ma khop-é-r-an*
I.OBL cough-CAUS-3SG.PRS/FUT-S
'I am coughing.' (lit. 'Something is making me cough.') (– control) (Bashir 2015: 6)

(10.92) *toq ma γun-é-t-ay*
mud.DIR I.OBL get.stuck-CAUS-PST.D-3SG
'I am stuck in the mud.' (lit. 'The mud has stuck me in it.') (– control) (Bashir 2015: 6)

Some of these formally causative verbs of experience are derived from adjectives. For example, from *qayí* 'heavy' comes *qayeék* 'to be heavy'; from *trang* 'tight' comes *trangeék* 'to be tight (clothes, shoes)', as in (10.93).

(10.93) *phuphúk trang-é-r-an*
a.little tight-CAUS-3SG.PRS/FUT-S
'It is a little tight.' (SWKA in Bashir 2023b)

Some are expressed with conjunct verbs consisting of a noun plus the transitive verbaliser *kor-* 'do', as in (10.94) and (10.95).

(10.94) *kamí* *kó-ni-an*
shortage do-3PL.PRS/FUT-S
'There aren't enough (bricks).' (lit. 'They are making a shortage.') (EB field data)

(10.95) *má-te* *ʦeqí* *k-óni-an*
me-DAT smallness do-3PL.PRS/FUT-S
'They are too small for me.' (lit. 'They are doing smallness for me.') (EB field data)

The causative/desiderative form *-áru* conveys an involuntary emotion or desire, as in (10.96) and (10.97). In construction with *sóra* 'by' expressing the agent, it can also accommodate a cause of the unavoidable feeling, like the humorous words in (10.97). In this construction, the *-aru* form expressing an involuntary feeling or action is the grammatical subject of the verb *g-* 'come', and the experiencer appears in its oblique form.

(10.96) *ma* *keł-áru* *g-óy-an*
I.OBL weep-CAUS.DES come-3SG.PRS/FUT-S
'I can't help weeping.' (SWKA in Bashir 2023b)

(10.97) *namakín* *lú-o* *sóra* *ma* *hos-áru* *h-ay*
humorous words-OBL by I.OBL laugh-CAUS.DES come.PST.D-3SG
'The humorous words made me laugh.' (MYS in Bashir 2023b)

10.8 Expression of emotions

The internal experience of emotions or sensations is also expressed with *g-* 'come' and an oblique experiencer, for example 'anger' in (10.98) or 'dizziness' in (10.99).

(10.98) *ma* *saxt* *qahár* *g-ití* *žiré-t-am*
I.OBL severe anger come-PFV.PTCP digest-PST.D-1SG
'I was very angry (but) I tolerated it.' (MNN)

(10.99) *sér-a* *phar* *nis-áv-a* *ma*
bridge-LOC1 across emerge-IPFV.PTCP-LOC1 I.OBL
žanaγéri *h-ay*
dizziness come-PST.D-3SG
'As I was crossing the bridge, I felt dizzy.' (MS)

The idea of 'liking' or 'be pleasing to' is expressed with the conjunct verb *pon d-* 'be pleasing to', as in example (10.100). 'Dislike' or 'hatred' is expressed with another oblique experiencer construction, as in *avá toγó diš* 'S/he hates/dislikes me' (lit. 'I am bad/displeasing to him/her'), in which the person who likes or dislikes the subject appears in the oblique form.

(10.100) *haya ḍaq ma nán-o-t pon.dóy-an*
this boy my mother-OBL-DAT be pleasing.3SG.PRS/FUT-S
'My mother likes this boy (as a marriage prospect for me).' (RKB)

The overt expression of emotion usually is expressed transitively with a conjunct verb employing *kor-* 'do', for example, *méher koŕík* 'to love, be affectionate to' or *phíri koŕík* 'to stroke with affection/love (for example, a child)'.

The sense of 'want to' is sometimes conveyed by the present/future specific form, as in (10.101) and examples (4.60) and (9.101) above.

(10.101) *xúr di kya lu d-ós-an-aá*
other also any words give-2SG.PRS/FUT.S-Q
'Do you want to say something else?' (DSAL)

10.9 Phasal constructions

Phases of an action or event, from its origin to its conclusion and result, can be expressed as illustrated in the following sections.

10.9.1 Be ready to/be eager to/try to V

The oblique infinitive plus *čaq* with nominal meanings 'inclination', 'trend', 'tendency', 'likelihood', 'readiness' and adjectival senses 'eager', 'ready' plus a finite form of *b-* 'become' expresses the ideas of 'be ready to' (10.102), 'be eager to' (10.103), or 'try to' (10.104).

(10.102) *khoṭ qorqór b-íti boṣ-ík-o čaq*
clouds thick.full become-PFV.PTCP rain-INF-OBL readiness

b-íti š-er
become-PFV.PTCP be(INAN)-PRS.3SG

'The clouds have become thick and full, and it is ready to rain.' (MNN)

(10.103) *avá pišávur-o-te b-ík-o čaq mágam tat ma*
I Peshawar-OBL-DAT go-INF-OBL eager but father me
no laák-oy-an
NEG allow-3SG.PRS/FUT-S
'I am eager to go to Peshawar, but my father isn't allowing me.' (DSAL)

(10.104) *ma išṭok-é-ik-o čaq mo b-os*
me play-CAUS-INF-OBL eager PROH become-IMP.2SG
'Don't try to use me for your own purposes.' (lit. 'don't try to play me') (MNN)

10.9.2 Be about to V

This construction consists of the oblique infinitive of the verb denoting the event about to take place plus the perfective participle of *b-* 'become' and a finite form of 'be' (10.105) or an oblique infinitive + *baṣ̌* (10.106).

(10.105) *kyaáγ.ki tonǰ b-ík-o b-ití*
which.REL lost become-INF-OBL become-PFV.PTCP
š-éni
be(INAN)-PRS.3PL
'… which are about to be lost' (RAKR)

(10.106) *ko háni keł-ís-an xłikh-ík-o baṣ̌*
why so.much weep-2SG.PRS/FUT-S gasp-INF-OBL NEC2
'Why are you crying so much that you are about to gasp?' (MNN in Bashir 2023b)

Actions which were about to happen but did not are expressed with the past incompletive (PST.INC) form (Section 6.8.2.3).

10.9.3 Begin to V

The main inceptive construction, 'begin to V', is with the LOC1 form of the infinitive plus a finite form of *d-* 'strike', as in (10.107). Also, the past direct form of some verbs denoting activities, for example 'to pain/hurt' or 'to shiver' can carry an inherent inceptive sense, as in (10.108).

(10.107) *or-áru g-íti zomo-ík-a*
sleep-CAUS.DES come-PFV.PTCP yawn-INF-LOC1
pr-ay
strike.PST.D-3SG
'When s/he became sleepy, s/he began to yawn.' (DSAL)

(10.108) *andáv sóra d-ík-o doł-ít-ay*
fever on strike-INF-OBL shiver-PST.D-3SG
'When s/he suffered an attack of fever, s/he began to shiver.' (DSAL)

10.9.4 Be V-ing

Being in the midst of an ongoing action is expressed with a durative tense-aspect form, like the present/future specific, *avá kórum kóman* 'I am working' or the past imperfective, *avá kórum koráv ošótam* 'I was working', illustrated in example (10.109).

(10.109) *çhétr-i sor ʦop-áv o-š-ot-am*
field-LOC2 ears collect-IPFV.PTCP AUG-be-PST.D-1SG
'I was collecting (fallen) ears (of grain) in the field.' (DSAL)

10.9.5 Finish/complete V-ing

A construction meaning to finish doing something employs the perfective participle of the verb naming the action plus a finite form of *nási nezík* (~ *neék*) (lit. 'to take out to the edge') 'to complete' (10.110), or *khuleék* 'to finish' (10.111).

(10.110) *host nig-íni kor-í nási.né-t-ay*
hand wash-INS.N do-PFV.PTCP finish-PST.D-3SG
'He completed making a vessel for hand washing.' (oral text, Village Sorech)

(10.111) *xá:y roy-án tu neyl-í*
oh people-OBL.PL you swallow-PFV.PTCP
khul-é-t-av
finished-CAUS-PST.D-2SG
'Alas, you have finished swallowing up all the people.' (oral text, Village Bang)

10.10 Discourse continuity

10.10.1 Clause chaining

Sentences like the English ‘I will go home and eat dinner’, or ‘I went to the bazaar, and a shopkeeper called out to me’, in which two simple clauses, each with a finite verb and having the same or different subjects, are joined with a conjunction like ‘and’, are not expressed in Khowar with *očé* or *va*, the words for ‘and’. The most frequent ways of expressing a sequence of more than one event utilise a non-finite form for the first (subordinate) clause and a single finite verb for the second (main) clause. The non-finite forms used are the oblique infinitive and the perfective participle. These morphological strategies usually indicate whether the subject of the two clauses is the same (perfective participle) or different (oblique infinitive).

10.10.1.1 Different subjects: oblique infinitive

When the subjects or agents of two linked clauses are clearly different, especially in scenarios involving transitive verbs and volitional actions, the clauses are usually linked by the oblique infinitive. In (10.112) the subjects of the two clauses are ‘someone’ and ‘rock’; in (10.113) they are ‘dog’ and ‘I’; and in (10.114) they are ‘person$_a$’ and ‘person$_b$’. In all cases, the subjects of both clauses are in the direct case form. This pattern holds whether the verbs of the two clauses are transitive or intransitive.

(10.112) *bohrt-ó zuq d-ík-o tsraq tán no*
stone-OBL push give-INF-OBL motion EMPH NEG
a-r-ér
AUG-do.PST.D-3SG
‘When (someone) pushed the rock, it didn’t even budge.’ (GMKH in Bashir 2023b)

(10.113) *reéni ma don ço̜k-ík-o avá žiríy a-ré-tam*
dog me teeth attach-INF-OBL I shriek AUG-PST.D-1SG
‘When the dog bit me, I shrieked.’ (SWKA in Bashir 2023b)

(10.114) *pušúr buł-ík-o no o-y-óy*
meat fry-INF-OBL NEG AUG-eat.PST.D-3SG
‘When s/he$_a$ fried the meat, s/he$_b$ didn’t eat it.’ (DSAL)

10.10.1.2 Same subjects: perfective participle

One of the main functions of the perfective participle[9] is to link two or more clauses, usually when the grammatical subjects of the linked clauses are the same.[10] The primary meaning of the perfective participle is temporal sequence, from which other meanings like causality or manner develop. Sometimes such linkages express the primary meaning of temporal sequence, as in (10.115). Often, combined temporal and causal senses develop, as in (10.116) and (10.117).

(10.115) *mandók-o* *band* *kor-í* *uɣ-ó* *yuú*
sluice.gate-OBL closed do-PFV.PTCP water-OBL down.here
laák-e
let-IMP.2SG
'Close the sluice gate and let the water flow down here.' (MNN)

(10.116) *paysán* *khul-é-i* *luč* *b-ití*
money finish-CAUS-PFV.PTCP penniless become-PFV.PTCP
as-úr
be(ANIM)-PRS.3SG
'He has finished his money and become totally penniless.' (MNN)

(10.117) *lušt* *bóht-a* *ç̣hun-í* *ušup-ít-am*
smooth rock-LOC1 step-PFV.PTCP slip-PST.D-1SG
'I stepped on a smooth rock and slipped.' (MNN)

Examples (10.115), (10.116), and (10.117) all display the pattern familiar from many other Indo-Aryan languages, in which both the perfective participial clause and the main clause have the same grammatical subject. In Khowar, however, this is not a strict rule, as can be seen in examples (10.118), (10.119), (10.120), (10.121), and (10.122). In these sentences, the relation between the two events is that the event mentioned in the participial clause is the cause of the event reported in the main clause. The grammatical subjects of the two clauses in each of these examples are different: in (10.118) 'gall bladder' and

[9] The perfective participle in this function is traditionally referred to in the South Asianist linguistics literature as 'conjunctive participle' and more recently 'converb'.
[10] This topic is often discussed as 'tail-head linkage'.

‘an animal’, in (10.119) (my) ‘ankle’ and ‘I’, in (10.120) ‘sunshine’ and ‘apples’, in (10.121) ‘clouds’ and ‘thunder’, and in (10.122) ‘snow’ and ‘ground’. In all of these examples the predicates of the main clause are non-volitional, in most cases intransitive, events.

(10.118) *uṣakí-en thałxá oxó-i o-br-ít-ay*
cold-INS gall.bladder swell-PFV.PTCP AUG-die-PST.D-3SG
Lit. ‘Its gall bladder swelled up from cold and it died (of an animal which dies spontaneously in winter).’ Sense: This is an ironic idiomatic usage, said jokingly when a hunter fails to hit his mark (when the speaker knows that a hunter can’t hit his target). (DSAL)

(10.119) *ḍang.kół bóht-tu d-íti ǰabaǰá*
ankle rock-LOC3 strike-PFV.PTCP unable.to.move
hó-t-am
become-PST.D-1SG
‘(My) ankle struck a rock and I was unable to move.’ (DSAL)

(10.120) *yor b-íti paloóγ poč-ít-ani*
sunshine become-PFV.PTCP apples ripen-PST.D-3PL
‘It became sunny and (the) apples ripened.’ (RKB)

(10.121) *khoṭ g-íti bumburéṣ k-óy-an*
clouds come-PFV.PTCP thunder do-3SG.PRS/FUT-S
‘Clouds have come and it is thundering.’ (RKB)

(10.122) *him buru-í zemín ʥa b-oy*
snow melt-PFV.PTCP land wet become-3SG.PRS/FUT.NS
‘When the snow melts, the ground becomes wet.’ (RKB)

In all of these cases, the event in the first clause, reported with the perfective participle, has what Lindholm (1975: 78), discussing the Tamil adverbial participle (AvP), has called ‘natural relevance’ to the event of the main clause. Lindholm says: “What a Tamil speaker responds to in using the AvP is the perception of a relation between the semantic content of two clauses that can best (though grossly) be labelled ‘natural relevance’.” Lindholm gives the sentence in (10.123) as a simple Tamil illustration of this.

(10.123) *pāmbu kaḍiccu avan settān*
snake bite.AV.P he died
'The snake bit him and he died.' (Lindholm 1975: 31, cited from Ramanujan and Annamalai 1967: 164)

This same situation can also be represented in Khowar with the perfective participle (10.124).[11]

(10.124) *ayí d-íti hasé o-br-ít-ay*
snake strike-PFV.PTCP REM.SG.DIR AUG-die-PST.D-3SG
'A snake bit him/her and s/he died.' (RKB)

Importantly, this analysis of the functions of the Tamil adverbial participle and the use of the Khowar perfective participle is not based on a structural/syntactic notion of grammatical subject, but on speakers' perception of semantic relevance.[12] Sometimes either the perfective participle or the oblique infinitive can appear, but with slight differences in meaning: with emphasis on simple temporal sequence (oblique infinitive) or suggestion of a causal relationship (perfective participle) between the two alternatives. Example (10.125) illustrates such a case.

(10.125) *haté kórum ma yád-i g-íti /*
REM.DIR task my memory-LOC2 come-PFV.PTCP /
g-ík-o avá b-ayát-am
come-INF-OBL I go-PST.D-1SG
'When I remembered that task, I left.' (RKB)

10.10.1.3 Quotative particle/complementiser from SAY

In Khowar, *reé*, the perfective participle of *re-* 'say', has developed grammaticised functions as well as retaining its lexical meaning 'having said'.[13]

[11] It can also be represented using the oblique infinitive, as in (b).

(b) *ayí d-ík-o hasé o-br-ít-ay*
snake strike-INF-OBL REM.SG.DIR AUG-die-PST.D 3SG
'When a/the snake bit him/her, s/he died.' (IF, p.c.)

[12] Masica (1991: 401) gives some Sinhala examples illustrating the same point, for example (c).

(c) *mahattayā gihillā maṭa mokut karanna bæri unā*
'The master having gone, I couldn't do a thing.' (Fairbanks et al. 1968: II. 90)

[13] Quotative particles and complementisers developed from SAY are also found extensively in many other languages of Central Asia and the Greater Hindukush Karakoram area. See Bashir (1996b) for discussion and examples of these.

It has two perfective participle forms—*raá* and *reé*. Both of these are used in forming complex tense-aspect forms, and *reé* functions as a quotative and a more general complementiser. The basic/original function of a quotative is to introduce direct speech, the usual way of reporting speech in Khowar. This basic function can be seen in (10.126), where the direct utterance is 'Bring flour!' and (10.127), where what s/he did not think is 'Is it easy or hard?'.[14]

(10.126) *peṣíru angyé reé yád-i dré-t-am*
flour bring-IMP.2SG QUOT memory-LOC2 put-PST.D-1SG
'I reminded (him) to bring flour.' (SWKA in Bashir 2023b)

(10.127) *askán-aá girán reé no dun-í kórum*
easy-Q hard QUOT NEG think-PVF.PTCP work
a-ré-r
AUG-do.PST.D-3SG
'S/he did the task without thinking whether it was easy or hard.' (Bashir 1996b and field notes)

A complementiser links a subordinate clause with its main clause. Extended functions of *reé* have developed, involving many verbs of speech or extended speech (order, announce, write, think, intend, fear, worry, hope). With such verbs, *reé* is the naturally occurring complementiser, especially in oral discourse. It typically appears in sentences like (10.128), (10.129), (10.130), and (10.131).

(10.128) *ispá hardí šan-ít-ay tu hardiphát*
our heart worry-PST.D-3SG you lonely
b-os reé
become-2SG.PRS/FUT.NS COMP
'We worried that you would be lonely.' (lit. 'thinking that you would be lonely') (IF in Bashir 2023b)

[14] In this discussion *reé* is sometimes labelled as QUOT and sometimes as COMP, depending on how close the clause is to the original function of reporting.

(10.129) *yá xodáy keły-án-te kya vaqyá*
O God sheep-OBL.PL-DAT what occurrence
h-oy reé tseq di ma
become.PST.D-3SG COMP a.little also my
hardí šen-ít-ay
heart worry-PST.D-3SG
'Thinking, "Oh God, what has happened to the sheep?", I too became a little worried.' (from short story *keɫivál keɫítay* [The shepherdess wept], Faizi 1989.)

(10.130) *ma grambéṣ-an má-su bo thušé-ni-an*
my neighbour-PL.DIR me-with much flatter-3PL.PRS/FUT-S
kya ǰoš-án ispá-t d-oy-aá reé
some fodder-OBL.PL us-DAT give-3SG.PRS/FUT.NS-Q COMP
'My neighbours are flattering me a lot, hoping that I may give them some fodder.' (lit. 'maybe he will give us some fodder.') (Village Parwak, in Bashir 2023b)

(10.131) *hayá ta poš-í buhtu-ír-an*
PROX.SG you.OBL see-PFV.PTCP fear-3SG.PRS/FUT-S
šunǰ ç̣ak-é-ir-an reé
needle stick-CAUS-3SG.PRS/FUT-S COMP
'Seeing you, she (a little girl) is afraid that you are going to give her an injection.' (lit. 'She is afraid, thinking "she is going to give (me) an injection".') (NKN in Bashir 2023b)

Sometimes the (extended) thinking is about a reason, as in (10.132), or a purpose, as in (10.133).

(10.132) *čhuy drungár reé avá pisá-t šiloóy d-óm-an*
night long COMP I you.PL-DAT story give-1SG.PRS/FUT-S
'Since the night is long, I am telling you a story.' (Bashir 1996b: 226)

(10.133) *avá salím-o paš-ím reé g-ití*
I.DIR Salim-OBL see-1SG.PRS/FUT.NS COMP come-PFV.PTCP
as-úm
be(ANIM)-PRS.1SG
'I have come (hoping) to see (meet) Salim.' (Bashir 1996b: 230)

A further function is to name something, as in (10.134) and (10.135).

(10.134) *qadím-a çhetrár-a ǰešṭán ḍekeék*
old.times-LOC1 Chitral-LOC1 mischievous.spirits to.chase.away
reé i rásum š-áu-r
QUOT a custom be(INAN)-PST.HAB.I-3SG
'In the old days in Chitral there was a custom called *ǰešṭánḍekeék* (driving away the mischievous spirits).' (indirect knowledge) (RAKR in Bashir 2023b)

(10.135) *siyahát e hátim reé farsí kitáb š-er*
travels of Hatim QUOT Persian book be(INAN)-PRS.3SG
'There is a Persian book called *Travels of Hatim*.' (MAK in Bashir 2023b)

10.10.2 Discourse particles

Several particles important in enhancing meaning and structuring discourse have appeared in the preceding chapters without specific focus on them. In this section, I draw some of them together and discuss their contributions in more detail. Several frequently occurring particles serve to express various emotional nuances as well as structuring the discourse.

10.10.2.1 Affirmative and negative particles

The affirmative and negative particles are *dií* 'yes' (10.136) and *no* ~ *noh* 'no', *no* occurring pre-verbally and *noh* utterance-finally as the negation of a nominal sentence (10.137). When negating a nominal sentence, *noh* can be glossed 'is/are not'.

(10.136) *dií g-ití as-úr*
yes come-PFV.PTCP be(ANIM)-PRS.3SG
'Yes, s/he has come.' (EB field notes)

(10.137) *aṭíli uγ pi-ík-o láyq-a noh*
muddy water drink-INF-OBL fit.for-LOC1 NEG
'Muddy water is not fit to drink.' (RAKR in Bashir 2023b)

A tag question expecting a positive response, like English 'isn't it?' or Urdu '*hæ na?*'; or a cajolative particle (CAJ) is expressed with *nó:*, as in (10.138) and (10.139). Note the expressively elongated *o* in the cajolative and tag question particle.

(10.138) *b-ísi nó:*
go-1PL.HORT CAJ
'Come on, let's go (positive response expected).' (MA in Bashir 2023)b

(10.139) *baçhóɫ-o kuṣ-ís nó: thul b-ík-o*
calf-OBL slaughter-2SG.PRS/FUT.NS TAG fat become-INF-OBL
'You'll slaughter the calf, won't you, when it gets fat.' (MA in Bashir 2023b)

Contrasting in pronunciation with *dií* 'yes' are *di* 'also' (10.140), 'both… and' (10.141), and in negative contexts, 'even' (10.142), and stressed *dí* 'now' (10.143).

(10.140) *hamó di boγ-á-ve*
PROX.SG.OBL also go-CAUS-IMP.2SG
'Erase this (one) also.' (MS in Bashir 2023b)

(10.141) *baṣ-ír-an di kuçhuní di d-óy-an*
rain-3SG.PRS/FUT-S also hail also strike-3SG.PRS/FUT-S
'It is both raining and hailing.' (RKB in Bashir 2023b)[15]

(10.142) *hasé ṣóy-a g-íti di no paš-ír*
REM.SG near-LOC1 come-PFV.PTCP even NEG see-3SG-PRS/FUT.NS
'S/he can't see even from close up.' (SWKA in Bashir 2023b)

(10.143) *dí b-ísi*
now go-1PL.HORT
'Let's go now.' (MNN in Bashir 2023)

[15] Example (9.52) is repeated here for reader convenience.

di also can function as a sort of indefinitiser, '... -ever', as in *kyá di* 'any at all', 'whatever' or *kará di ki* 'whoever'.

10.10.2.2 Sentence-final particles

Several sentence-final particles convey speaker commitment or attitude toward the utterance. The important particle *la* has several senses, all of which involve speaker closeness (CLO) or intimacy, either affection or respect for the addressee, or commitment to the accuracy or importance of the utterance.[16] When used with imperatives, it softens the imperative force and conveys politeness or affection, as in (10.144). It is often used between husband and wife' (10.145), and in Laspur only between husband and wife, according to Inayatullah Faizi. Speaker commitment is shown in (10.146), and affection in (10.147). When *dií* 'yes' is followed by *la*, its vowel is shortened and loses its low pitch (10.146). In (10.148) the sense conveyed is that the speaker has direct personal knowledge of the things he is speaking of.

(10.144) *nišé* *la*
sit-IMP.2SG CLO
'Please have a seat.'

(10.145) *mó* *k-o* *la*
PROH do-IMP.SG CLO
'Don't do it (please, dear)' (MNN in Bashir 2023b)

(10.146) *dí-la*
yes-CLO
'Yes indeed.'

(10.147) *ǰám-la* *ma bulbú:l* *yaá* *ang-yé*
good-CLO my nightingale.VOC here bring-IMP.SG
'Good, my darling (lit. 'nightingale'), bring it here.' (oral text, Village Bang)

(10.148) *hatét* *nakám* *la*
REM.PL.DIR unsuccessful CLO
'They/those are unsuccessful.' (MNN)

[16] In this work, *la* will be labelled as CLO (CLOSENESS), in an attempt to capture a generalised function of this particle.

In addition to *la*, several other particles convey speaker attitude toward the content of the utterance. The stressed utterance-final emphatic particle *dí* ~ *día* 'now' as in *dí bísi* 'now let's go', 'so', or emphatic particle, must be distinguished from unstressed *di* 'also' discussed above. It must also be distinguished from utterance-initial *dí* 'now' seen in example (10.143) above. It is illustrated in (10.149) and (10.150).

(10.149) *hateγ-én d-íti avá no b-aγát-am dí*
REM.SG.OBL-INS give-PFV.PTCP I NEG go-PST.D-1SG EMPH
'On account of that, I didn't go.' (MS in Bashir 2023b)

(10.150) Question: *hayá dar phox-aá ḍang*
PROX.SG wood soft-Q hard
'Is this wood soft or hard?'

Answer: *ḍang – boxt-ó žav día*
hard – rock-OBL son EMPH
'Hard. It is hard as a rock!' (IF in Bashir 2023b)

Stressed *vá*, when appearing sentence-finally, adds a sense of speaker commitment to the (emotional) content of the utterance; this is glossed as emphasis in (10.151) and 'regrettably' in (10.152).

(10.151) *ohó the hes haṣ abathá moóš vá*
oh so DIST.SG.DIR such irresponsible man EMPH
'Oh, so he is such an irresponsible man.' (MS in Bashir 2023b)

(10.152) *ǰam palóγ-o ingár gúç-i d-oy-án*
good apple-OBL for.no.reason base-LOC2 strike-3SG.PRS/FUT-S
vá
EMPH
'He is cutting down a good apple tree for no reason (regrettably).' (MNN)

ko is an utterance-final particle indicating uncertainty (UNCERT), illustrated in (10.153).[17]

[17] Example (10.83) is repeated here as (10.153) for reader convenience.

(10.153) Question: *axmát ṣapík žu-tí as-úr-aá?*
Ahmad meal eat-PFV.PTCP be(ANIM)-PRS.3SG-Q
'Has Ahmad eaten?'

Answer: *žu-tí as-úr-aá ko*
eat-PFV.PTCP be(ANIM).PRS.3SG-Q UNCERT
'He may have eaten, but I am not sure.' (SWKA in Bashir 2023b)

Utterance-final, stressed *kyá* also conveys speaker commitment and focuses on the significance of the content of an utterance; it can carry an implication that some further action or response is expected. Examples (10.154), (10.155), and (10.156) illustrate these senses.

(10.154) *ṭhor b-ós-an kyá*
fallen become-2SG.PRS/FUT-S EMPH
'You are going to fall down.' (said to a child running carelessly) (SWKA in Bashir 2023b)

(10.155) *hamóṣ kyá*
thus EMPH
'Like *this* (indeed)' (can indicate satisfaction in having accomplished something successfully, or emphasis on how something should be done) (MS in Bashir 2023b)

(10.156) *é: žav, angár boγdú kyá*
O son, fire go.PST.I.3SG EMPH
'Son, the fire has gone out.' (implied: respond appropriately) (SWKA in Bashir 2023b)

Stressed *kí*, an emphatic particle pronounced with close juncture immediately following an imperative form, conveys speaker investment in the outcome of the command. Several examples follow as (10.157), (10.158), (10.159), and (10.160).

(10.157) *tu tán he korm-ó kor-é-kí*
you self.EMPH that work-OBL do-IMP.SG-EMPH
'You do that work yourself!' (MYS in Bashir 2023b)

(10.158) *ma báče bazár-ar savdá ang-yé-kí*
I.OBL for bazaar-ABL things bring-IMP.SG-EMPH
'Bring groceries from the bazaar for me!' (MYS in Bashir 2023b)

(10.159) *mraç çhan-úr-kí*
mulberry knock.down-IMP.PL-EMPH
'Knock down some mulberries (with a long stick)!' (DSAL)

(10.160) *hasé ré-t-ay.ki ispá mo*
REM.SG say-PST.D-3SG-THAT we PROX.SG.OBL[18]
lał-ísi-an hayá išnáry-o
look-1PL.PRS/FUT-S PROX.SG thing-OBL
ispá-te d-et-kí
us-DAT give-IMP.SG-EMPH
'He said, "We want to look at this. Give this thing to us!"' (oral text, Village Kari)

An utterance-final imperative interjection *očhé*, with variant pronunciations *očhét, očhót, očhó*, and plural form *očhór* follows an imperative form and means something like '(for) now'.[19] It sometimes conveys impatience (10.161) and (10.162); it can suggest or imply that something else will follow, as in (10.162). In (10.160) and (10.161) it co-occurs with the utterance-final emphatic particles *kya* and *kí*. A plural form, *očhór*, also appears with plural addressees (10.163).[20]

(10.160) *sábar k-o: očhé kyá*
patience do-IMP.SG wait.IMP.SG EMPH
'Be patient; just wait a minute!' (SWKA)

[18] *mo* is the short form of *hamó*.
[19] I am glossing *očhé* and *očhór* as 'for now' (cf. Urdu *filhāl*) pending a more complete understanding of its meaning.
[20] These clearly imperative forms originate in Burushaski, viz. Hunza Burushaski forms *ʌčo* (SG) *ačo:in* (PL) 'wait!' (Lorimer 1938: 8) and Yasin Bur. *ʌčʰo* (SG) *ačʰo:in* (PL) 'wait' (Lorimer 1962: 3). The sense of 'wait' shows up clearly in example (10.160).

(10.161) *é: ma laák-očhé-kí ma ko band*
hey I.OBL release-now-EMPH I.OBL why bound

k-ós-an ré-t-ay.ki
do-2SG.PRS/FUT-S say-PST.D-3SG

'He said, "Hey, let me go now! Why are you tying me up?"' (oral text, Village Bang)

(10.162) *haníse ma γoš no b-óy-an*
now I.OBL free.time NEG become-3SG.PRS/FUT-S

b-oγé očhé darbát-a niveš-ím
go-IMP.SG wait.IMP.SG little.while-LOC1 write-1SG.PRS/FUT.NS

'I don't have time now. Go, wait a bit, I will write it in a little while.' (RAKR)

(10.163) *hanún pisá prušṭ ho-ó-te mo b-oγúr očh-ór*
today you.PL facing DIST.SG-OBL-DAT PROH go-IMP.PL wait-IMP.PL
'Today (you) don't go out to receive him!' (implied: 'for the time being') (oral text, Village Chapali)

10.11 Semantics of reduplicated forms

Reduplicated forms are iconic signs in which the form of the sign resembles some aspect of the meaning: multiplicity, intensity, extension, or sound (onomatopoeia). Reduplication is, in essence, a self-referential mechanism, which usually, by virtue of repetition, generates a meaning of increase—plurality, distributivity, intensification, discourse emphasis, multiplicity of location, states, points of view, or events—or extended duration. Reduplication is basically a strategy of the spoken language, and in order to observe the variety of its forms and meanings, one has to work with oral rather than written data, since only some forms of reduplication can readily be represented in writing (mainly types of full reduplication).

Various forms of reduplicated structures were introduced in Section 3.4. This section focuses on meanings conveyed by these types of reduplication.

10.11.1 Plurality

Plurality is conveyed by two types of partial reduplication. First, with some monosyllabic adjectives with CVC structure, the base form is preceded with a CV copied from the base form. For example:

phuphúk 'small (plural)' (← *phuk* 'small'), for example, *phuphúk alú* 'small potatoes'
ʦeʦéq 'small (plural)', also 'children' (← *ʦeq* 'small')
thuthúl 'fat', 'thick' (plural) (← *thul* 'fat')

Second, plurals of some words are indicated by a partially reduplicated CV syllable with a vowel change, as with:

lilóṭ 'big (plural)' (← *loṭ* 'big')
žižáv 'sons' (← *žáv* 'son')

Some fully reduplicated adjectives also indicate plurality, for instance *ǰamǰám* 'good' (plural) (← *ǰam* 'good').

10.11.2 Distributivity

Distributivity is indicated by a reduplicated numeral word suffixed with *-gán*, which carries the distributive sense 'each', as in *kandurigán* 'how many/much each?' (10.164) and (10.165).

(10.164) *ʦeʦéq-an-te i-gán i-gán biskóṭ d-et*
children-OBL.PL-DAT one-each one-each biscuit give.IMP.SG
'Give the children one biscuit each.' (SWKA)

(10.165) *hamí dur-én ǰu-gán ǰu-gán*
PROX.PL.OBL house-LOC.PL two-each two-each
navkár kórum k-óni-an
servant work do-3PL.PRS/FUT-S
'Two servants are working in each of these houses.' (SWKA in Bashir 2023b)

10.11.3 Intensification

Intensified meaning can be conveyed by full reduplication with elongation of the stem vowel and accompanying low pitch contour in the reduplicated copy, which precedes the base word, as in the following words.

Full reduplication with vowel elongation in the copy:

dudeéri dudéri 'very very far' (MNN)
ẓaáng ẓáng 'very high' (MNN)
ṣoóy ṣóy 'very near' (MNN)

Partial reduplication too signifies intensification in forms where the initial CV of a CVC word is repeated, with its vowel expressively elongated and pitch lowered similarly to what happens in the fully reduplicated examples immediately above.

laáláš 'very very slowly' (MNN)
koókóš 'covered with blisters' (MNN)

In these forms, the doubled vowel symbol in the first syllable with stress marked on the second vowel indicates both lengthening and a low pitch on that syllable. Main word stress remains on the final syllable. Examples (10.166) and (10.167) show full reduplication without elongation of the vowel in the reduplicated copy.

(10.166) *toó* *sot* *žur-gíni* *ʥrapʥráp*
REM.SG.OBL seven daughter-PL close.together.REDUP
por-í *as-úni*
lie-PFV.PTCP be(ANIM)-PRS.3PL
'His seven daughters are sleeping right next to each other.' (oral text, Village Bang)

(10.167) *uy* *łámłam* *palé-r-an*
water scalding.hot burn-3SG.PRS/FUT-S
'The water is too hot to use. (it is scalding [me])' (MNN in Bashir 2023b)

10.11.4 Multiplicity of physical locations, states, or events

Multiplicity of physical locations is often indicated by reduplicative sequences in which a reduplicated noun referring to a spatial concept is followed by one of the locative case endings: LOC1 in (10.168), LOC2 in *prašpráš-i* 'here and there' (lit. 'on all sides'), or LOC4 in *prašpráš-o* ‘on both sides’ (← *praš* ‘side’). Other forms attested in my data include *nasnása* ‘side-by-side’ (← *nas* ‘side’, ‘edge’), *guçgúça* ‘here and there at the lower edges’ (← *guç* ‘lower edge’, ‘base’).

(10.168) *γečγéč-a ašrú kor-í osoéni-o*
eye.RED-LOC1 tears do-PFV.PTCP handkerchief-OBL
sóra ašrú-an maž-áv o-š-óy
with tears-OBL.PL wipe-IPFV.PTCP AUG-be-PST.D.3SG
‘Weeping in both eyes, s/he was wiping her/his tears with a handkerchief.’ (oral text, Village Bang)

A complete or fully developed state is conveyed by *ǰamǰamí* ‘state of full welfare or happiness’ (← *ǰam* ‘good’), illustrated in (10.169).

(10.169) *ǰamǰamí-a khyo-t keł-ís-an*
complete.welfare-LOC1 what-DAT cry-2SG.PRS/FUT-S
‘Why are you crying when you are in a very good state?’ (MNN in Bashir 2023b)

Multiple iterations of an action or event are exemplified by *γernaγér* ‘turning again and again’, ‘zigzag’ (← *γer-* ‘turn’) (10.170).

(10.170) *ravléy-tu pon γernaγér kór-i*
Lowari.Pass-up.on road zigzag do-PFV.PTCP
š-er
be(INAN)-PRS.3SG
‘On Lowari Pass the road has been made zigzag.’ (DSAL)

10.11.5 Temporal extension/repetition of activity

Iteration and repetition are meanings frequently conveyed by reduplication, as with *kyávat* ‘when’ and *kyávat kyávaxt* ‘sometimes’, or *yorána yorána* ‘yearly’. Example (10.171) shows a frequently occurring expression *barbár* ‘again and again’.

(10.171) *barbár loł-í kyam b-ós-an*
time.time look-PFV.PTCP how become-2SG.PRS/FUT-S
‘Why are you (just sitting and) looking repeatedly (instead of doing something)?’ (MNN)

In oral tellings of folk tales, temporal extension of the hero's travels is shown by the repeated verb, as in (10.172). In (10.173) the elongated *i* iconically indicates temporal extension of a state (sitting).

(10.172) *rahí.kor-í* *baγ-áy baγ-áy baγ-áy baγ-áy baγ-áy-*
depart-PFV.PTCP go.PST.D-3SG (REDUP 4 times)
i bačaí-a *baγ-áy*
a kingdom-LOC1 go.PST.D-3SG
'He set off and travelled and travelled and travelled and travelled. (Finally) he came to a kingdom.' (oral text, Village Kari)

(10.173) *niš-áni* *niš-áni:* *gur bík-o*
sit-PST.D.3PL sit-PST.D.3PL.REDUP late become.INF-OBL
ré-t-ay.ki …
say-PST.D-3SG …
'They sat and sat (for a long time). When it got late, he said …' (oral text, Village Bang)

10.11.6 Onomatopoeia

Reduplicated onomatopoetic words for animal cries and other sounds are so widespread cross-linguistically and numerous in Khowar that a few examples will suffice: *braxbráx* 'sound of hard objects hitting each other', *ṭopṭóp* 'sound of plopping', *khúṣukhúṣu* 'whispering'.

Akin to onomatopoeia, in that they repeat the sound of an utterance rather than imitate the sound of some extra-linguistic referent, are calls to summon or drive away various animals. Some of these are:

bažáło bažáło 'here, kitty, kitty' (call to summon cat) (Laspur usage) (IF in Bashir 2023b)
dóh dóh dóh 'come! come!' (call to summon dog) (MNN, IF)
čigoó čigoó 'come! come!' (call to summon goat) (MNN in Bashir 2023b)
ḍyéh ḍyéh 'come! come!' (call to summon chicken) (MNN in Bashir 2023b)
khíṣ khíṣ 'shoo! shoo!' (call to drive away chickens or other birds, and used to drive away *ǰešṭán* during *ǰešṭán ḍekeék* rituals) (RAKR in Bashir 2023b)

10.11.7 Self-referentiality

Also akin to onomatopoeia is the very frequently, and mostly spontaneously, employed pattern of complete repetition of an entire utterance. This can also be considered a type of quotative marking, in which repetition of the exact words of the utterance focuses self-referentially on the exact form or sound of the utterance. Example (10.174) shows two instances of this.

(10.174) *łeng-í* *ré-t-ay.ki* *ma*
sway-PFV.PTCP say.PST.D-3SG I.OBL
kyaní k-ómi-an *ma* *kyaní k-ómi-an* –
what do-2PL.PRS/FUT-S I.OBL what do-2PL.PRS/FUT-S
mat *qaí* *h-óni* *áči* *petsh-úr*
I.OBL-DAT heavy become.PST.D-3PL back throw-IMP.PL
áči *petsh-úr*
back throw-IMP.PL
'Swaying, he said, "What are you doing to me, what are you doing to me? They are (too) heavy for me, throw them back, throw them back!"' (oral text, Village Sorech)

10.11.8 Attenuation

I have not recorded many instances of the attenuative function of reduplication in Khowar. However, reduplication of *phuk* 'small' in *phuphúk alú* was noted by MNN as meaning 'smallish potatoes'.

10.11.9 Multiplicity of viewpoints

Nor have I recorded any instances of reduplicative utterances which signify 'pretend', as in Panjabi examples like *bačče skūl skūl kheḍ re ne* 'The children are playing "school".'

10.11.10 Narrative summary

In oral narratives, especially long folk tales with embedded stories, on arrival at a new place the protagonist is often asked to relate his prior adventures to a newly met character. In such situations, where the protagonist has to repeat what the listeners have already heard, the storyteller, instead of repeating the entire sequence of events, will employ the element *hamóṣ̌* or reduplicated *hamóṣ̌ hamóṣ̌* for multiple events, as in the question and response in (10.175). This is a storyteller's device which refers back to a whole section of previous discourse and avoids repetition. The listener understands that in the world of the story the protagonist actually recited the full narrative of his previous adventures.

(10.175) *žib-ík-o* *wahagamíote* *khyo-t* *g-ití*
eat.INF-OBL suddenly what.OBL-DAT come-PFV.PTCP

as-t-áv? *kar-ó* *gúç̣-a* *b-i*
be(ANIM)-PST.I-2SG ear-OBL base-LOC1 go-PFV.PTCP

é: *hamóṣ̌* *hamóṣ̌* *kórum*
hey like.this like.this events

'When he_a had eaten, (he_b) suddenly (asked), "What did you come for?" Going close to his_b ear, (he_a said,) "Hey, this and this happened."' (oral text, Village Sorech)

APPENDIX
Jeshtanan Shilogh, a folk tale rendered by Mumtaz Hussain

Introduction

The text *Jeshtanan Shilogh* 'Story of the Jeshtans' was given to me in written form by Mumtaz Hussain of Village Charun Owir, near Booni in Upper Chitral, for which I owe him my sincere thanks. He tells me that it was originally told to him by his (now deceased) mother in 2003, written down by his daughter, and then checked and revised with his mother's help. Mumtaz Hussain has spent his entire career in education, teaching Pakistan Studies. He retired in 2019 as Principal of Government College, Chitral. Since retirement, in addition to writing on Chitrali history and culture, he has developed and is managing the website Mahraka.com, an online resource the purpose of which is to make materials on Chitral and other parts of the northernmost parts of Pakistan readily accessible to students and researchers.[1]

Since *jeshtans* are prominent characters in Chitrali folklore, a few words about them are appropriate here. *Jeshtans* were conceived of as dwarf-like supernatural beings which lived hidden in the houses of humans and sometimes created mischief in the house. As winter approached in November, there used to be a custom called *Jeshtan Dekeik* 'driving the *jeshtan* away', during which they were swept out of the house with a rough thorn broom while the people shouted '*khiṣ khiṣ*'.[2] According to Rahmat Akbar Khan Rahmat,[3] on the day of driving the *jeshtan* away, people would wear old ragged clothes, put *surmá*

[1] I am grateful to Mumtaz Hussain for his help in translating the song sung by the *ǰeštans*.
[2] This is the same call used to chase chickens.
[3] These details were told to me by Rahmat Akbar Khan at his home in Chapali in January 1990.

'antimony' in one eye but not in the other, wear a shoe on one foot but not on the other, wear a shalwar with one leg rolled up above the knee and the other not, and wear a shirt with one sleeve put on and the other not. After the *jeshtan* had left, the people would say that now the house is free of the *jeshtan*, cook something sweet, and say a prayer entreating God that the *jeshtan* not come back to the house.

This text is presented in its original Perso-Arabic script as written by Mumtaz Hussain (read right to left), with individual sentences numbered for easy reference to the English translation, and with morphological analysis of each sentence. Since this is a story about supernatural beings in a legendary past, which could not have been seen by the storyteller, verbs in the main narrative appear in their indirect forms, as in sentence (1). On the other hand, verbs which report perceptions of a character in the story appear in their direct forms in his own voice, as in sentence (12).[4]

جیشتانان شلوغ

(1) وختہ مائی وختہ ای موش بیرائے۔

(1) *váxt-a-máy-váxt-a* *i moóš biráy*
Once upon a time-LOC1 a man become.PST.I. 3SG

(2) موش بو عقلمین، اوچوتو۔

(2) *moóš bo aqulmín ucútu*
man very wise intelligent

(3) مگم ہتو بُوکہ لوٹ گوروڑی شیرائے۔

(3) *mágam ható búk-a loṭ gurúłi širáy*
but his neck-LOC1 large goitre be(INAN).PST.I. 3SG

(4) گوروڑی اونگی اونگی ہانی لوٹ بیرو کہ ہسے موڑو لوڑیکو نو باک بیرائے۔

(4) *gurułi ung-í ung-í háni loṭ birú*
goitre grow-PFV.PTCP grow-PFV.PTCP so big became
ki hasé múł-o lołík-o no bak biráy
that he down look-INF.OBL not able become.PST.I. 3SG

[4] Some native English speakers may object to my maintaining the Khowar usage of direct speech in reporting verbs of speech and perception instead of changing it to the English usage which follows 'sequence of tenses' conventions and changes verbs of reported speech and perception to past-tense forms. See the connected translation which follows the sentence-by-sentence analysis to see this. A similar effect in English can be produced by using the 'historical present' in sentences like 'So I go there and see that the house is on fire' to report an event that took place in the (recent) past.

(5) استورو سینہ التی اوغ دیاوا بیارو کوری ہوئے دیاک بیرائے کہ اے برار
یئی لوڑے کی، مہ استور اوغ پیرانا نو۔

(5) *istor-ó sín-a alt-í uγ*
horse-OBL river-LOC1 take-PFV.PTCP water
dy-áʋ-a biyár-o
give-IMPFV.PTCP-LOC1 across.river-OBL
kúri huy dy-ak biráy
somewhere call give-AG become.PST.I 3SG
ki é: brar yií lołé kí ma istór uγ
that hey brother here look EMPH my horse water
pír-an-aá nóh
drink.3SG-PRS/FUT-S-Q not

(6) ہتوغو اصلی نام کیاغ بوئے، مگم روئے ہتوتے گوروڑی خان راک بیرانی۔

(6) *hatoγó ásli nam kyaγ boy mágam roy*
his real name something become.PRS.FUT.3SG but people
ható-te gurúłi xan r-ak biráni
him-DAT Gurułi Khan say-AG become.PST.I. 3PL

(7) ہسے گوروڑیو کوری تان عالمار اہتی بیرائے۔

(7) *hasé gurúłi-o kór-i tan alám-ar ahtí biráy*
he goitre-OBL do-PFV.PTCP REFL trouble-ABL fed.up was

(8) مگم کیانی کوئے، قدیم زمانا گوروڑیو کیہ علاج دی نو اوشوئے۔

(8) *mágam kyáni koy, qadím zamaná-a gurúłi-o*
but what do.3SG.PRS/FUT.NS old times-LOC1 goitre.of
kya iláǯ di no ošóy
any cure even not was

(9) ای انوس گوروڑی خان استورو سورو نیشی سفرہ بوغاو استائے۔

(9) *i anús gurúłi xan istor-ó sóro niš-í*
one day Gurułi Khan horse-OBL on sit-PFV.PTCP
safár-a b-oγáʋ as-t-aáy
travel-LOC1 go-IMPFV.PTCP be-PST.I-3SG

(10) یور ڈوکو دیتی شام اوتیکو بَسوتے کورا آبادیہ توریکو نو بیرو۔

(10) *yor dók-o d-íti šam utík-o*
sun horizon-OBL touch-PFV.PTCP evening enter.INF-OBL
bas-ó-te kúra abadí-a
night.stay-OBL-DAT anywhere settlement-LOC1
torík-o no birú
reach.INF-OBL not be.able.PST.I.3SG

(11) براٹ ہتوسوم شیرانی، سینو نسو بی براٹار ژوتی، کورا پوریکوتے بوہتو کین کھوشش کاردو۔

(11) *braṭ ható sum š-ir-áni, sin-ó nás-o*
bread him with be(INAN)-PST.I-3PL, river's bank-LOC4
b-i brat-ár žut-í kúra poríḱ-o-te
go-PFV.PTCP bread-ABL eat-PFV.PTCP somewhere sleep.INF-OBL-DAT
boht-ó ken khošíš kardú
rock-OBL shelter attempt did

(12) دودیری روشتی گیکو لکھی ہتیرہ بوغدو کی ای کینی روشتی شیر، ہوازہ دی گویان۔

(12) *dudéri roští gík-o lakhí hatéra b-oγdú*
far light come.INF-OBL quickly there go-PST.I.3SG
ki i kén-i roští šer, haváza di góyan
when a shelter-LOC2 light there.is voice also is.coming

(13) خوشان بیرو کہ موݰ بندگان لیتام۔

(13) *xošán b-irú ki moṣ banda-gán*
happy become-PST.I.3SG that in.this.way person-PL
lét-am
find.PST.D-1SG

(14) استورو ہتیرہ کورا کوئی بوتی ایھ اوتیر کہ لوٹ ختانو بہکی کین۔

(14) *istor-ó hatéra kúra kú-i bot-í*
horse-OBL there somewhere somewhere tie-PFV.PTCP
ayh utír ki loṭ xatán-o báhki ken
up ascends when big house-OBL equal.to shelter

(15) موڑا انگار پھومبراش دیتی نسین ای ڈیشتی جیشتانان بشیاؤ پھانِنیان۔

(15) *múž-a angár phumbaráṣ dít-i nas-én i*
middle-LOC1 fire bonfire strike-PFV.PTCP side-LOC.PL one
ḍiští ǰestan-án baše-áv phan-íni-an
handspan jeshtan-PL play-IMPFV.PTCP dance-3PL.PRS/FUT-S

(16) جیشتانان موشو پوشی مینو ہائے، مینو ہائے رے قوژد کاردو۔

(16) *ǰeštan-án móš-o poš-í menú hay menú hay*
jeshtan-PL man-OBL see-PFV.PTCP guest came guest came
re-é qužd kárdu
say-PFV.PTCP shout did

(17) موشوتے راردو کہ گیے تو دی پھونے۔ گوروڑی خان راردو کہ اوہ تھے جم پھوناک اوشوتام مگم ہنیسے ہیہ گروڑی مہ کیژیبیکو نو لا کویان۔

(17) *móš-o-te rárduki gye tu di phoné. gurúłi xan*
man-OBL-DAT said come you also dance! Gurułi Khan
rárdu ki avá the ǰam phonák ošót-am mágam haníse hayá
said that I TOP good dancer be.PST-1SG but now this
gurúłi ma kižibík-o no lák-oy-an
goitre me move.INF-OBL not let-3SG.PRS/FUT-S

(18) پھانیمان کیچہ بیتی۔

(18) *phan-ím-an kíča b-íti*
dance-1SG-PRS/FUT-S how become-PFV.PTCP

(19) ریکو ای جشتان پھار خڜپ کوری گوروڑیو نیزی بیلوغہ لکھیرو۔

(19) *rék-o i ǰeštán phar xaṣáp kor-í gurúłi-o*
say-OBL one jeshtan over grab do-PFV.PTCP goitre-OBL
nez-í bilóγ-a lakh-íru
remove-PFV.PTCP wall.niche-LOC1 put-PST.I

(20) گوروڑی خان خلاص بیتی پھونیکوتے اف دیرو۔

(20) *gurúłi xan xalás b-íti phon-ík-o-te*
Gurułi Khan free become-PFV.PTCP dance-INF-OBL-DAT
af dirú
down came

(21) جشتانان پروشٹو تان ہانگو پیخھی ہنیسے ہموش راو پھونیکا دیرو

(21) *ǰestan-án prušṭ-ó tan hang-ó petsh-í*
jeshtan-PL before-OBL their tune-OBL abandon-PFV.PTCP

haníse hamóṣ rav phoník-a d-irú
now like.this say.IMPFV.PTCP dance.INF-LOC1 strike-PST.I.3SG

استور بوتہ موش چھونگوڑیہ

istór bót-a moóš čhungúłi-a
horse evening.meal-LOC1 man skin.bag-LOC1

(22) موش ہوش کاردو کہ ہمیت بوتہ مہ خسمت کوری اوراری درے استورو ژیبونی چھوچھی روپھی ہاسیہ مہ تان ژیبونی۔

(22) *moóš huṣ kárdu ki hamít bót-a ma xesmát*
man understanding do.PST.I that these night-LOC1 me tired

kor-í orár-i dreé istor-ó
do-PFV.PTCP sleep-LOC2 put.PFV.PTCP horse-OBL

žib-óni čhúčhi ruph-í hási-a
eat-3PL.PRS/FUT.NS morning get.up-PFV.PTCP breakfast-LOC1

ma tan žib-óni
me EMPH eat-3PL.PRS/FUT

(23) چھوئے باو گیکو پھونیک دی پِین باو گیرو۔

(23) *čhuy b-av gík-o phoník di*
night become-IMPFV.PTCP come.INF-OBL dancing also

pin b-av gíru
fast become-IMPFV.PTCP come.PST.I

(24) موش دی تان خیالہ استائے، تیز غیردی گیاوا کینو بیلوتے گیتی مہمیز کوری بی استورو سوری غیری چاغیز دیرو۔

(24) *moóš di tan xyál-a as-t-aáy, tez γerd-í*
man also his thought-LOC1 be-PST.I-3SG quickly turn-PFV.PTCP

gyáv-a ken-ó biló-te
come-IMPFV.PTCP-LOC1 shelter-OBL entrance.OBL-DAT

g-ití mahméz kor-í bi istor-ó
come-PFV.PTCP leap do-PFV.PTCP come.PFV.PTCP horse-OBL

sór-i γer-í čaγéz d-irú
TOP-LOC2 turn-PFV.PTCP whip strike-PST.I.3SG

(25) جیشتان ہتو اچہ اے مینو حال بوس لا ، بس نو بیتی کوئے بیسان راو تھمامو دیرو
مگم ای ڈیشٹی جیشتان تاژیان استورو اچہ کورا تارونیان۔

(25) *ǰeštán ható áča é: menú hal.bos la, bas no*
jeshtan him after hey guest, stay please, night not

b-íti kúi bí-s-an rav thamámu
stay-pfv.ptcp where go-2sg.prs/fut-s say.impfv.ptcp all.effort

d-íru mágam i ḍiṣ̌ṭí ǰeštán taži-án
strike-pst.i but one handspan-sized jeshtan Tajik-obl.pl

istor-ó áča kúra tar-úni-an
horse-obl after where reach-3pl.prs/fut-s

(26) روشتی خومیکو گوروڑی خان دورا توریکو لڑینی کہ گوروڑیو دراک نیکی۔

(26) *roští xomík-o gurúłi xan dúr-a*
daylight descend.inf-obl Gurułi Khan home-loc1

torík-o łał-íni ki gurúłi-o
reach.inf-obl look-3pl.prs/fut.ns that goitre-obl

darák níki
trace is.not

(27) روئے ہیغار ہموغاربمبارکو گیرو۔ گوروڑی خان ریشو کوشی ژیری کاردو۔

(27) *roy he-γár hamo-γár bumburák-o girú*
people there-abl here-abl congratulations-obl came.

gurúłi xan reṣú kuṣ-í žéri kárdu
Gurułi Khan bull slaughter-pfv.ptcp feast do.pst.i.3sg

(28) گوروڑی خانو خیرو برار دی گوروڑی بیرائے ، مگم ہتو گوروڑی ہانی لوٹ نو
بیرائے۔

(28) *gurúłi xán-o tsiró brar di gurułí biráy,*
Gurułi Khan-obl younger brother also goitrous was,

mágam ható gurúłi háni loṭ no biráy
but his goitre so big not was

(29) گوروڑی خان گوروڑیو سار خلاص بیکو ہتو دی بو ارمان بیرو۔

(29) *gurúłi xán gurúłi-o sar xalás bík-o*
Gurułi Khan goitre-obl from free become.inf-obl

hatoó di bo armán birú
his also much wish become.pst.i

(30) براروتے راردو کہ اوا دی جیشتانان ماڑہ بیم، کیہ ہیہ گوروڑیو سار خلاص بوما۔

(30) *brár-o-te rárdu ki avá di ǰeštan-án máł-a*
brother-OBL-DAT said that I also jeshtan-PL.OBL den-LOC1

b-im, kya hayá gurúłi-o sar xalás
go-1SG.PRS/FUT.NS what this goitre-OBL from free

bo-m-aá
become-1SG.PRS/FUT.NS-Q

(31) گوروڑی خان راردو کہ ائے تو لاش تھی نیشے۔

(31) *gurúłi xán rárdu ki é:i tu laš*
Gurułi Khan say.PST.I.3SG that hey you carefully

thií niš-é
be.still-PFV.PTCP sit.down-IMP.SG

(32) اوا نو بیتی گوران اپکار نسی ہاتم۔

(32) *avá no.bíti gor-án apák-ar nis-í*
I accidentally witch-OBL.PL mouth-ABL emerge-PFV.PTCP

hát-am
come.PST.D-1SG

(33) تو بار بار لوڑی تان سورو کو گوران گوڑوکوسان۔

(33) *tu barbar loł-í tan.sóro ko gor-án*
you time.time look-PFV.PTCP yourself.OBL why witch-OBL.PL

gół-o k-ós-an
gullet-LOC4 do-2SG-PRS/FUT-S

(34) مگم څیرو برار نو منیرو۔

(34) *mágam tsiró brar no man-íru*
but younger brother not agree-PST.I

(35) آخیرجہل کوری گوروڑی خانو سار ہتے ژاغو نشانو گنی بیکو تے تیاری کاردو۔

(35) *axír ǰáhal kór-i gurúłi xán-o sar haté*
finally stubbornness do-PFV.PTCP Gurułi Khan-OBL from that

žaγ-oó niṣán-o gan-í
place-OBL directions-OBL take-PFV.PTCP

bík-o-te tayarí kardú
go.INF-OBL-DAT preparations do.PST.I

(36) ﺧﯿﺮو ﺑﺮار اﺳﺘﻮری ﺑﯿﺘﯽ ﺑﯽ ﭼﮭﻮﺋﮯ ﺑﯿﮑﻮ ﮨﺘﮯ ژاﻏﺎ ﺗﻮرﯾﺮو۔

(36) *tsiró braár istorí b-íti bi*
younger brother mounted become-PFV.PTCP go.PFV.PTCP

čhuy bík-o haté zaγá-a tor-íru
night become.INF-OBL that place-LOC1 reach-PST.I

(37) ﻻڑﯾﺮ ﮐﮧ ﮐﯿﻨﯽ روﺷﺘﯽ ﮔﻮﯾﺎن۔

(37) *lał-ír ki kén-i roští góy-an*
see-3SG.PRS/FUT.NS that shelter-LOC2 light come.PRS/FUT.3SG-S

(38) اﺳﺘﻮرو ﺑﯿﺮی ﺑﻮﺗﯽ اﯾﮭ اوﺗﯿﺮو۔

(38) *istor-ó béri bot-í ayh ut-íru*
horse-OBL outside tie-PFV.PTCP up enter-PST.I

(39) ﺟﯿﺸﺘﺎﻧﺎن ﮨﺘﮯ ذﯾﻠﮧ ﺗﺎن ﭘﮭﻮﻧﺎو اﺳﺘﺎﻧﯽ۔

(39) *ǰeštan-án haté záyla tan phon-áv as-taá-ni*
jeshtan-PL that manner EMPH dance-IMPFV.PTCP be-PST.I-3PL

(40) ﻣﻮﺷﻮ ﭘﻮﺷﯽ اﺋﮯ ﻣﯿﻨﻮ ﮔﯿﮯ ﻻ ﮐﻮره ﮨﺎؤ رے ﺗﻮ ﭘﮭﺎر ژﯾﻨﮕﯿﺌﺮو۔

(40) *móš-o poš- í é:i menú gye la kúra*
man-OBL see-PFV.PTCP hey guest come please where

h-av reé toó phar ẓingé-iru
come.PST.D-2SG say.PFV.PTCP him across pull-PST.I

(41) ﺟﺸﺘﺎﻧﺎن راردو ﮐﮧ ﺗﺘﮯ ﻏﯿﭻ ﮐﻮراو اﺷﻮﺗﺎم، ﺟﺎم ﮨﻮو۔

(41) *ǰeštan-án rárdu ki tá-te γeč kor-áv*
jeshtan-PL say.PST.I that you-DAT eye do-IMPFV.PTCP

o-šót-am ǰam ho-u
AUG-be.PST.D-1PL good become.PST.A-2SG

(42) ﮨﻨﻮن اﺳﭙﮧ ﺳﻮم ﺑﺲ ﺑﻮس ﮐﯿﮧ ﮐﮧ ﻗﺪر ﺣﻮال ﺑﯿﺮاﺋﮯ ﺗﺘﮯ ﺧﺴﻤﺖ ﮐﻮﺳﯽ۔

(42) *hanún ispá sum bas bos kya.ki qádur.havál*
today us with night be whatever respectful.treatment

biráy tá-te xesmát k-ósi
become.PST.I-3SG you-DAT service do-1PL.PRS/FUT.NS

(43) ڈپیکار پروشٹی ای اولیئے اشٹوک کہ کوسی کیچہ بوئے۔

(43) *ṣapík-ar prúšṭi i avlie išṭok ki k-ósi*
meal-ABL before one round.of dancing if do-1PL.PRS/FUT.NS
kíča b-oy
how become-3SG.PRS/FUT.NS

(44) تو دی یو گیئے کہ اسپہ سوم پھونے۔

(44) *tu di yuú gye kí ispá sum phon-é*
you also down come.IMP.SG EMPH us with dance-IMP.SG

(45) موش راردو کہ اوا پھونیکوتے کیہ عار کومانا، مہ ہیا گوروڑی متے
ناواہخ بویان۔

(45) *moóš rárdu ki avá phoník-o-te kya ar*
man say.PST.I that I dance.INF-OBL-DAT any shame
k-óm-an-aá ma hayá gurúłi
do-1SG.PRS/FUT-S-Q my this goitre
naváts b-óy-an
uncomfortable become-3SG.PRS/FUT-S

(46) ریکو ای جشتان ہتو گوروڑیو نیزی بیلوغہ لکھیرو۔

(46) *rék-o i ǰeštán hatoó gurúłi-o nez-í*
say.INF-OBL one jeshtan his goitre-OBL remove-PFV.PTCP
bilóγ-a lakh-íru
wall.niche-LOC1 put-PST.I

(47) موش ایھ لڑیر کہ گوروڑی خانو ہتے گوروڑی دی ہتیرہ لکھی شیر۔

(47) *moóš ayh lał-ír ki gurúłi xán-o*
man up look-3SG.PRS/FUT.NS that Gurułi Khan-OBL
haté gurúłi di hatéra lakh-í šer
that goitre also there place-PFV.PTCP be(INAN).PRES.3SG

(48) پھونیک شروغ بیرو۔

(48) *phoník šurúγ birú*
dancing begun become.PST.I

جشتانان موشو موژا دیتی (49)

(49) *ǰeštan-án móš-o múž-a d-íti*
jeshtan-PL man-OBL middle-LOC1 put-PFV.PTCP

استور بوتہ موش چھونگوڑیہ

istór bót-a moóš čhungúłi-a
horse evening.meal-LOC1 man skin.bag-LOC1

استور بوتہ موش چھونگوڑیہ

istór bót-a moóš čhungúłi-a
horse evening.meal-LOC1 man skin.bag-LOC1

راو پیٹیرینگ بیتی گیرو۔

r-av peṭering b-íti girú
say-IMPFV.PTCP spinning become-PFV.PTCP come.PST.I

موش دی ژانو سوم بیتی غیرداو گیرو۔ (50)

(50) *moóš di žan-ó sum b-íti γerd-áv*
man also life-OBL with become-PFV.PTCP turn-IMPFV.PTCP
girú
come.PST.I

غیردی غیردی پھوک ڑینگ نیسیکو موش اف مہمیز کاردو۔ (51)

(51) *γerd-í γerd-í phuk łeng nisík-o*
whirl-PFV.PTCP whirl-PFV.PTCP a.little gap emerge.INF-OBL
moóš af mahméz kárdu
man down leap do.PST.I

ہیہ بارا جیشتانان دی خیالہ استانی۔ (52)

(52) *hayá bára ǰeštan-án di xyál-a as-taáni*
this about jeshtan-PL also attention-LOC1 be(ANIM)-PST.I.3PL

ایوالی ایھ خشٹپ کوری بیلوغار ہتو گوروڑیو یو گنی ہتیغین لکھیرو۔ (53)

(53) *iváli ayh xaṣáp kor-í bilóγ-ar hatoó gurúłi-o*
one up reach do-PFV.PTCP niche-ABL that goitre-OBL
yuú gan-í hate-γén lakh-íru
down take-PFV.PTCP it-INS beat-PST.I

(54) گوروڑی بی موشو گردانہ دیتی ثراپ ہتئے چوکی حال بیرو۔

(54) *gurúłi bi móš-o gerdán-a dit-í*
goitre go.PFV.PTCP man-OBL neck-LOC1 strike-PFV.PTCP
tsrap haté-i çok-í hal.birú
tightly it-LOC2 stick-PFV.PTCP stay.PST.I

(55) موش گردانہ کیاغ پرائے رے اچی غیریکو ہتے ای گوروڑئین لکھیرو۔

(55) *moóš gerdán-a kyaγ pray reé*
man neck-LOC1 something strike.PST.A.3SG say.PFV.PTCP
áči γerík-o haté i gurúłi-en lakh-íru
back turn.INF-OBL that one goitre-INS throw at-PST.I

(56) ہسے بی پازہ دیتی ہتیرا چوکیرو

(56) *hasé bi páz-a d-ití hatéra çok-íru*
it go.PFV.PTCP chest-LOC1 strike-PFV.PTCP there stick-PST.I

(57) موش استورو سوری غیری ژانو بچ کوری دورہ توریرو۔

(57) *moóš istor-ó sóri γer-í žan-ó bač*
man horse-OBL on mount-PFV.PTCP life-OBL saved
kor-í dúr-a tor-íru
do-PFV.PTCP home-LOC1 reach-PST.I

(58) مگم ایغو ژاغا جو گوروڑیان گنی، ای اچہ ای پروشٹہ۔

(58) *mágam iγ-ó žaγá-a ǰu gurułi-án gan-í*
but one-OBL place-LOC1 two goitre-PL take-PFV.PTCP
i áč-a i prúšṭ-a
one behind-LOC1 one front-LOC1

(59) تھے عقلمین روئے رے اسونی کہ کوس اونگوڑی کوروم نو کوریلیک۔

(59) *the aqulmín roy reé asúni ki kos*
so wise people say.PFV.PTCP be(ANIM).PRES.3PL that someone
ungoł-í kórum no kor-élik
imitate-PFV.PTCP deed not do-NEC

Jeshtanan Shilogh—English translation

(1) Once upon a time there was a certain man. (2) A very wise and intelligent man. (3) But there was a big goitre on his neck. (4) The goitre grew and grew and became so big that he wasn't able to look downwards. (5) (One day) he took his horse to the river and while giving it water called to someone across the river, saying "Hey, brother look here! Is my horse drinking water or not?"[5] (6) His real name was something else, but people called him Gurułi Khan.[6] (7) He was fed up with his problem caused by the goitre. (8) But what could he do? In the old days there was no cure for goitre. (9) One day Gurułi Khan mounted his horse and was going on a journey. (10) When the sun touched the horizon and evening fell, he was not able to find a settlement anywhere to spend the night. (11) He had bread with him; going down to the riverbank he tried to find a rock shelter to sleep in. (12) When light appeared in the distance, he quickly went there (and saw) that there is light in a shelter (and) sound is coming. (13) He was happy thinking "I have found people like this." (14) Having tied his horse there somewhere he goes up (and sees) that there is a rock shelter as big as a large house. (15) Inside a fire has blazed up and around it jeshtans the size of a handspan are playing (instruments) and dancing. (16) Seeing the man, the jeshtans shouted, "A guest has come, a guest has come." (17) They said to the man, "Come, you dance too!" Gurułi Khan said, "Indeed I was a good dancer, but now this goitre doesn't let me move. (18) How can I dance?" (19) When he said this, one jeshtan reached over, took the goitre out and put it in a wall niche. (20) Being free (of the goitre), Gurułi Khan jumped down to dance. (21) The jeshtans stopped their previous tune and now began to dance, saying, "For our evening meal the horse; the man in a skin bag for later on. For our evening meal the horse; the man in a skin bag for later on." (22) The man understood that tonight they will tire me out, put me to sleep, and eat my horse. In the morning they will get up and eat me for breakfast. (23) As it got darker, the dancing got faster and faster. (24) The man was also aware of this, (and) quickly whirling around, came to the entrance of the shelter, leapt on his horse and struck it with a whip. (25) The jeshtans were calling after him, "Hey guest, please stay with us. Where are you going without spending the night?" They tried their best (to catch him), but how could a handspan-sized jeshtan catch up with a

[5] He had to ask someone else because he could not look downward to see whether the horse was drinking or not.

[6] *gurułi* 'goitre'. People were often characterised and nicknamed by a distinctive, often negative, physical characteristic.

Tajik's horse? (26) When dawn broke and Gurułi Khan reached home, (the people) see that there is no trace of the goitre. (27) People came from far and near to congratulate him. Gurułi Khan slaughtered a bull and gave a feast. (28) Gurułi Khan's younger brother was also goitrous, but his goitre wasn't as big. (29) When Gurułi Khan got free of his goitre, he (the younger brother) also wished (for that). (30) He said to his brother, "I will also go to the jeshtans' den; maybe I will be free of this goitre." (31) Gurułi Khan said "Hey, you be careful and sit quietly. (32) I accidentally got out of the mouth of the witches and have come (home). (33) Why are you looking (at me) again and again and putting yourself in the gullet of the witches?" (34) But his younger brother did not agree. (35) Finally, stubbornly he got directions to that place and prepared to go. (36) The younger brother mounted his horse and when night came reached that place. (37) When he looks (he sees that) light is coming (from) a rock shelter. (38) He tied the horse outside and went up (to the shelter). (39) The jeshtans were dancing in the very same way (that they were before). (40) Seeing the man and saying, "Hey, guest, please come; where have you come" pulled him over. (41) The jeshtans said, "We were waiting for you; it's good (that you've come). (42) Today you will spend the night with us; whatever respectful treatment there is, we will serve you. (43) How would it be if we do one round of dancing before the meal? (44) You also come, dance with us." (45) The man said, "I might not be embarrassed to dance but this goitre of mine is a hindrance." (46) When he said this, one jeshtan removed the goitre and put it in a wall niche. (47) When the man looks up (he sees) that that Gurułi Khan's goitre is also placed there. (48) The dancing started. (49) Putting the man in the middle (and) saying "The horse for our evening meal, the man in a skin bag for later on. The horse for our evening meal, the man in a skin bag for later on", they spun swiftly and came (toward the man). (50) The man, fearing for his life, came whirling. (51) Whirling and whirling, when he found a gap, the man jumped out. (52) The jeshtans were also paying attention to this. (53) One of them reached up, took down that goitre, and threw it at him. (54) The goitre went, struck the man's neck, stuck firmly and stayed there. (55) When the man, thinking that something has hit me in the neck, turned back, (they) threw that other goitre at him. (56) It went, struck him in the chest and stuck there. (57) The man, mounting his horse, saved his life and reached home. (58) But instead of one goitre, there are two goitres—one behind and one in front. (59) So wise people have said that one should not imitate someone and do things.

References

Abdramanova, Saule. 2017. 'Basic color terms in the Kazakh language', *Sage Open* 7(2). Accessed 7 July 2024. https://journals.sagepub.com/doi/full/10.1177/2158244017714829.

Akhgar, Ismail Wali. 2008. 'Major themes in modern Khowar poetry'. In *Proceedings of the Third International Hindu Kush Cultural Conference*, edited by Israr-ud-Din, 296–302. Karachi: Oxford University Press.

Akhunzada, Fakhr-ud-Din. 2013. 'Mini-Chitral in Swat'. Accessed 5 April 2023. http://www.mahraka.com/bashqar.html.

Akhunzada, Fakhr-ud-Din. 2021. *Changing language-in-education policy in Pakistan*. Accessed 17 February 2024. https://www.researchgate.net/publication/354324960.

Ali, Afsar. n.d. Unpublished ms. Redublications [sic].

Anbreen, Shagufta, Fakhira Riaz, and Yasmin Akhtar. 2020. 'English and Khowar: The study of social media linguistic practices of Khowar speakers', *Global Language Review* V(I): 125–34.

Aydin, Erhan. 2009. 'Data regarding Yenisey inscriptions in T. Gerard Clauson's etymological dictionary', *Turkish Studies* 4(4): 93–118.

Baart, Joan L.G. 1997. *The sounds and tones of Kalam Kohistani*. Islamabad: National Institute of Pakistan Studies, Quaid-i-Azam University and Summer Institute of Linguistics.

Baart, Joan L.G. 1999. 'Tone rules in Kalam Kohistani (Garwi, Bashkarik)', *Bulletin of the School of Oriental and African Studies* 62(1): 87–104.

Baart, Joan L.G. 2003. 'Tonal features in languages of northern Pakistan'. In *Pakistani languages and society: Problems and prospects*, edited by Joan L.G. Baart and G.H. Sindhi, 132–44. Islamabad: National Institute of Pakistan Studies, Quaid-i-Azam University and Summer Institute of Linguistics.

Baart, Joan L.G. 2004. 'Contrastive tone in Kalam Kohistani', *Linguistic Discovery* 2(2): 1–20. Hanover, NH: Dartmouth College.

Baig, Rahmat Karim. 1997. *Hindu Kush study series, volume two*. Published by author and Peshawar: Rehmat Printing Press.

Baig, Rahmat Karim. 2004. *Chitral: A study in statecraft (1320–1969)*. Karachi: IUCN Pakistan.

Bashir, Elena. 1988a. *Topics in Kalasha syntax: An areal and typological perspective*. PhD dissertation, University of Michigan Ann Arbor.

Bashir, Elena. 1988b. 'Inferentiality in Kalasha and Khowar'. In *Papers from the 24th Regional Meeting of the Chicago Linguistic Society, Part One: The general session*, edited by Lynn MacLeod, Gary Larson, and Diane Brentari, 47–59. Chicago: Chicago Linguistic Society, The University of Chicago.

Bashir, Elena. 1996a. 'Khowar and areal linguistics'. Paper presented at the Second International Hindu Kush Cultural Conference, 19–23 September 1990 in Chitral, Pakistan. In *Proceedings of the Second International Hindukush Cultural Conference*, edited by Elena Bashir and Israr-ud-Din, 167–79. Karachi and Islamabad: Oxford University Press.

Bashir, Elena. 1996b. 'Mosaic of tongues: Quotatives and complementizers in northwest Indo-Aryan, Burushaski, and Balti'. In *Studies in Pakistani popular culture*, edited by William L. Hanaway and Wilma Heston. Lahore: Sang-e-Meel Publications and Islamabad: Lok Virsa Publishing House.

Bashir, Elena. 1997. 'Khowar/Burushaski commonalities'. Paper presented at the Third International Himalayan Languages Symposium, 18–20 July at the University of California at Santa Barbara.

Bashir, Elena. 2000a. 'Relative clauses in Khowar'. Paper presented at the Sixth Himalayan Languages Symposium, 15–17 June at the University of Wisconsin at Milwaukee.

Bashir, Elena. 2000b. 'Spatial representation in Khowar'. In *Proceedings of the 36th Annual Meeting of the Chicago Linguistic Society*, 15–29. Chicago: Chicago Linguistic Society, University of Chicago.

Bashir, Elena. 2001. 'Khowar–Wakhi contact relationships'. In *Toḥfa-e-dil: Festschrift Helmut Nespital*, edited by Dirk Lönne, 3–17. Reinbek: Dr. Inge Wezler, Verlag für Orientalistische Fachpublikationen.
Bashir, Elena. 2003. 'Dardic'. In *The Indo-Aryan languages*, edited by George Cardona and Dhanesh Jain, 818–94. Abingdon/New York: Routledge.
Bashir, Elena. 2007. 'Contact-induced change in Khowar'. In *New perspectives on Pakistan: Contexts, realities and visions of the future*, edited by Shafqat Saeed, 205–38. Karachi: Oxford University Press.
Bashir, Elena. 2008. 'Artificial glaciers: Trajectories of idea and practice'. In *Masters of understanding: German scholars in the Hindu Kush and Karakoram, 1955–2005. Journal of Asian Civilizations*, 31–2, edited by Hugh van Skyhawk. Islamabad: Taxila Institute of Asian Civilizations.
Bashir, Elena. 2009. 'Wakhi'. In *The Iranian languages*, edited by Gernot Windfuhr, 825–62. London/New York: Routledge.
Bashir, Elena. 2015. 'Two micro-areal developments in northwestern South Asia: Causative involuntatives and causee marking postpositions', *Journal of South Asian Languages and Linguistics* 2: 29–62.
Bashir, Elena. 2022. 'Khowar and Kalasha: Similarities and differences in their micro-areal contexts', *International Journal of Diachronic Linguistics and Linguistic Reconstruction* 19: 1–59.
Bashir, Elena. 2023a. 'Copular use in Khowar, Kalasha, and neighboring languages'. In *Roots of Peristan the pre-Islamic cultures of the Hindukush/Karakorum*, edited by Alberto M. Cacopardo and Augusto S. Cacopardo, 237–76. Rome: ISMEO.
Bashir, Elena. 2023b. 'A Khowar–English glossary [HL Archive 12]', *Himalayan Linguistics*. Accessed 22 October 2024. https://escholarship.org/uc/item/955239w9.
Bashir, Elena and Thomas J. Conners. 2019. *A descriptive grammar of Hindko, Panjabi, and Saraiki*. Mouton-CASL Grammar Series, Volume 4. Mouton de Gruyter: Berlin.
Bashir, Elena, Maula Nigah Nigah, and Rahmat Karim Baig. 2022 [2005]. 'A digital Khowar–English dictionary with audio' [DSAL]. Accessed 22 October 2024. https://dsal.uchicago.edu/dictionaries/khowar-2nd/A_Digital_Khowar-English_Dictionary_with_Audio-second_edition.pdf.
Beg, Fazal Amin, John Mock, and Mir Ali Wakhani. 2022. 'Recent developments in Wakhi orthography'. In *Languages of northern Pakistan: Essays in memory of Carla Radloff*, edited by Joan L.G. Baart, Henrik Liljegren, and Thomas E. Payne, 131–46. Karachi: Oxford University Press.
Berger, Hermann. 1960. 'Bericht über sprachliche und volkskundliche Forschungen im Hunzatal', *Anthropos* 55: 657–64.
Berger, Hermann. 1967–8. 'Türkische Pferdewörter bei einem Sanskrit-Lexikographen?', *Indo-Iranian Journal* 10(2/3): 177–80.
Berger, Hermann. 1974. *Das Yasin-Burushaski (Werchikwar): Grammatik, Texte, Wörterbuch*. Neuindische Studien 3. Wiesbaden: Harrassowitz.
Berger, Hermann. 1998. *Die Burushaski-Sprache von Hunza und Nager, Vol. I Grammatik*. Wiesbaden: Harrassowitz.
Berlin, Brent and Paul Kay. 1969. *Basic color terms: Their universality and evolution*. Berkeley: University of California Press.
Birahimani, Ali. 2021. 'Reviewing the history and development of aspiration in Eastern Balochi', *Journal of Historical Linguistics* 11(3): 457–98.
Bodrogligeti, András J.E. 2001. *A grammar of Chagatay*. Languages of the World/Materials 155. Munich: Lincom Europa.
Bosworth, Clifford E. 2001. 'Notes on some Turkish names in Abu al-Faḍl Bayhaqī's *Tārīkh-i Mas'ūdī*', *Oriens* 36: 299–313.
Buddruss, Georg. 1982. *Khowar-Texte in arabischer Schrift*. Mainz: Akademie der Wissenschaften und der Literatur and Wiesbaden: Franz Steiner Verlag.
Buddruss, Georg. 1989. 'Kommentar zu einem Kivi-Vokabular aus dem sowjetischen Pamir', *Studien zur Indologie und Iranistik* 15, 197–205. Reinbek: Verlag für Orientalische Fachpublikationen.
Buddruss, Georg. 1996. 'Shina-Rätsel [Shina riddles]'. In *Nānāvidhaikatā: Festschrift für Hermann Berger*, edited by Dieter B. Kepp, 29–54. Wiesbaden: Harrassowitz Verlag.
Buddruss, Georg and Almuth Degener. 2017. *Materialen zur Prasun-Sprache des afghanischen Hindukusch*. Department of South Asian Studies, Harvard University. Cambridge, MA: Harvard University Press.

Burrow, T. 1973 [1955]. *The Sanskrit language.* London: Faber and Faber.

Burushaski Research Academy. 2006. *Burushaski–Urdu lughat* [Burushaski–Urdu Dictionary], 3 volumes. Karachi: Director, Bureau of Composition, Compilation & Translation, University of Karachi.

Casaretto, Antje and Carolin Schneider. 'Vedic local particles at the syntax-semantics interface'. In *Language change at the syntax-semantics interface*, edited by Chiara Giancollo, Agnes Jäger, and Doris Penka, 223–60. Berlin/Munich/Boston: De Gruyter Mouton.

Catford, J.C. 1977. *Fundamental problems in phonetics.* Bloomington: Indiana University Press.

Charles, S. 2012. *Philosophical writings of Peirce*. New York: Dover Publications.

Chitrali, Rehmat Aziz. 2019. Draft ms. *Chitrali–Urdu–English Dictionary*. Karachi: Khowar Academy.

Comrie, Bernard. 1989. *Language universals and linguistic typology: Syntax and morphology*. Chicago: University of Chicago Press.

Corbett, Greville G. 1991. *Gender*. Cambridge/New York: Cambridge University Press.

Decker, Kendall (ed.). 1992. *Languages of Chitral*. Sociolinguistic Survey of Northern Pakistan, Volume 5. Islamabad: National Institute of Pakistan Studies and Summer Institute of Linguistics.

Delancey, Scott. 1977. 'Mirativity: The grammatical marking of unexpected information', *Linguistic Typology* 1: 33–52.

Demircan, Ömer. 1987. 'Emphatic reduplication in Turkish'. In *Studies on modern Turkish: Proceedings of the Third Conference on Turkish Linguistics*, edited by H.T. Boeschoten and L.T. Verhoeven, 24–41. Tilburg: Tilburg University Press.

Di Carlo, Pierpaolo. 2011. 'Two clues to a former Hindu-Kush linguistic area?' In *Selected papers from the International Conference on Language Documentation and Tradition with a special interest in the Kalasha of the Hindu Kush valleys, Himalayas*, edited by Carol Everhard and Elizabeth Mela-Athanasopoulou, 101–14. Thessaloniki: School of English, Department of Theoretical & Applied Linguistics, Aristotle University of Thessaloniki.

Dixon, R.M.W. 2009. *Basic linguistic theory, volume 2: Grammatical topics.* Oxford: Oxford University Press.

Emeneau, Murray B. 1956. 'India as a linguistic area', *Language* 32: 3–16.

Emeneau, Murray B. 1966. 'The dialects of Old Indo-Aryan'. In *Ancient Indo-European dialects*, edited by Henrik Birnbaum and Jaan Puhvel, 123–38. Berkeley: University of California Press.

Endresen, Rolf Thiel and Knut Kristiansen. 1981. 'Khowar studies'. In *Monumentum Georg Morgenstierne I.* Acta Iranica, Deuxième Série, Volume 7, 210–43. Leiden: E.J. Brill.

Erdal, Marcel. 2004. *A grammar of Old Turkic.* Leiden: Brill.

Fairbanks, Gordon H., James W. Gair, and M.W.S. De Silva. 1968. *Colloquial Sinhalese: Parts I & II.* Ithaca, NY: Cornell South Asia Program.

Faizi, Inayatullah. 1989. 'Keɫiʋál keɫítay ["The shepherdess wept"]'. In *Khowar* (an annual journal). Chitral: Anjuman-e Taraqqi Khowar.

Faizi, Inayatullah. 2021 [1982 ms]. 'Dying words and new vocabulary of Kohwar'. Accessed 22 October 2024. https://www.mahraka.com/faizi/khowar_old_new_words.html.

Faizi, Inayatullah. 2021 [1985 ms]. 'Different dialects of Kohwar'. Subsequently published in *Annual Journal of Khowar*, 1989, 19–28. Chitral, Pakistan: Anjuman-e-Taraqqi-e-Khowar, Chitral. Now also accessible with the title 'Difference of morphology, phonology, and vocabulary in Khowar language spoken in different parts of Chitral'. Accessed 3 July 2024. https://www.mahraka.com/faizi/language_varity_khowar.html.

Fernández Leborans, M.J. 1995. 'Las construcciones con el verbo estar: Aspectos sintácticos y semánticos', *Verba* 22: 253–84.

Fussman, G. 1972. *Atlas linguistique des parlers dardes et kafirs.* Tome I: *Cartes.* Tome II: *Commentaire.* Paris: École Française dé Extrême-Orient.

Gambhir, Vijay. 1993. 'Complex verb phrase: A diachronic and synchronic view'. In *Complex predicates in South Asian languages*, edited by Manindra K. Verma, 77–96. New Delhi: Manohar.

Goodman, Nelson. 1955. *Fact, fiction and forecast.* Cambridge, MA: Harvard University Press.

Greenberg, Joseph H. 1966. 'Some universals of grammar with particular reference to the order of meaning elements'. In *Universals of language*, edited by J.H. Greenberg, 73–113. Cambridge, MA: MIT Press.

Grierson, George A. 1919. *Linguistic survey of India, Volume 8, Part 2: Specimens of the Dardic or Piśācha languages (including Kāshmīrī)*. Calcutta: Superintendent Government Printing, India.

Grjunberg, A.L. and I.M. Steblin-Kamensky. 1976. *Vakhanskii iazyk. Teksty, slovar', grammaticheskii ocherk* [The Wakhi language. Texts, glossary, grammatical outline]. Moscow: Nauka; French translation (1988) *La langue wakhi*. Paris: Editions de la Maison des Sciences de l'Homme.

Heegård Petersen, Jan. 2015. 'Kalasha texts—with introductory grammar', *Acta Linguistica Hafniensia* 47(sup 1): 1–275.

Hock, Hans Henrich. 1989. 'Conjoined we stand: theoretical implications of Sanskrit relative structures', *Studies in the Linguistic Sciences* 19(1): 93–126.

Hussain, Mumtaz. 2016. *Shilogh: Chitrāli baččõ kī lok kahāniā̃.* [Folk tales: Folk tales for Chitrali children]. Islamabad: National Book Foundation.

Islam, Bibi, Tariq Khan, and Aziz Ahmad. 2019. 'An analysis of lexical effects of English language on Khowar (Chitral's regional language)', *Pakistan Journal of Languages and Translation Studies* 7(2): 165–72. Accessed 3 July 2024. https://uog.edu.pk/downloads/journal/PJLTS_Issue_07_No_02.pdf.

Jäger, Gerhard. 2001. 'Topic-comment structure and the contrast between stage level and individual level predicates', *Journal of Semantics* 18(2): 83–126. Accessed 11 November 2024. https://doi. org/10.1093/jos/18.2.83.

Khan, Afsar Ali. 2016. *Khowar matalan gurzain* [A garden of Khowar proverbs]. Islamabad: Forum for Language Initiatives.

Khan, Khan Sahib Abdul Hakim. 1902. *Translation of the Ganj-i-Pukhto into the Khowar dialect*, edited by B.E.M. Gurdon. Calcutta: Office of the Superintendent of Government Printing, India.

Khan, Sami Ullah, Dolat Khan, Munir Khattak, and Nigar Gul. 2021. 'English loanwords adaptation into Khowar', *The Discourse* 7(1): 87–98. Accessed 6 April 2023. https://www.researchgate.net/publication/355193526.

Kieffer, Charles M. 2009. 'Parachi'. In *The Iranian languages*, edited by Gernot Windfuhr, 693–720. London/New York: Routledge.

Kim, Alan Hyun-Oak. 1988. 'Preverbal focusing and type XXIII languages'. In *Studies in syntactic typology*, edited by Michael Hammond, Edith Moravcsik, and Jessica Wirth, 147–69. Amsterdam/Philadelphia: Benjamins.

Kochetov, Alexei, Paul Arsenault, Jan Heegård Petersen, Sikandar Kalas, and Taj Khan Kalash. 2020. 'Kalasha (Bumburet variety)', *Journal of the International Phonetic Association* 51(3): 468–89.

Kulikov, Leonid. 2007. 'Reciprocal constructions in Vedic'. In *Reciprocal constructions*. Typological Studies in Language 71. Volume 2, edited by Vladimir P. Nedjalkov, with the assistance of Emma Š. Geniušienė and Zlatka Guentchéva, 709–38. Amsterdam: John Benjamins.

Lambton, Ann K.S. 1957. *Persian grammar*. Cambridge: Cambridge University Press.

Lehr, Rachel. 2014. *A descriptive grammar of Pashai: The language and speech community of Darrai Nur*. PhD dissertation, The University of Chicago.

Levin, Beth, John Beavers, and Shiao Wei Tham. 2010. 'The typology of motion expressions revisited', *Journal of Linguistics* 46(2): 331–77.

Levinson, Stephen C. 1994. 'Vision, shape, and linguistic description: Tzeltal body-part terminology and object description', *Linguistics* 32: 791–855.

Levinson, Stephen C. 1996. 'Frames of reference and Molyneaux's question: Crosslinguistic evidence'. In *Language and space*, edited by Paul Bloom, Merrill F. Garrett, Lynn Nadel, and Mary A. Peterson, 109–70. Cambridge, MA: MIT Press.

Levinson, Stephen C. 2000. 'Yélî Dnye and the theory of basic color terms', *Journal of Linguistic Anthropology* 10(1): 3–55.

Liljegren, Henrik. 2010. 'Where have all the verbs gone?', *Himalayan Linguistics* 9(1): 1–79.

Liljegren, Henrik. 2013. 'Notes on Kalkoti: A Shina language with strong Kohistani influences', *Linguistic Discovery* 13(1): 129–60.

Liljegren, Henrik. 2014. 'A survey of alignment features in the Greater Hindukush with special references to Indo-Aryan'. In *On diversity and complexity of languages spoken in Europe and North and Central Asia*, edited by Pirkkho Suihkonen and Lindsay J. Whaley, 133–74. Amsterdam: Benjamins.

Liljegren, Henrik. 2016. *A grammar of Palula*. PhD dissertation, Stockholm University. Studies in Diversity Linguistics 8. Berlin: Language Science Press.

Liljegren, Henrik. 2017. 'Profiling Indo-Aryan in the Hindukush–Karakoram: A preliminary study of micro-typological patterns', *Journal of South Asian Languages and Linguistics* 4(1): 107–56.

Liljegren, Henrik. 2019. 'Gender typology and gender (in)stability in Hindu Kush Indo-Aryan languages'. In *Grammatical gender and linguistic complexity: Volume I: General issues and specific studies*, edited by Francesca Di Garbo, Bruno Olsson, and Bernhard Wälchli, 279–328. Berlin: Language Science Press.
Liljegren, Henrik. 2021. 'The Hindu Kush–Karakorum and linguistic areality', *Journal of South Asian Languages and Linguistics* 7(2): 239–85.
Liljegren, Henrik. 2023. 'The languages of Peristan through the lens of areal typology'. In *Roots of Peristan: The pre-Islamic cultures of the Hindukush/Karakorum* edited by Alberto M. Cacopardo and Augusto S. Cacopardo, 391–431. Rome: ISMEO.
Liljegren, Henrik and Afsar Ali Khan. 2017. 'Illustrations of the IPA: Khowar', *Journal of the International Phonetic Association* 47(2): 219–29.
Liljegren, Henrik and Fakhr-ud-Din Akhunzada. 2017. 'Linguistic diversity, vitality and maintenance: A case study on the language situation in northern Pakistan', *Multiethnica*. Meddelande från Centrum för multietnisk forskning, Uppsala universitet, ISSN 0284-396X, 36–37: 61–79. Accessed 6 July 2024. https://www.diva-portal.org/smash/record.jsf?pid=diva2%3A1155268&dswid=402.
Liljegren, Henrik and Erik Svärd. 2017. 'Bisyndetic contrast marking in the Hindukush: Additional evidence of a historical contact zone', *Journal of Language Contact* 10: 450–84.
Liljegren, Henrik, R. Forkel, N. Knobloch, and N. Lange. 2021. 'Hindu Kush areal typology (Version v1.0) [Data set]'. Accessed 30 June 2024. https://www.diva-portal.org/smash/record.jsf?pid=diva2%3A1695535&dswid=-2134.
Lindholm, James M. 1975. *The conceptual basis of the Tamil adverbial participle*. PhD dissertation, The University of Chicago. Chicago: The University of Chicago ProQuest Dissertations Publishing.
Lorimer, D.L.R. 1937. 'Burushaski and its alien neighbours: Problems in linguistic contagion', *Transactions of the Philological Society* 36(1): 63–98.
Lorimer, D.L.R. 1938. *The Burushaski language. Vol. III, Vocabularies and index.* Oslo: Instituttet for Sammenlignende Kulturforskning.
Lorimer, D.L.R. 1962. *Werchikwar–English Vocabulary*. Instituttet for Sammenlignende Kulturforskning. Oslo: Norwegian Universities Press.
Luján, M. 1981. 'The Spanish copulas as aspectual indicators', *Lingua* 54(2–3): 165–210.
Lunsford, Wayne A. 2001. *An overview of linguistic structures in Torwali, a language of northern Pakistan*. MA thesis, The University of Texas at Arlington.
Mamatov, Jahangir, S.G. Harrell, Kathy Kehoe, and Karim Khodjibaev. 2005. *Tajik–English Dictionary*. Springfield, VA: Dunwoody Press.
Marín, Rafael. 2009. 'Spanish individual-level and stage-level adjectives revisited'. Accessed 3 July 2024. https://www.researchgate.net/publication/228704358.
Masica, Colin P. 1991. *The Indo-Aryan languages.* Cambridge/New York: Cambridge University Press.
Menges, Karl H. 1968. *The Turkic languages and peoples: An introduction to Turkic studies.* Wiesbaden: Otto Harrassowitz.
Mexas, Haris. 2016. 'Mirativity as realization marking: A cross-linguistic study'. MA thesis, University of Leiden. Accessed 22 July 2024. https://www.academia.edu/30875827/.
Mock, John H. 1998. *The discursive construction of reality in the Wakhi community of northern Pakistan.* PhD dissertation, The University of California, Berkeley.
Morgenstierne, Georg. 1932. *Report on a linguistic mission to north-western India*. Serie C III – 1. Oslo: Instituttet for Sammenlignende Kulturforskning.
Morgenstierne, Georg. 1934. 'Notes on Tirahi', *Acta Orientalia* 12: 161–89.
Morgenstierne, Georg. 1935. Preface to Lorimer 1935–1938, Volume I, vii–xxx.
Morgenstierne, Georg. 1936. 'Iranian elements in Khowar', *Bulletin of the School of Oriental Studies, University of London*, 8(2/3): 657–71.
Morgenstierne, Georg. 1947. 'Some features of Khowar morphology', *Norsk Tidsskrift for Sprakvidenskap* 14: 5–28.
Morgenstierne, Georg. 1955. 'A Khowar tale', *Indian Linguistics* 13: 163–9.
Morgenstierne, Georg. 1957. 'Sanskritic words in Khowar'. In *Felicitation volume presented to S.K. Belvalkar*, edited by Sarvepalli Radhakrishnan, 84–98. Reprinted in: *Irano-Dardica*, 256–72. Wiesbaden: Dr. Ludwig Reichert Verlag. Issued under the auspices of the Dr. S.K. Belvalkar Felicitation Volume Committee. Banaras: Motilal Banarsidass.

Morgenstierne, Georg. 1961. 'Dardic and Kafir languages'. In *Encyclopedia of Islam*, new edition, 138–9. Leiden: Brill.

Morgenstierne, Georg. 1973a [1967]. *The Pashai language: Grammar.* Indo-Iranian Frontier languages, 2nd edition, Volume III. Oslo: Universitetsforlaget.

Morgenstierne, Georg. 1973b. *The Kalasha language.* Indo-Iranian Frontier Languages, Volume IV, Instituttet for Sammenlignende Kulturforskning, Serie B: Skrifter. Oslo, Bergen/Tromsø: Universitetsforlaget.

Munnings, David. 1990a. 'Syllable structure in Khowar'. Unpublished research paper. Arlington: University of Texas at Arlington.

Munnings, David. 1990b. 'Towards a sociolinguistic profile of the Khowar language'. Unpublished research paper. Arlington: University of Texas. Accessed 5 April 2023. http://www.anusha.com/munnings.htm.

Naji, Naji Khan. 2008. *Khowar–Urdu lughat* [Khowar–Urdu dictionary]. Shotkhar, Torkhow, Chitral: Naji Sons.

Naseem, Sher Nawaz. 1987a. 'A prominent Kohwar poet', *The Frontier Post*, 20 March. Accessed 6 August 2024. https://mahraka.com/naseem/5.pdf.

Naseem, Sher Nawaz. 1987b. 'Baba Ayub, ghazal producer', *The Frontier Post*, 3 April. Accessed 6 August 2024. https://mahraka.com/naseem/3.pdf.

Naseem, Sher Nawaz. 1987c. 'Prominent Kohwar poets—III: Gul Nawaz Khaki', *The Frontier Post*, 17 April. Accessed 6 August 2024. https://mahraka.com/naseem/6.pdf.

Naseem, Sher Nawaz. 1987d. 'Prominent Khowar poets—IV, Mirza Firdous Firdousi', *The Frontier Post*, 8 May. Accessed 6 August 2024. https://mahraka.com/naseem/2.pdf.

Naseem, Sher Nawaz. 1987e. 'Prominent Kohwar poets—V, Amir Gul Amir', *The Frontier Post*, 14 May. Accessed 21 October 2024. https://mahraka.com/naseem/4.pdf.

Naseem, Sher Nawaz. 1987f. 'Kohwar poets, Amin-ur-Rehman Chughtai', *The Frontier Post*, 24 July. Accessed 6 August 2024. https://mahraka.com/naseem/7.pdf.

Naseem, Sher Nawaz. 1988. 'Father of modern Kohwar, Shahzada Hisamul Mulk', *The Frontier Post*, 29 January. Accessed 6 August 2024. https://mahraka.com/naseem/1.pdf.

Newman, Paul. 2012. 'Pluractional verbs: An overview'. In *Verbal plurality and distributivity*, edited by Patricia Cabredo Hoffherr and Brenda Laca, 185–209. Berlin: de Gruyter.

Nichols, Johanna. 1986. 'Head-marking and dependent-marking grammar', *Language* 62(1): 56–119.

Noburu, Yoshioka. 2012. *A reference grammar of Eastern Burushaski*. PhD thesis, Tokyo University of Foreign Studies.

O'Brien, Captain D.J.T. 1895. *Grammar and vocabulary of the Khowâr dialect (Chitrâli), with an introductory sketch of country and people.* Lahore: Civil and Military Gazette Press.

Özyürek, Asli and Sotaro Kita.2020. 'Expressing manner and path in English and Turkish: Differences in speech, gesture, and conceptualization'. In *Proceedings of the Twenty-first Annual Conference of the Cognitive Science Society, 1st edition*, edited by Martin Hahn and Scott C. Stoness. New York: Psychology Press.

Papke, Julia Kay Porter. 2010. *Classical Sanskrit preverb ordering*. PhD dissertation, Ohio State University.

Paxalina, T.N. 1987. 'Materiali po jazyku kivi. [Materials on the Kivi language]'. In *Iranskoye jazykoznaniye, yezhegodnik 1982*, 112–14. Moscow: Nauka.

Perder, Emil. 2013. *A grammatical description of Dameli*. PhD dissertation, Stockholm University.

Radloff, Carla F. 1999a. 'The finite verb in Gilgiti Shina'. Unpublished ms.

Radloff, Carla F. 1999b. *Aspects of the sound system of Gilgiti Shina*. Islamabad: National Institute of Pakistan Studies and Summer Institute of Linguistics.

Radloff, Carla F. 2003. 'The solution to a linguistic mystery: The absence of diphthongs in the Shina language of Gilgit (with implications for writers and learners of Gilgiti Shina)'. In *Pakistani languages and society: Problems and prospects*, edited by Joan L.G. Baart and Ghulam Hyder Sindhi, 145–53. Islamabad: National Institute of Pakistan Studies, Quaid-i-Azam University and Summer Institute of Linguistics.

Radloff, Carla F. with Ahmad Shakil Shakil. 1998. *Folktales in the Shina of Gilgit (text, grammatical analysis and commentary).* Islamabad: National Institute of Pakistan Studies, Quaid-i-Azam University and Summer Institute of Linguistics.

Rahmat, Rahmat Akbar Khan. 1989. '*Chetráro rásm.o.riváǰan sum khowár alfáz*, [Customs of Chitral and associated words]'. In *Khowar adab: Proceedings of the Second 2-day Conference, September 1988*, 44–53. Chitral: Anjuman-e-Taraqqi Khowar, Chitral.

Ramanujan, A.K. and E. Annamalai. 1967. 'Preliminary studies for a reference grammar of Tamil' (mimeographed ms). Chicago: University of Chicago.

Raza, Farid Ahmad. 2014. *Auray: Khowar afsana* [Morning breeze: The Khowar short story]. Islamabad: Forum for Language Initiatives.

Raza, Farid Ahmad. n.d. 'The changing trends of indigenous Khowar names for human beings'. Accessed 5 April 2023. https://mahraka.com/khowarNames.html.

Raza, Farid Ahmad and Zahoor ul-Haq Danish. 2019. *Khowar folktales, volume 1.* Islamabad: Lok Virsa. English and Khowar versions. Accessed 30 July 2024. https://khowari.com/?page_id=1014.

Rubino, Carl. 2005. 'Reduplication: Form, function and distribution'. In *Studies on reduplication*, edited by Bernhard Hurch, 11–29. Berlin/New York: Mouton de Gruyter.

Satoko, Yoshie. 2005. 'The sound system of Gojal Wakhi', *Area and Culture Studies* 71: 43–81.

Saunders, Barbara. 2000. 'Revisiting basic color terms', *The Journal of the Royal Anthropological Institute* 6(1): 81–99.

Schmidt, Ruth Laila and Razwal Kohistani. 2008. *Grammar of the Shina language of Indus Kohistan.* Wiesbaden: Harrassowitz.

Shafket Ali, Shumaila. 2020. 'Conceptualization of worldview through proverbs: A comparative study of Kalasha and Khowar proverbs', *Journal of Social Sciences and Humanities* 28(2): 67–88.

Shah, Syed Anwar Ali and Muhammad Ismail Wali. 2021. 'Manifestations of CONTAINER metaphor of LOVE in English and Khowar: A cross-cultural linguistics study', *Ilkogretim Online—Elementary Education Online* 20(5): 2071–7.

Shah, Wazir Ali and Georg Morgenstierne. 1959. 'Some Khowar songs', *Acta Orientalia* 24: 29–58.

Shahzad, Muhammad Yousaf. 1989. '"Rajuli". [a short story] In *Khowar* (an annual journal), 21–2. Chitral: Anjuman-e-Taraqqi-e-Chitral.

Skyhawk, Hugh van. 1992. 'The Jamáal Qháan story of Alíi Gouhar of Ḍomošáal (Hunza)'. In *Languages of northern Pakistan*, edited by Joan L.G. Baart, Henrik Liljegren, and Thomas E. Payne. Karachi: Oxford University Press.

Sloan, Muhammad Ismail. 2006 [1981]. *Khowar–English dictionary: A dictionary of the predominant language of Chitral.* New York: Ishi Press.

Slobin, Dan and Ayhana Aksu. 1982. 'Tense, aspect, and modality in the use of Turkish evidential'. In *Tense-aspect: Between semantics and pragmatics*, edited by Paul J. Hopper, Typological Studies in Language, Volume 1, 397–405. Amsterdam: John Benjamins.

Steblin-Kamensky, Ivan M. 1999. *Etimologičeskij slovary vaxanskogo jazyka* [Etymological dictionary of the Wakhi language]. Saint Petersburg: Saint Petersburg State University.

Strand, Richard F. 2005. 'The sound system of Degano'. Accessed 4 July 2024. https://nuristan.info/IndoAryan/Pashai/Degan/DeganLanguage/Lexicon/phon.html.

Strand, Richard F. 2007–11. 'Transcription and pronunciation of the Nuristani languages'. Accessed 4 July 2024. http://nuristan.info/Nuristani/phon.html.

Strand, Richard F. 2011. 'Khowar lexicon'. Accessed 17 December 2022. https://nuristan.info/lngFrameL.html.

Strand, Richard F. 2012. 'The sound system of Khow`ar'. Accessed 4 July 2024. http://nuristan.info/IndoAryan/Chitral/Khow/KhowLanguage/Lexicon/phon.html.

Strand, Richard. 2022. 'The role of phonatory location in the evolution of the far-northwestern Indo-Âryan languages'. In *Languages of northern Pakistan: Essays in memory of Carla Radloff*, edited by Joan L.G. Baart, Henrik Liljegren, and Thomas E. Payne, 449–95. Karachi: Oxford University Press. Accessed 4 July 2024. https://nuristan.info/PDFs/Strand%20-%20Phonatory%20Location-2016-06-07.pdf.

Talmy, Leonard. 1975. 'Semantics and syntax of motion'. In *Syntax and Semantics, Volume 4*, edited by J.P. Kimball, 181–238. New York: Academic Press.

Talmy, Leonard. 1985. 'Lexicalization patterns: Semantic structure in lexical forms'. In *Language typology and syntactic description 3: Grammatical categories and the lexicon*, edited by T. Shopen, 57–149. Cambridge: Cambridge University Press.

Talmy, Leonard. 2007. 'Lexical typologies'. In *Language typology and syntactic description 3: Grammatical categories and the lexicon*, 2nd edition, edited by T. Shopen, 66–168. Cambridge/New York: Cambridge University Press.

Tiffou, Étienne. 2014. *Dictionnaire du Bourouchaski du Yasin: Bourouchaski–Français et Français–Bourouchaski*. [Dictionary of Yasin Burushaski: Burushaski–French and French–Burushaski]. Louvain-la-Neuve: Peeters.
Tiffou, Étienne and Richard Patry. 1995. 'La notion de pluralité verbale: Le cas du Bourouchaski du Yasin. [The concept of verbal plurality: The case of Yasin Burushaski]', *Journal Asiatique* 282(2): 407–44.
Tikkanen, Bertil. 1988. 'On Burushaski and other ancient substrata in northwestern South Asia', *Studia Orientalia Electronica* 36: 303–25.
Tikkanen, Bertil. 2008. 'Some areal phonological isoglosses in the transit zone between South and Central Asia'. In *Proceedings of the Third International Hindu Kush Cultural Conference*, edited by Israr-ud-din, 250–62. Karachi: Oxford University Press.
Trail, Ronald L. and Gregory R. Cooper. 1999. *Kalasha dictionary—with English and Urdu*. Islamabad: National Institute of Pakistan Studies, Quaid-i-Azam University and Summer Institute of Linguistics.
Turner, Ralph Lilley. 1962–6. *A comparative dictionary of the Indo-Aryan languages*. (includes three supplements, published 1969–1985) London: Oxford University Press. Accessed 6 July 2024. https://dsal.uchicago.edu/dictionaries/soas/.
ul-Mulk, Nasir. 1921. *Hurūf-e tahjī-e zabān-e Khowār* [Alphabet of the Khowar language]. Lahore.
ul-Mulk, Samsam. n.d. *Khowar qaida*. [Khowar primer] Peshawar: Idāra e Išā'yat Sarhad.
ul-Mulk, Samsam. 1966. *Khowar (ya Chitrali zaban ki) graimar* [Khowar grammar]. Peshawar: Pashto Academy, Peshawar University.
Whitney, William Dwight. 1981[1889]. *Sanskrit grammar*. Cambridge, MA/London: Harvard University Press.
Windfuhr, Gernot. 1979. *Persian grammar: History and state of its study*. The Hague/New York: Mouton.
Windfuhr, Gernot (ed.). 2009. *The Iranian languages*. London/New York: Routledge.
Yorulmaz, Gamze and Buket Baran. 2022. 'Comparative analysis of the horse-related vocabulary in the Tatar and Tuvian languages'. Accessed 27 October 2024. https://www.academia.edu/117039726/COMPARATIVE_ANALYSIS_OF_THE_HORSE_RELATED_VOCABULARY_IN_THE_TATAR_AND_TUVAN_LANGUAGES.
Zoller, Claus Peter. 2005. *A grammar and dictionary of Indus Kohistani, volume 1*. Berlin/New York: Mouton de Gruyter.

Further reading

Bashir, Elena. 2003. 'Dardic'. In *The Indo-Aryan languages*, edited by George Cardona and Dhanesh Jain. Abingdon/New York: Routledge.
Haig, Geoffrey. 1998. *Relative constructions in Turkish*. Wiesbaden: Harrassowitz.
Lorimer, D.L.R. 1935. *The Burushaski Language. Volume I: Introduction and grammar*. Oslo: Instituttet for Sammenlignende Kulturforskning.
Matsumoto, Yo. 2003. 'Typologies of lexicalization patterns and event integration: Clarifications and reformulations'. In *Empirical and theoretical investigations into language: A Festschrift for Masaru Kajita*, edited by Shuji Chiba et al., 403–4. Tokyo: Kaitakusha.
Munnings, David. 2006a [1990]. 'Reduplication in Khowar: An autosegmental treatment'. Unpublished ms., subsequently included in Sloan (2006 [1981]).
Munnings, David. 2006b [1990]. 'Khowar lexical phonology'. Unpublished ms., subsequently included in Sloan (2006 [1981]).
Schmidt, Ruth Laila 1998. 'Typology of Shina pronouns'. Paper presented at the 15th European Conference on Modern South Asian Studies, Prague, 8–12 September.
Schmidt, Ruth Laila and Vijay Kumar Kaul. 2010. 'A grammatical sketch of Guresi Shina'. In *Anantaṁ Śāstram: Indological and linguistic studies in honour of Bertil Tikkanen*, edited by Klaus Karttunen. Published as *Studia Orientalia* 108. Helsinki: Finnish Oriental Society.
Stilo, Donald L. 1987. 'Ambipositions as an areal response: The case study of the Iranian zone'. In *Select papers from SALA-7: South Asian Languages Analysis Roundtable Conference held in Ann Arbor, Michigan May 17–19, 1985*, edited by Elena Bashir, Madhav M. Deshpande, and Peter Edwin Hook, 308–36. Bloomington: Indiana University Linguistics Club.

Index